Advance Praise for THE LOST TRAVELLER'S DREAM

"Combine Sir Toby Belch's cakes and ale with Holden Caulfield's ruthless criticism of everything phony. Knead it with the discipline of Thomas Merton's quests for The Human One. Liberally salt it with Mel Brooks and then radically pepper it with a pinch of blithe Brooklyn sass, and you will have made a cake from the *manna* of an authentic prophet. Joel Kovel has recorded a pilgrim's progress for this millenium, full of *joie de vivre* and anti-capitalist grace, mirth, and music. With steel-tipped boots called Freud and Marx he kicks ass against the Beast, and with ballet slippers he dances around, through, and out of Academia. He walks shoulder to shoulder with the *compas* in Nicaragua, California, Palestine, South Africa, Cuba, and Turtle Island. His soul is hammered out by William Blake upon the anvil of the world where it is washed with tears and buoyed by laughter. This is a righteous dialectical Yalie, a brilliant shrink, a stalwart comrade, a non-Jewish Jew, a Green presidential candidate, a gentle prof, and a Marxist Christian meek and bold. Here he remembers it all through that holy membrane that permits interfluence between words and deeds or ideas and actions. He is accompanied by the one who will use that which is not to bring to nought that which is. Call it Revolution, or with him call it Ecosocialism! Whatever. The lost traveller can bring us home!" — Peter Linebaugh

Advance Praise for THE LOST TRAVELLER'S DREAM

"*The Lost Traveller's Dream* is a moving and unforgettable account of a personal, political and spiritual journey. Even more significantly, it is the author's profound and personal expression of the age-old song of freedom, the redemption song, that we so desperately need at this moment in history. Kovel presents us with an engaging account of his life as a student, seeker, physician, radical psychoanalyst, teacher, scholar, writer, heterodox Marxist, engaged revolutionary theorist, and Blakean Christian mystic. At its deepest level, his story reveals the eternal dialectic between our constraining conditions of life as they are given in personal, familial and social reality, and a powerful, transformative and liberatory force, a force that some call Spirit, that is striving to emerge in the midst of things. In Kovel's version of this song of freedom, we are shown how a profound but fleeting revelation in youth finds concrete social and material affirmation in the communities of liberation and solidarity of revolutionary Nicaragua, and how this leads to a lifelong and dedicated struggle to realize the deepest truths of history and spirit in personal and communal reality, here and now." — John Clark

The Lost Traveller's Dream

ALSO BY JOEL KOVEL

White Racism: A Psychohistory
A Complete Guide to Therapy
The Age of Desire
Against the State of Nuclear Terror
In Nicaragua
The Radical Spirit: Essays on Psychoanalysis and Society
History and Spirit
Red Hunting in the Promised Land
The Enemy of Nature
Overcoming Zionism

THE LOST TRAVELLER'S DREAM

A MEMOIR

JOEL KOVEL

AUTONOMEDIA

DEDICATION
To Earl Kooperkamp: Pastor and Friend

ACKNOWLEDGMENTS
Needless to say, if one writes a memoir, then literally
everyone encountered over a lifetime is to be thanked.
But there are some who also gave material aid
(including a listening ear) to its composition and
publication over the past seven years. Herewith, a selection:
The final team: Jim Fleming, publisher nonpareil;
and Sarah Dziedzic, whose contribution has been
invaluable in so many ways. And over the long march:
DeeDee Halleck, Molly Kovel, Alex Kovel, Quincy Saul,
Ben Barson, Jerrod Brady, Jesse Lemisch, Jaime Yancovitz,
Jorge Chica, Peter McClaren, Christopher Myers,
Michael Löwy, Marc Estrin, Peter Linebaugh, Harry Clark,
Fran Goldin, Ria Julian, Mel Wulf, Marguerite Collins,
Rowland and Amanda Watermeyer and young Jane,
John Clark, Billy Adams, Jim White, Kanya D'Almeida,
Kym Roberts, Mary Foulke, Edwina Unrath, Barry Samuels,
Erin, Greg, Owen and Josephine Fitzsimmons, Peter Lam-
born Wilson, Jacquie Soohen, Salvatore Engel di-Mauro,
Colin Robinson, Philip Weiss, Roy Bourgeois,
Brigetta Gynther, Jonathan and Liam Kovel.

Autonomedia
POB 568 Williamsburgh Station
Brooklyn, New York 11211-0568 USA
info@autonomedia.org
www.autonomedia.org

Contents

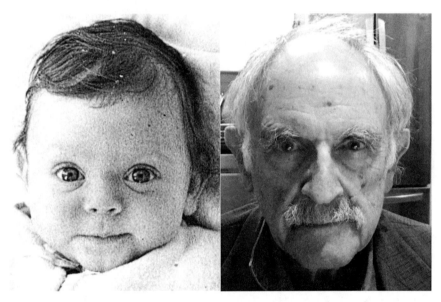

THE AUTHOR, THREE-AND-A-HALF MONTHS.
THE AUTHOR, NINE-HUNDRED-SIXTY-THREE-AND-A-HALF MONTHS.

Foreword
Peter McLaren

*T*he *Lost Traveller's Dream* is an extraordinary account of a life's journey, fiercely intimate and set about with such remarkable nuances of memory that at times it reads like an engrossing novel populated by the many well-known intellectuals, political figures, and artists who became at one time or another Joel Kovel's personal friends and collaborators.

It would be restrictive, however, to focus Kovel's narrative on elites. Though the dominant literary influence on Kovel's life and thought is the visionary William Blake (from whom the work's title is drawn), another case can be made for Geoffrey Chaucer, whose humanism stirred him from his first days at Yale. There is something of Chaucer's Tabard Inn in these pages, which become a gathering place for humanity in solidarity encountered over the years, from Black co-workers in Rockaway beach resort, to Caribe Indians in the Suriname rain forest, to patients wheeled at night through rat-infested Bellevue hospital, to Sandinista Nicaraguans battling US imperialism, or ANC militants against the Apartheid south African State, or Cubans for whom he helped lift the US blockade and citizens he approached during his Green Party campaign for the US Senate in 1998, and the presidential nomination in 2000, these latter guided by the prime contribution of his later years, the cause of Ecosocialism.

Yet it is also an account that ardently captures the complex interconnections between politics and biography, the material and the spiritual, grace and the soul, history and spirit, following the example of Chaucer's Clerk of Oxenford, that "he wolde gladly lerne and gladly teche."

The memoir is organized around a driving question: How did the precocious son of immigrant parents who grew up in Brooklyn under the dominion of an extreme right-wing, fascist-leaning father become so devoted to ruthlessly criticizing capitalism and devoting his life to the quixotic goal of bringing it down? Kovel, first and foremost a teacher, provides instructive illustrations, drawn from his life as well as from art, literature, and spirituality to answer this question.

As the reader moves from chapter to chapter, scientific literary, and political, references abound, woven into a tapestry of personal disclosure with an increasingly religious theme that falls away from his Jewish upbringing and toward a Christian calling that represents, for him, the destination of the Lost Traveller's Dream. Throughout, Kovel is able to make complex ideas accessible and evocative to readers regardless of their familiarity with Freud, Marx, Blake or the dozens of other thinkers he engages throughout his tale. In so doing, he models Paulo Freire's notion of "armed love," carefully, and often humorously, teaching what it means to be dedicated to the relentless struggle for social justice, even when that means personal vilification and isolation from those who have the power to reward compliance in the form of financial security, political victory, and academic prestige.

What stands out is Kovel's steadfast example of personally demonstrating through his actions his beliefs and political convictions, at great cost incurred twice at the top of the academic ladder. Such personal sacrifice does not lead him to fall into the trap of mounting a triumphalist defense: one man's personal victimization as a result of daring to challenge the regnant horrors of capitalism and its hydra-headed tentacles that reach inside every state institution in the country, savaging everyday life in the process. Kovel is much too sagaciously introspective and searingly self-critical to walk that path. Instead, *The Lost Traveller's Dream* is as much a form of self-analysis as it is fearless and courageous exposition, rife with jarring honesty.

Any path-breaking journey entails the risk of getting lost, even as in the process one finds oneself learning a great deal from those one never expects to meet. Like Chaucer, Kovel details the panorama of his society—late, disintegrating capitalism—with inspiring hopefulness.

The Lost Traveller's Dream chronicles a lifelong journey with such specificity that the reader will come to see that there's no singular path to becoming found, whether it be through education, political revolution, fortuitous meetings, or spiritual conversion. Kovel's achievements have secured for him an honorable place in the history of resistance to corrupt power, while his memoirs open the possibility for others to chart their own path toward the same destination.

PETER McLAREN is Distinguished Professor in Critical Studies, College of Educational Studies, Chapman University and author of numerous award-winning books, including *Che Guevara, Paulo Freire and the Pedagogy of Revolution* and *Pedagogy of Insurrection: From Resurrection to Revolution.*

To The Accuser who is
The God of This World

Truly My Satan thou art but a Dunce
And dost not know the Garment from the Man
Every Harlot was a Virgin once
Nor canst thou ever change Kate into Nan

Tho thou art Worshipd by the Names Divine
Of Jesus & Jehovah: thou art still
The Son of Morn in weary Nights decline
The lost Travellers Dream under the Hill

19

Preface

To The Accuser who is
The God of This World
Truly My Satan thou art but a Dunce
And dost not know the Garment from the Man.
Every Harlot was a Virgin once,
Nor canst thou ever change Kate into Nan.
Tho thou are Worshipd by the Names Divine
Of Jesus & Jehovah: thou art still
The Son of Morn in weary Nights decline
The lost Travellers Dream under the Hill.

— William Blake

The title of this memoir is drawn directly from the last line of this epilogue to an enigmatic work of 1820: "For the Sexes/THE GATES OF PARADISE."[1] It may have been the last line of poetry Blake committed to a copper plate. A copy of the engraving—with an image of a demon hovering over sleeping humanity and these lines above—was a parting gift from Catherine O'Neill, with whom I worked in my waning days as a psychotherapist in the 1980s. I do not recollect how she became aware of my fascination with Blake, but I deeply appreciated the gift and hope she reads this. I mounted it at eye level in front of my desk in our house in Willow, upstate New York, so that the spirit of Blake could be absorbed as I worked there. Years later, when the decision to write a memoir came, choosing a title was the easiest part. It was as though Blake's internalized voice had been urging me on all the while.

Here is a one sentence summary of what *The Lost Traveller's Dream* is about: a Jewish youth has a mystical experience of grace at age seventeen and then spends the next sixty years here, there and everywhere, until he ceases being Jewish, comes home to Christ Jesus, and is baptized. You see what I mean? I was lost, I travelled, and I dreamt. Except for being ridiculously stretched out, the story is not at all atypical. In fact, what I am going to write is essentially the theme of what has been far and away the most popular and influential hymn of the English speaking peoples over the last two centuries:

> Amazing grace! (how sweet the sound)
> That sav'd a wretch like me!
> that once was lost, but now am found,
> Was blind, but now I see.

To me grace indicates a kind of suffusion of the self with an all-benign, unbidden love. "All is grace," Robert Bresson's Country Priest said as he died, releasing another of my early mystical moments. As I have come to understand it, Christian life is centered about a praxis of grace organized about being human in relation to the universe. It is not a reward for good behavior, but an alignment, a harmonization between the individual, no longer isolated, the social collective, and the cosmos, no longer estranged and now manifest, as Blake called it, in "minute particulars."[2]

It is also manifest as Christ's activity in gathering followers. Albert Schweitzer's framing of this was famous. Jesus, wrote Schweitzer,

> comes to us as One unknown, without a name, as of old, by the lake-side, He came to those men who knew Him not. He speaks to us the same word: "Follow thou me" and sets us to the tasks which He has to fulfil for our time. He commands. And to those who obey Him, whether they be wise or simple, He will reveal Himself in the toils, the conflicts, the sufferings which they shall pass through in His fellowship, and, as an ineffable mystery, they shall learn in their own experience Who He is.

Of this two things can be said here. First, that Schweitzer was advancing the notion that Christ must be continually rediscovered through a historical lens, hence, that each epoch can do no more than get the Jesus it needs. And second, that the same principle applied to Schweitzer himself yields an obnoxious portrait of late-nineteenth century authoritarian paternalism, as also proved the case for his famous hospital at Lambaréné, Gabon.

In my own threading of a path through a life lived from 1936 to the present I became in midcourse deeply affected not only by Jesus and Blake, but also by Karl Marx. Out of this emerged the promotion of a well-known moral aphorism, that of "ruthless criticism," into a principle of depth and range, which refers to a need to overcome both fear of authorities and one's self-resistance. The theme shall return throughout the later phases of *The Lost Traveller's Dream*.

Earl Kooperkamp referred me to Schweitzer when I connected with St. Mary's Episcopal Church in Harlem, in 2009, after having been thrown out of Bard College—my second sacking from a prestigious professorship for left-wing agitation, and like the first, which was from the Albert Einstein College of Medicine, proof that I was not made to fit into this world.

In any case, the long journey to St. Mary's began with the Jewish neighborhoods of Brooklyn, moved to the enclaves of Nassau County, then to various high-powered educational settings (Chapters 1, 2) where I studied science (Chapter 3) and met up with Blake while browsing in the Yale library. I lurched from straight science to medicine, with some interesting adventures (Chapter 4), and then from medicine to psychiatry (Chapter 5) and Freudian psychoanalysis, following which a tour of duty within the Vietnam War provoked a massive crisis of values, moving me sharply leftward and confirming a new identity as a writer and an anti-imperial agitator (Chapter 6). The response to my first book, *White Racism*, brought me to Marx and led to all sorts of complications, including a break with psychoanalysis (Chapter 7) and my various sackings and bannings, along with new avenues of struggle, which I hope I have told with sufficient art (Chapters 8, 9, and 10).

Regarding this eighty-year journey as a symphonic tone poem, the religious motif enters at year seventeen, is eclipsed for decades and then returns in my forties, primed by political radicalization and major changes in personal attachment (Chapters 2 and 8). Much of the 1980s was spent in defending the Sandinista revolution in Nicaragua, the first in modern history to be animated by Liberation Theology, which I embraced whole-heartedly. Indeed, I would have converted then, were not the only available location the Roman Catholic Church, utterly unacceptable because of its male hierarchy.

Fascination with the spiritual side of things continued as two new themes came to occupy my later years: contending with the ecological crisis, which passed into the development of ecosocialism; and increasing outrage over the Jewish State of Israel, evolving into anti-Zionism. These define the stormy events of my later years at Bard College, which ended in separation from that institution, opening the path to St. Mary's and its denouement, described in Chapters 11–14, and rounded off with an epilogue.

I am not so foolish as to claim that I have in fact been found where I once was lost and can see where I was once blind. But I can assuredly say that I have fought the good fight (1 Timothy 1:18–19), and will continue to in this epoch of generalized collapse, happily outraged in outrageous times, for the sake of the little ones and their Kingdom of God.

And now, my story.

Notes

1 David Erdman, *The Complete Poetry & Prose of William Blake* (New York: Random House, 1988) 269. All Biblical references are from NRSV unless otherwise noted.

2 Erdman, "Jerusalem" Plate 91, 251. See also *passim* S. Foster Damon, *A Blake Dictionary*, rev. ed. (Providence: Brown University Press, 1988).

3 Albert Schweitzer, "The Quest of the Historical Jesus," Wikipedia, last modified November 12, 2012, https://en.wikisource.org/wiki/The_Quest_of_the_Historical_Jesus.

Chapter 1
Loomings

The bags had been unpacked, my mother had quarreled with Ben Wood's mother over which of us would get the better closet, we had met the third roommate, Walton Burr Sumner from somewhere in Texas, he who would bitterly protest the Supreme Court decision in *Brown v. Board of Education of Topeka* the next spring, and also our very liberal Freshman Adviser Allard Lowenstein of the Law School, who lived at the bottom of Durfee entryway. Later that day I went for a New Haven walk with my new friend from across the hallway, A. Lynn Williams, Jr, and learned that his father worked for the company with the odd name, at least to me in September 1953, of "International Business Machines" on its storefront. "What does he do?" I asked, and was told that A. Lynn Williams, Sr., was Executive Vice President of IBM. And so the fact was underscored that Yale, though physically placed in a small and run-down city not very far on the map from Long Island, was a long way indeed from my home in Baldwin on the South Shore of Nassau County. We were not, as Dorothy had put it, in Kansas any more.

THE PRESENTIMENT

A FEW DAYS LATER I learned something else about Yale when the Class of 1957, more than a thousand young men newly processed including by the ritual mortification of nude posture photos, gathered in Woolsey Hall for the inaugural lecture of our higher education. The setting was grand and we were formally attired in tweeds and neckties. Hardly anybody knew one another, excepting the several hundred boys from Andover, Exeter, and such places, who knew each other, it seemed, by birth; and it seemed no one knew of the speaker, an unprepossessing man named Richard Sewall. As for me, I knew nothing about anybody except that I was feeling lonely and es-tranged. I of course did not know that Sewall, born the same year as Rose Kovel, 1908, was an exceptionally beloved teacher of English literature who would in 1974 win a National Book Award for his study of Emily Dickinson—nor, needless to add, could I have guessed that I would be a finalist for the same award in 1972. I did not know that he loomed large enough in the affairs of the university as to become the headmaster a few years later of newly opened Ezra Stiles, one of Yale's residential colleges, where he would appoint the aforementioned Lowenstein to be one of its Fellows, supporting him when he led the call for the resignation of President Johnson for his waging of war in Vietnam, and intervening on behalf of Black Pan-thers and student radicals when they threatened to tear the campus apart in that epoch of protest. Nor did I know that Sewall was the son of Reverend Charles G. Sewall, himself the thirteenth son in an unbroken sequence of Congregational ministers. Or that his mother, Kate Strong, was the daughter of Reverend Augustus Hopkins Strong, Baptist, perhaps the leading Protestant theologian of the late nineteenth century and personal minister to John D. Rockefeller.

As Sewall's lecture settled into its rhythm my estrangement was replaced by rapt concentration. He started off with a nicely wrought discourse on the conduct of life, and shifted towards the close of his speech into higher gear, a rhetorical pattern in which a series of virtues were postulated, as though a succession of steps each rising from the place of the step before, three steps to be exact, painstak-ingly made from common words, each very convincingly drawn so that as one paused on a step to consider what it was about, it seemed as far as one could go, only to become abruptly confronted by the surpassing step beyond. Faith was the first step, yes, the inner belief in something beyond ourselves and the persevering in that belief; that was very fine indeed, and seemed as good as things got. But no, there was, beyond faith, Hope, a kind of faith which actively sought the future, faith in a kind of goodness in the world, a good-ness we could bring about because of faith in a world-changing power within us. That was better, was it not? And it, too, seemed as far as we could go and as good as it got…. But then the next step arrived and we stubbed our toe on it, until Sewall helped us upward. It was a step he called—and here I remember the exact words—"the greatest of these: Love…"

Love!… I melted: became aware of an exalted kind of feeling such as I had never felt before, a great crescendo, or better, since it wasn't quite that abrupt, the welling up of a liquid on which I was now floating. Words are feeble here, but it matters to say that the emotion was joyous in the extreme, at least by the standards of one whose joy had until then been measured out as attached to something concrete, like watching Jackie Robinson on the basepaths. The joy Sewall was spreading had no object to it: it was just that, an "it," suffusing everything, including myself. Trailing this affect, as the sky for a swimmer might be clouded by a spume tossed up by waves, was a kind of puzzlement, for I hadn't the least idea of what "Love" meant in Sewall's sense, except that it did not correspond to the meanings I gave the word in ordinary speech—that I "loved" books, sports, movies, chess, pizza, Mother's borscht, learning new things, Shakespeare, and mathematics. I was fond of my friends, but that was that; I had never come close enough to a girl to even haltingly try out that word; my family was composed, with one exception, of beings toward whom I felt a cacophony of emotions among which love was but one, clouded part; and as for loving myself, well, that was a poor joke given my habitual state of mind. Sewall was propounding a reality that swept everything else before it that remotely belonged to the world I knew—and yet was inextricably tied to and suffusing everything in this world. And I had known nothing of it.

No mystery about that: there had been nothing in life to prepare me for such an ecstasy. The great majority of Christians in the audience would likely have had little trouble in picking up the quotation from 1 Corinthians 13:13, though habit would also likely have dimmed the reaction of many. Meanwhile, I knew nothing of what to do with what I had felt. Thus my reaction proved transient. I was not ready for it by virtue of immaturity and Jewish upbringing, had no knowledge, much less understanding of a Saint Paul, had nowhere to go with what I felt and knew no coherent desire to go anywhere beyond the pressing demands of the university. Swept aside, my first Pauline moment became a lonely outpost in memory, eclipsed by lesser but more urgent events. It faded and became isolated in its clearing, as if surrounded and choked by weeds.

The second presentiment, two years after. We had in New Haven a small theatre near the campus to which one repaired for low-cost "art" cinema. I remember seeing Olivier's *Hamlet* there and also his *Henry V*—this my second viewing, ten years after Mother and I traipsed down to the movie house on Coney Island Avenue, where our neighbors held rallies in support of the heroic Soviet armies, to behold with slackened jaw the dazzling transforming of the coarse Elizabethan stage into a tapestry of the imagination.

Nothing dazzled the eye now. The images on the screen utterly lacked Shakespearean eloquence and splendor, indeed they lacked any ostensible appeal. What had led me to such a gloomy and grainy production as Robert Bresson's *Diary of a Country Priest*? I believe the night was rainy, else I would have quit the cinema for the streets. Who needed this misery? Everything on screen was going wrong, everybody was awful, uncomprehending, or wracked with pain. A wretched priest made dreary rounds through a dull countryside. Little was said; the sound track was mostly taken up with off-screen rustling noises like the raking of leaves or footsteps walking away from what passed for action; this included being mocked by a girl who pretended, first to know her catechism, and then to be romantically drawn to the priest. Eventually the priest got an aristocratic lady to face the death of her child, only to have her die the next night—himself blamed for it. And he himself was dying. Like Kafka's "A Hunger Artist," the priest can not get the right food; and the nourishment he does get is killing him. A wealthy parishioner shoots a rabbit and offers him a tasty stew—but the priest can only eat dried bread and wine. He goes to his grave a complete failure, his final words, spoken off-screen by a friend who cared for him at the end, were that "all is grace."

During the second half of the film I was in a more or less continuous and incomprehensible state of tears. Too ignorant to pick up the symbolism of the sacrament and its failure, too obtuse to see that the priest was Jesus mocked and scorned, unable to situate Bresson in the circuits of French Catholicism and history, I nonetheless sat and wept. And then I went out into the rainy New Haven night—perhaps to go back and study my physical chemistry and the laws of thermodynamics, perhaps to go with the Group to the Colosseum Diner for scrambled eggs and potatoes laced with enormous amounts of tasty grease and ketchup and accompanied by witty camaraderie into the morning hours. One thing I am certain would not have happened was a discussion in our booth about the little priest and what he meant for us and the world. Nobody would have dreamed of such a thing.

BOOLA BOOLA DAYS

WHERE DO SUCH THINGS come from so that they burst upon the mind like thunderclaps? Nothing in my childhood could be said to have prepared me for them; and yet there must have been something within me that met them on their path. As for the locus of that time, Yale, its influence was ambivalent—for on the one side it was Christian to the core, quite capable of evoking presentiments of Jesus; while on the other it was one of the great Mills of Satanic success: the Devil citing scripture; AntiChrist peering out from the shroud of our Savior. After Sewall's evocation of St. Paul, the assembly burst into one of those Protestant marching hymns that stir the soul and prime it for conquest. The spirit was roused, all right, but the trappings remained and turned the Love intended by Paul into idolatry. I'm still trying to sort out these things. But for that moment, in the first autumn of the Eisenhower administration, with foreign policy under the devoutly Presbyterian, atom-bomb waving, Massive Retaliation terror of John Foster Dulles, with the CIA recruiting in President A. Whitney Griswold's office, and Senator McCarthy and his kind casting thick clouds of repression over America, what chance was there for God's Love to flourish as Agape and realize the Priest's grace? What chance, indeed, at mighty Yale, where, as its minimally critical voices averred, the "bitch goddess of success" was worshipped and the National Security State was being spawned.

My life to this point could serve as a sociological case study of cultural displacement, one that left me without an integral sense of who I was while providing me with an inchoate drive to "make it" in order to fill in the missing spaces. I hailed on both sides from an Ashkenazi clan fleeing the darkness of Tsarist Ukraine—dark in that sense common to millions of Jewish immigrants from Eastern Europe who for all practical purposes had no history; for even though we knew that like all human beings, we had a history, we had no way of gathering it, given the neglect of the Jewish population, the lack of vital statistics, the rude interruptions of the transition to the New World and the great cataclysms that befell so many, especially in thrice backward Ukraine, during much of the 20th century.

And so we were primed for Americanization. Efforts to retrieve entry data from Ellis Island have failed on several occasions; while a serious attempt to trace the genealogy of Rose Kovel's "Farber" side of the family fizzled after a promising beginning. Thus my history came to be almost entirely imagined; there was nothing in it, really, that could anchor a sense of myself except what I picked up from the environment. The only success I can record in learning anything about the generations prior to grandparents came many years later from paying *National Geographic* one hundred dollars and sending them a scraping from inside my cheek in order to identify the paternal line through the Y-chromosome.

This informed me that about twenty thousand years ago, an Ur-Kovel went more or less straight north from the Rift Valley. Passing along the eastern end of the Mediterranean, he journeyed through Asia Minor and northward to what is known as Macedonia and Bulgaria, before disappearing from the genetic record, and, like the tree falling unheard in the forest, from existence. So much for that—though it was useful also to know that at least one strand of the Kovel line had departed Canaan many thousands of years before it became the setting for the drama of the Israelites. So possibly I am a descendant of those central Asian converts to Judaism in the eighth century CE, the Khazars. I have been told that I look like a Cossack, and who can say what dalliance or rape occurred down the line of that great mixing pot we call the human species? But it can be said,

Above: LOUIS KOVEL FAMILY, CIRCA 1910. LOUIS AT LEFT.
Below: THE FARBER FAMILY, CIRCA 1919. FROM LEFT, FRIEDA,
HER MOTHER (DIED 1919), ROSE STANDING NEXT TO HER
FATHER JULIUS, BESS SEATED.

for better or worse, that I am no "Semite," a point driven home when I met a classmate at Yale, George Lasry, a Sephardic Jew, hence actually "Semitic," whatever such a silly appellation is worth, who was from Morocco, and decidedly different in bearing and identity, being, so it seemed, much more sure of who he was than was I.

None of this was any concern to the Kovel and Farber families as they adapted to the New World. Grandfather Meyer Kovel, a housepainter from Dnepropetrovsk fleeing the Tsar's draft (twenty years for the Jewish recruit) and desperately poor for most of his sojourn in the Promised Land, was wont to tell people that they should "kiss the earth" of America. Some years later Julius Farber brought his bride from Zhitomir following a scandalous elopement and was forced to live under the conditions of extreme crowding that characterized the Lower East Side in the early years of the twentieth century; he adapted reasonably well as a repairer of watches, albeit with some dreadful turns of event that shall be recounted later on.

Louis Kovel (b. 1901) and Rose Farber (b. 1908) were each the eldest of a set of five, both were immersed in the vital world of New York Jewry—a great machine for swirling together tradition and modernity—and neither landed very far from the family tree. Both were poor. They chiefly differed from their parents in having English as a first language and Yiddish as the second, hence were enabled to partake of the great cultural wealth dispersed by New York in those days to its immigrant workers. Without perturbing the ties that bound them to the Jewish community, Lou and Rose adopted a white-collar way of life: for him, an accountant's job, specializing in taxes; for her, that of a personal secretary, at one point to the well-known author and convert to Catholicism, Fulton Oursler, who wrote *The Greatest Story Ever Told*.

Rose and Lou met through the circuits that enabled young New York Jews to find companions and, hopefully, partners. Of course there were no Club Meds in those days. However, the Catskills were well-stocked with affordable and accessible alternatives, and it was in one such resort, Green Mansions, that Lou and Rose found one another and began a courtship, leading to marriage in 1935. The world was mired in the Great Depression; but prudent Lou Kovel had managed to obtain a position with the Internal Revenue Service. This permitted a decent honeymoon to Italy on the *Andrea Doria* and afterwards, a relatively secure if modest life. As the economic climate improved, Lou switched sides and became a tax accountant specializing in helping prosperous men stay so. Eventually, he became one of them at the lower end of the upper-middle class, nonetheless a perch that enabled some exploitation of the great expansion of the United States economy in the post-war era.

LOUIS KOVEL AS A YOUNG MAN

From an economic standpoint, then, the life I grew up into was unremarkable in the extreme, and bourgeois—or should we call it *petit-bourgeois?*— through and through. In any case, we were a real, live nuclear family. Lou left every weekday for his nine-to-five job; and Rose left her job for the life of a housewife and perfected the arts of domesticity with the ferocity that was her hallmark, even learning how to fold contour sheets. The proper succession of dwellings followed *en suite*—from plain rental, to an exceedingly modest semi-attached Brooklyn home on East 10th Street purchased in 1941 for about eight thousand dollars, then in 1949, the Hegira to the suburbs, Long Island where I attended high school, and a succession of homes with lawns and picket fences, well-tended apartment complexes when houses became too much trouble, and the final resting place after 1973, Century Village in West Palm Beach, where on occasion one could even find a long-lost neighbor from Zhitomir or Dnepropetrovsk sitting by the pool. My youth had its troubles, but economic hardship was not among them.

I WAS THE FIRSTBORN and both extended families marveled at me. It has been the same for millions and millions of babies, including those I have fathered, but this was no statistic and no observation from without. It was me—this protozoan—assembling his being. What did I know or care that we were a bunch of Jewish nobodies living on a leafy street in the Midwood section of Brooklyn? There were books, were there not? Each one was for precocious little Joel, another diorama of the limitless inner world. Grandpa Meyer Kovel, may his soul be blessed, taught me to read and to play chess; and I was so fired up as to weep bitter tears after my first day at PS 99's kindergarten. "Mama!," I was said to scream, "They didn't teach me anything! ONLY BLOCKS!"... an early sign of alienation from machinery and dissatisfaction with authority, but much more important, of love of learning, of knowledge for itself and for transmission to others. I learned my Chaucer from Joseph Toy Curtiss at Yale, and of all its beautiful lines one descriptive of his Clerk from Oxenford (i.e., a student of philosphy at Oxford) most stuck in mind: "And gladly wolde he lern, and gladly teche." I should like it to be my epitaph.

BECOMING A MODERN AMERICAN

AS A JEWISH YOUNGSTER I was heir to a tradition that had given numberless generations an identity whose strength depended upon tribalism, dispossession and a sense of victimization; from another perspective, whose power to organize the inner world was yoked to a lack of power to organize the world at large. Traditionally, then, Jews survived as Jews by being strong at close range, in matters defined tribally, to compensate for weakness at long-range. We knew who we were, but who we were did not count for much.

The Jewish generations who followed the period of emancipation entered modernity with a vengeance, and, if truth be told, with something of a vengeance in mind, to show the Goyim just what we could do. This was especially fateful for the Jews of the United States, who have enacted the most remarkable success story of any ethnic group within a modern liberal democracy. Mine was the first generation to break through on a large scale to higher, meritocratic ground. This I experienced as follows: we Jews were going to make up for time lost to centuries of victimization at the hands of anti-Semites; we were going to prove our ethical and intellectual superiority, get the hell out of the ghetto, and find our place in the sun. This was to be done through hard work and discipline and by embracing the values of modernity in spades. These latter were chiefly, as I saw it, those of science. And indeed we did. PS 99, my modest school on East 10th Street, just across from our house at 1139 and so it seemed, 100% Jewish, had what is called a Rapid Advance Class, where the brightest kids were gathered (Allen "Red" Koningsberg, the future Woody Allen, was one, and a member of a little "rat pack" that sowed some mischief). Four or five of our graduates were among the forty finalists in the national Westinghouse Science competition four years later—not including me, alas, even though I won the Science Medal. When I went to Yale it was under a strictly enforced 10% quota and I knew but one Jewish faculty member: Charles Blitzer, a lovely gentleman, melancholy and lonely, perhaps because he was gay. Fifty years later, Jews comprised some 17% of the faculty, including the last two Presidents, utterly unthinkable in the era of A. Whitney Griswold.

BOTH ROSE AND LOU Kovel were cultured, and in their separate ways, politically engaged. Mother's family had been musical—one of her uncles, Mark Markoff, became an opera singer and voice teacher in Los Angeles, while Grandpa Julius could often be heard pleasantly plucking his mandolin. Opera became Rose's great love, photography, model building and painting, that of Lou. She sang in the Second Chorus of the Metropolitan Opera, and regaled me with tales of great sopranos and recordings of the works of Richard Strauss and what was for her the supreme moment of art: Lotte Lehmann as the Marschallin in *Der Rosenkavalier*, a tale of an aging Grand-dame who sacrifices her love for a young man (sung by a woman: Freudians, take note!).

Father, emerging from no discernable cultural lineage, was to my view the greater talent, a true mute inglorious Milton. Wandering with Leica or Rolleiflex in hand, he produced austere black-and-

NEW YORK AS PHOTOGRAPHED BY LOUIS KOVEL

white cityscapes of real merit; indeed, I was struck a few years ago at an exhibition of the Leica photography of the outstanding painter Ben Shahn—who happened to have been an acquaintance of Lou Kovel in the years before I was born—that one could substitute some of father's photography for that of Shahn and nobody would know the difference. Needless to say, their paintings were at entirely different levels. Even here, however, though clearly an amateur, Lou Kovel was no slouch. Excelling more in scenes of buildings than por- traiture, there is yet an oil painting of me at age four, awkwardly hi- eratic, that hangs at the top of our staircase in Willow and adorns the cover of this book.

If only they could have restricted themselves to the arts and left politics aside! Mother's Zionism played no special role for me in this phase of life, though a great deal later on. Not so for Lou Kovel's pol- itics, which crashed into me like a wild bull from my first days of awareness. I have mentioned Ben Shahn. Father never discussed Shahn's paintings or photographs so far as I can remember. Not so for Shahn's politics. Evidently Lou Kovel in the late '20s and early '30s ran in the same circles as Shahn, a leftist well known for sympa- thies with workers and the oppressed. Somewhere along this line a violent veering took place in my father's soul, moving him precipi- tously to the political right. This was chiefly manifested as rage against those who betrayed civilization, America, and so it seemed, himself, by not appreciating the menace inherent in Communism, the USSR, and Josef Stalin. Among these Fellow Travellers, Ben Shahn held a place of special treachery, as I heard on many occasions, though given my tender age and Lou Kovel's predilection for violent decla- mation rather than reasoned argument I never had the slightest un- derstanding of what this Shahn had done or believed. Nor was Shahn alone in league with the devil, even among artists. The great Picasso and the great Casals were also singled out, chiefly, it seemed, for the mortal sin of exiling themselves from the Spain ruled by one of Fa- ther's heroes, the fascist Generalissimo Francisco Franco: a truly stag- gering realization, the fascist sympathies of one's father. Franklin Roosevelt, no surprise, came in for a heavy dose of hatred as well, as I learned in fright during the 1944 election campaign when I brought

JULIUS, ROSE, FREIDA AND BESS

home to show Daddy a flyer extolling FDR handed to me on the street by a Democratic Party campaigner, to be met with a towering fury that made me fear for my life. For Lou Kovel had serious problems with anger management, and his existence was sown with dire threats. He would at times threaten me with a fearsome whip, the "cat-o'-nine-tails," to underscore the gravity of his charges—not very helpful for a growing boy's sense of security. The company of the damned radiated outward to include family and friends—fewer and fewer of whom remained friends of Lou Kovel in view of the fact that Father was given to throwing them out of his house for betraying civilization with their poisonous beliefs. Such catastrophic events, accompanied by screams and bellows, happened on more than one occasion, and became routinely inflated in significance by the pressure cooker that was my imagination.

A weird irony ensued. At one, delusional, level were the warnings regularly dispensed by father to the effect that the whole world, and most definitely, the whole United States, was about to be overrun by the Communists and their Fellow Travellers; at another, factual, level, it was indeed the case that our neighborhood, the Midwood

district of Brooklyn, was extremely left-oriented, with a very substantial presence of flesh and blood Communists and Soviet sympa-
thizers. Thus Lou Kovel's delusion was instantiated locally.
Everywhere I bicycled, from Avenue I to Kings Highway, and from
Ocean Parkway to the trestle for the line of the F Train on 16th Street,
one could see evidence of Communist presence. A child can be for-
given for limitations of mind that would lead him to generalize this
information to the whole of the United States along the conceptual
grid supplied by his lunatic father—though it must be added that
this child never had much aptitude for forgiving himself.

Soon enough I found my accuser. By early adolescence, partly
from imbibing the surrounding Zeitgeist and partly from an emerging autonomous humanism, I indeed began to evince certain forbidden democratic and left tendencies. And so began the domestic
Inquisition of incipient Communism in the province of 1139 East
10th Street, Brooklyn, NY, pretty much synchronized with what was
beginning in society at large except that the punishment was all subjective—and was to be developed with what I was to write about
forty-five years later in *Red Hunting in the Promised Land,* a comprehensive study of the persecutory tendency in America.

It is no surprise that so much of my later work came to be centered
about a politically inflected dialectic between inner and outer, subject
and object, differentiation and splitting. The world with its history,
and the self with its inwardness; matter with its thingness and spirit
that breaks the chains of matter. All of this drew me to Blake himself,
and to associated figures like Jacob Boehme or Paracelsus, figures I
scarcely touch upon within the confines of this memoir: all these entities are also aspects of problems that defined my early years and
were carried forward. They were not caused by the relations in my
family I describe in these opening chapters—which themselves were
shaped extrinsically. But what happened between me and my father
shaped my thinking and gave me a stage and vocabulary to represent
what mattered.

The wars with Lou Kovel went on until a time came, in 1960,
while on a visit home from medical school, another monster quarrel
broke out between father and son, the former now on his downhill

path and the latter rising though by no means the flaming Red he would become in mid decade. I forget the subject, which matters not except for being the nth variation on the same old theme. We went round and round, two weary pugilists, then paused, looked at one another, and weeping uncontrollably, fell in each other's arms.

That was the last battle between us. Eventually, I came out of it all with an intricate set of identifications with Father and also resistance to what I cannot but see as his deeply misguided life. No doubt, the influence of Lou Kovel on me is profound, first, in tendencies to see perfidy and menace in certain groups; second, a reversed signification of who was to blame and whom to protect; third, a sharper sense of how to go about things, including self-criticism as well as criticism of others; fourth, linked with this, a capacity or at least the goal, to see all sides of an argument and a hope, as I never abandoned with Lou Kovel, of reconciliation. I identify with Father in being extreme and not moderate in my views; and as a corollary to that, of resisting going along with the crowd. And the dichotomy between the direction of our views led me to differentiate between persons and the ideas or states of being they embody and represent. Thus all persons have sacred rights, even evil-doers who have to be brought to justice, and certainly Lou Kovel, who was not at all evil, but in the grip of pathological and deluded ideas. Thus ideas and ideologies have no inherent rights at all; and bad ones, like all forms of chauvinism, or the idea of the inferior rights of women, should be thrown into the proverbial dustbin of history.

No end of conflict, then, for the firstborn of Lou Kovel, but a profound gratitude to father, for making me thoughtful and sharpening my wits.

An especially important moment of reconciliation came to pass in the weighty decision of which institution of higher learning to seek. I was desperate to get out of the bland suburban Hell of Baldwin, Long Island; Lou Kovel was desperate to see his talented son in the most prestigious possible university; there were several decent choices, but one, Yale, was the clear winner, especially after the two of us bonded to each other there on a fine day in May 1952, through the luminous haze that seemed to bathe the neo-gothic buildings, the exquisite courtyard of Branford College at the foot of Harkness Tower, the great Sterling Library and Gymnasium—all redolent of that grandeur toward which Lou Kovel sought, like a moth its flame, a grandeur that both adorned and projected the might of his New Rome, as depicted by his favorite authors, Gibbon and Spengler. It must have seemed to my father the Golden Palace at the end of the long road from Ukraine; while to his son, who was to be what his father was not, it seemed a Golden Door. Was this laying the ground work for my epiphany at Richard Sewall's address sixteen months on?

There were two little bumps on the road to New Haven—the first, discovery of a book, *God and Man at Yale,* composed by a recently graduated Roman Catholic—scarcely an outsider but member of both Skull and Bones and the CIA—William F. Buckley, who averred that the university had been drifting away from the firm beliefs of its Founding Fathers and toward a dangerous "relativism," i.e., left-leaning and godless thought. The second was receiving a Regents Scholarship to the perfectly respectable, indeed, excellent, "safe school," Cornell, in upstate New York.

Not to worry: Father may have recognized Buckley's tantrum for what it was—a demand of the *arriviste* Catholic bourgeoisie for a seat at the table of Protestant power, and a sign that the forces of political reaction were making their move to control the terms of debate; in any case, he took it in the spirit that there was no such thing as bad publicity. As for the threat of a scholarship to my dreams of Ivy League glory, I am ashamed to say that I went to bed the night of its receipt in a dismal state of mind, anticipating an outburst of Lou Kovel's fathomless anxiety about money. It turned out, however, that the specter of poverty that hung over all his days could be pushed aside like a gauzy curtain by the breath of his dream. The next morning I awoke to find an envelope by my bed. Inside was the letter from the Regents, and on it, written in father's fine hand, were the words, "Joel, you don't have to go to Cornell for this." From Dnepropetrovsk through Williamsburg, so poor that he had to work at extinguishing street lamps each morning on his way to Boys' High School, he who had sacrificed immeasurably to support

JOEL (LEFT), WITH PAUL CHEVIGNY, ROY JACKSON AND ANDRE SCHIFFRIN

a family with two chronically ill siblings kept at home because of poverty and shame, and who became a legendary penny-pincher and radiated penury all the days of his life…. Lou Kovel was sacrificing again, to send his boy to Yale.

AT ITS BEST, YALE PROVED an occasion to gratify my endless curiosity and thirst for knowledge. At its worst it was the occasion to give reign to a ridiculous level of competiveness. I recall with shame the baffled look on my Classical Civilization instructor's face as I came raging into his office because he gave me a mere B+ for my midterm grade. This was well before the era of grade inflation, and B+ was a quite respectable, indeed, excellent grade—but not for this future Junior Phi Beta Kappa student. How dare he! Why, didn't he know who he was dealing with?… He practically threw me out while passing on the advice that I should relax and just try to enjoy my learning. How could I explain that my competitiveness ran parallel with, but did not consume my curiosity and love of learning? In any case, I never took a course considered "gut" but only what I loved.

I immensely enjoyed my studies, auditing three courses faithfully in addition to my heavy course load and browsing like Nietzsche's camel becoming a child among the shelves of the great libraries. The longing I had expressed my first day in kindergarten, that somebody had better teach me something, was finally being gratified. So, despite my rapacious greed for high grades, I really loved studying Classical Civilization, Lou Kovel's *Glory of Greece and Grandeur of Rome,* so much so that the next year I audited the great Bernard Knox's two-semester sequence in Athenian Tragedy.

Knox was British. When he was eighteen—my age when I attended his lectures—he was leading study groups in Marx at Cambridge; three years later he was fighting for the Spanish Republic and came within an ace of losing his life; in WWII he joined up as a regular soldier, but soon became bored, volunteered for the OSS and was dropped behind Nazi lines, where he spent the rest of the war fighting with left-wing partisans in France and Italy. While holed up in an Italian villa, Knox discovered a trove of ancient Greek and Latin literature and acquired the vocation of a Classical scholar. After the war he made the round of great universities, became a legendary teacher, and was showered with honors until his death in 2010 at age 95.

So what? Well to me, whether at age eighteen auditing Knox or at 75 writing about him, quite a bit: it seemed in 2011 as it did in 1954 that here, in the person of Bernard MacGregor Walker Knox, was a life worth living, full of glory and heroism. And of course, the corollary needs be noted: measured against Knox, my life is paltry and conformist. Nothing, you see, will ever be good enough for this unquiet soul. Mind you, I never knew Knox beyond a glancing greeting at his classes. But he slips into a role I have set for him on the inner stage, of the good father who loved the past without dishonoring the present or future, who lived into ripeness and did not slip into an ignominious, terrible end as shall be recounted for Lou Kovel in the next chapter. Knox, this lovely stranger, is poised in memory as one of earth's honored guests, not the unlovely heath-storming Lear that was my poor Lou Kovel. And in comparison to my restless self (for there are dyads here and the self is multitudinous), he had an integral sense of presence and identity beyond my reach. Bernard Knox knew to fight the fascism that Lou Kovel admired, risking all, while I, at comparable age, had no sense of commitment worth mentioning. I was stirred, to be sure, by the great surge of Civil Rights movements that surfaced during my college years; and I became aware of an affection for Black people that took me by surprise as their struggle evolved. But I never seriously thought of doing anything about this until 1966 when my writing career commenced; and even then my sentiment was not connected with an impulse to make a difference in the world except through my writing, much less to risk anything beyond neglect or ridicule for my *outré* beliefs.

My backwardness could be explained by the suffocating political atmosphere of the 1950s; or by petit-bourgeois acculturation; or the excruciating situation of having a father who himself was a fascist sympathizer. And what, in any case, is there to justify? Have I not managed to evince a fair amount in the way of commitment as the years went by, enough to qualify as an exception to the rule that a man of sound mind sheds his youthful leftist ideals as he matures, calms down, takes his place in the world, and gets his proper reward?

This puts the shoe on the other foot where Bernard Knox is concerned. Were the fires of revolt banked in him after his war days so that he could move up the ladder and find his reward? Did Knox become more sensible and abandon his revolutionary verve? Was he the better man for doing, or I, who wandered, lost, in search of a vision? This is perhaps silly speculation—though Knox does seem to have spent a great deal of time in contributing to the *New York Review* in his later years, not the kind of publication that circulates the views of ardent supporters of the Spanish Republic. So if I were twenty years older and as militant in 1936 as I am now, instead of merely being born as the Spanish Civil War broke out… who knows? Would I, all afire with the ardent radical left *zeitgeist* of the '30s, have joined the Abraham Lincoln Brigade, perhaps to die in Spain next to my *compañero* Bernard Knox, perhaps to survive to channel my gifts into a lifetime of reward from those institutions that have made me a pariah?

My time at Yale, 1953–57, was one of eclipse for the Left. Nevertheless, a small but significant light shone down from the sanctum of Norman Thomas' League for Industrial Democracy, or to be more exact, the "Student" version thereof. In little more than a decade, SLID was to metamorphose into Students for a Democratic Society and become a bellwether of the New Left. During my college days this was, shall we say, a premature tendency—though not absolutely so, thanks to the leadership of one of my closest Yale friends, André Schiffrin. He brought a level of talent and sophistication that mattered to the organization and a lot more to me, who had no inkling that people of my generation could think strategically about politics, participate in the high political and intellectual culture of Europe, or be so insouciant about meeting the standards of the university. Bearing the wounds of many frantic hours of staring at blank pages as deadlines were counted down, I marveled at Schiffrin's ability to toss off first-draft papers at the rate of one thousand words per hour, confident of getting through with flying colors, and of his comprehensive and effortless grasp of Socialism as absorbed in a French childhood amongst intellectual elites. I was also impressed by the self-confidence that permitted him blithely to walk about conformist Yale in double-breasted suits of European origin. This was not by choice but a manifestation of penury deriving from the dislocation and tribulations of war: the suits were all André—who lived with

JOEL (LEFT), WITH ANDRE SCHIFFRIN, PAUL CHEVIGNY AND ROY JACKSON

his widowed mother in the only address on Park Avenue south of 96th Street which could be classified as poverty housing—possessed.

Schiffrin launched the Yale chapter of SLID under the marginally more auspicious name of the John Dewey Society. It was ostensibly a provider of a lecture series bringing social democrats like Irving Howe to campus; and also, and more meaningfully, a social club where an embryonic left could assemble and enjoy one another's company. Befitting an elite university, we were a group of irregular and talented fellows, more clever by half than most others, and by and large destined for successful lives (though three of our circle were to end as suicides). The JDS included Paul Chevigny, who has become an eminent legal scholar and critic of the reactionary police practices within advanced democracy; Jonathan Weiss, son of the legendary Yale Philosopher Paul Weiss, and pioneer in bringing legal services to the poor and elderly; Jesse Lemisch, who was to become a distinguished and embattled leftist historian; and though "small and weak" by his own estimate, certainly not least, Roy Jackson, scion of degenerate WASP landed gentry in Danbury, CT, whose aortic valve was scarred by rheumatic fever in childhood, who became celebrated for dressing down Senator Joe McCarthy at age twelve when the latter paid a visit to his home town, and as his all-too short and doomed life went downhill, became a kind of Lucifer as he squandered his inheritance in pursuit of venery.

Thus there was a species of Left politics at Yale in those days; but how far, and to what left, might be inferred from two of our brightest and best members, Richard Posner and Robert Rifkind. The former is famous as the prolific and right-wing Libertarian member of the Seventh Circuit Court of Appeals and has been called the greatest legal scholar of our time. The latter we knew as "Young Robby Rifkind," because in his case, there was a then-famous father to take into account: Judge Simon Rifkind, attorney for Jacqueline Kennedy among many others, and said by William O. Douglas to have been the best lawyer ever to argue before the U.S. Supreme Court while he sat on it. Born in the same year, 1901, as Lou Kovel, and like him an early-century immigrant from Eastern Europe to these shores, Rifkind the Elder (we also called him "Old-Robby") was a poster boy for the fabulous success of American Jewry and its capacity to remain integrated with the public affairs of the Jewish people.

He took a leave in 1946 to work with Holocaust victims and became devoted to the cause of Israel. Little did anyone know just what this involved. Even now, when the story has been uncovered by Grant Smith, hardly anybody knows—and more to the point, cares—what Judge Rifkind was doing for an obscure Jewish-American organization, the American Zionist Committee, to enable it to evade the requirements of the Foreign Agents Registration Act of 1939. This stipulates, as its name implies, that those who represent a foreign power within the United States turn over their records to the Justice Department and allow their affairs to be inspected and regulated by the host government. As anybody of modest wit knows by now, the State of Israel is not regarded as a foreign power within the political culture of the United States of America; to the contrary, it substantially controls the foreign policy of its host government. And for this we are substantially indebted to the indefatigable Simon Rifkind's success in evading FARA on behalf of the AZC, which, freed from onerous regulation, took the name of the American-Israel Public Affairs Committee and went on from there to take charge of the United States government on behalf of Israeli interests, chiefly by being a Zionist brokerage house controlling the flow of campaign funds to elected officials.

Young Robby Rifkind does not have the fame of his father, but this fruit did not fall far from the tree. A different top-drawer law firm—the father's Paul, Weiss, Rifkind and Garrison being replaced by Cravath, Swaine, and Moore—and a different set of public positions within the enduring institutional framework of our ruling class; but the same high bourgeois identity, the same insistence on the righteousness of the Jewish State of Israel and the same relentlessness in hammering away at the forge of Zionist interests. Young Robby actually has gone further in this direction than Simon, who must have been very happy when, nine months before his death at 95, his son, now President of the American Jewish Committee, sat down with Pope John Paul II at the Vatican, to praise the Pontiff for the improvement in Jewish-Catholic relations and warn him against people who distort the history of the Holocaust. That's right: Young Robby Rifkind was lecturing the Pope!!! Oh, the power and the glory of Jews who trod the path of Zionism! From the pushcarts to the boardrooms, with patient, painstaking organizing according to a plan that never had to be written down: first accumulate the money and take care of our own, then move our people through the great institutions like Yale and into Civil Society, then buy the politicians until the state is under control. Then, use the WASP state to midwife the Jewish state, then control the foreign policy of the WASP state to make it subservient to the Jewish state, and always, always, keep control of the discourse by beating back the opposition with the eternal "Look what you have done to us," which grows into the allegation of anti-Semitism for those who criticize Zionism.[1]

TWO YEARS AFTER TEACHING Wojtyła a lesson, Robert Rifkind assumed the presidency of the Charles Revson Foundation, a substantial portion of whose charity is given in the cause of Hasbara, that is, normalizing Israel and painting it in progressive and humanitarian hues. His college buddy Richard Posner took a different path consistent with his Libertarianism, and has been substantially critical of Israeli jurisprudence. In any case, in 1955, the State of Israel meant nothing to me; and I only knew Bob Rifkind as a very decent, very bright, and somewhat stodgy friend, who, like Posner and all the rest made me proud to be in such a group as the John Dewey Society—whose collective identity also underscored the judgment of Tom Cohen, son of the founder of *Commentary* magazine, and one of the closest of my companions in those days, that perhaps it would better to rename ourselves as the "Don Jewey Society."

Relishing our cleverness and sense of superiority kept the John Dewey Society insulated from the world around us. This has been the way of fraternities and cliques within colleges from time immemorial, but Yale elevated the tendency, because, after all, Yale was a breeding ground for superior beings, and its men needed to see themselves as high above the masses. This attitude was at its worst in the 1950s, when the "town" of New Haven was depressed and shabby and the "gown" of Yale was stained with all the bad effects of a single-sexed environment in a period of political reaction. The odor of class-based contempt for townies was quite disgusting—or would have been so in my case had I a working consciousness of the phenomenon of class.

ONLY A BIT OF THAT was vouchsafed to me, and that during the summer holidays, when I ventured into what was known as the real world, to earn a modest supplement to the largesse of Lou Kovel. I had done caddying and lawn-mowing before then in a desultory way. The summer of 1954 introduced me to economic reality, first through the charms of industrial production in a local plant that was stamping out business forms; and then, after becoming an appendage of a machine proved unbearable, to a longer sojourn, thanks to Father's connections, at the Hotel Del Mar, in Rockaway Beach.

The stay at the Del Mar was more extended and more complex. Now I was employed in the service industries, hence "social relations," as we say in the prevalent jargon, were in play. I was to be a busboy in a seedy but convenient Rockaway seaside resort frequented by middle-aged Jewish couples, the women parked for the summer while the men went back and forth to work in Manhattan. My job was first of all to produce clean tables between courses and after the meals laced ultra-high with animal fat, a round-the-clock diet of Prime Ribs of Beef obtained by the Del Mar's proprietors, George and Teddy Topper, from a mysterious source. I also turned on the charm to make the customers feel good about the Del Mar experience. Pecuniary motives were entailed inasmuch as my actual wages were miniscule and the scale of tips depended upon one's relationship to the tipper. But it was not entirely pecuniary (a word deriving from cattle, as I recall), since I found the work so appalling as to make schmoozing with the clientele a kind of refuge of sanity. I am not what one would call a "Hail fellow, well met," but beneath the severe and preoccupied exterior I know how to talk to people, a facility that has served me well as a physician, psychoanalyst, teacher, and candidate for political office. In any case, the following fragment of a conversation took place between one such wife, the kindly Madame Y, and myself after about three weeks on the job:

> Y: Joel—why are you so nervous all the time? I've never seen anybody so nervous.
> J: I didn't know that I was [a lie]; maybe the job is stressful.
> Y: Well, I don't know about that. But you should do something about it. You know, you could become a great man, maybe if you weren't so nervous.
> J: What!? How can you say something like that?
> Y: I don't know. You just impress me like that.

A shocker! Did my panic show so badly? And what was this stuff about being a great man? It's one thing for me to think that; but what could Mme. Y have meant? I was, of course, a grandiose fellow, even messianic at times. But what made her think it could be real—not that I minded a judgment so close to my own opinion?

But all thought of success, much less, greatness, was suppressed by the charnel house known as the Hotel Del Mar. The Topper brothers were as odious a pair as I have ever met, the wheezing rotund George, his fat face studded with innumerable blackheads, and Teddy, chattering like the squirrel he resembled. Police would stop by at all hours, as well as dubious figures who gave an impression of being mobsters. As for the workers, the Topper enterprise was a cesspool of old-fashioned Dickensian exploitation. Tales of stealing tips were rife, along with egregious victimizations such as the hiring of a pathetic alcoholic as a dishwasher and remunerating him strictly with booze, thus saving on dollars while keeping the poor devil working at the edge of the DTs. Then there was the foul smelling, dank, dark and windowless basement assigned to us by the Toppers, the male staff making do on a collection of ramshackle cots with essentially no privacy.

For me, however, the chief horror was the work itself. It became the leading edge of a complex that in later years I would draw upon when I wanted to describe the alienation of labor and the injuries of class; and its arena was mental rather than bodily injury. I had left Yale for the summer, flush with academic achievement and packing Great Books to read in a project of continuing self-improvement. I planned to start with *The Magic Mountain* and intended to follow with the closer-to-home *The Grapes of Wrath*. After a week Chez Topper, however, I began to notice a wandering of mind unable to attend to the complexities of Thomas Mann. Better switch gears, I thought, pick up the Steinbeck, polish that off, and then return to Mann. But after another week my attention continued to wander despite Steinbeck's magnificent evocation of the world of the Joads. Puzzled, I said to myself, well, let's relax a bit and just read newspapers a while. So I went to the hotel shop and picked up *The New York Times*. Might as well stay abreast of current events! But it wasn't very long before I found the *Times*, which is to say, the Great World outside Rockaway Beach, opaque and utterly boring. So I switched gears again and picked up the *New York Daily News*. At last! I had found my level: trashy, reactionary, anticommunist, fear-mongering, violent, celebrity obsessed—in a word, sensational. I had joined with the mass mind, my independent critical spirit washed down the drain of alienation. And so it remained until rescued at end of summer.

In the midst of this misery and as if by dispensation from a just and loving God, two very good things happened, though the effects of the first I would not realize until years later. The workers in Topper's basement were a fairly mixed lot, but the great majority were food servers of African descent. The thought of sharing close quarters with Black men sent a strange twinge of apprehension through me. Yale's Class of 1957 had about two or three Black students, one—surprise!—our basketball star. This corresponded to what I had known throughout my life. It was, simply, the great splitting of the American social body, naturalized, made routine, and concentrated as one climbed the social ladder. Black people had never been real except as cutout figures to my parents and much of the extended family, in whose everyday speech one could discern a racist element, casual yet overlooked. Now here they were, as real as the next row of cots.

It soon became apparent, however, that whatever my problems at the Hotel Del Mar, the proximity of Black fellow workers was not to be among them. In fact, just the opposite occurred. As the dreary summer wore on, I found that I liked these men, indeed, felt more comfortable in their presence than with my own kind. It was not a question of close friendship but of mutual acceptance. The differences between us included age and the entire configuration of life except that part joined by our common fate as workers Chez Topper.

Thus Smiley and company went off on their jaunts after hours and I stayed with the other Jewish boys hanging around the kitchen, gossiping and mooching morsels of prime beef and other snacks like dogs around a campfire. But when Smiley and his friends came back something in me lit up. I loved to hear their melodious voices, took pleasure in their grace, spontaneity and sober, shrewd and good-humored conception of a hard world. I laughed with them and shared stories of the rottenness of the Del Mar and its extension to the great city and its crooks and cops. It would be fatuous to claim that these men were soulmates, a term that meant nothing to me in any case. I never learned anything of the inner Smiley, or of his history or family circumstances, or of what became of him or his friends. The connection, however, was to extend from its superficies, through the universality of class, to the whole history of domination and the overcoming of domination, that precious, frail, mutual ground of recognition of humanity.

The other very good thing was glaringly manifest. When Lou Kovel came to pick me up at summer's end we discovered that the Toppers had been up to their old tricks: my tips had disappeared into their slimy hands. Tip-Toppering! Shocking! Now, however, father evinced a spirit I could scarcely believe. He immediately came to the rescue and demanded that I be paid what I had earned. A considerable *meleé* ensued. There was Lou Kovel, shouting and defending the rights of the worker-son he had so often excoriated, screaming now not at his boy but at the Toppers, who were sputtering and jumping up and down in a veritable mutual conniption fit. I thought George's blackheads would come popping out. The men very nearly came to blows, not a prudent course of action in view of the extensive Topper contacts with the New York City Police and who knows else.

Somehow this got resolved and I was saved for another terrific year at Yale, leaving Smiley and the guys to stay and endure the Hotel Del Mar. But I should think the whole affair lived on within me, though not to be realized until much later. The most unusual bonding with my father and admiration for his courage, the realization that our Jews, ostensibly high-minded and long-suffering people, could be crooks and oppressors of people of darker color, my affection, indeed, preference, for these others, even a pang of conscience for leaving them to their fate—all these spirits, and many others, too, entered my being like little larvae, burrowed down and went to sleep in their cocoons, until awakened by events to come.

Note
1 Grant Smith, *America's Defense Line* (Washington, DC: Institute for Research, 2008): 141–144.

JOEL AND PARENTS ON VACATION

AT AUNT BESS'S HOUSE

ROSE WITH ALEX AND JOEL (RIGHT)

Chapter 2
The Yaller Dog

The Mother of All Contradictions

My difficulties began immediately upon entry to the world, in the course of which I was said to have injured my mother after a very long and arduous delivery. Then my voraciousness gave her mastitis when I was a month old, causing an abrupt weaning. The effects shadow me like a cloud raining down axiomatic convictions that life is full of surprises, many unpleasant, that one can never count on anything, and that if something goes wrong it is likely my fault.

A peculiar discovery from my 43rd year tells me that this was not merely subjective. It was related directly to me by Rose Kovel as we walked from the Jacobi Hospital parking lot on Pelham Parkway on a breezy Autumn day in 1978, I assisting her on a follow-up visit to Dr. Louis Del Guercio, who had recently performed a partial mastectomy for carcinoma of the breast. I was supporting her on my arm, and she, still weak and in pain and in her very bad mood over recent changes in my marital life, was muttering, partly to me, partly to herself, and partly to the wind:

> You know, when I think of you I feel this pain here [indicating where her breast had been] and it's like somebody is scratching and picking at me [as she raked her fingers over the surface of her coat]

So that was it! Am I a reincarnation of the Mesopotamian god Marduk, destroyer of his mother, Tiamat, the Dragon goddess of the sea, who not only gave this mother of mine her mastitis, but planted the seed of her cancer! The words were startling, yet eerily familiar, an ancient curse to define an irremediable guilt. Did it begin at ground zero, when I finally tore my way free from Rose's body, wounding her as I went; or at one month, when my uncomprehending sensorium had suddenly to contend with absence of breast? Or, more broadly, what would my stormy being have to do with the relationship with the Empress of Storms, Rose Kovel, herself?

Now let it be said: Rose Kovel *née* Farber was by objective measure a fabulously good mother who took superb care of her children and their home. She forced on me a spoonful of cod liver oil every day, to the point where I actually grew to like the stuff; and the happy fact that I seem to have a sturdy constitution and to have avoided major illness all my life so far must to some degree be chalked up to her care. She endowed me, too, with the good moral lesson of not reflexively accepting the recommendations of experts, as by refusing to go along with the stupid regimen medical experts were foisting on us around the time of my birth, that babies had to be fed at fixed two-hour intervals; and when I was older, by refusing to sacrifice me to the fashion of routinely having tonsils removed. This I especially appreciated inasmuch as a developmental abnormality had cursed my childhood with frequent and devastating nosebleeds; these lasted from roughly my sixth to thirteenth year, then blessedly ceased as sturdier tissue grew in. The nosebleeds required a number of emotionally traumatic cauterizations and considerably aggravated my wild-minded disposition toward anxiety, focusing it on fears of having my face invaded. I was a boy whose doctors would throw their hands up at examining his throat, and who once, at age nine, upon seeing in a comic book at a friend's house the image of a man whose lower jaw had been mutilated into a bleeding terraced mass like an Asian rice paddy, ran screaming all the way home, and for long after that moment could not even think about that image without horror. How good it was then, to know that I had a mother who would protect me from harm and would always be there for me!

Yet, which was the mother I had? Why did I develop a sharply delineated fantasy at around age six that I had two mothers, and that when one left the room there would be no telling who would return, she who was loving, whom I loved in return, and who saw to it that my physical, cultural and intellectual care was first rate; or the other, the Mr. Hyde mother, who would scream at me, impose Draconian rules, constantly criticize, never be satisfied, and could, I believe, be physically violent? This latter event was no doubt rare, maybe it took place only in my mind—but as sure as I am sitting here I had through my childhood a blurry, synaesthetic, yet very compelling memory of feeling and seeing her nails on my skin in one of her rages. So Rose may have done to me what she claimed decades later I had done to her!

My double-mother fantasy was part of a strategy for dealing with a very tough, formidable and possessive woman. I felt the threat from her rage, and also the need to resist her—which as any fool should have been able to see, only aroused her rage. This took place across many years of life. I kept on trying to explain her to myself and to understand why I so often felt the need to refuse to be what she wanted me to be, a good Jewish boy who would grow into a good Jewish man who could fall in love with a Jewish woman just as well as a *shiksa*, (and as she often said as well, a rich girl just as well as a poor girl), and not a renegade who flouted the rabbi's advice and went off the first time around with an Irish-American nurse, a lapsed Catholic from a working-class Bronx family. Would it not have been reasonable for me to become a decent Jew who would have his son circumcised, instead of an ideologue driven by an obscure health-cult and who refused what he took to be pointless mutilation; or a proper man who would enjoy the fruits of his first-class professional training and settle down into comfortable Upper West Side psychoanalytic life, maybe even getting one of those West End Avenue apartments that now go for one hundred times what they cost forty years ago, and where the elevator opened directly into the parlor... but no, the ingrate had to run off the second time around with an even worse choice, a free-spirited left-wing artist, also poor, to become a communist and reject everything properly civilized about our world, including, worst of all, that refuge of the Jews, the Jewish State of Israel? How could such a promising boy do such things? "Such a *Kopf*!" mother would tap her head, sigh, and lament teary-eyed in my direction: he could have had it all, and instead, look what he did.

Both Rose Kovels, harridan and angel, condensed into one ordinary person. So far as the world could see, she was a normal bourgeois Jewish woman who wanted nothing more than the love of her sons, a

SAD JOEL

well-appointed home, and a nice fur coat to impress our wealthier and more accomplished relatives, for example, Dr. Morris Bauman, a morose dermatologist with a bad liver and a fabulous library and record collection, who was to show me a book from his shelves by a Czech-Jewish writer named Kafka, whom I might like to read someday: good choice, Morris! Accompanying Morris was his talented, enterprising, fluttering, sickeningly perfumed and shockingly rouged miniature wife, mother's Aunt Rae, and their math genius son Norman, whose brilliance I felt I could never match—a good-hearted person who bowed to family pressure, became a doctor like Morris, eventually did research for Big Pharma, and joined the nuclear freeze movement.

Then there were client-friends of our family who were closer to the status of Big Bourgeoisie, like Sol Foreman, manufacturer of fancy tableware who lived down 10th Street at Avenue I, had a box at the Met, sent his kids to the Orthodox Yeshiva, and years later became the proprietor of Peter Luger's steakhouse near the Williamsburg Bridge, only to die at age 99, after, so the *Times* obituary put it, having ruined his health by consuming a Porterhouse steak every day for

HAPPY JOEL

fifty years. Well, almost every day; we have to include that day, in 1947 I believe, when it was roast beef heroically prepared by Rose Kovel for what was perhaps the grandest moment of her life: a dinner for the entire Foreman Family—Sol, Marsha, Marilyn, Amy, and the very bright and charming, though hydrocephalic and short-lived Bobby—along with, of course, the four Kovels, nine souls around one table in a very small dining room at 1139 East 10th Street, a table that had naturally to be extended for the purpose, so that it became a proverbially groaning table, and then, so cruel is fate, a teetering and, no!, a collapsing table once Rose set the main course upon it, the contents of which were set going, such is the implacable force of gravity, onto the floor after pausing to stain the laps of various Kovels and Foremans. Oh what a dreadful day! Made worse yet also ameliorated by brevity, for all things must pass, even gravy-spattered Foremans out of our tiny though well-tended house. It was at least as mortifying as the occasions when Lou Kovel would cause people to walk out by his philippics about treasonous fellow travellers, although of course more amiable and full of friendly regrets.

I should think, though, that it was not as painful for Mother as the eventual realization that her fondest, though strenuously denied, hope, for a union between Marilyn Foreman, Sol and Marsha's oldest daughter, very wealthy and solidly Orthodox, and her firstborn was not going to be realized. I tried to cooperate, driving to Brooklyn for a date from our Baldwin, Long Island home soon after obtaining a license. However, the chemistry, as they say, was simply not there, and we will never know whether it was kindly Marilyn or I who was the more ill-at-ease, or how I would have liked all those never-to-be-mine Porterhouse steaks which the mink-clad Foreman women were to learn how to select in the great refrigerators of the Meat District.

But Rose Kovel, *née* Farber, was no quitter. Frequently ill, accident-prone, often at odds with others, possessed of great determination, she bore the burden imposed by history, and lived her life through a hectic, identity-rending era, from Zhitomir (birthplace of Sviatoslav Richter seven years after herself) to the fantastically crowded tenements of the Lower East Side, to the Bronx, Brooklyn, the South Shore of Nassau County, eventually to sojourn like an elephant come home to die, in Century Village, West Palm Beach, as desolate a place—to me, that is—from which to depart this world as can be imagined. She had energy and will-power to spare, and lived in the early transitional period of women's rights. Yet perversely, Rose chose actively to champion the vile patriarchal ways put in place to crush her powerful female will. Uncrushed, enraged, Rose nonetheless allowed herself, nay craved like a Dostoyevskian heroine, humiliation, a down-payment, one might suppose, on her vengeful fury. She would slavishly prepare the monthly accounts for presentation to her husband, who would glance at them, sign the checks, hand them back for posting, and return to his brooding in the overstuffed chair. Meals in the Kovel household were ritualized according to a simple rule: nothing could be eaten until the master of the house sat down; and nobody could do anything to prepare the food, as well as clean up afterwards, other than the slave-queen of the house. Later, when her grandchildren Jonathan and Erin would visit her in Century Village, she would insist that Erin serve her older brother, in accordance with the Law, and nobody could dissuade her.

Childhood tragedy had scarred Rose. Her mother, beautiful and vivacious, was also unfaithful—perhaps promiscuously—and played the two-backed beast with the boarder they had been forced by necessity to take into their tiny tenement apartment. Who knows what Rose saw? Then, in 1919, her mother, the grandmother I never knew, became a statistic, one of the 50–100 million taken by the Spanish Flu, leaving eleven year old Rose the lady of the house and surrogate mother for Frieda and the infant Bess; leaving Julius Farber in a despair that took him to the precipice of one of the city's bridges. Pulling back from suicide he saved himself and the girls by marrying my step-grandmother Fanny, essentially a mail-order bride from Ukraine. Next, two more daughters, Gertrude and Rima on the way; then, the hopelessly bad relations between Rose and her step-mother, eventuating in open rupture of the never-speak-to-the-other-person kind, not just with Fanny, but also Rima. I never fathomed much about this, but I saw first-hand the ferocity of mother's feelings in hate and love, a woman who had seen too much, felt too much and never got over some things. After her beloved kid-sister Frieda pre-deceased her by some seven years, Rose would break down weeping for the rest of her days whenever the lost sister was brought to mind. As Freud put it, in some people we find a kind of "stickiness of the libido." Such a person was Rose Kovel.

No-Good Boy-O[1]

I WAS ONCE a sniveling little fellow, and it must be admitted, something of a mama's boy. There was a first time I was a lost traveller, not seriously, mind you, not lost for more than a few minutes, and never in outward danger: just a four year old who became separated from his mom in the Dime Savings Bank on the corner of Coney Island Avenue and Avenue J until reunited by sympathetic people. But the terror that entered me, the sheer, existence-threatening panic, who can fathom it? In any case, I was born with raw nerves, more touchy, "sensitive," Mother called me, than most, and more easily sent to the edge of the abyss. I have been told several times that I used to have "spells," or visions from a very early age, around two, during which I would shriek in terror. I remember none of this—indeed, the earliest memory I have is pleasant, a red dog (possibly an Irish Setter) cavorting on the Hamptons beach we used to visit in the summers.

But it seems that everything became branded onto my sticky psyche. I remember presentiments when I was very little, people worrying about me, I worrying about myself. I remember Jacob Abel, my closest friend on 10th Street when I was five, son of a toystore owner, no less, telling me, "Joel, what is the matter with you? Why do you walk with your eyes on the ground? Why do you worry so much?" All I could think was: how does he know? Am I so easy to see through? Yes, I was the original worry-wart, capable of worrying about the fact that I was a worrier. Do not get me wrong. I was a very lively child, precocious and lionized and capable of laughter and joy. But joy and terror congregated together in my inner being. Split apart, they drifted into separate packages; at least, that could be said of the moments of fear, which coalesced into a kind of regime.

A cloud of fear seems to have hovered over my early years, so much so that I longed for adulthood. Once, I suppose I was seven or eight, I went to mother—Rose Kovel in good mother mode, that is—in distress over the rages and outbursts of my father, which were extremely disturbing whether directed at me or the many people who got under his skin, including herself. She confided in me that yes, he was a troubled man, but a very good one at heart, who deeply loved everyone in his immediate family, and certainly loved me. She went on to say that Lou Kovel knew himself to have a violent, uncontrollable side and the realization tormented him with guilt—and then, as though a door opened within her, she paused and continued, prefacing the story with words to the effect that she didn't know whether she should tell me this or not but that perhaps it would help if she did. For there was a time, when I, not quite two, had been in a high-jinxy, obstreperous mood, and would not settle down despite father's exhortations, when he suddenly went into a rage, picked up the little boy he loved so much, bellowed at me, shook me violently and—here the account lapses into uncertainty—may even have struck me, he a fairly powerfully built man and I less than thirty pounds of trembling flesh. But whether he struck me bodily or no, there could be no question but that he had struck me with fear of Biblical proportion and inflicted a wound that took very long to heal—if heal it ever has. Father was seized immediately with remorse, and went into a terrible depression over what he had done to me. But though he may have sworn on the spot to never do anything of the sort again, my memory is littered with evidence to the contrary well into the future, and it must be, *mutatis mutandis*, back into my earlier years as well, for the Lou Kovel I knew could never contain his bellowing, his ranting and his threats, nor overcome the deep misery that gave rise to them. And many was the time I heard the words, "Just wait until your father gets home!"

Then there was the awful moment in January 1940, when, aged four years and four months, I was given my month-old brother Alex to hold and briskly proceeded to drop him from the couch in our little house on Avenue I and 7th Street; no bodily harm done to the tough little fellow, mind you, and no external reprisal; but a howling, savage lash of primordial child guilt within me and a lifelong obsession with clumsiness and other slip-ups ahead. Whatever the fuller picture, there can be no doubt that this little event charged, or triggered, or enhanced, or gave emblematic meaning, to an enduring pattern of violent self-castigation, a lashing by the terror demon. This established itself as the severe, monumentally critical voices of my beloved, feared parents within my own nascent being. And it remains. Let me cite one instance: as if on cue during the writing of this chapter, I chanced to let slip the computer mouse from my hand, sending it clattering to the floor. "You son of a bitch," I literally screamed at myself, "how the fuck can you be so clumsy!" What slaves are we to our inner tormentors!

And then, a fateful sequel. A few weeks later, more or less, an outbreak of streptococcal illness occurred in the Kovel home. It somehow affected Alex so that, this being the pre-antibiotic era, it was decided in accordance with sound medical practice to quarantine the house. This meant keeping me away from exposure. And so it was that I came to be sent to my Aunt Bess and Uncle Hy's home a few blocks away on 13th Street for the duration of the crisis, which was to last a month or so, eternity to the child mind.

I recall being brave about it. I was fond of Bess and Hy, and their proximity permitted frequent visits from mother and father. Externally, therefore, my predicament was not so bad. But tell me how a "sensitive" child, though too young to know the meaning of the word, exile, would have not have felt, deep inside, exiled from home; and how, since explanations tend to be inserted into chains of events to smooth them together, could I not interpret this exile as a consequence of what happened on the couch? How could it not become inscribed in mind as a kind of retributive vengeance by the higher powers for the terrible dropping of baby Alex, not a crime defined by the world, but branded as such by the fires of Hell on my vicious conscience?

There is another haunting question. Could it have been that these events congealed into and defined a consequential kind of template, an extended setting of Fate, that did not simply indicate or define, but came in some measure to demand and even determine a life in which I see myself, and have actually become, a permanent outsider, a stranger and an alien? Freud wrote of those who became "criminals from the sense of guilt." In other words, that our conscience, the moral regulator of our lives, may also have an executive function.

> But that's always the way; it don't make no difference whether you do right or wrong, a person's conscience ain't got no sense, and just goes for him anyway. If I had a yaller dog

that didn't know no more than a person's conscience does I would pison him. It takes up more room than all the rest of a person's insides, and yet ain't no good, nohow. Tom Sawyer he says the same.

—Mark Twain, *Huckleberry Finn*

CONSCIENCE—ABSTRACTED BY FREUD into Superego—is the directed and/or evaluative way we talk to, or watch over, ourselves. The noisier this becomes, the more conscience consumes the self and stands in its place, a real monster, a beast, a Yaller Dog, as Huck Finn called it. It is the precipitate in mind of all savage earlier relationships, modified as best we can with morality, which in the bad times approaches a state of delirium and even real madness.

As Mark Twain put it (I should think, drawn from self-reflection) this monster is perfectly normal, and quintessentially all-too-human—not in any prefigured form, mind you, and always woven with social existence, always with us after we leave infancy, and never with any other of God's creatures. It depends upon structures that have mass and neural connection, but it itself cannot be weighed or anatomized except figuratively. In that sense conscience is an all-too-real work of the imagination; yet it endures and evolves through a life, now allowing some cheating or forbidden pleasure, now driving to self-annihilation, even suicide, now imbued with grace and standing against tyranny and evil even unto death: what a wonder it is!

In present circumstances, however, it is an entryway to a series of especially stormy episodes that have shaped a stormy life.

THE DEATH OF AUNT BETTY

SHE WAS LOU KOVEL'S youngest sister and hands down, my favorite relative. She was also my father's favorite, despite being a left-winger. Who else could poke fun at him and coax a smile out of the gloomy fellow? For me, Betty was the only person of the family in whose presence I felt joy and enthusiasm: a kinship of spirit to go along with that of blood. She was the first liberated woman offered me by life and the model for my propensity for woman's liberation, she whom I felt loved me as much as I loved her and who stood for the possibility, proffered by Sarastro of *The Magic Flute*, of a *"besserer Welt."*

AUNT BETTY

Then there was the matter of religion, where Betty made no bones about disliking Judaism, to the point of one day simply renouncing it. I didn't quite know what to make of that; and had no inkling of what lay ahead.

The stunning news was received early in 1953: Betty had come down with a cancer of the worst kind—ovarian, a stealthily disfiguring predator of the abdominal cavity and a death sentence at age forty. Here are two recollections from her last days, plus one from the days that followed.

I drove with mother to visit her, cringing in anticipation, to find a reality worse than imagination. My beautiful, powerful aunt had turned into something resembling a pear, her abdomen swollen to gigantic proportion by ascites and her emaciated, elongated face looking at me with a wan smile and eyes of death. I can't recall what was said, because there was nothing, really, to say. But when mother and I made our good-byes, went out to the car, and turned on the radio—there, as if served up by a celestial disc-jockey, floated into the air the one piece of music most revered by Rose Kovel in the entire universe: the trio from the final act of *Der Rosenkavalier*—and with Lotte Lehmann, Crista Ludwig and Elisabeth Schwarzkopf, no less! The liquid radiance of the female voices induced in us a kind of ecstasy. Sharing in grief, we were closer than I can ever remember.

Some time later—I believe it was in late summer near Betty's impending death—I chanced upon father asleep in his overstuffed chair. He loved his sister very much, and his sadness, revealed in his repose, caused an anguish to flow through me. But there was something worse, far worse. For the weight of his head had pinned his mandible to a supporting hand, and this had caused something of an elongation of his face by holding the upper portion of the jaw stationary and allowing gravity to pull down the tissues of the lower. Suddenly I foresaw the same process that had horribly altered the appearance of his dying sister at work in the skull of my father. His jaw now appeared elongated, and also sickle-shaped, like hers. I visualized, then, not just an emotion of grief but his flesh withering away and dissolving as in a story by Poe. I saw my dying aunt in the face of my father. Shuddering, I foresaw the flesh necrotized.

All this hung over my first days at Yale; and, it could be, played some role in the spiritual awakening occurring at my matriculation in September.

When Betty died in October I went with leaden heart by railroad from New Haven to New York, and then on to the funeral chapel on Brooklyn's Grand Army Plaza. It was a dreadful ceremony, secular in the worst sense, with eulogy delivered by a hack who had not known Betty and spoke from notes. Afterwards we went to her home for a forlorn collation. I wandered about disconsolately, numb and wretched. Then I heard voices of three women behind me. They were complaining bitterly, not about the inadequacy of the service to capture the spirit of the dead woman but about the spirit of the dead woman herself…

"Just like her…" said one;
"So selfish…" said another;
"Yes, couldn't even provide us a Jewish service…" said the third.

I turned, gaping, as if encountering the Witches from *Macbeth*. But no, these were my aunts, whom I will not identify further. I had known them all my life, shared innumerable family gatherings, stayed at their homes, and never dreamed this could happen. Stunned, I said nothing. None appeared to realize what I had heard, or that it could have been problematic. After all, what value surpassed Jewish tribalism in their moral universe?

Silently I moved away and kept moving, to the coat rack and out the door, to get the 4 train to Grand Central. Later, I made some lame excuse for the abrupt departure. What could I have said: that from that moment I had inwardly severed my membership in the Jewish community and religion? In other words, the truth. I had just turned seventeen. I felt too weak and insecure to tell anybody of this; there was nobody to talk with about it. I could only make a pact with Betty to inwardly keep the faith with her, and pledge to myself to deal with the revelation tacitly, without revealing to the world the depth of my rage. Somehow I would have to figure out a way to do this, meanwhile appearing as just another modernizing, irreligious Jewish boy going through the motions.

WHEN I BECAME ENGAGED to Irish Catholic Virginia Ryan, a nurse I had met during my medical internship nine years later, my mother squeezed from me an agonized promise that we would visit a nice rabbi in Riverdale who would tell us how to make a Good Jewish home. Sure, Mom, whatever you say. And just wait until the time arrives for the circumcision of our son Jonathan, who was going to be born at our most modest little flat in City Island, myself having absorbed in the meantime some, shall we say, radical ideas about things of this kind, and by now completely severed inwardly from the Jewish faith.

Although she was not one of the Macbethian coven, I had no doubt from a mountain of evidence that Rose Kovel shared their attitude. And so she, too, was drawn into the circle of my estrangement. This awaited a much more extensive process to be recounted considerably further on concerning my antipathy toward Zionism and the Jewish State of Israel. But that fateful October day in 1953 had given it a foundation.

DEATH IN CENTURY VILLAGE

I HAVE BEEN TOLD that there is a passive verb in the legal lexicon, to be "koveled." For its provenance one need only google "United States v. Louis Kovel." There you may find considerable detail about the September 1961 encounter of my father with the Law, which ended in the Second Circuit Court of Appeals before the great jurist Henry Friendly. I learned of the matter through a phone call, received while discharging my medical internship at the Bronx Municipal Hospital Center. Father had been arrested! Removed from a courtroom on the charge of Contempt, Lou Kovel was handcuffed, arraigned, and bailed out to await trial, on the grounds that he had refused to disclose information given by a client in a tax fraud case. His claim was that an accountant shared the right of confidentiality held by an attorney so long as they shared responsibility for a given case. Eventually, Judge Friendly, bless him, agreed, and so Lou Kovel entered history as one of those stubborn refusniks who succeed in carving out a little space where the intrusive State could not enter.

I had been too swamped with the duties of an intern to see father at the time of his arrest. But as we followed the matter over the months ahead it became plain that courage had cost him greatly and had been but momentary, leaving in its wake a growing fear. Lou Kovel's extreme politics had, I think, set him up for this, in that he made his compact with power in order to stave off menace from demonized political and social forces. Their outward form came in two guises: the communists who were about to take over America thanks to the perfidy of liberals; and the subhuman Blacks he held in nameless dread. There was hell to pay, then, when fate made him the outsider, and an enemy—in contempt, no less—of that state whose earth he had, like his own father, urged us to bend down and kiss. I remember vividly the trip to Washington in 1948 to see father's client ex-Senator Albert Hawkes from New Jersey, Republican of course, who shook my twelve year old hand and gave me his blessing. After seeing the august chambers of the Senate we made a tour of FBI headquarters. It was the zenith of J. Edgar Hoover's reign as the persecutor of "Communism" and all things un-American, and here we were in his Temple, with firing ranges and big, blocky gentiles in fedora hats making us feel secure and important. After all the ranting about Communist fiends and their imminent takeover, it was most reassuring to visit the headquarters of the force that protected us every day from the Red Menace. But what of the day when the tables were turned, and the State, its authority indivisible, descended upon Lou Kovel!?

After his acquittal, the case of Louis Kovel, from having been an example of integrity before the Law, became a medical horror show.

LOU KOVEL BEFORE HIS CONFINEMENT

His incarceration and trial ushered in a vicious cycle, in which fearfulness begat withdrawal and withdrawal begat fearfulness, until his once-powerful mind disintegrated. He ceased intimate relations with mother, then insisted upon a separate room, where the monsters of the inner world could breed promiscuously during the sleep of reason. His work fell apart leaving him less and less of it to do, and more and more time to fret his life away. Father's fearfulness now became monumental. I saw its ravages in 1965 when my parents paid a visit to our Seattle home while I was doing my durance vile for the National Security State during its Vietnam War. Wanting to show them the beauties of the Pacific Northwest, Virginia, Jonathan and I packed Lou and Rose into the family car on a rare Seattle sunny day and drove the 80 miles to Mount Rainier National Park, presided over by the great snow-capped volcano visible from our home. We arrived in the parking lot at the base of the peak, I leapt out of the car to share the magnificent scene, so gorgeous and thrilling that I had been contemplating staying on in the boring Northwest after my tour of military duty. "Look, Dad, look!" I shouted, and waited for Lou Kovel to emerge, and waited… and waited in vain. For he was too frightened to leave the car. As in Melville's meditation on whiteness in *Moby Dick*, my father was struck down by awe, perhaps a metaphysical dread stirred by a perception of the great emptiness of the universe revealed in an expanse of white. Or maybe it was just that so much snow made him feel cold, a complaint that he increasingly made as his condition deteriorated.

Father's perpetual fear of the cold dovetailed with an instinct widespread in the community of Ashkenazim immigrants, whose trek had begun in a Slavic northern bioregion, took them to the great cities and the proliferating suburbs, and from there to the sunny South where a gaggle of retirement communities was arising from Floridian swamps. Among the first and largest was Century Village, new home to thirty-five thousand elders of the Ashkenazi cohort, 90% Jewish. Here, on the flatlands stretching west from West Palm Beach, in subdivisions with proper Anglo names like Westminster, Paddington and Somerset—they found comfort and recreation. So what that everything looked identical to everything else or that a visitor (myself, for instance, over twenty years) would continue re-liably, maddeningly, to get lost. So what that there were security checkpoints around the perimeter effectively separating the Century Villagers from the *schwarzers* who cleaned their homes and trimmed the lawns. So what that stretching away on all sides of this enclave were orthogonal, perfectly straight roads with intersections too wide to be crossed on foot and a forest of poles and wires servicing every mass-market establishment in America; for who ever, ever was fool enough to go walking there? So what that this demi-paradise was as different as could be imagined from the real circumstances of their origins, with history erased and nature consumed into a mesh of golf courses and swimming pools, all chemically toxic and spiri-tually alienated to the core—yet experienced as fun by those who felt entitled to a decent retirement as a rounding off of life's journey. From the *shtetl* they had come to urban cauldron; from cauldron to shabby but decent row houses of Brooklyn, Bronx and Queens; from there to the lawns of suburbia, all increasingly bourgeois; now, at last, to a well-earned place in the sun, a pleasure palace, eternally warm, and an awaiting grave.

The part about being warm was all Lou Kovel needed to hear. It led to a most rare agreement: let's head south, where nobody ever was cold, and everybody was happy. And so in 1972 they bought the condo of Somerset I–131 and moved to Century Village—that is to say, Rose Kovel, trained in the practical ways of the world from the days of a secretary to those of a housewife under patriarchy, capably made the arrangements, while the faded patriarch followed in tow.

Upon arrival in Century Village, the last threads of what had made Lou Kovel's life intelligible were broken. And so his mind broke as well, this time permanently. He took to standing facing the wall for hours at a time, essentially resigning from the human race. Language, the key to human existence, was jettisoned, as was the semblance of coherent relations with others. He ceased, in a word, to exist, though his bodily organs were to continue working for some two years.

No, this is wrong, a distortion induced by the extravagant pain of those days, the most unrelievedly awful I had ever known. There was an entity in the nursing home under the name of my father, Louis Kovel of Century Village. But he was no longer a person who recognized those near and dear to him or possessed the remarkable personal traits of "enigmatic Lou Kovel," as he was called by my high school friend, Tony Ehrlich—the only friend from my adolescence I have remained close to all these years. Lou could make sounds: a continuous babbling of phonemes unconnected to any possible signification. His being was beyond the layering required to call something enigmatic; nothing, no conscience, no misery, no despair, no speculation, no shame, lay behind the mask, now torn apart, of the Self.

And yet, though the saturnine human being Lou Kovel was gone, the ruined replacement still had a kind of existence. I could not fathom just what it was, so I gave up trying and just let impressions run freely. Then I could not stem the thought, outrageous amidst my pain, that the creature who had been my father looked happy for the first time. He had shucked us away, the oppositional ones, those against whom his will had crashed, those whom he had dominated or who dominated him, or whom he had to shout down, who made fun of his obsessions, or who made too much noise, or spent too much money. No longer worried about the Communist menace or the decline of the West, and quite indifferent to everything else, what had been Louis Kovel just lay there and serenely babbled. The regime of dread was over. Having nothing, he had nothing to lose.

But he was not alone. As in a surreal Piéta, the fallen figure was being cradled by a caregiver, salaried but genuine in his affection, a large and very black man, from the Islands, who smiled at what had been my father and took him as he was. I shook his hand and learned his name but to my shame, no longer recall it. It was beyond irony that the tormented racist who had been Louis Kovel should have found his peace in such arms as these.

STORMY WEATHER

AS DEMENTIA AND PSYCHOSES can be inherited, how could I not brood as to whether the same fate awaited me? My paternal grandmother—of whom I have no recollecton—was said to have died in a state of mental derangement, and a younger sister (though older than Betty) was evidently a kind of schizophrenic who was given the Mrs. Rochester treatment and sequestered for years because of poverty and shame in a back room of the Williamsburg apartment until she passed away. Father was prone to hypertension, a factor in dementia, as am I; but where I have had the benefit of excellent medical care for this and have been in "normal" range for years, he had none so far as I knew, indeed, probably aggravated everything by smoking cigarettes—something I have eschewed with revulsion since trying one on East 10th Street as a nine-year-old.

Extensive experience in the health professions taught me that the way one lives has a lot to do with health. I knew Lou Kovel to be the quintessential nay-sayer; and as he screamed at me, the betrayer of his reactionary values, so did I come to react against reaction, negating the negation, and defying him as well as living the fuller life that he had refused. It turned out to be, I should think, a powerful antidote to cerebral involution. More—inasmuch as Lou Kovel's death had occurred on the threshold of my 40th year, the standard time for a midlife crisis, I now found myself provided with a day to be seized after long immersion in endless night.

IT WAS THE SPRING OF 1976. An anarcho-communitarian educational collective was being put together under the felicitous name, for a lefty psychoanalyst, of The Free Association. I joined in and submitted an evening course on Freud's *Interpretation of Dreams*. A radical artist named DeeDee Halleck signed up. We would chat after class; I found myself drawn in by her intensity; we exchanged phone numbers and began seeing each other in the fall. Plainly, one thing was going to lead to another. Having done nothing of this kind during fourteen years of marriage, I entered in a spirit of exploration… and soon discovered I had found the love of my life. So began a period of ecstacy and agony unlike anything else I have undergone. It would take another volume to do it justice, and I have no intention of doing so, beyond saying that we all survived, though I could have been killed on three occasions which shall be left unexplained.

In mid 1977 I did the most painful thing of my life and moved out of my home with Jonathan and Erin, and into a new place nearby with DeeDee and her three sons from her first marriage, Ezra, Peter and Tovey. After a "trial period" of about a year we decided to go forward and so I have, taking a huge beating in the courts and losing at least half of my friends in the process.

To treat this crisis adequately here is simply impossible: it would take another full-scale book to do it justice—though there is no justice here, certainly not to Virginia, but simply the working out of life, which sometimes happens. This is no *Anna Karenina*; for the ending is a happy one, unevenly distributed and full of rough edges, and though this happy family, per *contra* Tolstoy, is not at all like every other.

JOEL AND NEWBORN MOLLY

The key to its success was the birth of Mariana Louise Drosten Kovel, a.k.a. Molly, on December 5, 1979, and the reaching out of DeeDee, and also Virginia, and even Rose Kovel, a process which allowed the tendrils of love to radiate and give connection to the fractious bunch. Thus we went forward into the Era of Grandchildren, from Rowan to Liam, to Tolan, to Owen and Josephine, and at length, Desmond and Andisheh.

DeeDee and I have clocked 39 years, not bad

JOEL AND MOLLY

for a coupling that was supposed to crash and burn in short order. I would estimate (not good science!) that we have had ten thousand stupid quarrels in this time, for we are both querulous idiots in playing the contact sport of love. I'm not sure what good I have done her, but very sure that she has enabled me to become myself—if a *cliché* may be drawn into the text. Of special importance is what has been empirically demonstrated for couples who last, that the partners enjoy each other's company and find what they say interesting. Yes, pillow talk is the secret to the "marriage of true minds."

THE LATER YEARS OF A DIFFICULT RELATIONSHIP

ROSE KOVEL SURVIVED HER HUSBAND by almost twenty years, dying of congestive heart failure brought on by diabetes in February 1993, nearly 85 years of age. She had scarcely been disease-free, witness the breast cancer reported at the beginning of this chapter, but she was able to enjoy an active life until her last year, when a downward cardiac spiral overtook her and made the final days miserable. The burden of father's disintegration, needless to say, had descended primarily upon Rose and tried her spirit most awfully. But she carried through the unspeakable ordeal with admirable strength of character.

Unfortunately, except for a truce imposed by Lou Kovel's condition, discord prevailed between my mother and me right up to the last few years of her life. I was the instigator, with a succession of personal changes that would have vexed a saint—and whatever Rose Kovel was, she was no saint. In fact, she seemed notably to harden after the death of her husband, as though she kept him within her by identifying with the authoritarianism of his soul. But I certainly gave her ample provocation. Once I ceased being the prize-winning Golden Boy and started defining a, shall-we-say, controversial path in the world, she responded with great severity. Others—most notably my brother Alex, as he grew in years—shared in one degree or another this attitude, and carried on the function exemplified by Lou Kovel, albeit without the fanaticism, to inform me that I was no longer the anointed one who could do no wrong and brought honor to the family, but a scandal and a fallen angel. How often mother reminded me of the forsaken opportunities—for fame, power, influence, I had squandered thanks to my dereliction. At times this was expressed in tones of bitterness, as when I ventured to ask one day on the beach as we were watching the children playing in the sand, whether she could give me a general kind of idea of how the family estate was arrayed, only to be met with scorn: "How could you be trusted with such knowledge? You would only ruin the estate if you ever got your hands on it." Well, so much for that.

The chief battlegrounds were our sharp differences *vis-à-vis* the State of Israel—of which more in Chapter 12—and conflicts concerning my life partners. Relations with Virginia—"Joel's Irish Rose"—were very tense for some time, and flared terribly upon my refusal to have Jonathan circumcised, culminating in an awful quarrel which led me to sever relations with mother for six weeks. But lo, this passed on, and eventually Virginia and Rose Kovel got along just fine and even formed a kind of alliance.

Things were much tougher with DeeDee because of the scandal that ripped through our lives, and more deeply because both parties were very strong outspoken characters separated by profound ideological differences. This, combined with at-times ferocious conflicts stemming from the fact that the two sides joined together included five children born in the space of less than four years.. But here, too, amelioration set in as soon as Molly came into the world, and Rose, like everyone else, fell in love with her.

For all the harshness, let it be said that there was an easing of relations with Rose as her end drew near. Her strident hatred of Palestinians, which extended at times to calls for their genocidal extermination, slackened as the pressure of her bad conscience relaxed under the influence of the oncoming shroud; so, too, did the ultra-Zionism that no longer served any purpose. During her last year, Alex and I worked out a schedule of successive visits to Century Village, where we camped out on the divan in the second bedroom and tried to meet her needs along with a visiting nursing staff. She was too weak and ill for any emotional demonstrations, but a kind of tenderness came forth which I am sure comforted us all; at least

I know it comforted me, until that day arrived when, the two sons not being present, she began slipping away. According to a nurse who was there, mother's breathing became shallower as the end approached. The nurse approached and asked Rose if she was dying. The "yes" was faint but unmistakable, and that was that.

A few days before, as Alex was winding up his tour of duty, there had been a knock on the door, and an itinerant Rabbi entered, not an uncommon sight in Century Village. He let himself in and began shuffling about and mumbling a series of prayers and incantations over supine Rose Kovel. His davening done, the Reb got up to leave. But as he headed toward the door, mother seemed to draw herself together and gain some energy. Half propping herself up, she gesticulated toward Alex and bid him approach, and bend down to hear her as she whispered with the last gasp of her old ferocity, "DON'T PAY HIM ANYTHING!"

Finally, we agreed on something.

MOTHER'S TRAY

THEY ARE BURIED in small shabby adjoining graves very close to an awful West Palm Beach express road, with trucks rushing past and America's air-conditioned nightmare spreading into the distance. It is one of the first places scheduled for submersion according to the logic of climate-driven sea-rising. I've been there once in the twenty years since her departure and have no plans to return. They visit now and then, usually without the other, in a reasonably cheerful dream, and I like that. They should be remembered for their works—Mother's water colors and excellent crafts, especially a gold-leafed tray that took her about six months to lacquer; Father's photographs, model ships and paintings, chiefly, I confess, for selfish reasons, the one of me at age four.

Oh, yes—and his heavy plodding step as he came up the stairs at 1139 East 10th Street, the sounds reassuring to his light-sleeping boy.

Note

1 From Brendan Behan's play, *Borstal Boy*.

Chapter 3
Mr. Science

The memorabilia collected by my parents at my birth included the inaugural issue of Henry Luce's *Life* magazine with its dramatic cover photo of the Fort Peck Dam, symbol of America's hope that massive technology could rescue us from grinding depression. I felt the power as a toddler when I was taken to the World's Fair of 1939 to behold, godlike, General Motors' immense Futurama—five-hundred thousand miniature buildings and fifty thousand model vehicles spread out over thirty-six thousand square feet, soaring gently over the city to come. Thank you, GM, bringer of the automotive age.

Nine years on, the Great Depression now but a dim memory, I saw Robert Flaherty's *faux* documentary *Louisiana Story*, about drilling for oil in the bayous. Very serene it was, everything gentle and under control. Yes, the Standard Oil Company of New Jersey had financed the project with its Pulitzer Prize winning score of Cajun music by Virgil Thomson. Who would complain about that? So thank you, too, ESSO, for powering the automotive age, and inspiring Herbert Schwartz, my buddy at PS 99, and me to submit entries in GM's Fisher Body design competition. Herb became a patent attorney, and I… well, I loved science and was very good at it, but it has been a bumpy road.

Consider that sunny day in August, 1945, when distant shouting interrupted the torpor of Camp Mitchell and Harlee. I roused myself from my bunk, ran out to trace the sound and found a group of counselors jumping up and down and screaming as they waved *The New York Times*, across whose front page was emblazoned the great news of our super-weapon capable of destroying a Japanese city with one blow. What joy! Brighter than a thousand suns, The Bomb stood proud at the head of a long line of military hardware celebrated by young minds over the years of deadly combat. This one, the greatest weapon of all, promised victory over evil.

Then it became the evil, as the Cold War and its nuclear arms race flooded our souls with terror. I remember a conversation with Bobby Meyers, another PS 99 buddy, as we walked down the street one evening, listening to the distant sound of a plane overhead, wondering whether this was the Russians coming to wipe us out? Sleep no more!

Somehow the fear becme controlled by the effort to understand and then master the architecture of nature. Clumsy in the laboratory and talented at theory, once at Yale I drifted into a science major with the unlikely choice of chemistry, whose elegant presentation of nature's innards may have reminded me of that magical moment in 1939 when my three-year-old mind contemplated GM's miniature cosmos.

For a time mathematics ruled supreme. I was no prodigy but had been a pretty decent math student who won some prizes, loved the beauty and elegance of the subject, and envisioned it as a foundation of my as-yet unspecified future in science. As junior year began, that expectation was enhanced when I joined a seminar in advanced algebra taught by Shizuo Kakutani, an indisputably great mathematician and the luminary of Yale's department. It was generally considered the Mount Parnassus of the undergraduate math program and its most difficult course; and here I was, confounding my fears and expectations by doing far better than I had any right to expect. I was shocked to find myself sailing through the deep waters of set theory and related matters with intellectual joy and a dispatch that seemed miraculous. Imagine: multiple infinities! An infinity of infinities!

The man who was guiding this journey had a mind like a buzz-saw and the personality of Mr. Rogers, for Kakutani was as gentle and unassuming in manner as he was soaring in intellect. He could fill a blackboard with elegant little chalk marks as fast as they could be spoken, whether the chalked blitz was an off-the-cuff response to a query demanding an original proof or refutation of a theorem. All the while he would be wryly musing about how God immediately saw all mathematical possibilities while mere humans had to work to make the connections. That I could even imagine being positioned some way along the continuum was astounding. I went so far as to browse histories of mathematics. Was this to be my future as well?

And then the second semester began.

I COULD NOT AVOID the notice in the Berkeley College dining room announcing tryouts for the forthcoming spring drama, which was to be our own in-college production of *Twelfth Night*. Now here was something different, not entirely new for this bookworm, but nevertheless a depth of engagement with literature several levels beyond where I had been before, levels I told myself I had to explore. And so I went, and read for the play, and was offered the part of Sir Toby Belch, and of course accepted, notwithstanding that this was likely severely to stress my intellectual efforts, chiefly those under the aegis of Professor Kakutani.

And so it did. From being engrossed in the Empyrean heights of mathematical abstraction to being engrossed in acting a darkly comic Shakespearean role is quite a stretch. Had I a more substantially developed inner math apparatus—a more robust innate endowment as against one that had to lean upon the genius of my professor—the matter might have worked out differently. But as it transpired, I had been riding a train to mathematical glory; and when, as trains will, it pulled out of the station, it left this preoccupied passenger behind. Class after class, I could feel the point of Kakutani's inspired proofs slipping away from me. I just couldn't concentrate! And since everything in this course built upon what had gone before, there was a kind of exponential quality to my defect, like the collapse of a sand castle chewed away by waves, first bit by bit, and then all at once.

The midterm exam was a catastrophe and an exercise in mortification.

Kakutani was shocked. "What happened to you? You were the best student in the class. And now this; nothing is right." I am further ashamed to say that I do not remember my reply. I couldn't blame it on Shakespeare, and I can't even remember how we resolved the mess, though I recall Kakutani's decency and kindness in the process. I took it as a kind of mercy killing.

But there was no killing, and life went on. I retained sufficient math skills and theoretic ambition to take an elective course open to seniors and graduate students which had the great attraction of bringing the subject into apposition with the thrilling breakthroughs of the twentieth century in quantum physics, and also of giving me an opportunity to prove that I still had something in the tank. Here I had the good fortune to study during my senior year with Michael J. S. Dewar, from Oxford, who was visiting for a semester and gave a seminar in molecular orbital theory of the chemical bond, a subject to which he had made major contributions. Checking in my attic in Willow I found the final exam for the course, filled with mathematical scrawls I can no longer understand, but testimony that I did at least achieve the launching point of what could have been a decent career in what is stupidly called, especially where the mysteries of the quantized world are concerned, "hard science."

But the moment was no more than that and had gone. I had opted out of a career in science and was resigned to the fact that I would never become a great scientist or any other kind. Perhaps Sir Toby had gotten to me after all, that old Trickster and reprobate whom I loved playing, and who on Shakespearean wings had shown me dimensions of the self that I neither understood nor could let go.

I put the question—What is to Become of Me?—to a practical test by electing to take a summer job after junior year in the huge General Electric plant in Pittsfield, Massachusetts, where they made transformers and needed a chemical facility for the purpose, chiefly to fabricate insulation. I knew nothing of the fact that here were being concocted the toxic PCBs that would play so dramatic a role in the environmental politics of the Hudson River. What did I care? For as Marx had written, the alienated worker loses touch with the productive process into which capital inserts him. And that is what

I felt and was: alienated and inserted into a big, brooding, and dreary lab where I had no control over anything—except over the question I had put to it: if this, too, is chemistry, and if the yokels who surrounded me were chemists, was this really the kind of life I wanted for myself, even though there were many more desirable pathways in chemistry I could have chosen? It was a stupid question, a mere trick framed to allow me to say openly what I really knew all along but could not admit, that chemistry, chemists, and the whole trail I had been blazing was not for me. And so I said goodbye to science and math.

As to where I would go next—well, that was chosen with the same degree of perspicacity and impulsivity, again at the GE lunch table as I recall, now on one of those frequent solitary meals taken for lack of interesting company, my sole companion *The New York Times*. And there on the obituary page was the announcement of the death of a physician, with a photo and a one column bio, a nice looking man, evidently Jewish, who had lived well and done good, with a comfortable life and a Mount Sinai appointment and some worthy research and, it appeared as well, a loving family. That settled it! I decided on the spot to go to medical school, because it connected science with the human world. And so I set forth on a 29-year journey I never actually wanted to take, because I didn't know who I was and had to rely on fantasies of insertion into surrogate selves.

The first step in my medical career was remarkably simple. Amazingly, the top medical schools sent cadre to hotshot places like Yale. The Columbia Physicians & Surgeons team, headed by an internist named George Perera, was the hands-down winner. It had nothing to do with the school, everything to do with the fact that I and my Don Jewey Society wanted to relocate to New York. Everything should be so simple.

A bit more on Sir Toby. He points back to the liberating, terrifying figure of the Trickster, ubiquitous among First Peoples and a universal feature of drama, and indeed all myth. As Stanley Diamond was to explain twenty years later, Trickster stands for primordial ambivalence and the Hermetic wanderings of the self, as folded into the Athenian drama taught to me by Bernard Knox. His like was loathed by Plato, but keeps on slipping through the cracks never-theless. The motif surfaced in Rabelais and Cervantes, was brought to the highest level of realization by Shakespeare, and felt by me on the stage of the Berkeley College Players. Playing Toby meant mak-ing myself into Toby, somebody I truly was not. This called reason and truth into doubt, as his transgressions stirred my own way-wardness. Shakespeare does that by penetrating deeply enough into the undersides of the word to shake the foundations of self-hood. It was epitomized by Iago's motto: "I am not what I am." My God! Who are we, then? It is an annihilator of being, opening onto the un-bounded inner seas.

This made me lose my way, I do believe, from the austere, Apol-lonian path of science. Too much of a wanderer was I, too unruly and ever on the edge of disorganization, as great chunks of thought could calve like icebergs from the fracturing whole and slip into the sea. It was the path that was abandoned, however, not the dream. Unlivable as vocation, science, now retreating into speculation, lurked about the outer precincts. Perhaps as medicine it could an-swer my questions. Ultimately, it would mean a different, radical appropriation of Nature.

But first I had to get through the summer of 1957.

A SINE-WAVE SUMMER

THE NATIONAL MARITIME UNION (NMU) was a leftover from the glory days of the American labor movement and an emblem of its corruption. Founded the year of my birth and an adornment of the Congress of Industrial Organizations (CIO), the NMU was not just the guarantor of the rights of our mariners, but also the place where they went to seek employment. I don't recall the location beyond being in Lower Manhattan and the far West Side, but I re-member the seediness of the hiring hall, the torpor and the air of manipulation as sundry tars hustled for choice jobs while the cold wind of estrangement blew, driving my fine ideas about like chaff. Where now were the luminous abstractions about the logic of the universe, the summa cum laude that proved how excellent I was at playing with learning, the exquisite lawns of late spring Yale, and the plates of fresh strawberries given weekly to the deserving gentlepersons of Berkeley College? Back on the shelf, that's where, while I sat on the hard metal chairs, knowing nobody, and waiting hour after hour to hear my name, squirming inwardly at how I was going to explain the dubious stratagem of a hothouse creature like myself legitimately claiming employment on one of our country's merchant ships.

But there was really nothing more to it than pull, the grease of the world as applied by Lou Kovel through a tax client. It was quite routine. When my chance arose, after an eternity of waiting and the growing fear that I was going to spend the whole of the summer in this desolate fluorescent-lit room waiting for the job that never came, suddenly, undeservedly, the job came, more exactly, the badge that entitled me to it. Nobody was going to question the arrangement or ask difficult questions about my credentials. Some forms placed in front of me, a request for my identification photo and a small fee, and presto, I had joined the NMU, with a union card to prove it, proclaiming, to the infinite amusement of my friends, that Joel Stephen Kovel was authorized to work as an:

Ordinary Seaman
Wiper
Steward

on a vessel sailing under the flag of the United States—oh, how Tom Cohen and Jesse Lemisch had fun with that, imagining just what an Extraordinary Seaman Wiper would be! And soon after came news of where it all would be enacted: nothing less than the celebrated *SS United States*!

It was the fastest ocean liner ever built, its giant turbines capable of galumphing across the ocean in three-and-a-half days at a speed of thirty-six knots. The *United States* was a peculiar child of the era, sired by the phallus of war on the luscious body of peace. The U.S. Navy paid some two-thirds of the construction costs to enable rapid conversion to a troop ship that could transport an Army Division across the Atlantic in less than four days in the event we were to go, as Slim Pickens put it in *Dr. Strangelove*, "toe-to-toe with the Russkies": fifteen thousand GIs to replace the two thousand or so peacetime passengers who consumed its delights while being serviced by a crew of nine hundred, the great majority of whom were neither the "seamen" who worked on deck or aloft, nor the "wipers" who tended the massive engine room, but plain "stewards," who saw to the needs of the passengers.

I was one such, and it must be added, the unholy least of these. How did I know this? First, by the "sleeping" quarters to which I had been assigned. Think: what could be the minimally habitable space, on so enormous and swift-moving a vessel, as would be assigned to the most expendable mariner who did the least useful work? Find this spot, and the crew member to inhabit it would perforce be the lowest man on the SS *United States*. The prow would define such a location, where it narrowed to a colossal blade suitable for cutting through the waters—and not any point on that blade, either, but the point seven decks or so beneath the open air, where it actually breasted the water, creating in the narrow den behind the steel plates of the prow a roaring and hellish noise, this with two accompaniments, one physical—the twenty-to-thirty-foot displacement as the lighter front end of the boat, some one thousand feet from the massive propellers, would be now lifted, now dropped, according to the action of the waves upon the great linear bulk of the ship; and the other mental, for what was a person more likely to haul out of his thought-locker than the celebrated disaster of a half-century ago when another glamorous ship collided with an ice-berg, as happened to a certain doomed vessel that was, like the *United States*, considered the *non plus ultra* of a technologically advanced civilization? And who would die this time?

With *Titanic* premonitions I tossed and turned and arose and went upon my four-hour tour of duty—this the clincher that certified my status as the least of the nine hundred stewards, the man who does the most stupid work of all, labor utterly without skill or dignity. Consider: my assigned spot on the great vessel was to stand wearing a silly uniform at the control panel of the Cabin Class elevator as it took passengers on the five-deck journey from their rooms to the dining and recreation levels. All I had to do was to smile, say hello and goodbye, and push the button. This task was considered too strenuous for the clientele hence requiring the hand of a steward. The mechanically regulated ascent and descent of the elevator combined with the forward motion of the *United States* to inscribe a sine wave thousands of miles long. And when I descended into my nocturnal habitat, another sinuous course was tacked on, the nocturnal precipitous rise and fall of my bed combining with the great ship's path through the waters. Thus my dual sine wave summer, the one of ruthless *ennui,* the other of Jonah-like submersion into Leviathan.

I did this for four voyages, New York to Southampton to Le Havre and back. The *United States* allowed me to see something outside the United States for the first time, and also to purchase in England, for a mere eight hundred dollars, a splendid Zeiss microscope for my medical studies. When one adds this to the vantage point on the lives of my raffish fellow workers and the splendid meals we scavenged from the ship's galley, I would have to say that my days as a mariner were far from a total loss. It is not so often one gets to feel the elemental pulse of the sea, and at such close quarters. Further, my curious circumstances and exceedingly undemanding job cleared space for some serious reading. There was a little area on deck where one could stare off at the hastening waters, then look back to the text. I can't say this altered very much my reading of *The Charterhouse of Parma*; but as for the other books, well, who knows how it affected me? For example, *The Interpretation of Dreams*, by an influential man named Freud I had never considered before but now found utterly fascinating, so much so that I was able to pick up his three-volume biography by acolyte Ernest Jones for the latter voyages. Suddenly, the approaching years of medical training appeared in a radically different light.

Chapter 4
"For of the Most High Cometh Healing"

These words, of the second century BCE scribe Jeshua Ben Sira, loom on 168th Street over the portico of the very high, very grey, and very mighty Presbyterian Hospital. A few yards to the right, another, somewhat smaller, portico tells the visitor in letters of granite that he has arrived at the College of Physicians and Surgeons, the School of Medicine, Columbia University. Two dates are inscribed below, 1767 AD and 1926 AD, the years that Columbia founded its medical school and built its giant hospital.

Much has changed since I walked past those doors in 1957, new Zeiss microscope in hand, and took up residence in Bard Hall around the corner. The P&S medical complex, already gigantic in 1957, is now easily twice the size. It is amazing how the developers found and keep on finding spaces in which to shoehorn yet another gleaming tower. I still gasp a bit when huge billboards loom above our highways selling some medical institution as though it were a brand of beer, indeed, there is a notable example extolling the lofty Presbyterian hospital itself just after one enters the Henry Hudson Parkway at 125th Street near my Manhattan home: evidently, then, not the most high, for it is willing to submit itself to the hucksters. Nor is there anything in the entire consciousness industry to trump the adverts on prime-time TV promoting some wondrous pill to make the tear ducts flow more freely or help the ding-dong to stand tall and be counted, to which are appended the legally required provisos with their prudent warnings (call your doctor if you go into coma or if it stays up for more than four hours). The whole enterprise of medicine has undergone momentous change under the neoliberal regime of Capital, as doctors have had to contend with the gigantic profit-driven bureaucratic hierarchies that have turned many physicians into high-paid proletarians and smothered all under the tyranny of insurance companies and Big Pharma.

I do not want to give the impression that I was getting along fine in medicine and only got off the train because I had become sickened by capitalist abuses. The reasons lie deeper, personally because of that peculiar demon of mine which drives me away from the given and gives me no rest; and from the standpoint of our civilization, because although there were better paths within medical practice which I could have chosen, they all were in context of the transformation of science and medical science that entailed philosophical, political and existential positions I opposed as I grew into my mature self.

I did become a good physician, not just in the command of medical knowledge but in personal skills and clinical judgment. However, the logic of the profession and its hierarchies always gnawed at me with its ethos of objectification—what Foucault would call a discourse of the impersonal gaze, and what Blake would call "Urizenic" single vision—as the ruling mode of interaction.

There is much history to be learned here and many of my writings touch upon the subject. But the best and most comprehensive account is that of my friend Silvia Federici, which situates the rise of capitalism and its medical empire in a vast struggle against folk and female healers.[1] The end result was the preparation of the ground variously called Cartesian, Newtonian or Baconian—dissecting, rationalizing and placing the scientific doctor at the pinnacle of the universe and making him—and I mean, a *he*—Lord over the mighty institutions of medicine. It included that way of knowing that belongs pre-eminently to medicine and is tooled to place its practitioners at the helm of the medical establishment. They are the Lords of the List and Masters of the Decision Tree and the Citations from the "Literature"—not necessarily bad persons, but definitely constructed to be wheels in a gigantic medical machine. I knew them by names of John Lindenbaum, Milford Fulop, Ora Rosen (yes, women can do this as well as men, though not as often, nor did they change the patriarchy any more than Margaret Thatcher or Golda Meir) and her husband Sam, Stanley Luftschein, Lionel Grossbard, Arnold Drapkin, and Jeffrey Bernstein. God, they were smart, bursting with facts—and some quite compassionate as well, like Drapkin, who was our excellent family physician for some years and died too soon, taken out, I should think, by working himself to death.

There were many others shuffling for position at the end of the bed on rounds in order to make themselves known to the higher-ups, the Robert Loebs, Frank Stinchfields, and Irving Londons, so that they could replace them some day. I knew them as virtuosi of compartmentalization, of being able to smoothly rationalize a divided way of being into neat segments, medical science and humane caring coexisting in little boxes of professionalism. I could match lists and decision trees with the best, and was capable of administering various outposts of the Empire. I suffered no intellectual handicap in this game. There was, however, an idiosyncrasy of mine that cut me off from the others and eventually drew me away, for I was no good at compartmentalization. My intellectual and experiential sides couldn't co-exist in cubicles, but kept running, no, crashing and bleeding into one another. I could never split them apart, at least, not for long. I don't know who among us was better off or "mentally healthier." But the point is that they stayed at their post, generally well rewarded, while I moved off track, driven by the obscure passion that stormed about my mind and led me into strange places.

There were Gods in this Earth: exemplars of the Most High and sages of the good grey medical school. The supreme medical eminence was Robert F. Loeb, doctor nonpareil, and Apollonian ideal for the P&S student, he who stood at the foot of the bed during rounds, his calm gaze searching like stout Cortez for the correct diagnosis and his scathing verdict prepared for the slacker. Citizen of the world, beyond Jewishness (you pronounced his name Löb), recipient of enough rewards and academic medals to stuff one's soul and fill a whole trophy room with the leftovers, The Loeb-ian Ideal was to marry firm biophysio-chemical principles with care for the individual patient, grounded in painstaking and conscientious attention. The rub was that we needed a firm and beneficent class hierarchy in which everybody could expect a Robert F. Loeb as her or his physician, to stave off the infernal mechanistic logic of Cartesian science and yet to work within that science. The ideal retained some of the older values, though wouldn't go so far as my childhood doctor Lou Berlinrood, who would routinely make house calls, where those soft, strong fingers would palpate my chest—and surely played some role in directing me toward the healing profession. In my training days before the takeover by the insurance industry, pillpushers, and capitalism's totalizing of the commodity, medical-patriarchal science could still be administered with a soupçon of noblesse oblige. So it was for Loeb and other P&S dons, men like Yale Kneeland and Dana Atchley. So serene were they, so knowing of their place in the world's firmament.

I was at P&S during the cusp of Loeb's withdrawal as his retirement loomed. The '60s lay ahead and a light breeze of paradigmshift could be felt, offering plenty of cracks for a suitably irregular young doctor to fall through, though in truth it must be said that I had already done so, some years before, and in secret. And it may be that what I am about to relate opened a quest in my soul that no conventional medical career could satisfy.

A BIG BUMP IN THE ROAD

AS CADAVER X SLOWLY VANISHED under our busy hands, Irene and I became acquainted. It was alphabetically predestined. Here was Joel "Ko" and there was Irene "La," and as nobody else possessed a surname in between, so did the twain of us meet to become the team for that corpse dispatched from the city morgue for the edification of budding doctors. Irene was intriguing at first glance, because different from the other students: a bit older (seven years past my age), a bit saltier and more rough spoken, more worldly, a lot less Ivy League, and not at all Jewish.

I discovered just how different Irene was in early November when I showed her a remarkable piece in *The New York Times* that had caught my eye during our break period from dissecting. It reported on the death of a doctor and was reminiscent in that way of

86

the fateful obituary I had read in the summer of 1956 which had triggered the impulsive decision to become a physician. But this was a physician of a very different sort, and his death was not announced on the obituary page but in a full column in the news section.

The doctor's name was Wilhelm Reich, and his life had been sensational and scandalous in the extreme, witness the fact that he had died at age sixty in a federal penitentiary: scarcely the exit point for an eminent physician. Reich had been an early disciple of Freud, and was a force in the psychoanalytic world; but he was also a Communist, of the card-carrying variety. He had the remarkable, indeed unique, distinction to be driven out of both movements in 1935. Reich then wandered a bit, dallying in Norway and eventually arriving in the U.S., where his dramatic claim to have discovered a kind of life energy with cosmic ramifications—the Orgone—became the basis both of a therapy cult and a movement with scientific aspirations. There followed years of conflict with the United States government, in particular, the Food and Drug Administration, which took exception to his use of the "Orgone Accumulator" as a therapeutic modality. A trial ensued, after which Reich, having refused to accept the court's authority, was imprisoned on contempt charges.His books were banned (and even burned!2) and a brilliant, doomed career came to an ignominious end.

And Irene, bless her, knew all about it, because she was part of the Reichian movement, intended to become a practitioner, and was at P&S for the purpose, since Reich demanded of his followers that they be fully trained physicians. In her case this also meant going as an adult to college and acquiring the necessary science background from scratch. Irene never knew Reich personally. But she was close to the center of the movement because her own therapist, Dr. Simeon Tropp, formerly a surgeon, was one of Reich's closest friends and associates. Indeed, Tropp, Reich and their families had lived together at the Orgonon Research Center in the northwest corner of Maine.

Suddenly, Irene had become highly interesting. We began associating after hours, I joined her circle of friends, and spent what time the exhausting curriculum permitted in Greenwich Village, where she had a walk-up apartment on Sullivan Street. It was a good time and soon became better, as one thing led to another and I began spending nights and weekends with her. And then things started to become not so good, to my considerable distress. After a while we came to an amicable parting, there being little to sustain the relationship, especially after Mr. X, having achieved maximum entropy, was swept from the scene. Irene went on her way, never becoming a Reichian therapist as originally planned, but a regular psychiatrist. She lived an unhappy life as far as I could tell at a distance, and passed away a few years ago. As for me, I went on my way, quite unhappy and with the phone number of Dr. Simeon Tropp in hand.

When Tropp answered it seemed as if he had been expecting me for some time. Of course I didn't know what to expect at my end. But what I most certainly did not expect was a long drive on overly-familiar Long Island parkways leading to a large and nondescript gray split-level ranch house in, of all places, Babylon, well-out on the South Shore, not far from where I had gone to high school. In the driveway was a massive Packard, a conveyance Tropp used on his vacation trips to Florida. My adolescence had made me hate suburbia; yet here I was in the apotheosis of suburbia. Chez Tropp could not have been further from the ultra-radical image conveyed by the life of Wilhelm Reich. This was just fine with Tropp, indeed, according to plan. It was necessary, he claimed, to live a life of utter conformity to the social milieu in which one found oneself. If the neighbors were Republican, one voted Republican (the area was in fact conservative politically); if they went to church, one went to church; if they put American flags on poles outside the house, one went and bought the Stars and Stripes and did the same; and if they bought big American cars, one bought big American cars.

The reason was twofold. First, the government's campaign against Reich and Orgonomy was indeed an Inquisition, distinctly reminiscent—at least to Reich and the Reichians, and I must add, myself—of the persecutions of scientists who had troubled the world's sleep, people like Galileo and Giordano Bruno. Given this ever-present threat, the first line of defense would be to hide in full view, so to speak, in order to keep the persecutors off the mark. Second and more disturbing was a conviction that what Reich had brought forth, and what Tropp was continuing (though he never claimed any of the genius of his friend) had to be considered a profound revolution, so profound as to dissolve and redefine the very notion of what it is to be human by suborning it to the deeper realm of nature. It followed that what one did in the ordinary human world really didn't matter very much to the Orgonomist. What mattered was fidelity to the Orgone and its flow through our body—most important, its discharge in the convulsive moment of orgasm. This was the armature around which a comprehensive biopolitics was wound. It included an ethic, a theory of health and illness and what to do about it, a vision of child-rearing and of work, indeed, of society itself, even a cosmology propounded by Reich in his later years, according to which the Orgone was the secret to the universe, its veritable organizing principle.

All this was transferred to and enacted upon the Orgonomist's couch and in Tropp's heavily sound-proofed room. In my case it took place upon a body buck-naked except for a short, thick rubber hose inserted in the mouth so that the jaw would not be broken by the "primal screaming" unleashed by therapeutic technique. This consisted essentially of strict attention to breathing, especially expiration, along with kneading of various points, chiefly muscular, where the "armoring" of a life of orgone-negative living had settled in to block the flow, thus comprising one's character, or habitus in the world (as Reich had developed in several influential early works, such as *The Mass Psychology of Fascism* and *Character Analysis*). The process of therapy was to set going various flows of energy, some appearing as screaming, with accompanying recovery of emotions and memories. Alongside, comments by the therapist functioned as a kind of recitative according to his intuition, delivered before, during, and after the main encounter with the flows of primal energy. Thus commentary on the life-pattern of the patient was allowed, though it never became more than ancillary to the main action, which was, always, the mobilization of the Orgone.

My visits to Tropp were scattered over four very hectic years, with significant stretches of absence due to the exigencies of my fierce and demanding schedule and his sybaritic way of life. It happened more than a half-century ago, and appears in memory as in a moonlit, shadowy landscape studded with hillocks and arroyos, and scattered streambeds of desire, set flowing and drying out again or sinking into the sand. It was heady stuff, even if intellectualization was the least-utilized of all mental functions to arise in that cork-lined room. I mean, this was really not being in Kansas anymore, Toto! To this day, I'm not sure what it was. Nor am I sure who Tropp was, though I liked him a lot—for being shrewd, kindly, funny, intuitive, imaginative, and generous of spirit.

I know he was going through a very difficult time during our work together—because of Reich's imprisonment and death, and the crumbling of the Reichian movement; but mainly because of the death of his young wife, Helen, from cancer (at 42, pretty much the age of Aunt Betty's passing) and the burdens of caring for his two young boys. A string of female surrogates seemed to be trooping through the premises, discretion not being Tropp's strong suit, and concupiscence one of the leading features of his character. Already well into his sixties at the time, Simeon Tropp was not about to concede anything to age. He was an eternal voyager, and something of a troubadour.

It was the first of my experiences in what is loosely called "therapy." By no means the last, it was definitely the most *outré*, involving not just these, shall we say, unorthodox methods, but also logistics of serious difficulty. I usually saw him on weekday evenings, sometimes cutting out of my last class at P&S, and racing to the A train for the journey from 168th to 34th Street and a rendezvous with the Long Island Rail Road. Forty-five minutes later, I disembarked at the Freeport station, to be met by my puzzled mother, who was half-glad to at least see her difficult son, and more than half-worried at what was ailing him and why he wouldn't tell her or Lou Kovel what these visits were all about or how they were conducted. After a quick meal at their home in Roosevelt, I would commandeer the family Pontiac and press on toward the Southern State Parkway for the drive to the unfortunately named Babylon—though I doubt that any of its inhabitants, Tropp included, would have known or cared about this city's fabulous five-thousand-year role in human history, or all the layers of irony compacted into the space between its Biblical legend (imagine: the Great Whore!) and sedate bourgeois present. And then, my business with Tropp concluded, I would reverse my path, returning usually after midnight, eyes bleary with reading microbiology or whatever was on the menu at P&S.

What was the value of all this? Therapeutically, I am sad to say, rather little. I often felt that I had, so to speak, gotten a lot off my chest, and I suppose something worthwhile must have happened because Ellsworth Baker, who had assumed the scepter of what was left of Reich's movement, pronounced me orgonomically healthy when I went to him to train as a Reichian therapist a few years later—of which, more below. But the core of my disordered self remained fraught with fears and loathings amid the wild rollercoaster ride of my days. Nor could I shake the nagging feeling that I was running around like a rat in a cage instead of actively living my life.

Nor had the problems arising in my relations with Irene been resolved. In terms of Reichian discourse, I would not say that my time with Tropp had led to the *summum bonum* of orgastic potency.

Why these limits? I did my share of yelling and screaming on Simeon's couch, and often felt better at the end of sessions. But there are plenty of sublunary explanations for this, including suggestive infusions of Tropp's upbeat and charismatic personality; the cultish pleasures of running off in the night for a kind of witch's Sabbath with him; the simple expelling of tension such as can be evoked by all sorts of muscular and excretory events; perhaps, though never registering as such in my consciousness, some homoerotic gratification. All of these were possible, none of them dispositive either singly or in combination.

In fact, and more importantly, one can look at this from the other end, to realize that the structure of the orgone therapeutic encounter worked to eliminate an authentic transcendence, precisely because it entailed an intense "hands-on" relationship between therapist and patient which could not be subject to dialogue between the two. The enabler of this was the orgone hypothesis itself, an all-purpose override that made every other consideration secondary or residual.

With this Joker in his deck, the therapist can assert—as Tropp often did—that anything went so long as you get the energy flowing. But in my heart I could never accept this—could never, that is, really and truly let go so long as this man, however adept and however linked to the source of orgonomic wisdom, was standing above my nakedness and kneading my flesh. My good feelings about Tropp could never by themselves place him in a moment of authenticity so long as the fundamental relationship of the therapy was so lop-sidedly reductive to an energy flow. I am sorry, but a human being goes beyond that; and this fact alone meant that a therapy built on the extremity of Reich's insight could only go so far and no further.

THE READER MAY HAVE OBSERVED by now that the notion of the Orgone bears no small resemblance to the notion of Godhead put forth by the various religions across space and time. As evidence for this we have the words of no less an authority than Wilhelm Reich. Studying Reich's prison letters, Myron Sharaf, his biographer, concludes that "in his last months Reich repeated what he had been saying for years—that what was called 'God' and what he had formulated as 'orgone energy' were identical."[3] But if this was so, then Reich—and his followers, insofar as they did not regard such reasoning criti-cally—was stepping very far out on a limb.

Meanwhile all was not well in the House of Orgonomy, and the deity itself was suffering from a series of mishaps, the details of which are given in Sharaf's invaluable biography.[4] Some resulted from experiments that went seriously awry; but mostly, I think, it was a matter of context: the effects of Reich's persecution by the state and, looming over all, the grim shadow of the nuclear era and its massive testing of weapons of mass destruction. It was to Reich's great credit to recognize the deadliness of ionizing radiation well before the scientific/medical establishment got this through their thick skulls. However, his conclusion was deeply problematic, as problematic as the orgone hypothesis itself: that with the nuclear era, orgone energy had itself become contaminated. No longer the life force as such, it was now to be regarded as "DOR"—Dangerous Orgone Radiation—and its usefulness became curtailed.

One couldn't have it both ways: if the Orgone was God, then how could the Supreme Being be brought so low? Of course, one could insert the Devil at this point, as Reich often did in thinly disguised ways in his late works, notably, *People in Trouble, Cosmic Superimposition* and *The Murder of Christ*, in the latter of which the Savior bore a distinct resemblance to an exiled Austrian scientific genius whose efforts to save the world were foiled by Red Fascists and other avatars of the "emotional plague." But while all this was fascinating to follow, it led to a hopeless conceptual tangle. Nothing could erase the contradiction between the Orgone as subjected to this titanic and Manichean struggle and the Orgone as capable of scientific calibration. Reich literally drove himself mad as he became pinioned between these poles, hatching one delusion after another from his powerful mind.

Meanwhile, in Babylon, Simeon Tropp was of the opinion that his wife's fatal cancer was the result of exposure to DOR; and for the duration of my therapy, with one exception, his Accumulator stood forlornly in the corner of his therapy suite. There came, however, the day Tropp decided to put the infamous "Orgone Box" through its paces; and so he sat me down inside it for twenty minutes. But all it did was to make me feel hot, sweaty and uncomfortable, phenomena that could be well enough explained by sitting in any insulated and unventilated phone booth-sized cubicle on a muggy summer's day, as was the case. I was similarly unimpressed when, in an effort to give a convincing demonstration of this universal energy, he took me outside to the water's edge on another warm day, set up his telescope, and had me look through it at the surface of the sea, upon which one could definitely see busy wave-like currents in the air. These he called the motion of the Orgone. When I invoked Occam's Razor to opine that this familiar phenomenon could be readily explained by variable diffraction patterns caused by water vapor being played upon by the breeze, Tropp, unflappable as-ever, declared that we had more work to do to free up my orgonomic powers of perception.

By now, two subtexts had become intertwined. In one it had become clear that Tropp saw me as a leading figure in the next generation of Orgonomists. In the other, it was also becoming clear that he saw himself as retiring from the fold. Perhaps it was the DOR episode, eroding the totalizing power of the Orgone hypothesis. Or perhaps it was the loss of Reich, which released him from the bond of a discipline that ran contrary to the demands of his inner self. Sharaf writes that Reich esteemed Tropp more than anyone else in his entourage for his warm, lively and entertaining personality; but that he also despaired of his inconsistency and lack of rigor. And Simeon did wander, throughout the period of my work with him, and in an accelerated way as time passed.

He had heard the siren call of the fateful decade of the '60s, opening onto the minds of those inclined to "turn on, tune in, and drop out," as the saying *du jour* was to have it. The work of Timothy Leary and Richard Alpert with LSD and other psychedelics at Harvard was underway during this period; and while I have no knowledge as to whether Tropp ever knew these bellwethers of the Counterculture, it does seem that the star to which his spirit became attached as his Reichian phase declined was the ingestion of mind-altering substances. I lost contact with him after 1962, but would hear of this from various informants. And so it was that Simeon Tropp ended his days simultaneously as one of the oldest and youngest hippies, dying, if my source was correct, during the act of love.

As FOR MY PATH, the rather cold eye I have cast over orgonomy in these pages reflects a half-century of reflection and internal development, and not the actual picture during the period I am discussing, roughly from 1958 to 1962. It is more recollection and interpretation than description of a phase in which I had divided myself into two, Joel the assiduous medical student and House Officer in Internal Medicine and Psychiatry, and, after hours as it were, Joel the intrepid voyager in search of his Ultima Thule, seeking to be Magellan to Reich's Vasco da Gama; and seeking, too, to return from the destination and give the benefits to humankind. In this scenario, Reich was the great but doomed forebear whose path I would follow even as I avoided his tragic outcome. Accordingly, in the night kitchen presided over by Dr. Tropp, I sincerely represented myself as interested in going further with the practice of orgonomy; and did so on the basis of having already ventured into the domain of its theory. For I had become fascinated with the audacity and scope of Reich's mind. With that reckless curiosity of mine, insatiable to the extent that the extreme demands of medical education could be tossed aside in an instant while, like an overly generous host who would somehow find room for a guest unwanted by the conventional world, I raced off to prepare space for it.

What a thrill it was to receive my surreptitious copy of *The Function of the Orgasm*, smuggled from Europe in the baggage of a good friend from Yale—who shall remain incognito here just in case the statute of limitations for bringing in works banned by the U.S. government has not expired (Spoiler Alert: his initials are A.S.). It was a feast of the mind, encouraged by Tropp who cited Nietzsche's Zarathustra, that one should be like a camel and take aboard as much as possible for the long, hard journey through life, and thereby happily made a virtue of necessity for me.

So it was that I found room for plunging into the esoterica of Reich, no small task considering that the man had taken it upon himself to gobble up the whole of creation. Interestingly, the one zone of Reich's work that I did not pursue were his Marxist ventures. That would happen a decade later, when I would begin to more or less reverse Reich's trajectory, moving away from psychotherapeutics and toward social transformation. For now, I was still very much under the spell of the ancient dream of science, that it could unify our understanding of nature across all spheres of inquiry. Reich had been unafraid to follow the example set forth by Aristotle; and I was heartened to take up the mantle, especially as his emphasis on bio-physical inquiry matched my daytime participation in the life of a major research-directed medical school. I became a pest to a number of well-disciplined and important researchers, mainly on the theme of the recently activated furor about the origins of life, upon which Stanley Miller's experiments on biogenesis had recently cast some light.

It was integral to Reich's view that an actively formative life force such as the Orgone could give continual rise to living being.

A number of his experiments were in this direction. And so it became a Tropp-encouraged project of mine to sift through the accounts of so-called spontaneous generation for evidence that there was more here than what had passed through the excessively narrow gate of scientific legitimacy. Needless to say, I got nowhere in my efforts to reach the attention of the academics with this profound breakthrough. As one Ice Queen embryologist of British origin pronounced upon the matter in the course of dismissing me from her office, "I find this so inherently improbable as to be not interested in pursuing it further." The obstinate woman having confirmed Reich's postulate of universal blindness among the intellectuals toward the "Orgonotic functionalism" that moved the universe, I could retreat from this and similar encounters with my virtue intact.

Early in 1962, when I had begun my psychiatric residency at the Albert Einstein Medical School, I presented at a research seminar a speculative paper on the nature of hypertension as a generalized contraction of arterioles. This would require, however, a sense of what mediates the process, from the affect of anxiety and its associated influences to the walls of these tiny vessels. The larger conclusion was that we needed a view of the Whole in relation to physiological function. I reviewed the process carefully, leaving unstated the suggested conclusion that there could be an organismic force behind this, and was quite careful and circumspect about the mode of presentation. The paper was very well received. It sits in my attic in a box of early works—and still reads rather well. It also was the last thing I would declare about anything biological beyond abstractions of one kind or another.

In his generosity—and also, I should think, as a way of establishing for me a place in the lineage of Orgonomy—Tropp donated to Virginia and myself in the summer of 1962 the use of the vacation cottage that he and Reich had built in Rangeley, Maine, on the grounds of the research institute where Reichian Science was to flourish. It was a typical rustic wooden cabin, on the shores of the very large and very remote and very indigenous-sounding Lake Mooselookmeguntic. It was beautiful and peaceful, and so far as I could tell, ghost-free. The

Observatory sat nearby on a commanding hilltop, a sanctuary in stone for scientific dreaming about the universe.

It was a lovely farewell to Simeon Tropp, but not to Tropps altogether. For there was a younger brother, Oscar, also a physician-orgonomist, and his family, which included the formidable and deep-voiced Shawna ("Sean O'Tropp, the Orgonomist's Irish daughter," Jackson, Lemisch and I used to call her). I saw them often in these years, for Oscar dwelt in a stamping ground of mine, the Upper West Side. He provided a useful counterbalance to the rambunctious Simeon, as a man who would never say that one should live among the Yahoos to escape the gaze of Big Brother. No, Oscar lived his beliefs, which were of a firm Trotskyist persuasion. He lectured at the New School on sundry matters concerning mind, body and society. He was querulous, but like his older brother, generous and kind, albeit with well-reasoned gloom about the dreadful development of the world and America. He was also very fond of me, foolishly, stubbornly, and fatally so, as evinced in a phone call I received from Shawna early in March 1963:

> "Joel, Father is terribly sick, with severe chest pain. You must come over and see him."
> "But Shawna, I've had no more than a medical internship. Plus, I live in City Island. It'll take me an hour to get there. Call an ambulance!"
> "He says he doesn't trust any other doctor but you."
> "I'll come, but call an ambulance anyway!"
> "He says he doesn't want one, only you."

And so it went back and forth, as I grabbed my kit, raced out the door, jumped into my blue VW Beetle (gift of Lou Kovel as I graduated P&S, perhaps with the ulterior motive of sparing them the need to help me get to appointments with Tropp), raced—and I mean raced, in a way that broke every speed law and could well have made two-week old Jonathan an orphan—roaring (if a Beetle can be said to roar) onto Pelham Parkway, Bronx River Parkway, the Cross Bronx Expressway, and the Westside Highway, then off at 96th

Street, screeching to a halt in front of their West End Avenue apartment (no ambulance in sight), racing up the stairs, bursting in the door… to see poor Oscar gasping his last breath, his eyes rolling, his throat gurgling, unresponsive to CPR, my last and most distressing medical fatality.

It was heartbreaking, followed shortly by the farce of meeting Ellsworth Baker, to whom Simeon had referred me as the keeper of the keys to orgonomic training and science. Could this be the scion of Reich, the guardian of his flame, this dry and distant fellow, perfectly polite yet bored-looking with the immense trust placed in his hands? Baker tested me, pronounced me orgonotically fit, and passed me on to one of his "staff," who was running an evening class for future Reichian therapists.

It could have been a class for plumbers as advertised on matchbooks or in subway cars. Push this, pull that, watch the breathing, open the flow. *Oy!* I may have given it two sessions, maybe three. But in any case Baker-ism settled matters. Reich gone, Tropps gone, barbarians in charge of Orgonomic Functionalism…. I am a stubborn fellow, but I know when it is time to leave. I needed to regroup, and had a setting for that inasmuch as my day kitchen was already in the Psychiatric Program at the Albert Einstein College of Medicine. And so the Reichian night kitchen was shut down, never to re-open, although trailing clouds of influence continue in the concerns of my later years. The time had arrived to take seriously the figure of Sigmund Freud, whose acquaintance I had made some six years before on the deck of the *SS United States.* He had been waiting patiently in the antechamber of my mind and was ready to step forth now that my sojourn with his doomed disciple was done.

DUE SOUTH AND TRUE NORTH

BUT FIRST, THERE IS something else to be told.

The whole thing was preposterously unlikely. Suppose there had been a Thomas Kramer in the P&S class. As Kr comes between Ko and La, either he would have been my anatomy lab partner or Irene's. She and I wouldn't have worked together, hence it is quite unlikely that I would have shared my news story about Reich's death with her, much less begun an affair, the incubation of which involved day to day contact in the lab. Absent intimacy with Irene I would never have visited Tropp in Babylon and become inflamed with the grand, doomed specter that was Wilhelm Reich. In fact, had I not read the *Times* that day it is unlikely I would have ever had a Reichian period at all, for that cursory obituary was also Reich's ticket to oblivion.

Looking back over the interlude, it is not immediately obvious what good it did or even what imprint it made on me. The science became less and less plausible with the years, and the therapy as well. Eventually I lost interest in being a therapist entirely; but had I retained the calling, there is little chance that Reichian principles would have been directly incorporated into it. So what was the point? Was this a mere fling, to be excused as youthful excess and corrected by sober maturity?

Well, no, not at all. The opening was fortuitous, to be sure, but it was fortunate, too, because by opening onto something other than what the world demanded of me it provided my imagination a stage on which to expand. There was much that was foolish about my Reichian phase, but something grand about it as well. It was the first time I had chosen to do something radical; and being a radical therefore gained a toehold in my identity and played a part in what was to come. Reich shaped my dreams and permanently discredited the safe path of an ordinary career.

Reich's legacy also charged me with an embrace of nature, a biocentric ethic, if you will, accompanied by its logical correlate, the critique of civilization. Years later this would grow into the doctrine of ecosocialism. The tendency did not begin with the encounter with orgonomy, however. Since Yale days, ideas of this sort had been gestating thanks to my acquaintance with William Blake, whom I met in the Sterling Library reading room on breaks from the tedium of studies. Fascination with Reich was sown on soil prepared by Blake. Was it not Blake who had proclaimed in "The Marriage of Heaven and Hell" that "everything that lives is Holy"—as succinct a distillation of Reich's ethos as can be imagined? It took thirty years before

I went from being a Zarathustrean browser of Blake to one who recognized the scope of his magnificence and began serious study of his genius. For now, I was like the fourteen-year-old Blake himself in "How sweet I roam'd from field to field, and tasted all the summer's pride...,"[5] basking in beauty and the portents it stirred.

In the real world my sojourn in Reichianism focused the holiness of life on the actual life that Virginia and I sought in the mingling of our flesh: the infant Jonathan, born in February of 1963, after my parting from Simeon and just before the death of Oscar Tropp. It was infant Jon who needed protection against the life-negative forces in the world, immediately present as the baleful medical establishment which imposed civilized brutality on the naked newborn babies, and after that as the circumcision of male flesh in the name of a religion I had come to distrust.

I insisted, and Virginia agreed, that the boy was to enter the world at home and to be spared the trauma of circumcision. And so it was done with due diligence, and accompanied by due conflict with Rose Kovel, as has been related. But it is worth adding that these two refusals required of me a two-fold active opposition: to the establishments of medicine and of Judaism; these in turn prefigured the two leading struggles on a wider scale that would mature decades later—against the capitalist system, and against Zionism. Thus attention to the integrity of life and the essential dimension of spirit, both deeply influenced by my Reichian phase as nourished by Blake, came to shape my approach to politics.

As it was for individuals and social systems, so it became for humankind at large. Reich was distinctly in the lineage of Rousseau, indeed, no twentieth-century figure more forcefully advanced the notion that humans were born free and were everywhere in chains. To develop the point, Reich turned to the study of anthropology, where he hoped to find the scientific basis for Rousseau's insight in the ways of our "First Peoples." His early work contains glowing tribute to the discoveries of Bronislaw Malinowski concerning the sexual emancipation of Trobriand Islanders. The larger theme pervaded his work, and eventually found its way into Simeon Tropp's treatment room, where it roused in me "the search for the primitive," as my mentor Stanley Diamond was to put it years later.

Once again, fortune smiled on her young suitor. Medical education was a bloody four-year scramble, succeeded by the hyper-exploitation of being a House Officer. However, P&S gave a three-month moratorium for the first half of our last semester. And there, in the announcement of our choices, was a program in, of all things, tropical medicine; and in, of all places, the tropics, homeland to the Noble Savage! To be specific, in Trinidad, where we could see a leper colony and study in programs generously funded by the Most High Rockefellers; and, for the bulk of the time, Suriname, just emerging out of the chrysalis of Dutch control. Here our host would be the Most High Aluminum Company of America, which happened to have a large Bauxite mine near a town named Moengo, with a hospital that would enable us to study tropical diseases like malaria and develop the healing arts all around. But the *piece-de-resistance* was a three-week expedition by dugout canoe into the trackless interior.

I found the towns of Suriname to be depressing, endless displays of the blight wrought by centuries of colonialism culminating in extractive capitalism. The expedition into the roadless interior, however, was thrilling. As our boats—giant tree trunks hollowed out by fire—slipped away with the stream, I sensed the peeling away of the edifice called civilization emerging around each bend and taking human form. Or, here, two forms: those of the Caribe Indians, the archetypal folk whose kind met Columbus, and thereby met their doom; and those of the Bush Negroes, Guiana Maroons who slipped away from the plantations of the Dutch slave masters and rebuilt a model of West Africa along the shores of the great rivers.

Here, in the deepest rain forest, near the East-West Continental Divide with Brazil just to the south, our little band gathered. On one side, some ten medical students, their Surinamese Doctor/Chaperones, and about a dozen Bush Negro porters who saw to it that we got safely to our destination; and on the other, a small band of malnourished and very forlorn Indians. It was January 20, 1961 and the short-wave radio crackling with the inauguration of President John F. Kennedy imparted a surreal note to the occasion. As we listened to

"Ask not what your country can do for you..." the Caribe made an offer: one arrow, product of a full day's work, feathers attached, gorgeous, a real museum piece, to be evenly exchanged for one shotgun shell suitable for ordnance the Caribe had recently acquired. No doubt, each party thought he was getting the better of the other. I thought it was horrendous, in part because the Indian, to survive, had subordinated his labor to the machine, and mostly because it seemed that this whole "market" setting was for him one of decline, ethnocide, and looming physical extinction. A canopy of loss hung over our encounter, and drove the enchantment away before it.

The Caribe had appeared to materialize directly out of the forest, only to fade back into it. The Bush Negroes, however, arrived connected to a vital village community, the first of its kind I had ever seen. There was nothing suggestive of decline about them, quite the opposite. Our all-male crew laughed and sang and met every challenge with enthusiasm, including portages of great risk and exertion. We spent a number of nights in villages along the way defined by the Maroni River that divides Suriname from French Guyana (easily the most bedraggled, pathetic place I have ever seen, as befits the home of Devil's Island), and then, headed southwest into the deeper forest on the Tapanahony, along whose banks were spread a diadem of villages brilliant with color and sparkling. These had no paved surfaces; and all was what our language would have to call "dirt." But as Freud taught, dirt is "matter in the wrong place"; while what the Bush Negroes lived upon was matter ceremonially arranged and artfully assembled, so there was no question of calling the arrangement one of dirt unless one was a racist; just as there was no question of seeing the village as subject to the property relations and class divisions we have come to regard as "natural" in our own capitalist towns, suburbs and cities. It seemed here, rather, that everything was differentiated and yet interconnected in webs of mutual recognition. Play was not split off from work, nor art from life, nor the generations from each other or the land.

Now I say "seemed" because only a fool would think that he could grasp the reality of these folk on the basis of so immediate and glancing an impression. Yet this is no hasty generalization, either; but has been retrospectively assembled from years of pondering the matter and seeing things in various contexts, including association with Stanley Diamond which lay twenty years in the future. Returning to late January, 1961, I can only say that the period on that riverine world was received by me with a kind of permanent ecstasy accompanied by a kind of buzzy meditation, of how marvelous, how strange, and how different it was from the zone that was my normal habitat and to which I realized, always with a pang, I would have to return.

What puzzled me was that the Blacks did not seem to appreciate this. I remonstrated with them during moments of rest, a sophomoric, bumptious soon-to-be-doctor addressing folk whose life was embedded in 350 years of history. We were able to converse in a friendly fashion as the river babbled by, thanks to the free and easy argot of the pidgin tongue of taki-taki, open to the whole crazy-quilt that was Suriname, and accessible to the oncoming English-speaker. I held that this was the most beautiful place and way of life I had ever seen; how then could they do what so many seemed to be doing, leaving their paradise for the towns near the coast, for the false and delusive rewards of our industrial society; was Coca-Cola worth this?... They responded, in so many words, well, that was just the way things looked; from their perspective, life was more exciting in the town;, that's where the action was; it was the thing to do. And easier as well. Why go through the immense trouble of making a giant dugout canoe from a tropical tree—just think about how hard the work was, and how many fires had to be built—when manufactured canoes are there for those who have money? And the worst of this is it that it made a certain amount of sense. Damn sense then!

It is the story of the world, and pretty much the same for both indigenous peoples despite the evident differences between Caribe and Bush Negro, the one exchanging handmade arrows useful to the tourist trade for mass-produced and much-more-lethal shotgun shells, the other exchanging their labor for what the Calypso song would call the "Yankee Dollar," enslaving themselves now to another master, the whole brought to world-annihilating levels under capitalism, which is from this perspective nothing less than the codes devised to destroy what Rosa Luxemburg had called, in 1913, the natural economy whose wreckage was the condition for the accumulation of capital.

I would have to go home without the big answers I had sought, but with renewed fascination. A decisive shift was continuing to develop in me, away from the natural-science paradigm and toward the ways of humankind. It was a continuation of the rupture that befell my science career at Yale with *Twelfth Night*, except now the Shakespearean thread was given by *The Tempest*. Instead of studying nature as such, my thoughts were increasingly turning to the peculiarities of a creature whose being centered in the transformation of nature and whose identity we recognize as history. I was becoming a Marxist *malgre moi-même*, though more than a decade would pass before Marx himself would loom before my eyes; while figures such as Rosa Luxemburg were utterly unknown to me during my visit to Suriname.

Where stood the Noble Primitive (I never thought in terms of a "Savage"), then? Since Rousseau, since Melville's voyage recounted in *Typee*, since a countless succession of imitators, Westerners have taken the path down which I wandered in Suriname, and populated it with "The Other": fellow humans who were not truly fellow but screens on which the lost travellers could project what was missing or despised in their own lives, screens increasingly defined by empire and modernity. With me it had begun, I suppose, with *Bomba the Jungle Boy* and other trashy stuff voraciously read; it grew with Huck Finn floating down the Mississippi on a raft beside an escaped slave, took all kinds of shapes over the years and came to a kind of crescendo as I went along the banks of the Tapanahony, courtesy of Bush Negro labor. How to choose the stance toward these fellow human beings whose existence was enchained with imperialism, and whom we have over-valued, under-valued, and by all means, distorted for our purposes? What was their truth?

There is a book Tropp loaned me after praising it as supremely representative of the world-view that he, a disciple of Reich, would wish for me. I read it in the early '60s, and it made me wonder; writing these passages and realizing that I had forgotten much about it,

I got another copy of *Kabloona* (alas, through fiendish Amazon, massive exploiter of labor), and my wonder has increased.

GONTRAN DE PONCINS was a French artist and aristocrat, descended directly from Michel de Montaigne and born around the turn of the last century. He possessed in good measure the contempt for modernity consistent with his class. Finding himself nowhere at home, he set out, a lost traveller, to wander the world. He tarried in the South Pacific, but found it too soft. So de Poncins sought the end of the earth to find himself, thus he went in 1938 to the True North, the north beyond Edmonton, beyond the last trading station in the chain set down by the Canadians, until he found what he was looking for at Pelly Bay, just south of the Magnetic Pole. I wonder if he was conscious in doing so of moving along the same intellectual path as his immortal ancestor, Montaigne, whose 1580 essay, "On the Cannibals," became the first work within the Western tradition to explore the distinctions between the Indians and their European invaders in a way that criticized the latter by valorizing the former. That, in any case, is what Gontran de Poncins ended up doing.

De Poncins visited a place, so modern-day media tells us, where the lowest windchill ever recorded in Canada, −135° F, based on −60° F and winds of 35 mph—was observed, in January, 1975. De Poncins himself writes of weeks of −50° that had to be endured, with nothing but animal skins to wear, dog-pulled sleds to travel by, igloos built of snow to inhabit, and frozen fish and seal meat to eat, pretty much in the winter dark, all shared at very close quarters and for long periods with hosts who never asked for the pleasure of his company and took nothing in exchange except some tea he had brought for the purpose.

De Poncins observes that as he went further north from the last settlement, a pathetic forebear of the modern pre-fabricated outposts with all the comforts of home that are now airlifted in, he found the inhabitants, only a few dozen of them inhabiting thousands of square miles, more bearable and more admirable. It is necessary to observe that in all ways the process of acculturation was a difficult one. In the earlier phases of his travel de Poncins frequently comes across as a racist of the colonial sort, disparaging the lack of Inuit morality, and making claims such as that they had no "mind" in the recognizable sense we claim for ourselves. But as time went on (he was there some fifteen months), his racism unwound and was shed, both in opinion of the Inuit, and in his actual being as well. He now saw figures both recognizably human and also, in a deeply literal sense, tuned to the processes of nature—though perhaps I should not say "literal" so casually, since acculturation entailed a falling away of words; indeed, you could not call these Inuit illiterate because there was in their world no category of literacy to which they could relate.

Speech they had in plenty, as humans must; just so were they fully human in their devotion to their children (de Poncins writes of the whole caravan stopping at a child's wish and building an igloo on the spot); also of their at-times tragic sense of dignity (he describes a man brooding over his loss of hunting prowess until he commits suicide by garroting himself with a rawhide cord in front of the group); their submission to the eternal predicament of sexual jealousy, Iago's "green-eyed monster" (there are the often recounted casual wife-swappings, but also hair-raising stories of murders committed around the theme of sexual possessiveness); and most impressively the survival-dictated and brilliant ways and means of production through which a human body evolved for life in the East African savannah could endure under such extreme conditions. These are gender differentiated: the women showing amazing skill in fabricating clothing for sub-zero life, the tools as well as the materials taken from nature as formed in the animals they hunted; the unbelievable skills and endurance of the men who could stand for three days over a hole in the ice until the fish they had waited for would swim in range of their spear). To conclude this slender inventory of the Inuit there is this phrase which sets my mind spinning, and surely will do the same for those readers who have, like me, cringed at the thought of living under such conditions: that de Poncins found his hosts to be "a cheerful people, always laughing, never weary of laughter."

With this, the spiritual side as well. There was in this way of life a great silence before nature and its ultimate being, just as there is in our way of life an endless chatter that sheathes us from nature and its ultimate being. As de Poncins stayed with the Pelly Bay Inuit he found the latter way of being falling away and the former being restored, until at length, he found himself at one with the Inuit and as silent before the suchness of nature as any Zen Buddhist. And then he had to leave, the sense of silence enduring well into his re-entry and never, one supposes, fully passing away.

I would be remiss if I left out here something that didn't register in my first reading of *Kabloona*, namely, that there was another white man at Pelly Bay, though not a Kabloona. He was a priest who had been there six years before de Poncins arrived, Fr. Pierre Henry, beloved and certainly lovable as evinced in the text. Fr. Henry has since been described as a saint and for all I know may be up for canonization. Fr. Henry was indeed saintly—selfless, humble, loving, and with eyes on the ultimate; and it seems he fit like a glove over the Eskimo way of being. From one angle (which includes the fact that I didn't think much about this in 1960 when I first read *Kabloona*) Fr. Henry was a living testament to the great power of Christianity to enter into the life-worlds of the most remote peoples and gather their spiritual forms into itself.

From another angle, however, the priest who enchanted Gontran de Poncins was also a wedge into the integral world of the Inuit and harbinger if not instrument of their annihilation. Photos today show the spire of his little Catholic Church, erected I do not know when. By 1955 a Deep Early Warning antenna had been installed at Pelly Bay in case the Soviets decided to send a missile our way. By 1968 an airport was in place and wage labor had reached the local Inuit. It took another thirty years for cable TV to arrive, with the internet not far behind, and a modern school bringing literacy to all.

Today Pelly Bay is a tourist destination. Look it up on Google. It will no doubt adapt to the inevitable disappearance of the polar ice cap as our century wends its way toward oblivion. By 2100, Pelly Bay could be prime real estate for development, perhaps the site of a gated community with its golf course. It may be the last green real estate on Earth.

Who, then, is to be valorized? The original human, nakedly present before nature? Or the present-day human, internet-bound, capital-ensnared and sheathed from nature by a host of mediations? A very dumb question if taken as a matter of essences, but solidly necessary if seen existentially as an orientation in life. There are no essences in human being, but there are lineages of thought to be chosen as beacons of greater or lesser merit. This is the memoir of an eternally restless man who cast his lot with old Montaigne and his great, great… grandson de Poncins—and many others: Blake, Marx, Melville, Stanley Diamond, yes, even the doomed Reich, even, for a confused while, Old Freud.

All of which is to return in the discourse of ecosocialism.

Notes

1 Silvia Federici, *Caliban and the Witch* (New York: Autonomedia, 2004).
2 In Dusan Makaveyev's brilliant 1972 film, "WR: Mysteries of the Organism," there is a sequence showing federal agents actually shoveling Reich's book into an oven.
3 Myron Sharaf, *Fury on Earth: A Biography of Wilhelm Reich* (New York: St. Martin's Press, 1983), 472.
4 Myron "Mickey" Sharaf was Reich's Boswell over a ten-year period, deeply loyal though often betrayed and otherwise harmed by his Master. We knew each other a bit, and were on friendly terms.
5 Erdman, 412.
6 The Dutch had been preceded by the oldest Jewish community of the Americas, a remnant of which remained; and they added folk from the whole range of the colonized world. Thus most of the Creole population was a mixture of Javanese, Asian-Indian, and Chinese; all of which was reflected in taki-taki.
7 Rosa Luxemburg, *The Accumulation of Capital*, trans. Agnes Schwarzschild (New York: Monthly Review Press, 1968).
8 Gontran de Poncins, *Kabloona* (St. Paul: Graywolf Press, 1996). The word roughly means "stupid white man" as Amerindians say it, viz., Jim Jarmusch's great film on a related theme, "Dead Man." It was assembled with the aid of Lewis Galantiere from over a thousand pages of notes and line drawings by de Poncins.

It became a huge success in 1941, selling two million copies. It is now virtually forgotten though obtainable in numerous editions through used booksellers. The reader is urged to get the edition of 1980 by Time Life Books, which has maps, photographs, and considerable introductory material.

ALBERT EINSTEIN PSYCHIATRY DEPARTMENT, 1963.
STANDING, FROM LEFT WITH BOW TIES, ANDY FERBER (SEE CHAPTER 7)
AND LEON YORBURG (SEE CHAPTER 5), WHITE COAT AT RIGHT,
MILTON ROSENBAUM. SEATED, LEFT, IRENE LABOURDETTE
(SEE CHAPTER 4), JOEL, FOURTH FROM RIGHT.

Chapter 5
Psy Times

I t was late at night and late in my undergraduate medical training, during my sojourn on the surgical service. I was wheeling a
patient through the cavernous halls of the old Bellevue Hospital,
I believe, for an X-ray, listening to the scurrying of the rats, moving
past the wards filled with those slumbering and those moaning in
distress, sensing the mass of somnolent, suffering humankind, extending it in thought to the edges of the Earth... when I suddenly
became overcome by pure ecstasy. It was the first return of the
Agape love I had felt some eight years before at my matriculation
into Yale, though I didn't identify it as such. I just stayed with the
sublime, liquid sensation of love as it passed through me and the
souls of the living and the dead, and then back again, as though cir-
culating through the vessels of a heavenly body of which I was an
organ. I nearly fell to my knees. It was late in 1960 and Che Guevara
was at the time in Cuba building the revolution. I only knew dimly
of him and had no fixed opinion of what was going on, but years
later, when I earned of Che's principle that the revolutionary must
be guided by great feelings of love, combining them, so he added,
with the capacity for dispassionate discernment, I recognized that,
yes, I knew something of that.

I was twenty-four, wracked with guilt for what I had to do on
the Bellevue surgical rotation, for example, amputating the leg
below the knee of one old Black woman and stripping a varicose
vein from the leg of another, as the macho surgical residents looked

on and made helpful suggestions. Yes, it was exciting; and yes it was wrong, witness the fact that I knew the names of neither. Elizabeth Taylor, who was admitted shrieking to Harkness Pavilion, the luxury wing of Presbyterian, under her married name of Mrs. Fisher one evening while I was doing private duty nursing to earn some cash, she was never going to have to submit to the scalpel of a medical student. Not her, whose photo from the *Sunday News* had been on my bedroom wall in 1948. Perhaps my epiphany of Grace was compensation for the transgression of using poor, Black, nameless, and old patients as guinea pigs so one could take better care of the happy few.

My trip to Suriname and Trinidad loomed ahead, to be followed by two relatively easy months on a ward for patients with chest diseases, and then the winding down of medical school and the assumption of the duties of a medical intern at Jacobi Hospital in the Bronx, in a word, Hell.

Ninety-six consecutive hours of work over a hot July Fourth weekend put me in the hospital with septicemia stemming from an infected toe: not taking your shoes off for four days of work as an intern in a New York summer will do that. I was quickly restored to physical health with intravenous antibiotics, and sent back to the ward for three months of hundred-plus-hour weeks under conditions of extreme dehumanization. Jacobi, the city hospital of last resort for the East Bronx, received patients too sick and decrepit for the private and non-profit sectors. Over the year, I admitted two hundred patients, of whom forty died. The logic was that the best patient to be assigned was the "quick cool": one who perished between being admitted and worked up, thereby taking the attending doctor out of the rotation and giving a grim respite. I took all this rather badly; in fact, thought I was going to lose my mind and frequently locked myself in the toilet to escape the incessant chaos. I learned later that the Department of Medicine worried about me enough to put me on a suicide watch.

It was less physical stress than heartlessness that made me decide one evening late in July that I couldn't stand the idea of being a "scientific doctor." I had to find a way out.... But what else was there? I was in my little room in the intern's dormitory and began browsing amongst the texts.

And there was the big, fat and dull book about psychiatry. Though reading Freud's dream book on the high seas the summer before entering had roused my interest, psychiatry classes at P&S had extinguished it, smothering Freud's dialectic of the unconscious under the conformist blanket of an adjustment psychology, and causing this difficult young man to rebel in various ways and receive the lowest grade of his medical school career in psychiatry.

Now I could see that the oafishness of P&S psychiatry had artificially dulled my appetite for something toward which I was actually drawn, and that the long, now-declining, fascination with Reich had cleared space for it. I began to open my eyes and look about.

And what I saw outside my dormitory window was that the institution to which I was then attached, the Albert Einstein College of Medicine, was also the site of a dynamic program in psychiatry, socially innovative and psychoanalytically informed. Refocused, my spirits lifted and I got back on track. I was helped, too, by looking up Virginia Ryan, the feisty Bronx Irish nurse who had cared for me during my brief hospitalization. One thing led to another, we were married next April, and the following February, Jonathan, now a prominent cinematographer in South Africa, entered the world, to be followed in 1965 by Erin.

Einstein was the first medical school to open in New York City since 1897, and a mere six-year-old in 1961. It was the brainchild of Yeshiva University's President, Dr. Samuel Belkin, who approached the great physicist, socialist, anti-racist and humanitarian in 1951.

Remarkably, Albert Einstein was intrigued. He foresaw in a letter to Belkin that the project could become "unique" in that the school would "welcome students of all creeds and races." Yeshiva went further still. Working with the city, the new medical school became the first of its kind to be built conjointly with a public medical center. And so Jacobi Hospital was inaugurated as the new school's teaching hospital; a large and modern medical center arose on what had been East Bronx swampland, and Albert Einstein, a man of surpassing virtue, blessed the new medical complex with his name.

The new institution busily fulfilled its progressive mission for a considerable period. Partly this was due to the persistence of genuinely emancipatory potentials embedded in Jewry before Zionism commandeered the Chosen People. And partly it was due to an ironic dialectic embedded in the deep and darkly repressive '50s, epoch of McCarthyism and virulent anticommunism. It is loosely thought that this period merely displayed hysteria or was an instance of what Richard Hofstadter would call "the paranoid style in American life." But although there has been definitely such a dismal impulse, post-war America also contained a goodly number of actual communists and other radicals to persecute, having arisen during the great capitalist crises of the '30s. This defined the chief purpose of McCarthyite repression in all its guises, which was to break up the radical Left and clear it out of institutions— including, to be sure, academic and medical institutions. We do not tend to shoot our radicals in America unless they are Black. Hence the question arises, where do Left intellectuals go once persecuted? Well, in the case of the medical-communist Left of the '50s it can be said that some of them got lucky thanks to a burst of hirings in mid-decade at a new school with high ideals named after a great socialist intellectual. It was a passing moment, eventually yielding to the aging that most people of whatever political persuasion undergo, and the slow, steady repression carried out by normal capitalist means. Notwithstanding, the Einstein medical complex really was a hotbed of leftism of all kinds from its inception until the middle of the '80s, when the last specimen of this type was forced out. That was me, getting my anticommunist comeuppance, yet grateful for my exposure at Einstein to its first generation of radicals who were my teachers. For that was my professional home as my ship tacked leftwards.

ADVENTURES IN THE PSY TRADES

EINSTEIN WAS THE ONLY residency program I took seriously and with enthusiasm. But it must be said that the feelings were not reciprocated, indeed, I had the devil of a time getting accepted. Three factors were at play: the lateness of my application, which was only considered because someone already chosen had dropped out at the last minute; evidence of emotional instability, *viz,* the suicide watch requested by the Department of Medicine; and suspicions over my allegiance to Reich. Extra interviews kept being demanded as now one, now another, doubter had it out with me. Finally, Dr. Joseph Cramer, chief child psychiatrist, called me in to say that given my talent, the department was prepared to offer me a residency. He added, with impressive bluntness, that in his view I didn't belong in this profession, chiefly because he didn't see that I really wanted to be a psychiatrist. I have to admit that Cramer, a kind-hearted if crusty man who later became a good friend, had a point, although it took 25 years to verify.

As the story emerged it became clear that one person, and he alone, settled the matter: Milton Rosenbaum, chairman of the department and its peerless leader. Years later Rosenbaum confided that he had a kind of faith in me that no one else in his inner council shared. They saw my impulsivity, dubious and confused motivation, serious depression, and radical propensity, and were turned off; he saw someone who would settle down and make a real contribution—and whom he could allow to move on without recrimination once that contribution was made. And he was the boss. I have known thousands of people in this life. Many were more brilliant and creative than Milt Rosenbaum; many were closer to me, or more a soul mate. In fact, I can't say that Rosenbaum was a soul mate at all, or even a friend. I think, rather—and here I know I am treading on the path of cliché—that he was the father I had always wanted but lacked: steady, free from bombast, authoritative without being authoritarian because not possessed by demons, in command so you could be yourself without fear, very much of this world without succumbing to its temptations, no revolutionary but on the side of a decent and feasible progress. He would live into his nineties, active to the end, instead of disintegrating in his sixties like Lou Kovel. And of course, he would never scream at me for betraying Western civilization with my evil ideas.

Rosenbaum was a mover and shaker who lived out a Jewish life when Jews had choices before them that were less corrupting than now. He had desegregated the University of Cincinnati (his hometown) Hospital in the '40s. He had founded major psychiatric and psychological institutions in Israel up to the mid-'60s, and then, so it seemed to me, began quietly pulling back from the Zionist state. Before this he had scoured the world to round up psychoanalysts who had been scattered by Nazism; he brought them back to New York, in a number of cases parking them in the Pacific region, and further indebting them to himself, and secured their services to the Einstein psychiatric program, making it a world-class purveyor of Freudian ideas.

I can see Rosenbaum behind his large desk in a dimly lit office, a slender and measured man, tilting back in his chair, pencil between his hands, musing about this and that in his Midwestern twang, and when necessary, distributing emoluments to meet our needs. For this was American psychiatry's glory time. It seems unimaginable from the perspective of today's desolation, but we were then in Capital's most expansive epoch, and governed by people ridiculously enamored of the Psy world and its ideology of mental health.

There were two springs from which this flowed: the Kennedy family's devotion to sister Rosemary, who was born developmentally disabled and made worse by a prefrontal lobotomy at age 23; and an abiding impulse among progressive elites to counter the appeal of socialism with a positive image of mental health, such being a cornerstone of the liberal world-view.

In October 1962, JFK invited a junior faculty member and a first-year resident from a number of leading psychiatry programs to Washington for a *soirée* at the Shoreham Hotel. My friend Leon Yorburg—a child psychoanalyst of the Kleinian persuasion, and a fine woodworker in his spare time—and I were the representatives from Einstein. We traipsed to the Capital in my VW Beetle, deposited ourselves in the Shoreham's main ballroom, and were soon joined on the dais by all able-bodied members of the Kennedy clan to partake of a filet mignon dinner that still is my benchmark for supreme repasts, although given the spectacular company this can scarcely be accorded as an objective assessment. The President spoke, copper-colored skin and amazing hair glowing, and he was marvelous, telling the five hundred of us how important psychiatry was for his vision of the New Frontier and promising more good things to come. It seems preposterous that a man who would have to contend a few days later with the Cuban missile crisis (I imagine he was already thinking over some scary cables as he sat on the dais), the greatest sustained fright I can ever imagine enduring and the tipping point for nuclear Armageddon, could waste his time with such bromides.

Notwithstanding, within the year the Community Mental Health Act was enacted and we Psy folk, like piglets at the main teat, could come into our full being, which lasted until the fiscal crisis of the mid-'70s brought on the neoliberal desolation that will continue to endure for the foreseeable future. In a time when the collapse of community mental health facilities is routinely listed as causal for the latest school massacre or pushing onto the subway track, who among the psychiatriat can remember the bounty that was once ours, even including reimbursement by the federal government for our personal psychoanalyses? Are you kidding me? Had we not been anointed by the President himself?

And then came November 22, 1963. On the 24th, Milt Rosenbaum met with his weeping residents, which was kindly. He seemed stunned and at a loss for words to unravel the horror. In those days, nobody realized—hardly anybody does today—just how much the whole psy package, and its accompanying triumphalism had been the plaything of forces beyond our ken. Of course, this was the least of our problems. It took years of political maturation and sorting through official lies to get at the truth about JFK, that he was executed for offences against the National Security State he had once championed, to wit: preparing to end the Vietnam War, ending as well the Cold War and the nuclear arms race, making peace with Fidel Castro and other progressive leaders of the Third World like Sukarno of Indonesia. If the reader is curious, s/he may consult the august witness of James Douglass for an iron demonstration of these truths.[1]

Here is an associated finding of some relevance for me, which I was told by a friend whose mother was a secretary in the Selective Service Administration: that on November 25th, 1963, the Monday after the assassination, a command was received to draft a half million troops for the war in Vietnam that Kennedy had promised to liquidate. Entailed with this were regulations that would end the era of deferments for medical doctors, thus exposing privileged psychiatric residents to the reckoning of military service. Less than two years after the death of Kennedy, my residency done, I was off to Seattle for a fateful tour of duty.

Ignorant of the wider and deeper aspects, and protected from the real consequences until the crises of the '70s, Einstein Psy-folk lived in a bubble of bourgeois *jouissance* as humane technocrats who could debate the Big Issues, such as whether individual therapy under Freudian auspices was the way to go, as against group, or family, or community-based treatment.

Taken all in all, the years of residency and the early ones of my academic position were the most collegial I was ever to spend. Einstein in the '60s was a gathering of colorful characters who actually conversed from different points of the Psy realm and appeared to like each other. Everybody was bright, everybody was comfortable, everybody was hopeful that the future would hold more of the same, and that the clouds of war, empire and social disaster would remain on the distant horizon. The whole package was wrapped in the naïve assumption that we lived in ever-expanding times. Were we not riding the wave of the America Century?

Archetypical was Ed Hornick, director of inpatient services and in charge of the first-year residency program, who told us flatly that to get ahead in today's psychiatry, one had to get psychoanalytic training. "It's your credit card," said hard-boiled realist Ed. That was the program and we were expected to get with it.

Hornick was *sui generis* among the Einsteinians, being both un-Jewish and Midwestern. He was a Gatsby-like man, who burst onto every scene as if propelled by the momentum of running from something. Not that Ed evinced any desperation. This was a time when the notion of being "cool" was not yet in circulation. Had it been, Ed Hornick would have been entitled to the laurel for premature coolness. He was unflappable and frenzied in the same gesture, appearing above it all while racing here, there and everywhere. Hornick could not have slept more than three hours a night. He began seeing his patients in the wee hours, and after four or so sessions in the Eames chair, his pipe puffing (Ed was too cool to succumb to the oh-so-Freudian cigar-mania, though he consumed large numbers of cigarettes besides his pipe tobacco, I should think, to his doom) and his notebook filling up, would race to the medical center where he presided over his inpatient demesne and sprinkled his residents with tough love before coming back for some more income-extraction in the Eames chair. The day really began after dark, when Ed and wife Joy went out on the town. He said to me once that he considered an evening in which only one event was attended to be a kind of defeat. In any case, it was plain that he felt it to be such, as life for Ed Hornick was a kind of performance to show the world that here was a man who came from the sticks to really, truly live more fully than everyone else, and drink the most deeply from that wondrous fountain that was New York City. Ed Hornick was the man who never slept for the city that never slept.

Of course, life wasn't all going out. A performer wants a stage on which to strut; and this was admirably provided by his West 73rd Street mansion and Gatsby Palace. Six stories, with a roof garden and personal elevator, Chez Hornick was a true wonder of the *arriviste* world and the cynosure of mental-health eyes. Who needed a Park Avenue suite when a man could flank the entrance to his own brownstone with commissioned busts of FDR and Freud, and lead his guests to the custom-made whimsical furniture and up-to-the-minute art adorning the living room and entertainment center filling the third floor and provoking the oohing and aahing of gaping *cognoscenti*? I have no idea what the Hornicks paid in the '50s, but the building brought in some $8 million in 2007, when his three sons sold it to a developer. Beyond doubt, a fair portion of the frenzy of Hornick's life came from maintaining this extravagant dwelling for a salon of Proustian proportions, one that defined what it was to be a New York hipster-psychiatrist in that golden, fleeting age. With bills to pay for his lifestyle aplenty, and a three-month-long summer trek in the VW Microbus stocked with camping equipment and quotable books for next year's *soirées*, Hornick had to maximize his Labor-Day-to-Memorial Day earning power. This he did by charging top-dollar for psychotherapy and making clear to his clientele that if they didn't pay the fee on the spot when the bill was presented they needn't bother to come to the next session. After all, business was business. In sum, the very model of a modern mental maven of late capitalism.

I was at first uneasy about Hornick. This was to grow worse later on, as I shall relate, and then became excruciating as his life took a steep downward turn in the '80s. In the beginning, though, it was mainly a matter of fearing his scathing tongue, whose bracing venom was distributed equally to all the neophyte trainees. Nobody in all my years of schooling had spoken to me that way, in an open setting where the price of exposure was severe embarrassment. For example, during a ward meeting one day when I, presiding for the nonce and stumbling in the effort to keep the "group process" going in the presence of a garrulous, uncontrollable woman, had to bear the intrusion of Hornick tapping his pipe against the chair and pronouncing in his bluntest manner that "it looks like Mrs. Yifniff has Joel's left ball and half of his right one in her hand."

Once the laughter subsided, the pain faded and life went on; indeed, over time, exposure to Ed's cruelty had a salutary toughening effect. For along with his less-charming qualities, Hornick had the gifts of a sharp intelligence, a frank openness and, not too far beneath this, a generous and caring nature—not to mention a fine sense of humor. As he was a master at the nuclear psychotherapeutic gesture, of breaking through the frame of conventional discourse to destabilize the given relationships and open space for hopeful innovation, so was I able to learn something of this from him in the crucible of practice.

Over time I became pretty good at the same interventions, not, I hope, with cruelty, but by using the potentials granted to me to develop some skill not only with individuals but also groups. In the doing I grew almost as fond of Ed Hornick as I was of Milt Rosenbaum, seeing him as a kind of cheerful, avuncular figure, whose worldview attached a very different, happier set of meanings than was the case for the morose and demonized world of Lou and Rose Kovel. I especially appreciated the moment when Hornick pulled me aside and looking me straight in the eye, told me that my work showed real promise, adding that he still couldn't figure out what I wanted to do with my life, but awaited with interest the moment when I made up my mind; though when I started to do so, I don't think Ed was happy with the outcome.

And then there was José Barchilon, darkly handsome, charismatic and brilliant, as everyone knew. A Sephardic Jew from Morocco educated in France, Barchilon added a gallic touch to Einstein, opening the rude Bronx to great continental traditions.

Barchilon belonged to no psychoanalytic movement or school so far as I could tell, though he was a regular around the Temple to Freud that was the New York Psychoanalytic Institute on East 92nd Street. Very pleased with himself was José, as he demonstrated a standing backflip when we first visited his home in Rye. He also boasted of his skiing technique, and as though a true-blue Reichian, of his orgasms as well, forgetting that Reichians were not to boast, this being a sign of being stuck in the phallic phase.

He was our Training Director, a position I was to assume at Einstein a decade later; though if you had told me during my residency this was to be my fortune I would have blankly stared in astonishment, so far above our pedestrian minds did Barchilon seem to soar. In those years—I mean especially the period 1963–65—the opinion of José Barchilon, and particularly his opinion of me, mattered more than that of anybody on earth.

Freud's substantive contributions stemmed from the note he made to himself during the period of his exploration of hysteria, that "our patients suffer from reminiscences." Coupled with the notion that our impulses, and indeed, the construction of the body itself, were products of history, this had the potential to disassemble the Cartesian barrier between subject and object and went some way to reconnect the realms of science and culture.

José Barchilon camped on this ground, with the idea of extending Freud's insight that psychoanalysis, however much it set itself in the medical-scientific world, originally derived from the sphere of culture and never entirely left that sphere. This applied across the whole realm of collective representation, and nowhere more than in the matter of the word that Freud had used to construct the talking cure. Before this, words were the raw material of narrative and exfoliated across world literature, to become the art form most beloved by Barchilon, the novel. Now José shared with his Viennese progenitor the view that the imaginative writer was the precursor of the "scientific psychologist"; Barchilon went further, to pursue its corollary, that the scientific psychologists of the New Age could best learn their craft through the study of great fiction. And so the high point of the Einstein Psychiatric Residency program became the convivial and heady monthly gathering by the third-year residents at José Barchilon's elegant home in Rye, NY, for the psychoanalytic study of the novel.

Not everybody liked this, but most of us did, and nobody loved it more than I. Bless you, José, for allowing one of life's great pleasures to become a means of instruction. Ten years before, I had fallen away from the Apollonian track of studying mathematics under the tutelage of Shizuo Kakutani by the Dionysian pull of Shakespeare's Sir Toby Belch. Would this, too, become a destabilizing moment?

There was, however, nothing remotely Dionysian about it, because Barchilon had refined literature into a technology wholly subsumed into the logic of psychoanalysis, whence it became capable of being processed into a psychoanalytic production for professional advancement. As he put it in one of his writings on the subject, "A Psychoanalytic Study of *Huckleberry Finn*":

> We have assumed that the novels were the model of the modern case history…. Since the creative writer and the psychoanalyst were describing essentially the same phenomena, we tried to analyze Huckleberry Finn and some of his friends *as if they were real persons* [italics in original].
>
> In this analysis, we believe to have uncovered the exquisite psychological consistency of the character

of Huckleberry Finn. In fact, the interplay between his unconscious (reconstructed) nuclear conflict and its derivatives is so unbelievably congruent, that one could indeed make a fairly precise metapsychological formulation of Huck's psychic equilibrium. This finding, far from being an exception, has been confirmed repeatedly over the years in our seminar on the "Use and Place of the Novel in Psychoanalysis," and we have almost come to consider this kind of consistency as a hallmark of "great fiction."

Actually, Barchilon was the co-author of that essay, and the use of the first-person-plural pronoun was of the "royal we" sort. The other author was myself;[2] it was my first published work outside of vague mimeographs scattered over the years and some pieces in the *Yale Daily News.* I read a shortened version at a spring 1965 meeting of the American Psychoanalytic Association: my first public appearance before a professional-academic audience, and on the stage of the Waldorf Astoria, no less. A positively giddy moment, to be sure. I could hear the wings of great success beating overhead. Of course it was somewhat tasteless for the APA to flaunt its great prosperity by choosing such a setting at the pinnacle of bourgeois society. But I wasn't going to let that tiny cloud on the horizon spoil the great moment. I had discovered at my *bar mitzvah* at the Baldwin Jewish Center in 1949 that the deity had granted me, a fearful, clumsy, awkward, and all-too-often mumbling person, the gift of public speaking. And so I allowed myself to be in the moment, as they say, in order to relish the crowning success of my psychiatric residency.

The words quoted above were pure Barchilon-ese. He had done the beginning and the end of the essay, entrusting its body to me with a considerable amount of supervision. It was partly a sign of respect which I respected in return, partly a genuine desire to bring along a talented student in his chosen path, and partly a matter of necessity. For José Barchilon had writer's block. His fertile mind had problems transferring its product to the page; and so he required someone, a cross between an amanuensis and junior partner, to write something substantial. We discover in the bibliography of the Huck Finn essay, entry #6: "Barchilon, José, *et al., Use and Place of the Great Novels in Psychoanalysis.* New York: Pantheon Books, in press." I hope the reader will not be dismayed to learn that those last two words were a bit of a fib. José had me contact André Schiffrin, whose Pantheon Press was then underway. André showed definite interest—how could one simply dismiss so charismatic a mind as Barchilon?—and dispensed the publisher's mantra, that he'd love to see more. Somehow, this became an "in press," as I was to become José's "*et al.*"3

THERE WAS INDEED a firm hope on his part that I would become his partner and share his life's work. And there was certainly no indifference on my side. My habitual hypercritical attitude notwithstanding, our Huck Finn was a real achievement by two people sharing a task, and something of a labor of love, for I do love great literature. I myself am no stranger to writer's block, and if I could be recompensed for every hour spent staring at a page or screen wondering if I would ever write a decent sentence again, there would be no money worries in my life. I have grown accustomed to the need for a furnace of angst to anneal my writing, and so I soldier on. But I am not an ox, and cannot write simply as a result of flogging; there has to be a real desire. In this case, there was something of that desire, but there was more than that: an ambivalence, desire against desire.

While I could take satisfaction from having made definite contributions to the text of the Huck Finn essay, the fact remained that its frame of reference remained José's. And I had to admit to myself, that there was something that made me uneasy about Barchilon's method, which was essentially an extension of the orthodox psychoanalytic method, a bad taste that lingered, though I lacked the means of explaining it at the time.

José's idea went well beyond Freud's claim that the creative writer was the precursor of the scientific psychologist. He saw the creative writer as the provider of ore to be refined by the scientific and psychoanalytically informed critic, who could tell the writer what he really meant, thus burnishing his professional expertise concerning what people were really about. The "case study" of an individual was not simply an equivalent of the novel. The novel was a prefiguration of the case study, which to Barchilon's eye was its truth and scientific apotheosis: its higher and more technically sophisticated offspring. By saying that we were not only permitted, but obliged to treat the *personae* of the novel as if they were real persons, Barchilon asserted that the psychoanalytic method, a glass through which we saw darkly, nonetheless disclosed the reality of human existence. Captain Ahab was to him another motherless child, not the commander of a ship which could represent society itself, as directed by a psychotic capitalist command-structure bent on annihilating nature itself. There were no such categories in Barchilon's worldview—just as there were none in the psychoanalytic, or indeed, in the bourgeois worldview—capable of registering this and giving it life (as Melville found out when *Moby Dick* proved the ruination of his career, turning America's greatest writer into a nonentity).

I strove to follow Barchilon's guidelines for Huck Finn, obsessively detailing the absent mother, the deep depression, the death-wish, the Moses fantasy, the rebirthing, and related matters. Was this a real person? It seemed more like a kind of machine inhabiting an individual. Its goal was the case study. But was the case study of real persons, or of separated beings? Is the isolated individual the real person? Is not the real person the human being, and the separated individual the sign of alienation, a notion itself alien to Freudian psychoanalysis? John Donne speaks here:

> No man is an Island, entire of itself; every man is a piece of the Continent, a part of the main; if a clod be washed away by the sea, Europe is the less, as well as if a promontory were, as well as if a manor of thy friends or of thine own were; any man's death diminishes me, because I am involved in Mankind; And therefore never send to know for whom the bell tolls; It tolls for thee.[4]

Barchilon's discourse, which was the Psy discourse in its fully elaborated Freudian guise, isolated the self (from the Italian insulates, literally making it into an island as in the packaging of the psychic apparatus) as Huck was on the raft, separated from Jim and the society of the riverbank. But where Barchilon turned this into a fabric of lost infantilism, it seems to me that Mark Twain wanted us to experience the anguish of an imposed separation embodied in the great American crime of slavery, and its essential derivative, racism.

I had to write about slavery in the Huck Finn essay, it was simply too glaring to avoid. But slavery, though mentioned, was always secondary, a mere tag to what really mattered psychoanalytically, namely, the infantile strivings embedded in the mental apparatus. As for racism, there was nothing of it in the essay.

Was there not a link here with the elegance of the Waldorf Astoria, and the smartly attired and neatly bearded psychoanalysts professionally carrying out their function as the largely black staff waited on them, all within a society whose historically specific figure was "man as an island, entire of itself." I could not begin to think of such things at that time. But I do think it accounts for the bad taste I was feeling in the midst of the excitement and elation.

The year 1965 was a bloody one for racial struggle in the United States. On February 21st, Malcolm X was gunned down in the Audubon Ballroom; and from August 11th to 17th, the Watts district of Los Angeles exploded in a series of deadly riots that left 34 dead. There was of course much more violence before, in between, and after these landmarks, but the dates will serve to define the period during which the Huck Finn essay was prepared, presented to the APA, and discussed as part of the project of collaboration with Barchilon. He was about to move to Denver for an extended period, and I, too was about to move west, to Seattle, for my two-year mandatory service in the war effort, with no destination known after that. Perhaps I could join him after my discharge. Barchilon hyped the skiing and the free and easy life in the mile-high city, along with opportunities for psychoanalytic practice and theoretical development. Who knows? Perhaps we could develop his insight, freshly served by tunnel vision from the depths of depth psychology, that the matter of racism was the outcome of an inner desire for oppression on the part of the victim rather than any objective social conditions. To be precise, because the psychoanalyst, like any scientist, had to be precise in specifying the "instincts" at play in any human phenomenon, we could explore the Barchilonian theory of racism which he tossed off one day, that it resulted from a collective masochism of the Negroes. Ah, Science!

The importuning continued through the summer and on into 1966. But things were rapidly changing for me. Sometime in the New Year I wrote José to express my regrets at having to withdraw from our project. I had an ironclad excuse. For over the months of being in Seattle with a lot of free time to ponder the direction of my life, I had decided that I had to write a book of my own, on the subject, as it turned out, of White racism.

Notes

1 James Douglass, *JFK and the Unspeakable* (Maryknoll: Orbis Books, 2008).

2 José Barchilon and Joel Kovel, "A Psychoanalytic Study of Huckleberry Finn," *Journal of the American Psychoanalytic Association* 14 (1966): 775–814.

3 One tangible result: Schiffrin persuaded Barchilon to write a preface to Foucault's *Madness and Civilization,* which was then in press. This José was able to do.

4 John Donne, "Meditation XVII," in *Devotions Upon Emergent Occasions* (1624).

JON AND JOEL

Chapter 6
Dies Irae

You can see why the mountains are called the Cascades when viewing them along a north-south axis from the vantage of Crystal's seven thousand feet. Now they appear as a dazzling river of ice and rock, the entire mass cascading between and around still greater rocks of an ancient volcanic series. There, eighty miles to the north, sits shrouded Mount Baker; to the south is Hood, near Portland; then Adams and St. Helena's, and far, far away, the suggestion of California's Shasta. And here, right here, just behind my head, was Rainier, a reclining colossus, broad glaciated slopes his chest, benignly beholding us as though we were infants at play in the crook of his elbow. Rainier was twice the height of Crystal, which formed the giant's couch, and for us, an observation platform with an opening in the line of trees where commenced the three-thousand-foot descent to the base.

It was my first try at such an extended drop. I was barely adequate in the essentials of skiing, shocked to find myself on such a slope and, never one for heights or risky sports, elated beyond measure. Upon arrival at the bottom, intact and glowing, nothing seemed beyond my reach. The drive home would take us through glades of immense Douglas fir and Sitka spruce, there would be gorgeous waterways, moderate traffic, a friendly, low-key city poised on the edge of growth. Perhaps here was my opportunity to go west and leave behind the tired, dingy, and mean Old World defined by The Bronx. I had never been much of a nature boy. But the expedition to Suriname had opened my eyes. Now, the possibility of a serene, orderly life in close touch with earth's wonders began to take hold.

And then I remembered the deep misery awaiting me when I would return to the ticky-tacky home on the slight rise from which one could see Rainier eighty miles away on the occasional fine day. "If you can't see Rainier, it's raining. If you can see Rainier, it's going to rain," was a pet witticism of the locals. In the second of my Seattle winters it rained at least part of each day for 47 days in a row: sounds Biblical, though the total rainfall was no more than in New York, being mostly a little pitter-patter as the North Pacific winds, having wrung themselves out on the Olympic peninsula, saved the drips and drops for soggy Seattle. It contributed to a good case of cabin fever but in no way caused it. That was a function of what I was doing and who I was in relation to it.

When I chose Seattle's Public Health Service Hospital for my two-year obligatory wartime service it was with a dual ambition: try out a new part of the country and give the war in Vietnam a wide berth. At first the latter goal seemed attainable. Yes, there was a Navy officer's uniform to wear, but hardly ever in full regalia, I never had to pick up a gun, remaining all the while a good seven thousand miles from the war zone. All I had to do was take care of a motley population: Merchant Mariners conveying war *materièl* across the Pacific; Coast Guarders who… well, guarded our coast; other military personnel, mostly Naval with some Air Force and Army thrown in, who didn't have a psychiatrist assigned to their base; the families of said military folk; also retirees from the armed forces and their families; the staff of the USPHS itself; finally, Native American wards of the federal government, who dwelt in a "catchment area" (as the bureaucracy was wont to call it) that included Idaho, Montana, Oregon, Washington, and even Alaska: a mere 1,063,561 square miles, the mental health of whose aboriginal inhabitants had become the province of Surgeon (a rank equivalent to Lt. Commander, or Major) Joel S. Kovel, MD, freshly minted by one of the best psychiatry programs in the United States.

WITH THE EXCEPTION of housewives and their adolescent offspring, virtually all of whom bore the scars of military patriarchy, the bulk of my work was administrative, conducted outside of the

JOEL KOVEL

framework of the caring human relationship that humanizes psychiatry. I was therefore forced into becoming a dehumanized instrument of the state, for which the psychiatrist was a Reality Policeman and for which "mental illness" was defined as troublemaking.

Most devastating was trying to cope with what befell those descendants of First Peoples whose lives became shattered once their land had been seized by the United States. They flew one such to me whose trouble was intractable public drunkenness: thousands of miles at taxpayers' expense so that I could "have a look at him," not to help but to fill in a space on the form and sign my name. With the return flight virtually idling outside the door, I listened for about an hour to the rage of the handsome and articulate young man before me, and said what could be said, until the time was up and "my patient" was swept away to his fate. I received the courtesy of a follow-up about a week later, informing me that shortly after return, the young Indian consumed a bottle of vodka and fell dead upon the floor. Case closed.

In cases of this sort I was wretchedly passive; in others, however, there was something for me to do with one category of client of special important to the authorities. Roughly once a week there would appear in my office a person ordered to be seen psychiatrically by his commanders, not to have his distress relieved and his happiness and self-realization achieved, but to correct his bad behavior, and most important, give him a diagnosis—some kind of personality disorder, like "passive-aggressive" would do—that would facilitate his removal from the service for clogging up the war machine.

The military liked this option because it spared them a messy court martial. I loathed it, because it blocked whatever humanistic values I held dear as a psychiatrist, and it forced me to do what I had come to hate: namely, make a fetish out of the labeling called "diagnosis," and worse, for the purpose of railroading a kind of dissident. Under no circumstances could a label at the level of "personality disorder" do aught but conceal the truth of a human being at odds with his environment. I had managed to evade or soft-pedal this problem as a resident at Einstein, where the immanent authoritarianism of diagnosing was dissolved in a humanist ethos. Now the tables for sure were turned, and I faced the machine whose func-

131

tioning it was my job to facilitate, telling me to betray myself to do its work of aggressive war in Southeast Asia.

Objectively, a most minor complicity, and the tiniest particle of evil compared to the havoc being wrought in Vietnam. But it was the particle before me, within which the whole was compressed. Had not Blake told me countless times that we are capable of seeing a world in a grain of sand? To rub it in there were examples of resistance I could read about, like Dr. Howard Levy—years later to become a good friend—who had been imprisoned for refusing to train Green Berets posted to Vietnam. But Howard had no family to hold him back and, more to the point, was far more politically developed than I at this time. Week by week I was learning of the nightmare the United States was making in Vietnam, without being able to come to grips with it.

It ate away at my insides. I collapsed into the cavity it created and fell into one of my worst depressions ever, all the forces of life turning into self-loathing. Stanley Diamond was later to call the secret of so-called "innate" human aggression, that it was at root, "unlived life." So it was with me then. Not yet ready to live freely, my aggression turned inward and spilled over.

I recall feeling on the tennis court one day a shock of emptiness such as I had never felt before, a sensing of being alone in the universe, unloved and unlovable; the flat zone of the court seemed suddenly to stretch away in all directions, draining me of vitality. I cried out and staggered, troubling my partner, a nice young fellow whom we would visit in riot-torn Detroit on the way home in the summer of 1967. Being a clever dissembler, I was able to reassure him, as I did others, but the woes kept returning for months.

A TURN IN THE ROAD

A WHOLE YEAR HAD PASSED, we were in the summer of 1966, heading toward the 27th of August, when I would reach the decadal landmark of age thirty. The fretting machine was working away, spitting out self-accusations of worthlessness and failure. Little of this was evident from the outside, as I went about my daily rounds; I even kept in touch with friends from Einstein. One day a letter arrived from Donald Marcuse (no relation to Herbert), who had been a resident with me and, like me, had been planning a collaborative writing project with our charismatic Residency Director, José Barchilon, in this case, about the work of the Cubist masters, Picasso and Juan Gris. Marcuse was up-beat; he and José were really getting down to work and could look forward to some serious collaborative writing.… All very nice, except that I took the good news in a most ungenerous and self-centered way. Forgetting for the moment that I had excellent reason for avoiding my own collaboration with Barchilon, I stumbled about in envy and self-pity, until at some point I must have scraped bottom and bounced upward, for suddenly my lament took another direction and became an insight:

Here I am, almost thirty, and never written a book.

Wait a second! I never told myself I wanted to write a book… and at that moment, realized that I had plucked a vocation from the blue. To write a book, my own book! Not a collaboration with a racist psychoanalyst who thought the troubles of Blacks stemmed from their masochism—but something from, and of, me, something beyond the slough of desolation.

It would doubly alter my life, because I did not simply want to write a book, indeed, had no idea for a while what I wanted to write about. It was rather a decision to change myself, from the person whom my teachers had been urging to make up his mind to some-one who had in fact done so, deciding to devote himself to gather and process parts of reality and forge them into literature.

I did not think of making money, which was just as well, because I haven't. I did realize I needed to think in a different way and find new connections, and this was transformative. To write in this sense meant taking an argument to the limit, neither fearing my own con-clusions nor any conflict with authority. Indeed, much struggle lay ahead. But the struggle now had a purpose and direction. And so it became incorporated into my being.

What to write about? I thought of the war, which I hated more every day, but I was too far from the action to do so. No, it would have to be at closer range. And here the same theme kept rising: the "race problem" that had been agitating the nation for a decade. Seattle seemed relatively free from racial disorder; but then it also seemed without Blacks. Not entirely: after all, one of the officers at the USPHS Hospital was a Black man. He seemed to glide through the place, always polite, always calm and correct, always masked. Could his effacement be related to the fact that the USPHS had perpetrated the most heinous episode of scientific racism in our history—the deliberate withholding of syphilis treatment to Black men at its Tuskegee, Alabama facility? And what about the men who picked up the garbage we left in the back alley once a week? Why was it that, as young Jonathan perceptively asked, all these were Black men, and no Black faces were seen anywhere else?

There had been with me as well during this long depression a kind of torpid suppression of the matter of race. I had largely witnessed the great Civil Rights movement from the sidelines, with occasional flickerings of an uneasy conscience that soon subsided. I was aware that those close to me, including members of my family, seemed to have a kind of tacit complicity with overt racists though they never did anything out of line. But none of it held together. How easily had I let slip from my mind the Black workers at the Hotel Del Mar, with whom I had felt such solidarity during the summer of 1954!

Now, not instantly, but as a frozen hillside starts cracking in spring, the rumbling of an approaching avalanche began to be felt. I began to become aware that what was called the race problem would be better described as a kind of nightmare that pervaded our society and was warded off by its expert commissions, curricula, workshops, efforts to "improve communications," and the subsumption of race relations into psycho-jargon, reducing three-and-a-half centuries into a problem to solve. It not only missed the reality of racism, but somehow perpetuated it.

The truth could be evoked in song, as when Billie Holliday (and later, Nina Simone) sang "Strange Fruit," and it was copiously drawn in literature—not as in my Professor Barchilon's psychoanalysis of the text, that is, re-presentation, but as the direct transmission of something unspeakable. I had read my Faulkner, and my

Melville, whose Benito Cereno had gone to his doom muttering "the Negro"—that is, the inscrutable and silent Babo who led the slave revolt aboard his ship. And Conrad finished off *Heart of Darkness* with Kurtz's cry: "The horror! The horror!"

Something that had been split-off came alive in me as I dug and scraped. The more I understood, the more I felt, the less I feared and the more curious I became to travel on. It was visceral, attached to a kind of elemental awareness. Amidst my guilt and manipulated fears, I began to conclude that I really did know which side I was on; I just had to take the steps to make that knowing live. Taken back twelve years to a painful summer in the Rockaways at the Hotel Del Mar, memory now vividly recaptured my affinity for the Black workers whose quarters I shared, and made me feel I had to do something that would acknowledge the silence around race I had witnessed throughout my life. It was the least I could do for not having stood with them on the front lines.

As it became increasingly clear that this required standing against my kind, so I decided to not write about the "Black problem" that so agitated the state and liberal academics. My book, rather, would be about the rise of the actual Other: the Whites, the Master who was Other to himself. My book would be about whiteness, the ground upon which the figure of blackness was inscribed. White racism was to be the subject; and *White Racism* was to be the title—though this was not to be decided until some years later, by swift-thinking and practical André Schiffrin who, having agreed to be my publisher, nixed my lugubrious working title of "Darkness in the West." Why not just call it *White Racism*?, asked sensible Schiffrin—and so the infant was named.[1]

I am an inveterate browser, and from this point my browsings took two routes: one psychoanalytic, searching for deeper strata of mind; the other critical and integrative, taking apart the dominant ideology to find hidden patterns of power: my first venture on what would become a well-worn path. As these paths interwove, so was the bi-modal term, Psycho-History, needed: a term chosen for heuristic reasons, and that has always made me squirm.

I began by mulling over what José Barchilon had said: that racism stemmed from the masochism of blacks. This was pretty dumb, and racist, to boot; but the problem was arrogant presumption rather than any particular content. It was *ipso facto* goofy and totally wrong-headed: to think that he, a psychoanalyst, with all this implies in the way of class position and acculturation, could speak for millions of people who had endured four centuries in the New World, beginning as slaves who had been torn from African homes and shipped heartlessly to an inhuman social order in which their laboring bodies were commodities. Barchilon had evinced no curiosity about this. To undo his folly meant taking history seriously and as an entry into mind. It also meant regarding psychoanalysis from a radically different perspective.

I recalled an off-hand remark made during my residency by my supervisor, Robert Kabcenell, in response to a patient's dream which had featured a large number of black people running about. "Oh that," said Bob airily, "it always means the same thing: it's the representation of her shit. It's the same for everyone."

Kabcenell, though younger than Barchilon, could match him for self-confidence and exceeded him in elegance. He had an aristocratic bearing, and unlike José, never gave the impression of having to prove how brilliant he was.[2] Nor was what he said meant as a grand theory. Nobody in their right mind would believe that all people, in dreaming of blacks, were also dreaming of their own excrement, a proposition inconceivable to demonstrate in any case. But there was another resonance to it. For the lady in question was indubitably a white. She was not a white racist so far as I knew, and the more interesting for that. Because what I was fumbling toward could be that white folk might have a widespread, even universal, unconscious representation of "colored" people as colored, malodorous, and rejected products of their body—a negation of their identity as whites, if you will, and more powerful for being unconscious. Whether or not these whites were racists—and irrespective of the kind of racist they were (for I was already thinking of developing a typology of the phenomenon)—such connections belonged to the symbolic trove we carry about as a legacy and shaper of our history.

I now pondered what Freud, in his early essay, "Character and Anal Erotism," had written: that feces were suitable to represent possessions and later money. His disciples, Ferenczi and Fenichel, had extended the insight—thereby coming under Adorno's brilliant rubric that the truth of psychoanalysis lay in its exaggerations. Ferenczi had written that money was nothing but deodorized, dehydrated filth that had been made to shine. Imagine that! The audacity set my mind afire, and cast its light over Seattle, land of estrangement, where shadowy Blacks collected White folk's garbage.

Think: Black people had been possessed by Whites in the very peculiar version of slavery developed by the United States. Unlike any other variant across world history, slavery in the U.S. was structured by pre-racist assumptions as color-coded. It was a bedrock of a society in which blackness was the sign of property in human form, while whiteness became the sign of the owner—the "true" human being under the aegis of capitalism. Chattel slavery—slavery grounded in the sale of people following their conquest—defined property in terms of bodies. Chattel slavery so pervaded the history of the United States as to establish these signs as universals, organizers of the collective psyche at a level beneath the condensation of individual psyches. Thus a great, horrid cesspool sloshed beneath psychologies, both determining them and defining them. How bad was that? As bad as racism in American society, still reverberating in every murder by police of Black youth.

I had long been pondering that what we call "mind" was the product of history. Logically a truism—for we were once pre-human and could not have become human all at once without violating the laws of evolution. The concept haunted me, and continues to do so. But at that moment, one of sudden putting together, the collision of these ideas had produced a spark and from it a light had flashed, illuminating a path ahead.

I would not forget: that path was inscribed on real territory, which could not be evaded lest my study of racism become a dithering of fancy symbols. We had at the time a youngish government official and sociologist named Daniel Patrick Moynihan, who was to have a long and distinguished public career slipping back and forth over and around the numerous cracks in American society. At this time he was especially concerned with Blacks, and especially with the Black family, deemed by responsible opinion a running sore on the body politic. Moynihan epitomized *Homo liberalis,* as an inveterate occupant of all sides, a practitioner of "on-the-other-hand-ism," given to what was called "moderation" and the piecing together of compromise in the formulation of policy. In his lifetime of service to the State he was to earn endless praise for sagacity, and became rewarded by having public buildings named after him. Moynihan was an instrument of the liberal state. He rose to power at the moment when that state had embarked on a war in Southeast Asia that was to blight its reputation as a democratic, free society once and for all.

Moynihan seemed not in the least troubled by the cataclysm unleashed in Southeast Asia. He was concerned, rather, with racial matters at home. In 1965, as Assistant Secretary of Labor, he published a monograph, *The Negro Family: The Case for National Action.* It became known simply as the "Moynihan Report," and had a sensational effect on public debate and public policy. Arguing that pathology in Black families was the driving force behind the phenomena of racism, and, further, that this pathology centered on the woes of Black fathers and their widespread disappearance from families, Moynihan concluded that the restoration of dignity to Black males should be a leading policy aim of the government.

He was lauded for his advanced and bold thinking. But his Report also stirred much concern for its juggling of cause and effect, its recycling of patriarchal logic, and its slack treatment of structural and historical forces. The outcry led to a coining of the phrase, "blaming the victim," and a fine book of that title written by William Ryan.

To me, the Moynihan Report sparked a threefold reaction: first, outrage that this white liberal was defining what Blacks were; second, that the liberal state—and these years of the Johnson administration have been celebrated as the highwater mark of liberal democracy—could generate a different kind of racism (which I came to call "metaracism"); and third, that Moynihan had connected the process with the Vietnam War.

There was an ancillary policy directive in the report: that Black men should be encouraged to join the military, and rewarded for this with stable families and entry into society. In no institution of

American society were Blacks more equal to Whites than in the military. Where else could many Blacks command and discipline (however, at an NCO level) Whites? What better source of dignity for poor Black men than to share an honored hierarchy and the guilt-free violence of the state? In other words, the more liberal the intervention, the more effective the war machine, the more conducive to a more "equal" society at home in which all were to be equivalently subjugated, and the more effective in the laying of waste to Southeast Asia in a war racist to the core.

This closed the circle for me. I was passing beyond the perimeter of polite society, my nerves were raw from being rubbed in the complicity of my work with the National Security State in the Public Health Service, and Moynihan's social engineering imbued my reflections on race with mounting fury about Vietnam.

I was racing now; and after some hectic pacing, picked up a pencil, sat down, and wrote out an eleven-page *précis* of my book. It took all night, but by dawn, the shape of *White Racism* was before me. I wish I could lay hands on the document now, but I am wretched at organizing papers and fear it has long since been reduced to dust.

No matter, it was in my mind now. The *précis* and what came out of it signified a turn in my life. I knew without consciously dwelling on the fact that everything, somehow, had changed for me, and that as many low moments as I was to have in the future, I would not have to suffer them as a weakling who could not stand for himself against the imperial state. Not that the demons—or as the psychoanalysts would say, "bad introjects"—would go away; rather, that they would be met by strength and encountered dialectically.

I knew, too, that it would be no easy matter to translate my furious thoughts into intelligible and effective prose, inasmuch as I knew virtually nothing about the subjects that were now being tossed about in my brain. This daunted me not at all. After all, what was there to lose? I was free as the proverbial bird to do what I wanted; and what I wanted was to be my own university, and learn the whole damn thing by myself.

A terrain of bookshelves loomed, bearing the knowledge of the history of the Whites and the Blacks: the enslavement of the latter by the former; the development of slave society; the long and curious story of the imaginings of difference in literature and everyday life; the rise of "white" civilization; the forging of this collective identity out of a polyglot people; the connection of the history of racism with that of science and its furor of classification; the installation of the sub-humanity of Blacks in the Constitution of the United States; the economics of slavery; the sexual torments mediated by skin color and the erotics of bodily substance; the conventional social psychology of race relations; the evolution of these into a kind of typology; and so on and on, into the innumerable vicissitudes of racist being and racist becoming, and also passing beyond racism. It was glorious to learn.

One needed a solid foundation in theory to make sense of all this. Needless to say, I was free from any such encumbrance. I knew about the phase-spaces of evaporating fluids, something of set-theory, and a bit less about quantum mechanics; the Krebs Cycle was in my repertoire; also the electrodynamics of the heart and a wee bit about the double helix and the etiology of schizophrenia. But none of that was going to tell me how society was put together and how history happened, and how the one thing I knew fairly well, psychoanalysis, was going to fit in with the rest—especially as what I had been propounding, shall we say, ran against the prevailing psychoanalytic grain.

Through all my years of school, I had set aside the social sciences as being boring elaborations of the obvious, never dreaming that one day I would set out to write a book about how society, and mind, and suffering would tie together about vexatious White Racism. Once I picked up the spoor of the beast, however, all matters pertaining to its habitat became fascinating; thus began my brooding about the structure of society itself.

I flitted here and there, never one to be discouraged by ignorance, a butterfly in the garden of knowledge alighting upon the accumulated wisdom of the West. I encountered the powerful intellect of Max Weber, which passed swiftly through my system, leaving behind an appreciation for the structure of the human world that aided my typology of racism, and rue for his *Weltschmerz*. A much better impression was formed upon encountering Herbert Marcuse, who did not suffer from lack of hopefulness (at least then) and was on his way to becoming a philosophical bellwether of the New Left, including teaching friends I would soon make. Here it was, a book I could scarcely believe existed, *Eros and Civilization*, a dazzling appreciation of Freud and a challenge to Freud, written from the standpoint of a radical tradition that I could not identify, as Marcuse seemed strenuously trying to forget the traditional classes in favor of a kind of "new class" thriving on an epoch beyond scarcity.

Well, I didn't know about that, but I excitedly felt the utopian impulse and realized that his critique of contemporary modes of domination served my construction of a historical typology of racism slouching toward its *denouement* of metaracism. Marcuse—whom I never had the pleasure of meeting, though he was living at the time down the coast in San Diego—greatly heartened my investigations, and calmed a certain unease about how all these efforts would fit within the psychoanalytic career I envisioned for myself.

Surely, thought I, as the tour of military duty wended its way toward a conclusion, surely I should be able to combine the political vocation of a radical that I had by now fully adopted with a successful career in psychoanalysis. We were heading into the high '60s, were we not? The spirit of revolution was in the air, everything seemed possible, and a New Heaven and New Earth were felt in its breezes.

THE PLEDGE OF APOSTASY

THE ESSAY WAS TITLED "On the Responsibility of Intellectuals."It was by a linguist named Noam Chomsky, whom I had never heard of. And it appeared in *The New York Review of Books*, a ponderous publication that brought the larger world to our little Seattle home every other week. Chomsky worked in the manner of I. F. Stone, from sources already in the public record. But he was not a journalist like Stone, rather, a virtuoso in the exposure of turpitude, a kind of prosecutor who laid bare the colossal criminality of those who made the war in Vietnam, and those in the press and academia who sought to interpret this as a blunder, or an honest mistake, or as anything other than the cold and repellent exercise of empire behind the mask of democratic virtue.

The obligation of the intellectual was, therefore, turning to a somewhat worn but enduring phrase, "to speak truth to power." I may have been chronically uncertain about just what I was to be in the world, but I most definitely knew myself to be an intellectual. Of that there could be no doubt. I had already moved into Chomsky's camp by planning to write *White Racism*; and by this stage in my development there was also no doubt of how I stood on the war. So it would have been a simple matter to figuratively nod my head at Chomsky's essay, give it a seal of approval, and move on. However, I couldn't stop by simply speaking truth to power and then stepping back. No, Noam's moral force and intellectual power, along with the momentum of my internal growth, compelled me to turn what he had written into a manifesto. For there was something grander than just speaking truth to power, one had to address the power at its root and attack it, building new, alternative power as one went.

And so I pledged that the rest of my life would be dedicated to bringing down the power that, embodied in United States militarism, had made the war in Vietnam, and was bound to do more of the same in the future—as it most certainly has. This did not mean that I would do nothing else; it was rather a call to imbue everything I did with the larger purpose reflected in that pledge.

Such was my task. I realized right away that I could not rest until it was carried out, which meant I would not rest, period, until I had left this world, because though my pledge certified me as quixotic, I was not delusional, and I knew that what I had committed myself to was far, far greater than my power to bring it about.

Indeed, what I had undertaken was of such a scale that it could very well be that by the end of my life the world could be in even worse shape than it was at the time, so grand was the evil in things.

Alas, this has, I believe, proven to be the case.

However, neither triumph or worldly success were the criteria by which I would measure fidelity to my pledge. It was the process, my faithfulness to it, that mattered. This meant staying with things, not getting too far down, never giving up. That's what fidelity, requires (along with hope, as well).

Indeed, had I then the perspective these many years since have given me, I would have recognized that in this moment, I had embraced two-thirds of the Pauline trinity retrieved from Richard Sewall in September of 1953, on the threshold of my time at Yale, and would have wondered, too, just where the third and greatest part of the trinity—Love, or grace—would enter as well.

My pledge went so deep as to abolish the notion of merely being an intellectual. For if I was to be true to it, then I could neither be purely an intellectual nor a solitary actor, withholding myself from the world. My gifts were intellectual, but what is the worth of the intellect if not to discern its own limit, that point at which activity has to be expanded beyond the text and become activism? Just so, would the truth of activism be to expand its limit beyond the narrowly constructed individual in the direction of solidarity? Just so, the truth one seeks is to employ our power toward the universal.

Now, it may be asked, to whom was I making this pledge? To myself, one would suppose, but it could not be that simple, given the divisions in my being. I should think, rather, that the pledge itself, coming at the end of a rough time in my life, was a sign of a revision in that being, for I certainly felt differently as a person thereafter, as my whole life entered upon a different course. It was what Paolo Freire and others have called a "conscientization": it was a reworking of conscience from the savagery of what had been my "yaller dog" days as had evolved in childhood, to becoming a functional guidance system for a political and intellectual radical.

I never thought of it at the time in such terms, yet it must also be said that the change entailed a moving outside my constructed self, toward a "higher power" to whom I was appealing for realignment, and who had granted my wish. I do believe I drew strength from this. I did not sense this as an entity to be approached in prayer, nevertheless I think the inference is valid, for while we need to turn to our "inner" powers if we are to be saved, it is inconceivable that such powers are wholly internal. Were this the case, solipsism would be the case, framing a world frankly ridiculous and inconceivable, of wholly individualized egos drawing on purely material means.

While the "yaller dog" no longer held sway, its replacement was not benign. The Kovel conscience was a severe creature, capable of instilling fear and forcing its subject down difficult pathways. The impossible scope of the territory demanded by my pledge was to endow me with an inwardly rich but outwardly parlous life, at odds with all institutions and formed opinions.

In a word, trouble lay ahead. Over the years I sometimes complained of this, petitioning Fortuna to give me a better deal in this world, more commensurate with my talents. Why, I could have been a Department Chairman, or a fabulously wealthy ophthalmologist, or even a Senator or, yes, POTUS—that's right, President of the United States, the office for which I ran in the year 2000, confident I was better than the mannikins spun out by the system (Ralph Nader excepted) for these posts.

These gripes scattered and drifted away as I came to accept the fact that my transformed identity, while healing some wounds and ruptures of the inner self, also guaranteed a lifetime of tension with the outer ranges of things. No, I would not achieve a satisfactory career as a psychoanalyst, nor would I ever find an intellectual niche among the many groupings with whom I would become associated. How could these paths have been vouchsafed to someone who, in order to preserve his sanity, resolves to never give up until the world is turned upside down, knowing full well this will not come to pass? Who is going to follow him or allow him in from the cold?

BYE BYE SEATTLE

WE WERE GOING HOME. As the days in Seattle dwindled down to a not-so-precious few, the contours of the next phase took shape. My good professor, Milton Rosenbaum, had secured a Teaching Fellowship from the National Institute for Mental Health. This would give me time to work on *White Racism* and allow development as an educator, something that had always appealed to my spirit. A trip east, in application to psychoanalytic institutes, had produced rejection from the Great Temple of Freudianism, the New York Institute (which correctly foresaw my motivation to be dubious), but acceptance from its junior partner, the Downstate Institute, then affiliated with the Brooklyn Hospital complex of that name.

I was heading back to New York, True North. In celebration I let my moustache grow, in mimicry of the Beatles. It still resides on my upper lip 49 years later, not because I like it but because I didn't want the nuisance of explaining its absence to others. We packed the kids—Jon now five, and Erin eighteen months, into the back of a VW Beetle, put a whole bunch of bags on the roof and in spots I had never thought existed, and set out on I–90, a predictably nightmarish experience made worse when the poor, overloaded donkey of a VW developed a pinging sound outside of Rochester, a sign of fatal motoric disease.

Somehow we made it back to The Bronx (as great pain is often not remembered, I literally cannot recall how), where we stayed at Josephine Ryan's house until we found an apartment on West 78th Street, near the Collegiate School where Jacqueline Kennedy had sent her children, and the fabulous Apthorp, eventual site of my psychoanalytic office. Notwithstanding, the West Side was not nearly as sedately glitzy as we know it today; witness the pistol packed by our Super, Mr. B, and the salacious exhibitions by our neighbors in the brownstone across the street.

No longer a member, however ersatz, of the U.S. Armed Forces, no longer subjected to the Satanic war machine, I began counseling deserters at the nearest antiwar center, joined in planning for the great October march on the Pentagon, and commenced my doomed psychoanalytic career.

Notes

1 Joel Kovel, *White Racism: A Psychohistory,* 2nd ed. (New York: Columbia University Press, 1984).
2 Kabcenell trained at Einstein, became a pillar of the New York psychoanalytic community, and died horrifically in 1991, clubbed with a two-by-four by a street mugger as he was walking home from the New York Psychoanalytic Institute on East 92nd Street.

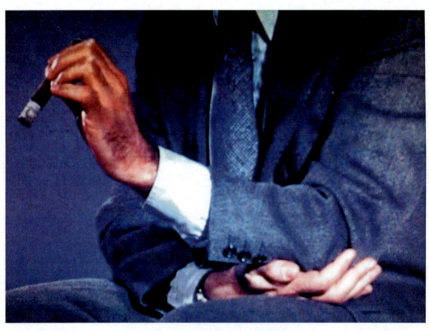

JOEL KOVEL PLAYS FREUD

Chapter 7
How Not to Become a Psychoanalyst

I had arrived. The greatest city in the world; faculty at one of the great medical schools; a prestigious fellowship at one of the best psychiatry departments; freedom to expand as a teacher of medical students; freedom to write my Opus #1; and capping it off, a top-flight institute in which to learn the greatest therapy, psychoanalysis, Freudian-style. That's what the doctor told the ten or so of us as we assembled deep inside Brooklyn at the Downstate Medical Center to begin formal psychoanalytic training: "Gentlemen (there were no ladies present): you are about to learn the best therapy in the world, Freudian psychoanalysis. Don't listen to what the others say; they're just envious. Because we have Freud to guide us, and Freud was the best."

I was taken aback, though everybody else seemed pleased with the news. A derogatory phrase from my half-buried Brooklyn boyhood lexicon came to mind. Why, they're like… "cloak and suiters," said I to myself, that is, low-level commercial men from the Garment District, men who would put anything together so long as it sold.

Such folk saw no problem with the sales pitch that Our Psychoanalysis was a better commodity than Their Psychoanalysis: the fabric firmer, the buttonholes neater, the zipper more reliable, the interpretations truer. What took me aback was the implication that psychoanalysis—the arcane and prestigious doctrine I had been yearning to explore—could turn into a mere commodity, and that I had arrived at a place where this was the way of looking and nobody minded.

I had begun learning psychotherapy during my first year of psychiatric residency. As time went on I became rather good at it, and good at teaching it and supervising trainees as well. After returning from Seattle in 1967 as a fully hatched Psy professional, I was obliged by economic need to set up a small private practice alongside of my academic work; this was later augmented by psychoanalytic training cases. What with adding my own training at Downstate to the mix, it could be said that I was developing into a competent psychotherapist and general all-around expert in the field. By the time I came to direct the Einstein Residency Training Program, I was leading seminars of supervisors, doing therapy behind the one-way screen for trainees, and teaching from videotapes of my work.

It was a time of "wild and crazy" proliferation of therapies, which I wove into my second book, conceived as a guide for the perplexed. Praised by *The New York Times*, *A Complete Guide to Therapy* was the most successful of my works in terms of sales and foreign editions—and the only one written with commercial success in mind, the goal being to raise funds to send Jonathan and Erin to college.[1]

There was one catch. The original title, *A Critical Guide To Therapy*, was nixed by the Book of the Month Club, which otherwise loved the book and wanted to buy 25,000 copies—provided I changed one and only one word: "Critical." This had to go, since no book ever sold in the United States with that word in the title. So it was to be a *Complete Guide,* or no deal. How dare they! I moped and I groused, I cursed the damnable pragmatism that defiled our culture, and concluded in about half an hour… well, everyone has his price, has to choose his proper battlefield, etc, and gave in. Happily, the Germans would only take it for translation in the original version, giving me the satisfaction of seeing *Kritische Leitfaden zur Psychotherapie* published by the culture that gave humanity the Third Reich.

The hurly-burly done, I distilled my concentrated experience over the years into a serviceable aphorism: that with a few marginal exceptions the psychotherapist could never cure anybody but could help everybody. Transformative ideologies tossed out the window, the secret of therapy remained simple and profound: cultivate the art of "being with" another person and mirror that being back to her, him, or them. Finding a way to bracket the fierce intellectual agitation that has marked my inner life, I became a serviceable therapist, though it must also be said that eternal restlessness and seeking of the infinite kept me from embracing the path for myself.

My Psy career took shape on the downslope of the '60s. Hopes that changing consciousness would in itself change the world crashed against brute reality; many emerged re-invented as the "New Age," and invested innumerable projects with utopian and grandiose claims. Often these took psychotherapeutic form and peddled "joy," or "primal screams," or "gestalt," or "revolution," or the "bioenergetic" second coming of Reich—Reich without the cosmic orgone—as curative of the human condition.

Some went beyond therapeutic goals and became cults, or took the shape of the Human Potential Movement, an egregious hallmark of bourgeois society, where capitalism and religion have often been hand in glove. In the '70s, our Grand Rounds lecture series once featured none other than Werner Erhard, *née* John Paul Rosenberg, of "est" fame. He could have stepped out of the pages of Melville's *Confidence Man*. A super-salesman, Erhard (still around as of this writing) wooed the spiritually desolate and made a goodly income in the process.

Others close to me took off on other, more exotic, paths, notably, my friend and Einstein colleague, Andy Ferber, who challenged Erhard in the question period of his lecture as to the superiority of his guru, the notorious Bhagwan Shree Rajneesh, or Osho. Erhard smoothly backed away from the pissing match, to general relief, for we were all weary of fretting over Andy and Rajneesh. A very bright and ambitious psychiatrist, Ferber was the leader of the Family Studies program at Einstein, which he invested with New Age Cosmic values. He and his wife Jane—an old friend from medical school days—and their children quit Einstein and went west to Rajneeshpuram, the former Antelope, Oregon, and now a utopian community, to begin life anew under Osho, whose chief claim to spiritual genius was an inordinate love of Rolls Royces, some thirty of which he acquired from adoring acolytes.

It ended catastrophically. Their marriage collapsed, and then so did Rajneeshpuram. Andy followed Osho back to Pune, India; and, after the Seer's death, to the Himalayas, where he became a gardener and herbal healer—about as good an end as could be woven out of such weird cloth, although he also held on to his medical license and has eventually settled in Florida to practice psychiatry, taking, so the internet avers, "all legitimate insurance plans."

Jane never got over the disaster, and died in 1990 of ovarian cancer. I fondly remember her as my medical school partner on the obstetrics service, where we watched Jason Robards in "The Iceman Cometh" while waiting for somebody's birth pangs to begin. She and Andy lived in a huge house once owned by D. W. Griffith on the New Rochelle shore, from which I embarked for the trip to Seattle in June 1965, giving Andy a farewell hug and driving the VW off into the early morning shadows.

Two years later I was back, and began my study of psychoanalysis, the crown jewel of the mental-health establishment in those years, proclaimed by Ed Hornick to be the credit card necessary for success in Psy.

Tales of the Couch

IN THE YEARS I WAS LEARNING how to do it, Freudian psychoanalysis had become austere and cheerless, with the length of treatment extending like the Great Wall of China, and the point thereof dissolving into opaque notions such as "resolution of the transference neurosis." The effect was a great deal of unhappiness for the trainees, and a brutal schedule. At the height of one's training—a plateau that often went on for five years—the trainee, by this time typically in his/her late thirties or forties with a suffering spouse and children, would have to spend at least 25 hours a week to learn the best therapy on earth over and above what was needed to provide for food, shelter, and whatever made life worth living, for example, August in Truro. The load included five hours on the couch for training analysis, plus two or three hours of supervision of one's own cases, plus of course travel time to these various locations under Manhattan's traffic and parking conditions. Then there was an equivalent number of hours of seeing private patients to earn the funds to pay the fees for the above; plus five or ten hours for unremunerated or minimally remunerated practice analysis on patients chosen from the Institute's clinic, along with the writing up of sessions so there would be something to tell the supervisors. Add in the bearing of office costs for this, and finally, attendance at seminars at the Institute, plus preparation for same (at Downstate we met on Wednesday evening and Saturday morning, after a long drive to Brooklyn on the then-rickety and serpentine West Side Highway). Indeed, the saddest and dullest parties on earth were those given by Freudian psychoanalysts, the saddest and most burdened of professionals.

The conversion of time to money goes a long way toward accounting for the decline of psychoanalysis into a profession for cloak and suiters. But the luminous insights that made Freudianism into a "depth psychology" could still be heard from time to time. I had, for example, a wizened Italianate supervisor whose townhouse in the West Village could pass for something along Venice's Grand Canal. From the shadows of his great office, with its stained glass window, the diminutive ancient related to me the real secret of psychoanalysis. Here it was: "Always remember, Dr. Kovel, the analyst has all the time in the world. That's right, he must never be rushed. The unconscious will reveal itself in time, and then, and then only, can it be gathered."

Well, yes, Freud had written that the unconscious was timeless; and clock time was imposed by the Ego's world. But hadn't the Ego been foregrounded in today's psychoanalysis? ... which meant that my Italian sage was more than superannuated, he was also an anachronism, a Proust *manqué*. And whilst Proust could park his *Recherche* in a space reserved for Art, the clinical practice of psychoanalysis would ever remain this-worldly, bounded and hounded by the ever-present needs of the belly, the requirements of social status, and the eternal fee.

My sagacious supervisor was therefore leaving out one detail: psychoanalysis was not just a solipsism in the mind of the analyst; the analysand-in-training was there, too, and he was in a rush because the parking meter was expiring outside, and the bills were coming due thanks to his ensnarement by capitalism, the world-ruling power of bourgeois society. And the same, of course, went for his supervisee in analytic training and *pari passu*, for the supervisee's relationship with his own psychoanalyst. For analytic training rested on the foundation of the training analysis at the end of whose yellow brick road lay the analyst's personal claim on all the time in the world.

The stillness of psychoanalytic treatment is a kind of greatly extended sensory-deprivation experiment of unlocking the gates to the inner self and bending the results to therapeutic ends. It is akin to falling asleep, that dissolution of reason which, according to Goya, bred demons; the therapy consists of restoring reason under psychoanalytic auspices, or, as Freud put it, where Id was, there Ego shall be.

He added that it was as the Dutch did with their Zuider Zee: the basic civilizing process itself, and it took place through reflection, not immediately on what brought the analysand into treatment in the first place, but on the "transference neurosis" emergent within the dyad of the analytic relationship. It's an inherently dicey business with pitfalls on every side, ranging from actual sleep by the analyst, to inattention and boredom, to various at-times nasty "countertransferences," which can go all the way to passionate arousal and its consequences.

Hence a training analysis is deemed essential. The training analysis is to be like a regular analysis in all respects but one—that the analyst is a senior member of the Institute, him- or herself vetted and seasoned over many years. The training analysts comprise the Council of Elders; they set policy, do supervision, and, as things go, get the prime cases, either for themselves or as referrals to qualified junior members. It follows, as the night the day, that every analytic trainee who wants a good career not only has to complete a training analysis along with everything else, but also must aspire to be like the training analysts-cum-elders whose hierarchy s/he will join once graduated. That is, to be a successful analyst, one has to join the club and become a successful bourgeois professional.

This arrangement is severely self-contradictory, and pretty much ruins the integrity of the Freudian project. The fatal flaw is that the free flow of subjectivity essential for psychoanalytic process is stifled by having one's analyst as a real authority figure, whose approval is essential to move on from the misery of the training period into the sunlight of "having all the time in the world." The Institute's elders tried to mitigate this by setting forth a policy of never discussing any specific content of the analytic process but only whether it is proceeding overall or not—a necessary but meaningless expedient, for it is the latter judgment that really counts. Thus psychoanalytic training bounces back and forth between the Scylla of shallow identification and the Charybdis of authoritarian indoctrination. In any case it is not to be recommended for the free-spirited.

I HAD TWO TRAINING ANALYSES, the first with Dr. C, a Hungarian *émigré* who resembled Peter Lorre and was largely in the background of the Institute; and the second, with Dr. S, younger than C, and a major figure in the life of Downstate. The switch occurred because of the sudden death by heart attack of Dr. C after more than two years of work, a fact I was informed of by his officemate over the phone. There was no invitation to the funeral. Most strange, to spend some four hundred hours on somebody's couch spilling one's free associations in his direction and to not know him to the extent of whether to miss him or not. My thoughts at the time of C's passage mainly oscillated around two instrumental poles: one, of "Goddammit; now this is going to stretch out my training yet further"; the other, of "Hmmm, now the schedule will be easier for a while; maybe I can take advantage and even make a move out of this trap."

There had been some fond memories of Dr. C, *viz.*, the time he relieved my guilt over something I was pondering about my taxes with the dicey remark that, where the IRS was concerned, questions of morality did not apply, only what one could get away with; or when he calmed some agitation on my part about how the manuscript of *White Racism* was roughed up by its editor, by saying that he had surmised, after listening to me for some time, that I must have a distinctive writing style, and that I should defend this against the publisher's instinct to make everything commonplace. Now that was really nice of Dr. C; however, it was also scarcely psychoanalytic in character, but rather, one shudders to say, supportive.

Then there were moments not at all nice. How could I forget the day after an evening spent in indulging in marijuana with Tom Cohen and other friends that Dr. C would greet my report with something as close to anger as could be imagined within the sedate confines of psychoanalysis? It was a double-barreled blast: the first blow, a phrase we applied to children and psychopaths who lack the internalized mental structures and cannot process conflicts in thought but must short-circuit and enact them instead, thus: "Dr. Kovel, This is *acting out!*"—not a crime in itself, but potentially a deadly flaw making an analysis, and especially a training analysis, impossible. And then the knockout punch: "If this happens again I shall have to terminate the analysis!"

Shock and panic flowed through me—and also a suppressed but definite outrage. For I had not just told C that I had indulged in marijuana, I had also told him that I rarely did so because I really didn't like the stuff, never had, and only went along to be sociable. I could have added that of all my mates I was in the lowest decile as far as indulging in mind-altering drugs went; this included alcohol, which I only consume in very limited quantities at parties to reduce my discomfort.

In fact, there has only been one instance of interest in my whole life of serious drug experimentation, a one-day stand during residency, using some research-grade LSD provided by a friend. This was definitely mind-bending, and justly provoked anger in Virginia, but was scarcely relevant at the moment. What was relevant, and had been told to C at the outset of the session, was that after two joints I had been seized by a world-shattering degree of paranoid anxiety, a feeling of menace to a degree I had never felt before in a whole life's history beleaguered by persecutory demons and "yaller dog" Superego; nor have I felt its like since, in these forty-plus years. It was the chill of the grave closing around me at this moment, no mitigation known: all in all, more than a man could bear.

I had told nobody at the time, and eventually contained it somehow, in part because of the comforting thought that I was going to see Dr. C the next day and that he, being a physician after all, would help me... instead of which I was threatened with termination of treatment for the crime of acting out.

My ire was such that the thought flashed through me—not for the first time, I might add, but suppressed and therefore, a "resistance" to analysis—that this would be the time to tell C, at the moment of his accusation, what had long irked me: that he should look to himself, and directly to his evidently uncontrollable chain-smoking of cigarettes that wafted toxically over the couch, entering my body as well as his. And I could have added that chain-smoking in context of such a sedentary profession as psychoanalysis was a recipe for serious health issues, as proved the case.

Perhaps I could have saved him. But fearful of authority, I did neither. He was, it seemed then and since in memory, a sad and lonely figure. With such a countertransference, one could imagine trouble with his son—not that I knew he had a son—who must have been as unruly as me.

THE RECORD SHOWS THAT I did not break with the Institute or move to California after Dr. C's death. Though there were certainly impulses in that direction, it seemed an utterly wrong-headed course of action; and so, after a decent interval, I resumed my training analysis with the younger and fitter Dr. S.

Dr. S., like Dr. C., must have been mad at me many times, none more so than when I came back to him some months after termination of my interminable analysis with the news that I had, uh... acted out, and entered into the affair with DeeDee that would cause the breakup of marriage with Virginia. Was this proof-positive of the worthlessness of eight years on the couch, as shown by my more-or-less instantaneous breakout upon release from the chains of the daily confession—or, contrariwise, of its remarkable power to free a man to find the woman he wanted?

I can say, however, that Dr. S's summary "advice" in that moment, that I "must renounce" this reckless course of action, belongs in the Hall of Shame of Really Bad Psychoanalytic Interventions. It nearly destroyed me at the time, pushing me to the brink of suicide, but also freed me to find a really good therapist from among the ranks of my ex-supervisors, Dr. Frank Berchenko, who made one or two shrewd interpretations while supportively allowing me to be who I was and am. The proof of this hypothesis is still evident some 39 years later.

Compassion is due Dr. S for having to listen all those years to my soundings off. No doubt I must have been a disagreeable analysand, super-judgmental, full of complaints, devious of mind and prone to rant. A characteristic theme centered about how my left arm would freeze up on the tennis court and let Steve Rittenberg, or John Pareja, or my brother Alex, beat me time and again, despite my superior serve, the only decent stroke in my quiver.

I expect he would have filed this under the heading of incipient transference neurosis; certainly it betokened how un-free I felt in the situation of the training analysis, whose power struggles were being recapitulated on the couch. But there was something more to it, that chewed away at me throughout the years of treatment, from the beginning to the end: that S and I just didn't get along, that we would not have been friends in the world, and that we worked in analysis across an invisible barrier.

I showed up dutifully and did my best to grind it out, as I am sure S did as well. But there was a lingering unease, perhaps even a hostility, which I suspect burst forth in his censoriousness when I came to tell him of my marital predicament. Two landmarks underscored this beyond the proverbial reasonable doubt, incidents that had I interpreted them properly at the time and followed out their implications conscientiously, would have led me to quit psychoanalytic training on the spot. But first, a bit of background.

SINCE MY RETURN from military service in September 1967, my life moved on two tracks, one for the orderly pursuit of professional advancement, the other for expression of the rage against the machine and its war that had turned my head sharply leftward in Seattle. Except for tactical details, there was nothing clandestine about these political ventures. I never joined a political party, never contemplated any violence, indeed for the most part I worked within my professional identity, as by counseling veterans or protecting draft resisters. Notwithstanding, an existential rift had opened between two simultaneously pursued pathways, the one more or less comfortably within the world, the other agitated by continual awareness that there was something terribly wrong with the world.

For the monstrous war was not simply a matter of tycoons, statesmen and generals sitting around green tables, but something nourished from below, something that could not be cleanly separated from the daily reproduction of society.

Tom Cohen had worked with Peter Davis on the film *Hearts and Minds,* which clearly showed how consent for war was propagated in everyday life, as by the rituals of football; and it was perfectly obvious that this was not something grafted onto and easily removed from consciousness, but rather implanted with the tenacity of a tick into the psyche of America. Nor was it simply a matter of conscious reinforcement; no less important, and indeed more subtle, pervasive, and malignant, was the bland and cultivated indifference of sectors of society who let evil occur by not rising up against it.

I realized then, as I do today, that if enough people say no and mean it, then nothing—no *gendarmerie,* no prison system, no state— can stand up to them. Although the resistance to war in Vietnam was enormous and was to indisputably play a role in temporarily inhibiting United States intervention, it was also by no means complete or deep enough, even in such left-leaning zones as the Albert Einstein medical complex.

I COULD NOT HELP but look about me and find in my professional life-world such things as my militant side would frown upon—inwardly at first, to be sure, but indelibly all the same.

I remember an antiwar event I had asked permission of my old professor, Ed Hornick, to hold at his Gatsby-esque townhouse on West 73rd Street. It was granted, and the event proceeded. But there was a certain torpor to it, which I could not help but ascribe to the lack of *esprit* of many attendees, some of whom were products of the residency and who now seemed more engaged in prancing about in their dazzling clothes than in rallying to the cause. Worse, Hornick himself—a man whose tough love had helped me overcome the anxieties of being a psychiatrist—began to cynically bait and mock me for my antiwar zeal, even to the point of expressing support for the U.S. presence in Vietnam.

Matters worsened as his marriage broke up, along with his career, and then his health, wrecked by excess. And although we kept in touch, I felt that I had let Ed down during his last days, and that this was a kind of vengeance on my side.

MEANWHILE, IT HAD COME TO PASS that the growing antiwar movement reached its grandest strategy—a shutting down of the city of Washington, D.C. itself. Tens of thousands of activists headed in late April 1971, to the Capital for what we called the May Day events. The caravan included two buses from the Einstein medical school in tow, proving its left *bona fides* as the only medical institution to do so. A subset of this, a kind of commando task force, was comprised of a dozen Einstein psychiatrists, myself in the lead, with a special mission ensuing from the fact that the American Psychiatric Association (APA) had chosen to hold its annual meeting at that very time, and in the national capital as well, indeed, at that Shoreham Hotel where nine years before, President Kennedy had charmed the *psychiatriat.*

Now the APA was using that space for a celebration of Nixon, or to be more exact, his Deputy Attorney General, Richard Kleindienst, soon to replace John Mitchell at that post, and who was to receive an award and make a keynote speech. And we, as representatives of the May Day movement, were going to put the quietus to that, with the dual aim of forcing the APA to disinvite Kleindienst and to pass an antiwar resolution. But first we would have to, as they say on the street, case the joint.

So it was on a Friday afternoon that a scruffy Joel Kovel and friends pulled up to the spiffy Shoreham after a long and sweaty drive from New York and traversed the elegant entrance… to find the lobby occupied by the breaking up of the previous psy conference, that of the fraternal American Psychoanalytic Association (APsaA), many of whose members were psychiatrists who would stay on for the APA.

Six years before, I had given my Huck Finn paper before the same gathering when it met at the Waldorf in New York. None of the APsaA members were anti-war radicals, certainly not Dr. S, with whom I had recently contracted to begin my training analysis in September, and who hove into view some twenty feet away, all suited up and chatting with colleagues. He seemed very comfortable. He didn't notice me, and I had no intention of breezily going up to him to explain my presence there. So I played the spook and vanished through another door into the labyrinth of the Shoreham, where we set about planning our little caper—or, not so little, for it is worth recording that our action was a splendid success, audacious, well-prepared and well-executed.

Gathering our forces and timing the charge perfectly, we made a multipronged attack on the dais during the APA's executive session. One of our number, Herb Schrier, who was chosen by lot, seized the microphone and proclaimed our demands; the others, myself included, controlled the floor mics and the doors and forced a debate, continually situating us within the framework of the May Day action.

And we won! because we presented our case well, and most of all, because we had considerable groundswell of support among the members. It took a while—a day or two as I recall—but we got the APA to disinvite the Deputy Attorney General of the United States, and got APA to endorse a resolution to pull out of Vietnam.

The only casualty was Schrier's psychoanalysis, which was terminated abruptly on his return the next Monday by his Downstate training analyst—who had been a supervisor of my analytic training—Dr. Mark Kanzer, for—you guessed it—acting out. I remember Kanzer as a fussy and uninspiring man, and learned some years later that he was a donor to the Sigmund Freud Endowed Chair at the Hebrew University in Jerusalem.

Schrier survived to become a successful child psychiatrist in the Bay Area. And I went back and resumed my professional life in New York. But the shock of seeing Dr. S in the Shoreham was great: the shock of non-recognition. It reverberated like an echo in a canyon, defining the positioning of the divided walls. It was in the mind, and it was real, because the mind enters reality when it alters the external world and is shaped into identities.

Had we flopped at the Shoreham… who knows?… I might have reconsidered the whole course of action and, in the word chosen by S, "renounced" my folly. But I doubt it, for I am a tenacious fellow very impressed by the audacity of Blake's "Proverb of Hell": that if a fool would persist in his folly he would become wise. Inexorably, over the years, I was finding Blake deeper and wiser than Freud.

In any case, we did not flop at the Shoreham. It was a small step but a real one, and kicked some sand into the war machine. These things matter, as does the elation of making them happen. The risk, the camaraderie with one's fellows: this is precious stuff, the solidarity required for the making of a new world. Such memories are also seeds. If they do not thrive in psychoanalytic soil, so much the worse for said soil, especially in view of Kanzer's summary dismissal of Herb Schrier.

I SAID THERE WERE TWO landmarks that deeply rattled my sense of myself as a member of the psychoanalytic community, with its orderly reproduction of the Directorate of Training Analysts. The second took place on a day of infamy, September 12th, 1973: more than two years following the May Day brouhaha. I strode into S's consulting room, virtually threw myself on the couch and proceeded to rage against Henry Kissinger.

"That fucking mass murderer! [Mimicking Kissinger's actual words]: 'I don't see why the United States should sit back because the Chilean people are irresponsible enough to choose communism!!!' What a shit! And you'll see; the CIA is behind this. Imperialism as usual…." And so forth.

Then wafted the words from behind the couch, counseling me against paranoia, introducing doubt, moving the discourse to the psychoanalytic high ground of my relationship with Lou Kovel, in those days sunk into dementia….

I could not believe my ears. Dr. S, my training analyst was arguing with me over the actual basis of what I was saying about the fascist overthrow of Salvador Allende's democratic socialism, pushing it into the thicket of analytic jargon instead of listening and learning. I was tremendously upset—after all, at that moment people were getting slaughtered in the Santiago soccer stadium, or, as in the case of the great singer, Victor Jara, after getting their hands cut off—should I not have been tremendously upset?

And I was obeying an excellent principle of psychoanalysis, where the core imperative is to say what "comes to mind." Why couldn't S just listen, which is another excellent principle and the core of psychoanalytic technique? Why intervene as though he was picking a fight with me, and with stupidities, no less, trying to invalidate my judgment when it was obvious that he knew nothing about the subject and was only filling the void with psychobabble while mouthing the mendacious interpretation of the Chilean coup offered by *The New York Times*?

It took no special skill or clairvoyance to see the hand of the CIA in the murder of Allende, or the imposition of a military dictatorship like that of Pinochet by U.S. imperialism, in what our boys called their "backyard." All one had to do was to change certain basic assumptions from those that tended to be passively imbibed by our professional bourgeoisie. Yes, this requires changing one's associations, mingling now with international networks of anti-imperial and socialist solidarity. There is, after all, a pattern, hellish but real and ascertainable, to U.S. foreign policy—just as there is to the state of Israel and our relation to it—though it is not too likely that the people, including Downstate analysts, who came out two weeks later, in ardent support of the beleaguered state of Israel, during the Yom Kippur War that almost brought it down, knew what was going on behind the headlines.

BY THIS TIME I had been seven years on that alternative track which began with anti-racism and anti-Vietnam war activism. I had not stood still. I am restless by nature; and so I had been moving on as a political animal while poring over Freud and learning the fine points of this symptom and that dream. Somehow the cognitive dissonance had not driven me crazy. But it was all too real. In fact, I had by September 1973 become somebody I was not yet when we took over the Shoreham Ballroom in May of 1971: an ardent although unorthodox Marxist, and a communist—lower case c—to boot. Rose and Lou Kovel's boy had undergone further changes.

SOME KIND OF A RED

WHITE RACISM: A PSYCHOHISTORY appeared in 1971. Its reception exceeded my fondest hopes, especially after nomination for a National Book Award (oddly, but presciently, in the category of "Religion and Philosophy") and made of me for a while a minor celebrity, with all the pleasant stimulation this entails. I found my work celebrated, among other publications, by *The New York Times,* which firmed this up by acquainting me with their book review editor, who recruited me as a regular for the *Sunday Book Review.* I would estimate that I produced a dozen reviews for them over the next decade on a wide variety of such topics as would fit into the flexible rubric of the "psycho-historical": Nazis, industrial magnates, R.D. Laing, and so forth.

This was no more than a reaping of the harvest of Psy to which many intellectuals of liberal society are addicted. All it requires is an antenna for the angst-ridden seams of our culture, a facility with the jargon of subjectivism, and above all, the propensity to defer or blunt any clear answer to our dilemmas. So many times over years of participation in forums of one kind or another have I heard of the need to eschew large answers, such as "the problem is imperialism," or at any rate to clothe them in weavings of "on the one hand—on the other hand." In other words, keep it complicated, keep it vague and fuzzy, do not let the mind, especially of the young, seize upon any clear understanding of the world such as might conduce to a transformative course of action.

There was also a hostile reaction, from the *New York Review of Books,* which seems to have had a long-standing grudge against me;[2] and in any case put Dr. Robert Coles on my case. Coles, a well-known child psychiatrist who aspired to the example set by the great James Agee, was a fierce advocate of bearing witness to the thing in itself, and took exception to the fact that I would try to categorize people as ideal types of one form of racism or another, or would see them as grounded in anything but the grittiness of the human spirit.

In a word, Coles hated Theory; and what he disliked about *White Racism* was my effort to integrate the immediacy of how people behaved around the matter of race with the ebb and flow of transpersonal structures over time. In a word, he took issue with the notion of my subtitle: Psychohistory.

I have no intention of resuming the boring intellectual quarrel between Coles and myself which appeared long ago in the pages of this august journal. Its details have no place here, nor, I should think, anywhere. But it does raise matters of significance. I called my book a "Psychohistory" out of an intimation of the shortcomings of Psy and a desire to overcome the primacy of subjectivism as a way of thinking in which ideas gave birth to each other. If it was alright for Freud to look at the biological basis of desire, it would also be alright to think in terms of structures that were supra-personal and evolved in a way that could be called "historical," insofar as racism—indeed, Mind itself—shows a definite, albeit complex, procession over time.

So I huffed and I puffed, and developed an elaborate theory—a word drawn from the Greek to denote a vantage point from which to optimally watch a drama—to try and bring this dimension into my study of racism. It was an honest effort, but very much, to my eyes, also a flop, and even an embarrassment, turgid and stuffed with psychoanalytic jargon. To this day I remain amazed the book was so well-received, given the shabbiness of its theoretical framework. All I could do was pledge to myself to try and do better in future work, in the meanwhile enjoying the stimulating role of an angst-ridden critic of our "cultural crisis," or something like that.

One day Schiffrin passed along a review from an obscure journal of radical philosophy called *Telos*. The reviewer was someone named Chip Sills, identified only as a teacher of karate in the Bay Area. Sills seems to have disappeared from the face of the earth, and if so, may be regarded as an Angel heaven-sent, for s/he bore the following life-changing message: that I had written a very fine book with a very serious defect: namely, the omission of Karl Marx, about whom I seemed to know nothing, even though I also seemed to be intuitively groping in search of him.

It was true: hemmed in by a bourgeois education under conditions of McCarthyist repressions and the delusions of Lou Kovel, I knew essentially nothing about Marx. Once I had glanced at the essay on alienated labor, and found it slightly interesting, but nothing more. Now the times had changed, opening upon sharply leftward perspectives; even as I had changed, gaining in strength through the realization that I did have my own voice, crude and unsophisticated, but with a certain power and originality, if I would give it rein. Where it wanted to go was away from the subjectivism of Psy in general and psychoanalysis in particular. And Karl Marx, with his axioms that social being determines consciousness, and that the self is the ensemble of social relations, came to define the destination.

I began, as is my wont, by browsing some anthologized passages from the mature work. I was thrilled, and soon realized that there was a special treasure in the writings of the young Marx from 1843 to 1848, which were not only essential for the understanding of *Capital*, but grew out of deep roots in philosophical and spiritual traditions. These provided linkages with Freud, and as I slowly came to realize, with Blake and—as Marx himself attests—with Jesus as well. That all evolved later, and will resume throughout this memoir; for now, I had made a thrilling discovery.

It was the brilliance of the thought, conjoined with an emancipatory urgency that had been ruthlessly suppressed in my Freudian training. "People," young Karl wrote in 1845, at age 27, "before really and truly framing ordinances and decrees, must at least have changed from top to bottom the conditions of their industrial and political existence, and consequently their whole manner of being."[3]

At least!! And their whole manner of being…. What a wonderful vista had been revealed! Here I was, in early career, a rising academic psychiatrist soon to be rewarded with the directorship of a major training program, suddenly discovering a whole world of which I previously had only the faintest idea—and immediately feeling myself at home in it.

Expert on one side, ignoramus on the other, scrambling furiously to catch up and play a role in something I had until quite recently known nothing about, I was in a continual whirlwind in one portion of my life while sedately measuring out the rest. So much to learn; such joy!

There were curious connections to my own past along with new associations in the present. I had known that Wilhelm Reich was active in the Communist movement as well as the psychoanalytic, and became expelled from both. Now I was reversing his path.[4]

A book named *Sex-Pol* appeared in 1972;[5] it contained Reich's writings from the 1920s, when he ran clinics to help German working-class youth with their sex lives. I read it avidly; and Bertell Ollman, who had written a fascinating introduction to that collection, became one of my first stalwart Marxist friends, and, with his foundational study of the *Economic and Philosophical Manuscripts of 1844*,[6] my guide to Marx's singular breakthrough into what Raya Dunayevskya felicitously called, "a new continent of thought."

A brilliant autodidact, Raya and I became good friends in the 1980s, shortly before her untimely death. Along with Ollman's study and István Meszáros' *Alienation*, these became my guideposts, and the astounding *1844 Manuscripts*, the intellectual foundation of my Marxism and increasingly, my orientation to life.

This committed me at the outset to what was variously called "Critical Theory," "Western Marxism," or what Raya and her coterie in *News and Letters* saw as the "Hegelian moment," as they gloried in erudite readings of *The Science of Logic* and combined these with reports from the shop floor.

A fortuitous meeting at the Austin, Texas airport, after a lecture on racism, introduced me to Paul Piccone, founder and chief editor of *Telos,* the very journal that had opened the Marxist door for me. The next thing I knew, I had joined the editorial board of this burgeoning radical philosophy journal, despite having had minimal exposure to the philosophers under study.

Piccone—now deceased—was an impulsive chap; and the deal was consummated just as my seat was being called for the flight back to New York, to my delight. Impulsive, indeed! He had been an immigrant laborer from Italy, barely literate, who came to the United States to work in the steel mills. Somewhere along the way he decided to advance himself by getting an engineering degree.

The school required each student to take one humanities elective. Paul had no idea what to take, so he stuck a pin in the catalogue, and it found "phenomenological Marxism."

Why not?, said Piccone, and the next thing he knew, he was a Marxist phenomenologist who founded *Telos* magazine. Paul could be brutal, and was known for editing contributions and running them in the journal without notifying the author. But even though our political views diverged over time, he was always gracious toward me, claiming with his thick accent that I was the only person with the journal who submitted clean copy. I think, also, he appreciated my independence of spirit, even if it led me to see things differently from the majority of editors. Over time, the whole *Telos* collective became burdensome and even obnoxious, as I realized that Western Marxism—billed as the "free" version as against Stalinism—meant Marxism for sophisticated Eurocentrics, and even, in many instances, Cold Warriors. Notwithstanding, the *Telos* experience was a great schooling in high-powered thought, and it acquainted me with the latest stuff from Adorno, Horkheimer, Marcuse and a number of others, including Ernst Bloch, who was to become my favorite.

Existentially, the encounter with Marx allowed a long-unrecognized passion for justice to move to the center of my life. Righteousness, an ever-flowing stream, Amos had called it; and it comforted me, even as Marx opened my eyes to what Dunayevskaya had called "a whole new continent of thought." No doubt, there was an orientation toward justice in me, deriving from reaction to my "yaller dog" conscience and seeking transcendence, that kept me from lurching onto the narcissistic paths of the New Age and human potential movements, to which I had been exposed throughout my Psy career. As this brought me toward Marx and a revolutionary politics and philosophy, it also opened a path toward the rejoining of my moment of Grace from 1953.

ON THE WORLDLY SIDE OF THINGS, however, I had asked for trouble. As the celebrated psychoanalytic culture-critic stopped being satisfied with laying out contradictions but insisted on fundamental—even revolutionary—change, the invitations from *The New York Times Book Review* faded like the morning dew, and the copious praise that had accompanied the arrival of my first two books swiftly evaporated. When my third book, *The Age of Desire,* appeared in 1981, I still had enough status to get attention in the daily book reviews.[7] Here, however, John Leonard, a Polonius among the intelligentsia, snidely chided me for blaming capitalism, trying to explain too much and missing the complexity of things. So sorry I am for my simplemindedness.

The turn toward Marx cost me my bountiful relationship with André Schiffrin, whose socialism was strictly that of Norman Thomas and Léon Blum. A liaison with Bob Young, Yale friend and British *émigré,* went some way toward recuperating this through his firm, Free Association Books, which published three of my next four titles. This foundered, however, when I decided to publish the seventh, *History and Spirit,* in the United States, with Beacon Press (see Chapter 9). In the meantime it had became evident that my star had set. The last mention in the mainstream press came in response to my my 1994 study of anti-communism, *Red Hunting in the Promised Land,* a severe attack on United States imperialism which I presented to Fidel Castro in Havana.

The *Times* took it seriously enough to run a second-page review in the Sunday book section of exceptional savagery, actually making up some content in order to smear the work, the three years of work embedded in it dutifully sinking like the proverbial stone. That may have been the low point of my writing career. I wish I could say I shrugged it off. But however these things hurt, and sometimes knock me down, they never still my resolve, which returns each time renewed.

The Age of Desire: Case Studies of a Radical Psychoanalyst is the most personal of my books, and a kind of watershed in which what came before my Marxist moment flowed into and joined with what came after. I represented this through a pastiche of multiple genres: fiction, allegory, history, sociological and anthropological critique, theoretical reflection, and autobiography.

I rendered an APA convention in Chicago as a Dantean excursion into the infernal regions and the annihilation of a psychotic inpatient as an episode from *The Iliad*. This latter was made up from whole cloth, while others were variously disguised actual cases I had worked with, mixed with allegorical flourishes and vignettes from my own life. Throughout—as I developed over the years to indicate just how important he was to me—could be found allusions to William Blake, supreme among the voices that rattle about my brain, because only in him could they all come together under the sign of the imagination. The excesses of "The Marriage of Heaven and Hell" were in my thoughts as I made *The Age of Desire* into a condensation of all the struggles I had waged over the '70s, as the political track of my life crossed and at times collided with the track of my professional Psy identity.

Thinking of this epoch, Blake's second proverb of Hell comes back to me: "Drive your cart and your plow over the bones of the dead";[8] and also the passage from Ezekiel in which its origins may be sought—the Valley of the Dry Bones (37:1–14): our prophetic obligation to bring new life out of the fragments of what is seemingly dead and gone.

In the moment defined by *The Age of Desire*, this was forged twice; first, as a grand theoretical encounter between the figures of Marx and Freud, set going by the exposure to the former in the context of my efforts to practice the doctrine of the latter, hence the hope of finding a kind of "synthesis" between them; and second, as a very existential matter of choice, for if some such synthesis could not be reached, then it seemed to me that the psychoanalytic, psychiatric, and, *pari passu*, medical phase of my life was over.

In fact, I never really decided anything, but just did what I willed until the authorities tossed me out of Psy in the mid–'80s. Friends of mine—Richard Lichtman, for example, and the late Victor Wolfenstein—were able to write fairer accounts of the Marx–Freud problematic than I, but maybe because they didn't have to get up every day and work in the mental health industry, as I came to call it in the mid-'70s, in my first extended critique along Marxist lines of the grim and ruthless turn toward biological thinking and repressive actions that arose in the wake of the great crisis in global capital that ushered in the neoliberal era.[9]

Hardly anyone appreciates just what a watershed the end of capital's post–1945 binge has been. Whether caused by the rebounding of our crushed WWII enemies or the "excessive" remuneration of the domestic working classes is a moot point; the fact remains that the crisis—shaken off here and there as a beast would flick away flies with its tail—has returned again and again over the past forty years, demanding warfare against labor and nature, and generating a vision of the future that appalls.

Thirteen years after JFK charmed us at the Shoreham, President Gerald Ford announced he would not bail New York City out of its fiscal distress. "FORD TO CITY: DROP DEAD" was the famous headline in the *Daily News,* announcing that Neoliberalism was here. The Health and Hospitals Corporation responded with a wave of layoffs; and Einstein Psychiatry once again jumped into a leading resistant role, myself playing an active part.

We won that one, and got more artful as the struggle went on in further skirmishes, the high point being devising a tactic wherein the staff would continue to give care while, however, refusing to sign off on the charts with the all-essential diagnosis. This shut off the life-giving flow of value through the system that allowed the various power centers—the drug companies, insurance companies and medical bureaucracies—their slurp at the great trough.

In other words, we were throttling the beast itself with a prefiguration of socialized medicine. It was a delightful *modus operandi,* though absent a sufficiently wide and deep-spread movement, doomed to transience. Like the noisy piglet at the Mama Pig's teat, perky Einstein got its job cuts restored, while the weaker sisters at other institutions down the row were only further cut off, leaving matters in some respects worse than ever.

The bitter irony was not lost on me. Here was the vaunted diagnostic system whose construction allowed psychiatry to preen itself as a bona-fide scientific enterprise—and one, moreover, with an intellectual apparatus that pressed the growing horde of pharmaceuticals through the brains of suffering humanity… and what good was it, really? Chiefly, to enable the commodification of the deeply spurious category, Mental Health. For the "mind" that was to be healthy or not—what was it but the fragmented, estranged ego-self wrought by capital, now turning humanity into a bag of molecules to which other molecules could be added.

And what was "health?" Was it a state of being that didn't suffer very much, only a little, so that a woman could worry about whether her armpit smelled bad enough to warrant a deodorant that would increase her chances of breast cancer—but not so badly as to feel for the person sleeping on a subway grate? Was Simone Weil mentally healthy? Or Franz Kafka? Or John Brown? Or Chelsea Manning?

The more I looked at it with lenses polished by Marx, the more did the mental health industry appear not just scientifically barren, but positively criminal, a perpetrator of massive fraud and the sacrificer of human being to an anti-human machine; the more, finally, did it seem that this principle defined what was mental health in the only cogent way possible. Therefore, the telos, or goal, of Psy's theory and practice was whether a person was capable of producing surplus value, or at least, not standing in its way by being disruptive and stirring up the underlings to rebellion.

I HAD NOT COUNTED on taking on Psy when I began rebelling against the war machine in 1966. But Marx held, justly, that theory and practice had to be aligned; and so I could not in conscience step back from the complicity entailed in being a psychiatrist/psychoanalyst any more that I could accept the comforts of being a USPHS functionary in Seattle during the Vietnam War.

There is an indivisibility about things, after all, however differentiated they might be in the immediate case. And so it was no longer a question of whether I would enjoy my chosen profession but of whether I could live with myself if I didn't fight its immersion in capitalism.

I achieved a little in this direction by retooling the Einstein program as its training director into the "Red Residency," seeking radically-inclined trainees and introducing Marxist content into the curriculum at a fundamental level. In a surfeit of vigilance, I would patrol the halls in spare moments looking for the smarmy "detail men" (often medical-school dropouts) who were there to push their corporation's pills on our staff and trainees; and then, with some genuine pleasure, tell them to get the Hell off the premises, at times escorting them and coming close to using physical force to do so.

But the most substantial thing I did to fulfill this mission, aside from writing *The Age of Desire* and some related pieces, was to attack the pernicious system of diagnosis then being institutionalized by the APA in its third *Diagnostic and Statistical Manual,* an infernal text which I set out to demolish. I do believe I gave the technocrats who devised it what-for, in open debates, and in the preparation of an ambitious critique, the excellence thereof being certified by the refusal of the APA to publish my critique of *DSM-III* in their journal, the pathetic and sole criticism being that the article was too long.[10]

ET TU, SIGMUND?

THROUGHOUT THESE YEARS the figure of Old Freud stood like a craggy rock at the entrance to a harbor beaten by waves. But water will eventually wear down rock; and eventually the Titan (of whom Auden said, upon his passing, that he was "no more a person now but a whole climate of opinion") was brought down to scale, at least in my mind. There was nothing simple about the process, just as there was nothing simple about Freud, a man of many faces: the illuminator of our dark crannies, the frustrated "stout Cortez," the night voyager, the jealous patriarch, the ambivalent Jew, the lover of antiquity, the biologist of the mind, the mystic *manqué,* and more as well, including, to be sure, the originator of a whole profession and its aura.

As the turmoil recounted here reshaped who I was, so did other sides of Freud come into clearer focus, a number of these thanks to revisionist accounts of his life and work by such as Frederick Crews and Jeffrey Masson, who challenged the hagiography of Ernest Jones and other propagandists. There now hove into view the cigar addict who kept smoking his seventeen-to-twenty stogies a day even after the appearance of the cancer that would kill him; the cocaine addict over many years who practically killed one of his friends by addicting him as well; the man who could never figure out "what women wanted," and was deeply contemptuous of them, as when he breezily wrote that the mother of his patient Dora suffered from "housewife's psychosis"; and most weird, a man who exonerated his crackpot otolaryngologist friend Robert Fleiss when the latter operated on the "hysteric" Emma Eckstein in the service of a wacky theory that he and Freud shared, about the connection between the nose and the genital tract... except that Fliess sewed up a piece of gauze inside her wound, nearly killing Emma. But that was all right, opined Sigmund, because even if Emma perished her case confirmed his "scientific" theory that hysterics were prone to bleed from the nose as an upward displacement of menstrual activity. Brilliant!

In his finer moments Freud could posit a kind of a sublime dualism of dialectical proportions between Thanatos, the Death Instinct from which arises our aggression, and Eros, "his equally immortal adversary," as the conclusion to *Civilization and its Discontents* has it. But no careful reading of his speculations along these lines can fail to see that Eros is at a continual disadvantage, and plays, as it were, with one hand tied behind its back.

For Freud, Eros is only possessive love, and therefore an instrument of the Ego. This is a useful notion, to be sure. But how paltry it becomes alongside the differentiation of Love into Eros and Agape—love toward the object on one side, and love from the object on the other: God's and Christ's love for us, the Love that Richard Sewall gathered for me that day in September 1953, the Love manifest as Grace, the selfless love offered by uncountable millions of caretakers. It is evident that Freud had insufficient experience of this sort. But does acquired misanthropy entitle him to pronounce the truth of human being? Or was it that his blinkering—which despises its poor and its caretakers, especially women—fit the needs of the patriarchal society that spawned him?

And so in his widely-praised critique of religion, which valorizes the still, small voice of reason over mere faith, we are told that the "masses are lazy and unintelligent," and that "civilization has little to fear from educated people and brain-workers."[11] The astounding stupidity of such remarks is compounded by the insouciance with which Freud tossed them off, with that sense of impunity granted to heroes of the dominant culture.

Evidence of ill-suitedness for a Freudian calling surfaced long before I had gained the wit to recognize them as such. Some time before the escapade at the Shoreham in 1971, at the very beginning of my analytic training in 1967, my guardian angel Milton Rosenbaum, impressed by what he had learned of my racism project, offered to set up an interview with none other than Heinz Hartmann.

Hartmann is no household name, neither now nor in the late-'60s, but if the world of Freudian psychoanalysis of the time could be compared with Christianity, it would be as if I had been invited to meet with St. Paul. The comparison is more than idle; for Hartmann, of a very upper-crust Viennese family, had the remarkable distinction of having been personally invited by Freud for a free psychoanalysis, a dubious bargain therapeutically but carefully calibrated to meet one of Freud's abiding concerns.

For not only was Hartmann a very distinguished academic, but a Christian as well. Thus he would fulfill the function wrecked by its first nominee, Jung, of providing psychoanalysis with respectability in mainstream academia and a bulwark against anti-Semitism.

And Hartman complied, at the cost—not at all inconsiderable, but definitely consonant with the motion of the center of the profession's gravity—of making psychoanalysis an "Ego psychology," thereby squeezing the lifeblood out of it, and turning it into a conformist academic discourse ("adaptation" was Hartmann's buzzword) incapable of any fruitful synthesis with Marx and other radical ventures.[12]

This was scarcely of concern to me at the time, as I was five years away from knowing I was a Marxist when I first met Hartmann. But I knew when a conversation was dragging as the courtly Hartmann and I had our chit-chat in his very large Park Avenue (where else?) apartment. Running out of things to say, I pulled the last card from my deck and asked him if he knew of a book written by a German *émigré* roughly of his generation, Herbert Marcuse's *Eros and Civilization*, which I was finding very stimulating.

"I am sorry, Dr. Kovel," came the swift reply, "but dot book has nothing to do with psychoanalysis. It is entirely outside of our professional discipline. In fact, I cannot say what it is about, except it is not psychoanalysis." And dot was dot, as I was shown the door.

I wonder what he would have said about Reich.

Hartmann died in 1975. At his funeral, which I did not attend, the chief musical work was "Des Baches Wiegenlied" from Schubert's *Die Schöne Mullerin*. Yes, that is something we could have shared.

EGO PSYCHOLOGY WAS initiated by Freud in the 1920s, codified by Hartmann in the 1930s, and thereafter reabsorbed by all that was conformist in psychoanalysis—including, and in spades, the Downstate Institute where I trained. It epitomized the difference between what had originally thrilled me about Freud and later came to bore and even disgust me. To accept the notion of a normative ego that was non-conflictual, innate, and largely autonomous was to me a throwing in of the towel; it *ipso facto* abolished any serious potential for resisting and transforming the conditions of existence, thereby trivializing the psychoanalytic project and turning it over to men with neatly trimmed beards and offices in suburban malls.

Meanwhile, I took the low ground, the path of negativity, and stayed with Blake and Marx while dragging my heels along the psychoanalytic path. I became known as the shrink for the disaffected and left wing, and helped a few people that way. And there were some interesting projects from the later years of my career, not that they resolved any of the contradictions:

• An essay against Erik Erikson, the liberal's Heinz Hartmann. It had the honor of being rejected by the *Partisan Review,* which had commissioned it, for having "Stalinist tendencies" (I beg your pardon!) as well as enraging Erikson himself, who, according to my friend Howard Kushner, an eye-witness, stormed into his San Francisco seminar waving it about while denouncing the unknown upstart who dared question his psycho-historical authority.[13]

• "Things and Words,"a long and substantial piece, written to establish my *bona fides* as a theoretician of psychoanalysis. It was a meditation on Freud's greatest "metapsychological" essay, "The Unconscious," and also a hopeful statement on the encounter between Marx and Freud, calling for a kind of synthesis. It was pretty good, and may have accounted for the fact that at the end of our sojourn together, the Downstate Institute saw fit to graduate me...[14]

• Last and least, though not to me and my circle, a brief but dazzling film career. Who could forget, in Lizzie Borden's 1983 *Born in Flames*, my cameo role as Dr. Lance Luftmann, a TV-shrink *Gauleiter* assigned to throttle the woman's revolution inside the socialist revolution. And how could Freud ever again haunt the man who played him in the minimalist extravaganza, *Sigmund Freud's Dora*, mouthing the very words of the epochal "A Case of Hysteria," and winding up by flicking the ash from his cigar? It was shot over two weekend afternoons in 1979, and reflected the fact that life with DeeDee (she took sound on the production[15]) had blossomed into immersion in the more-forward dimensions of the arts, especially film and video, her areas of immediate focus.

SHIFTS OF THIS KIND mitigated the *ennui* deriving from my alienation from Psy, though they could never eliminate it. That would require either leaving the field entirely, or seeing through the social revolution necessary for liberation—a process belonging to the question posed earlier in the present chapter: how to drain the dismal swamp posed by psychoanalytic education and its bizarre training analysis.

A nucleus of an answer may be posed as tersely as it is remote from present circumstances. To free psychoanalysis from the traps posed by the hierarchy between trainee and training analyst, all we have to do is to construct a communist world—or as I have come to call it, an "ecosocialist" one—in which such hierarchies would be dissolved in society at large through fidelity to the intrinsic value of nature.

Once society becomes responsive to the ethos of "to each according to need, from each according to ability," as a certain 19th-century *emigré* put it, then the market would dissolve and psychoanalysis would find its proper level. Until then... well, let the Devil take the hindmost. It is no longer my business to worry about.

Notes

1 Joel Kovel, *A Complete Guide to Therapy* (New York: Pantheon, 1976).

2 No paranoia, this. I once had a patient close to the directorate of the *New York Review* who reported after attending a dinner amongst them that my name had come up, sparking a general outburst of hostility. One is, after all, known by one's enemies.

3 Karl Marx, *The Poverty of Philosophy* (New York: International Publishers, 1963): 107.

4 However Reich, as I was told by Myron Sharaf, who escorted him to prison, declared "I am still a Marxist" even at the gates—the last words he spoke to Sharaf. I know of no evidence that Reich ever read Marx's early works—indeed, the *1844 Manuscripts* were only released in 1932, and not in the United States until 1956.

5 Wilhem Reich, *Sex-Pol Essays 1929–1934*, ed. Lee Baxandall (New York: Random House, 1972).

6 Bertell Ollman, *Alienation: Marx's Conception of Man in Capitalist Society* (Cambridge: Cambridge University Press, 1971).

7 Joel Kovel, *The Age of Desire: Case Histories of a Radical Psychoanalyst* (New York: Pantheon, 1982).

8 Erdman, "The Marriage of Heaven and Hell," 35.

9 Joel Kovel, "The American Mental Health Industry," in *Critical Psychiatry*, ed. David Ingleby (New York: Pantheon, 1980): 72–101.

10 Eventually published as "A Critique of DSM–III," in *Research on Law, Deviance and Social Control*, edited by Steven Spitzer and Andrew Scull, Vol. 9, 1988, pp. 127–46 (Greenwich, CT and London, England: JAI Press).

11 Sigmund Freud, *Future of an Illusion*, vol. XXI of *Standard Edition of the Works of Sigmund Freud* (1929): 7, 39.

12 This is elaborated in *The Age of Desire*, including the reasons for my rejection of the one major analyst who shared the view that Ego Psychology was conformist, Jacques Lacan.

13 Published thanks to Colin Greer. cf. Joel Kovel, "Erik Erikson's Psychohistory," *Social Policy* 4 (1974): 60–64.

14 Joel Kovel, "Things and Words: Metapsychology and the Historical Point of View," *Psychoanalysis and Contemporary Thought* 1 (1978): 21–86.

15 Anthony McCall, Andrew Tyndall, Claire Pajakowska, and Jane Weinstock, *Sigmund Freud's Dora*, 1979; cinematography by Babette Mangolte; sound by DeeDee Halleck (1979). *Dora* was an elegant exercise in Lacanian structuralism that used Freud's archetypal case study of Hysteria to illuminate post-Freudian phenomena such as advertising and pornography. An hour-long film, it was made for about six thousand dollars.

EL ENEMIGO DE LA HUMANIDAD

Chapter 8
Southward Bound

Once—I believe it was in the winter of 1977, during a tryst in Toronto—I cried out to DeeDee in a kind of ecstasy that we should found a new religion. The call was short on specifics and never got off the ground. But that it got onto the ground in the first place was a sign that something was rising within me, something unready and unknown, with a root sure to return.

It arose again around the turn of the 1980s, when the focus of politics turned to the anti-nuclear crisis accompanying the re-opening of the Cold War. This had entailed an accelerated nuclear arms race and reawakened the specter of end-times which had haunted me since that sunny day in August of 1945 when I joined my co-campers at Camp Mitchell and Harlee in wild celebration of America's prowess in destroying a whole city with one blow. Since then, I had been episodically seized by Nuclear Terror. Now the Second Cold War induced its dialectical negation, non-violent direct action. This moved to the center of resistance to the beast and eventuated in the writing of my fourth book, *Against the State of Nuclear Terror*, in 1984. It also drew me into placing myself on the line against the state and getting arrested, something I have undertaken about a dozen times in the years to come, most recently in 2012.

A complicated series of developments, played out over many years, was brought forward here. The dynamic seems to have been built in layers, as a sort of archeological construction:

• First, the epiphany from summer camp in 1945, charged with jingoistic elation for what "we" had done to the hated Japanese with our super-bomb, its memory persisting as that of an incomprehensible force set loose....

• Transfer of the menace to the Other: the Soviet Satan as constructed for me by Lou Kovel and anticommunism over the years....

• Now it combined into the disciplining of a "good citizen" who learned to fear the Bomb, respect the authorities and learn to obey their drills....

• All of which converged into the Mega Fright of October, 1962, in the standoff known as the Cuban Missile Crisis, the greatest pure fright the world has ever known. I virtually kept the car idling for days so that Virginia (pregnant with Jonathan) and I might escape looming Armageddon. Little did I suspect that JFK was preparing his own death by holding back General Curtis LeMay and Company from unleashing the Bomb....

• November 22, 1963 would not be comprehended at all for decades. It endured as a tocsin signaling a malignancy within my own country....

• And then came spring 1964, and I went with a group of friends to a movie by an esteemed filmmaker. Kubrick's *Doctor Strangelove* proved incalculably greater than what I anticipated: a black comedy, yes, but one transvaluing reigning values and bringing down the idols, dissolving nuclear terror into Homeric laughter. Five or six viewings have not dulled its power. Just the other night, reminded of Peter Sellers' concluding line, "Mein Fürher, I can walk!!" (improvised, like most of them), I nearly fell off my chair.

• Did this radical shift enter into the redefinition of myself two years later, recounted in Chapter 6, as a writer and enemy of the imperial and militaristic State? I have neither doubt nor proof of the fact. Certainly, *Strangelove* had torn apart the props of a conventional ordination of belief. More basically, the ensuing processes of political and personal change set into motion a long-deferred spiritual development that now, at the dawning of the eighties, began to take religious form.

I KNEW THAT RELIGIOUS FOLK such as A. J. Muste and Dorothy Day had marched against the nuclear state. But the significance of this meant rather little until the morning after December 9, 1980, when I awoke to learn that a group of Catholic clerics led by Daniel and Phillip Berrigan had broken into the General Electric nuclear weapons plant in King of Prussia, Pennsylvania, smashed the nose cone of an intercontinental ballistic missile, and poured their blood on files. It was a radical event in the history of nonviolent protest—although as could be expected for so truculent a bunch as the secular pacifists with whom I was then associating, there were those who held the Ploughshares people to be impure in their pacifism inasmuch as they had, after all, *broken a nose cone*—and with a hammer no less.

Observing the Berrigan brothers and other Ploughshares activists at a public lecture shortly afterward, I found myself struck by what at first seemed an unimportant detail of behavior: that in contrast to my buddies in the anti-nuclear movement who were by and large a somber and even gloomy bunch, these Christians radiated a serenity and even a cheerfulness, despite having put themselves in the deepest difficulties. It was plain they were under the direction of a higher, offsetting power, telling them to not be afraid.

During the spring of 1983, DeeDee, three-year-old Molly, and I found ourselves in Italy on holiday. I had been there before, with Virginia, and loved it. Now I found myself loving it again, with a subtle but definite difference, that there seemed to be an influence pulling me toward the sites of sacred art. Chief was the lovely town of Borgo San Sepolcro, home to Piero della Francesca. We saw the splendors of Constantine's dream and the enveloping Virgin; however, what I really wanted to see was the famous Resurrection, said by many experts (including Aldous Huxley) to be the greatest painting ever achieved. Rating masterpieces is a pretty dumb idea, but beholding the Risen Christ, his left side thickly draped and his right side pallid yet powerful, appearing as though the dirt of the grave was just being shaken off, and with that peculiar gift of Piero's of representing his holy figures looking wall-eyed out of the frame, their line of sight past the sleeping soldiers and directed toward infinity, one could understand why it could be given such a rank—and also wonder whether they, and we, would ever awaken.

Onward to Assisi, home of Francesco Bernardone, who talked to the birds and the wolves and wrote "The Canticle of the Sun." Giotto abounded there. I loved it of course, but felt a bit overpowered by the scale of the monument in proportion to the delicacy of its honoree. So I took a stroll one afternoon while DeeDee and Molly rested and wandered up the stone streets until I found myself in front of a little church, its door open. There was nothing about it in the tourist guide, no knockout representation by individual genius to be seen, just an ordinary church. I entered and found myself on the balcony of the nave, observing from above what was evidently a mass. Only a few old ladies sat below as the priest intoned something in Latin. I had never before been in such a setting.

I was struck first of all by the quality of the light. My eyes dazzled; everything seemed made of gold, and everything shone and reflected off everything else. I was transfixed, extraordinarily lightened. I could not understand it and decided not to try. Where were my exceptional powers of critical discernment? What was this happiness? What was happening to a Jew from Brooklyn, psychoanalyst and Marxist and everything else? Where had all the predicates gone? My being had been scrubbed of dross, leaving a naked wondering babe exposed to the universe. The doors of perception had been cleansed, leaving everything to appear as it is, infinite.[1]

THIS OCCURRED DURING the time I had become friends with Stanley Diamond, an anthropologist and poet at the graduate faculty of The New School and founder of a school of Marxist anthropology. I first observed Diamond at a conference, skewering some dull-witted academic; and as is my wont upon encountering certain extraordinary individuals, contacted him in the hope of making a friend—in this case, also, one might add, of improving my mind, as I perceived in Stanley a virtuoso in those skills of reasoning deriving from the Marxist tradition in which I was still a neophyte.

He answered the phone and after the first pleasantries launched into a monologue about how he knew of me and was grateful for the call, both for the sake of why I had made it and for the fact that I was a physician to whom he could relate his sad story. For he was becoming blind, owing to a tumor in his pituitary gland that in its expansion was pressing upon his optic nerve. This was not what I had bargained for, but as the song goes, you can't always get what you want. And so began an hour-long conversation that soon drifted, as did most of our conversations, into monologue, Stanley talking and Joel listening and making useful sounds every now and then. Much of it dwelt on illness, both his and his sister's, who was a schizophrenic and was driving him mad. Stanley spoke slowly but with such a command over cadence, such an inner intellectual force and insight, and such a charismatic suffering, that I had little space and less inclination for interrupting it with my own words.

Sadly, my time with Stanley was largely spent on his downward path, which continued after the pituitary tumor had been removed. This spared his sight and other brain damage, but the condition that replaced it was scarce improved, requiring as it did endocrinological replacement therapy of fiendish complexity and complication. His brilliant intellect endured, as did the beauty of his poetic language, but the general capacity for life withered, leaving shadows behind.

Diamond must have been quite a swashbuckler in his youth, when he enlisted in the British North African forces at the beginning of WWII, going on from there to do field work in Africa. Beyond doubt he was a fierce anti-fascist and anti-racist, who resigned and/or was forced out of UCLA and Brandeis in the McCarthy period, and who lived in bitterness as neoliberalism invaded the academy and slowly devoured the fruits of his work. Most of the time until cancer suddenly got him in 1991, I knew Stanley to be ill.

Notwithstanding, Stanley remained a powerful mentor to me for the better part of a decade. He sharpened my wits, made helpful interventions in editing various pieces I would write for the journal he had founded, *Dialectical Anthropology,* gave me a valuable exit strategy out of the Psy world through an adjunct teaching position in the graduate program at the New School (where, among other things, he and I co-taught a course in Marx and Freud), encouraged the open form of *The Age of Desire* that mixed fiction with social critique, and introduced me to new friends, most notably the great and persecuted Alger Hiss and the splendid Archie Singham, Sri Lankan/Jamaican anti-imperialist extraordinaire.

Beyond all this, Diamond's mentorship reawakened in me the notion of "natural humanity," or as one might say, the people of the South. I am fully aware of how problematic such North/South terminology may be, but we need some way to talk about First Peoples that reflects the profound dialectic between modernity and capitalism on one side and indigeneity on the other. I had begun this process under the influence of Wilhelm Reich during the Tropp years from 1958 to 1963. Reich's conceptual path devolved from the cosmos onto humanity through the mediation of the biosphere, and was grounded in a deep respect for the relationship of First Peoples to the earth. Something of this had happened as I engaged the riverine people of Suriname, and in my imagination, the Copper Inuit of Gontran de Poncins' *Kabloona*.

Diamond's path began with the study of humanity *in situ,* and moved outward from there, though he was not given to cosmological speculation and remained within the frame of the human world. Reich valorized "orgonomic potency," an integral, authentic relationship to nature chiefly expressed sexually. Diamond valorized the "primitive," a term mainly rejected nowadays,[2] that to him meant an integral relationship with nature no longer foregrounded as sexuality. Reich moved away from Marx, and in his narcissism claimed a new continent in thought for himself. In the process he reduced humanity to nature, bypassing what was human about human nature, causing me to drift away from his thinking. The notion of nature continued to fascinate me as it had done in the days when I studied the quantum bond. But for now Stanley Diamond's more modest location in the South suited me better from a number of angles, including my relationship to Marx.

Stanley often reminded me that Marx spent more time studying aboriginal humanity in the last decade of his life than anything else. He was spurred by a letter from a young *Narodnik,* Vera Zasulich, asking why the socialist revolution had to go through capitalism, with its manifold corruptions of the human spirit, rather than taking directly off from the communal "closer to nature" ways of First Peoples, including the Russian version thereof, the peasant commune known as the *Mir*. After much deliberation Marx replied that it depended on the circumstances, in other words, what Zasulich had propounded was a possibility that needed deep and serious study and radical application. This he set out to do, inconclusively, as death crept up on him. Such was the framework of Stanley Diamond's "dialectical anthropology," and that became the legacy bequeathed by Diamond to me, enfolding into the ecological and spiritual dimensions of my later thought.

I had approached Stanley with a two-fold vexation: first, trapped by the fetters of medical academia, and second, discontented with existing Marxisms and left movements in general. After a decade of left politics, I had no doubt about the need of resistance to the system, but little sense of where this should be taking me, and a lot of irritation with the visible possibilities for radical change.

Some of this had to do with not yet having worked through the layers of fearful inertia that had sedimented into my politics. This kept the blinders on and maintained my *naiveté* and confusion through the 1980s. I am ashamed to confess that despite knowing better, I had not yet, for example, given up on the possibility of rescue by some Democratic Party administration; indeed, kept voting for their candidates until psychopathic Bill Clinton at last purged me of the impulse. Yes, I was a Marxist and possessed facility in the standard Marxist alternatives, all of which seemed fine in theory and futile in practice—at least, among those practitioners I could see at first hand.

Being ornery Joel Kovel, I was not about to dismiss the record of the USSR and its derivatives just because the anti-communist consensus—which extended deep into academia—deemed it diabolic; but what I knew and reasoned could generate no enthusiasm either. Then there were the existing Marxist-Leninist alternatives—Stalinist, Trotskyist or Maoist, of the "Revolutionary Communist this and that" sort. These were commonplace in my circles of acquaintance, and because I had developed a degree of local prominence on the radical left, a number of them over the years assigned some cadre to follow me about and try to recruit me. Most of the folk I have met in these organizations have been sincere and dedicated. I could sympathize with their rage and desperation at having to live in the belly of the capitalist beast, but this was no excuse for being so tedious and strident. Thinking in terms of formulas, they all too often struck me as poor imitations of the religious fundamentalists they railed against. Worse, their limited conception of things invariably turned cultish, preventing the unification of a serious force against capitalism.

More distressing, yet—since it applied to a project in which I had invested much time and effort for the past decade—my sojourn with non-Leninist, critical-theory-type Western Marxism, chiefly through the *Telos* group, was turning distinctly sour. Meeting Paul Piccone may have gone far toward the alleviation of my despond about being part of the Psy world. But the longer I knew the *Telos*ians, the more they became reincarnations of those pettifoggers whom the young Marx and Engels had flogged as useless scribblers and pedants: Bruno Bauers all.

Worse than useless, for the intelligentsia's real connection to society was through academic institutions. Hence even the dissenters could come to manifest the occult and immanent goal of academia, which is to reproduce the capitalist order's technocratic elites, vastly more extensive in 1980 than 1945.

Our intellectuals, unable to see the mote in their own eye, systematically betrayed the universalist goals of the originators of modern communism. They became Eurocentrically racist and, from their comfortable perches in the university, signed aboard the then-emerging Second Cold War on the side of the West. This happened across several planes united by the deadly ideology of anti-communism, which was pumping life into the moribund Soviet Union in order to justify outrageous weapons expenditures, American imperialism and the nuclear arms race.

One famous Greek-French anarchist philosopher beloved by *Telos*, Cornelius Castoriadis (whom DeeDee and I visited in Paris in his very elegant apartment), went so far as to write an utterly delusional book in the 1980s, *Devant la Guerre,* the thesis of which was that the Soviets were imminently going to invade Europe. This he regarded with the degree of certainty that the sun would rise in the east; nor did such a pathetic argument diminish the esteem in which Castoriadis was held by the *Telos* crowd.

Furious quarrels ensued. Most aggravating was their display of a nauseating nonchalance to massacres in Central American countries, chiefly Guatemala and El Salvador, which had been revealed by courageous journalists like my friend Allan Nairn to be engineered by the CIA. My pointing out that we had better attend to what U.S. imperialism was doing right under our nose, rather than babble about the Great Power charade then underway, was met with hostility by the *Telos* bunch, who in their indifference to anything that did not directly involve the Great Axis from New York to London to Frankfurt to Tokyo, bore more than a superficial resemblance to the reasoning of Henry Kissinger.

And so they scorned me: how dare I waste their time with matters that had no relevance to the deep philosophical themes being debated in meaningful places like Paris and Frankfurt? What would Adorno say about El Salvador?

Well, Adorno was dead, hounded into a heart attack by his students in the late-'60s for supporting the U.S. in Vietnam—a dreadful fate it was for a dreadful betrayal of all that Marx stood for—yet here it was, coming around again. No doubt Adorno would have dismissed anything less-than-Western with equivalent scorn. Was Critical Theory to be the last stop on the line of revolutionary socialism, as far as it could go, given the deadly embrace of the late capitalism in which it had gestated? Even the great Marcuse had died in despair in gorgeous La Jolla on the Pacific, the only leading figure of the Frankfurt School to show courage and fundamental opposition, the only one who could escape Brecht's savage aphorism that its doyens were inhabitants of the Grand Hotel over the abyss. Their successor Habermas remained, grinding out turgid paeans to a hopeless liberal society in a less-than-grand hotel, perhaps a Comfort Inn, also teetering over the abyss.

And I, who had been in awe of Adorno, Marcuse and other Frankfurt School luminaries, who could have replied to Heinz Hartmann that day in 1970 when he deigned to tell me that Herbert Marcuse offered no path toward psychoanalysis, that if I could not be a Freud then at least I could aspire to be a Marcuse—what was left for me amidst this ruin of advancing neoliberalism, nuclear terror, and dithering leftoids?

This: in mid 1983, a student approached me in Stanley Diamond's shop at the New School. She seemed in a kind of ecstasy as she said, "Joel, I've just returned from Nicaragua. I thought of you while I was there. It's amazing, unbelievable. You've got to go; you'll never forget it!"

SANDALISTA DAYS

"A screaming comes across the sky. It has happened before, but there is nothing to compare it to now."

NOVEMBER 1983. Ten years after Pynchon's *Gravity's Rainbow* had famously opened with this evocation of a Nazi U-2 missile hurtling across the London sky, here was something to compare it to. The flyboys in the Pentagon, intoxicated by their glorious triumph over Grenada, center of the world nutmeg trade and home to the first successful Black revolution in the Americas since Haiti, were looking westward, and fancying the elimination with extreme prejudice of the mighty Sandinista juggernaut in nearby Nicaragua, now four years in power.

As Ronald Reagan intoned the Nicaraguan Threat—closer to Harlingen, Texas than Harlingen was to New York City!—harbingers of imminent invasion were heard screaming in the sky over Managua.[3]

And I was there to hear them. Every day, at any hour of the day or night, one could count on at least one of the sonic booms created by advanced U.S. fighter-bombers, announcing the presence of the Great Satan to the north, or as the Sandinistas preferred to call it, *"el Enemigo de la Humanidad."*

My sentiments exactly. I liked that, a lot. I loved the early evening gatherings when the ridiculous heat had abated and we could relax and sing sad songs in an amphitheater to the martyrs of the Revolution: Commandante Che Guevara, of course, but more salient, those to the martyr of the Nicaraguan revolution, Carlos Fonseca, trained in the Soviet Union and Cuba, stern-faced bespectacled ideologue and organizer of the FSLN—*Frente Sandinista de Liberacion Nacional*—a motley group of young intellectuals, men and women (this being an innovation of Fonseca's) imbued with the anti-imperial spirit that flourished after the Second World War. The FSLN set off on a revolutionary path that would gain a future through a retrieval of the past. Like Fidel, they would abide in the *selva,* or rainforest, for armed struggle. Here Fonseca met his death three years before the victory of the revolution, to live on as a martyr.

In these Managua evenings we would sing—or the Nicaraguans would sing and I, very halting in my Spanish, would tearfully listen, joining the culminating *"Presente!"* and the recital of *"el Enemigo de la Humanidad."* For a moment, at least, this traveller very far from home, had come home.

Fonseca was in a lineage of martyrdom that connected Che with Augusto Sandino, Nicaragua's national martyr, who gave the *enemigo's* Marines the devil of a time in the 1920s, until a kind of truce was established and he came out of the forest to be betrayed and murdered. The man responsible for this was Anastasio Somoza, head of the National Guard, who soon afterward founded the dictatorial regime from whose yoke the Sandinistas liberated Nicaragua 45 years later. It was Somoza about whom FDR coined the memorable phrase that, yes, he was a "son of a bitch, but our son of a bitch." FDR loved a good joke now and then.

I made four visits to Nicaragua. Each of the first three, in 1983, 1984, and 1985, were roughly two weeks in duration, and were followed by a three-to-four-month visit in 1986. On the maiden voyage of 1983 I was accompanying a talented team of video documentarians, including DeeDee, Karen Ranucci, Joan Braderman, Eddie Becker, and Skip Blumberg. Our collective purpose was to show something interesting about revolutionary Nicaragua, and we each had some special role to play. As the person with the least competence in making media, my job was to arrive a week before the others and be a kind of advance scout—also not my strong suit, especially given ignorance in Spanish, but an excellent immersion nonetheless.

What struck me the most from the moment I landed was the existential sense, noted above, of coming home, despite the incredibly strange and broken-down appearance of the country. Perhaps it had something to do with the fact that the policemen, all very slender and about 18 years of age, made me feel that they were somehow on my side, not in any specifically welcoming way, as tourists were greeted upon arrival in their tropical paradise in hopes of emoluments, but simply because they knew themselves to be part of a revolution and, recognizing me as a member of its international solidarity network, would gladly share it.

I had never been in a place so disheveled, dusty and chaotic, indeed so close to being a ruin,[4] and yet also so welcoming. Nor was this simply by the Nicaraguans; the country, scantly endowed with resources and desperately poor by all the parameters of the world, was rich in spiritual nourishment. We soon found little Nicaragua to be something like the spiritual capital of Latin America, not built with stone like Rome or Washington, but in the convergence of histories. Everywhere one went, especially in certain cafés that were universal meeting points for folk from all over the continent and beyond, there was instant fellowship: instantaneous but not at all shallow, for there is a common striving accessible to all inspirited by the notion of revolution, and which knows itself through mutual recognition.

I had some knowledge of this in advance, knew that it had happened before to many still living (we even had Spanish Civil War veterans trooping to Nicaragua), knew that it should not preclude the ruthless criticism that Marx demanded of revolutionaries, knew that there were many in FSLN Nicaragua who hated us and worked hand in glove with the *Enemigo* to destroy what we sought to build—and also knew that this spirit-force was absolutely essential if the world was to be transformed. I wept tears of joy that here, in the middle of life's road, I had finally received my aliquot of its nectar and imbibed it.

DURING THE SECOND WEEK, as our team wandered through town, we came upon a bank on whose front steps was lounging a grinning youth casually dressed, with an automatic rifle slung over his shoulder. *"Que pasa compa?"*—What's up, comrade?" we asked, to which he matter-of-factly replied, *"Esperando la invasion."* "I'm waiting for the invasion,"—and, implicitly, so are you. So here was the title of our little film, which won an award and enabled me to embellish my *curriculum vitae* with a deliciously non-academic piece of work.

The second and third visits mixed tourism and activism along with family matters, my stepson Ezra having followed our 1983 visit with an extended trip of his own that included working as a teacher and marrying into a Nicaraguan family.[5] Moments of solidarity took place throughout these sojourns and built in me the desire to go further. Chafing for a deeper involvement, I began preparations for the 1986 visit, ostensibly a project of medical-psychiatric work through a connection I had made with a Mexican collective organized by the legendary psychoanalyst, Marie Langer, who had escaped fascism twice, in Nazi-controlled Austria in the late 1930s, and Argentina under the dictatorship of the generals in the 1970s. It was a comfort to work with psychoanalysts and psychologists who did not make me ashamed of my profession. But it was apparent nevertheless that the slippage in my identity as a Psy professional was already fargone, and between this and my dilapidated Spanish, I am afraid that I didn't help Marie's worthy project very much.

In any case, the real purpose of the 1986 trip was not about Psy at all, and only partially about solidarity. It was also—and to be honest, mainly—to develop an encounter with Christianity that began shortly before my arrival in Nicaragua, as those scattered matters described at the beginning of this chapter, indeed, all the intimations of Christ from the beginning of this narrative, and indeed through a lifetime of reading and music, from Tolstoy and Dostoevsky, and Palestrina, Bach and Mozart, gathered into a new phase of my being, because they were intimations no more but part of a coherent reality of struggle and sacrifice: an actual, present Revolution.

Now they were, and were to remain, scattered no more, but for the rest of my days would periodically and increasingly cohere into Christianity's presence and not its manifestations. The edifice loomed not as distant thunder or flashes of inspiration occurring with a lover, or mystical moments that lit up my inner sky, or such musings such as had gone on with me since Richard Sewall knocked me over by evoking 1 Corinthians 13—but as a consolidated history more than two thousand years old confronting me and bidding that I declare myself before it. One might say there was to be a new centering, because Christ Jesus, though a man, also becomes the humanization of historical process. The Son of Man is also Nicaragua itself, as it struggles against empire and autocracy, and we unite with Christ as we enter that struggle.

Raised to existential intensity, these become Christian motifs; and while they were not sufficient at first to ready me for Jesus, I do believe they were necessary for my receptivity to what befell me in poor, beleaguered, communistic—*and* Christian—Nicaragua. It seems a miracle of sorts that at the very time in my life when I was casting about to find a better revolutionary alternative, a better way to be Marxist so to speak, here was Nicaragua undergoing a revolution, not just with Christian overtones but Christian substance: Nicaragua, the Yale of my middle years. It was the only revolution in the modern era in which Christian clerics played a major role, and Christianity entered deeply into its process and ideology.

One cannot regard Sandinista Nicaragua as theocratic, however. Despite the fact that the country had at the time perhaps the largest percentage in the world of believing Christians—some 95% Roman Catholics—there was no chance that Nicaragua would go the way of Iran, whose revolutionary triumph took place in the same year, 1979, and led to the Islamic Republic. The reason was obvious: the Catholic hierarchy in Nicaragua was firmly reactionary, and became a major force in the counter-revolution; and the revolution itself was largely an expression of the movement flourishing at the time as "liberation theology," in which Christianity was reinterpreted in terms of class struggle and its goals incorporated as those of socialism. Such is what was meant by the "option for the poor" announced by John XXIII at the Second Vatican Council.

Jesus was not simply a radical from the peasant class, though he was certainly that as well. He was the actual originator of the notion of communism within an already constructed class society (in contrast to the indigenous communism of First Peoples) whose class structure had been further divided by complicity with the Roman invaders. Despite the tantalizing references in the Book of Acts 2:44–45 that continued the Synoptic Gospels with a brief mention of the sharing of private possessions, it is not at all clear that the first Christians were practicing communists. It is perfectly clear, however, that this notion was part of the *zeitgeist* of Palestine in the First Century, even if mostly unknown throughout the rest of the Roman Empire, and that Jesus the man was its personification, and that as the Son of God Jesus called upon wealth and especially monetary wealth as anathema. What else did it mean to knock over the money-changing tables in the Temple? How else could it be that to follow Jesus meant thereafter to take the position of the dominated and exploited underclasses, not just to be helpful toward, to be sympathetic with, or charitable about, but, to *be* them as the precondition for self-transformation. Read Matthew 25:35–45, The Bible says it's so, and it is for humanity to figure out what this means in respect to Jesus.

Christianity was to brood over this problem as did no other religion, even as it became corrupted in innumerable ways over the centuries. Liberation theology was a particularly powerful instance of the perennial conflict as it seized the Christian mind, especially that of Latin America, in the great epoch of post-WWII emancipatory agitation. Sandinist Nicaragua was a focal struggle, in which revolution along socialist and anti-imperialist lines converged and became logically integrated with a struggle inside the Church itself, both locally and all the way up to the Vatican, where Pope John Paul II viewed the Sandinistas with pretty much the same consternation as did Ronald Reagan.

Pathetically weak in material terms, Nicaragua more than made up for it in spiritual intensity; and the wars to be waged against it by United States imperialism and the Vatican were astutely classified by Oxfam as being waged against the "threat of a good example." If the Sandinistas could build a democratic socialist society connected with a church liberated from hierarchy and class privilege, who could say how far this might spread? Better, therefore, stop at nothing to nip the menace in the bud.

It was certainly a good example as far as I was concerned; indeed, I could barely believe my luck, to find here in the world a process to induce what was gestating in my soul, bringing what was inside to the outside, to struggle with it and perhaps allow me to bring it inside again. I was preset to be bowled over by Nicaragua—nor did the country and its direction disappoint. Could it be that these presentiments of Jesus over the years since 1953 were what is meant by the Holy Spirit at work in a person, calling me to a salvation that could be mine insofar as it dissolved my egoic, separate individuality and united me with universal humanity, and through this, with the universe, human nature joining nature itself? And did this not indicate the contours of how to discern where Marxism had gone astray and where it needed to be redirected?

I say "indicate" because it would be preposterous to believe all this could snap into place at once. And indeed, the fact that I am writing this some thirty years after these events, using an aging and cranky body for the purpose while dogged by the realization that still, things have not snapped into place—and never will!—all this nags at me and causes dismay, but also a characteristic negation the absence of which will mean that death is nigh—because for me hope surges into the spaces worn thin by the grinding plates of reality and their receding phantoms. "I can't go on; I'll go on," said Beckett, and as it was good enough for him, so be it for me. And so, back to poor and valiant Nicaragua.

The Christian presence in Sandinista Nicaragua ranged from the highest levels of the state to the most humble places in civil society. I had some encounter with all of them. Miguel D'Escoto, a Maryknoll priest who spent much of his youth in Los Angeles, was, as Foreign Minister, the loftiest representative of liberation theology in the government.[6] I met him a few years later at Archie Singham's apartment in Brooklyn; and in 1985 I had the distinct pleasure of going on an evening march through the streets of Managua, Molly on my shoulders, in support of Padre D'Escoto's *huelga de hambre,* his hunger strike protesting US intervention, no doubt the first time a foreign minister had done anything of the sort. A photo of this *gringo* and his lovely daugh-

MOLLY AND JOEL IN *NUEVA AMANACER*

ter, both solemn, appeared some years later in an essay on liberation theology on the front page of *Nueva Amanacer.*

THE CARDENAL BROTHERS, Fernando and Ernesto, were ministers, respectively of Education and Culture. Fernando, a Jesuit, led the literacy campaign of 1980, in which a half million Nicaraguans learned to read. Ernesto was a Trappist monk, a famous poet and a disciple of Thomas Merton, whom I deeply admired and studied as well, especially when I realized that his journey to Christ came to traverse Taoism and Zen Buddhism and then terminate in Marxism. Terminate, indeed, as Merton perished under suspicious circumstances, after delivering his call for Christians to embrace Marx, electrocuted in his hotel room in Thailand through a faultily wired electric light as he came out of the shower.

Around this time I became friends with a wonderful man, Ping Ferry, a philanthropist and democrat who had also come under Merton's charisma and been his friend. From Ping I learned that Ernesto Cardenal had been counseled by Merton to not follow his path into hermetic monasticism at Gethsemane, but to practice his faith in the world and among the underclasses. Thus Ernesto went back to Nicaragua, to work in the tiny fishing community of Solentiname, an island in Lake Nicaragua. He transcribed the responses of various members of his parish as they read and commented upon passages from scripture. Published as *The Gospel at Solentiname*,[7] it moved me greatly, as an exemplary use of the Word, and was an excellent purgative of the baleful influence of the *Telos* bunch.

Ernesto achieved iconic status in 1983 when he was honored by toxic Pope John Paul II on the latter's state visit to Nicaragua. As he prostrated himself before the Pontiff the latter scolded him, and harshly demanded his resignation from the government on account of its hostility to the official Catholic hierarchy. Ernesto's faithful refusal went a long way to reinforce the way of liberation theology—though not, as events would warrant, long enough.

I met Fernando and Ernesto very briefly at *La Casa Jesuitica,* the Jesuit residence and a center for liberation theology in Nicaragua. The other Jesuits, including the now-deceased head of the mission, Jabier Gorostiaga, came to be a great influence on me, chiefly by example. One in particular, the *Norteamericano* Peter Marchetti, became a good friend, though his whirlwind mission centering around the development of a viable transition to socialism among the *campesinos* precluded more than fleeting contact.

I do believe that had my fortune been birth into a Christian family instead of being set down upon so peculiar, convoluted and excruciatingly long a path to the discipleship of Jesus that I was past life's midpoint by the time I awakened to its possibilities, that I would have become a Jesuit myself. I continue to maintain an interest in matters Ignatian to the present day (See Chapter 14), and the Society of Jesus's mixture of devotion, political engagement on the side of the people, and intellectuality has great resonance.

The idea behind the Popular Church was a simple one: that communities of faith should come forth out of the earth from which their members sprang, and not as authorized by the hierarchy of the church. Nicaragua was by no means the most populous and dynamic center of this movement—a distinction that belonged to countries like Brazil or Colombia—but as it was the center of revolutionary activity at the time, sympathetic souls came in great numbers to explore and share the lived doctrine.

The best known place in Managua for this was Santa Maria de los Angeles in Barrio Riguero. Here the Spanish Franciscan Uriel Molina Ulio from Matagalpa presided; and here one could routinely find a large and vocal crowd of Nicaraguans and *internacionalistas* from the Western Hemisphere and most of Europe carrying out a kind of Gospel, or Pentecostal service, even as the official religion was Roman Catholic, and no doubt while the local hierarchy and the hierarchy all the way to Vatican City sat gnashing their teeth in their elegant quarters.

AT WORK IN THE MINISTERIO DE SALUD

IT WAS ESPECIALLY fortunate that my Nicaragua period spanned the years 1983–1986, for in those years Santa Maria provided the setting for the Italian artist Sergio Michilini to paint the spectacular mural of the Resurrection that set so many hearts beating with joy, especially this one, who was not only experiencing the joy at being of the revolution but of sharing his first Christian service of any kind under the emerging canopy of Michilini's great representation.

Representation of what? Christ, to be sure…. But Christ is polymorphous as He passes through this world; this was not Piero's Christ solemnly rising over the sleeping soldiers, nor of course was it the dead Christ we see when viewing the image of Che slain by CIA thugs in Bolivia in 1967—which image could readily be transferred to Sandino and Fonseca. No, Santa Maria's Jesus was a muscular *campesino* youth, perhaps a resurrected Che or Sandino, with something like a turban on his head arising as from a whirlwind and descending into a turbulent crowd, whoosh!: Christ as revolution now, awakening the long slumbering Nicaraguan soul, as Blake, fond of whirlwinds himself, would make Albion rising the core of his Resurrection of Britain and humanity itself.

All of this was tremendously exciting and got the revolutionary juices flowing. But as it was spectacular, so could it turn one into a mere spectator event unless grounded in humble everyday practice. I planned my 1986 sojourn, therefore, about a number of useful activities—working with the Marie Langer group and the *Ministerio de Salud*; doing some sociological research into the condition of women within the revolution; traveling to the Atlantic Coast where conflicts had arisen between the FSLN and the English speaking people of the Miskito Coast: all well and good, but beside the main point, which was to deepen my relationship to Christ Jesus.

For this I needed a base of operations close to day-to-day life of liberation theology. My home base, then, should be a Christian base community, paradigmatic of how an emancipated church could arise autonomously from popular activity. There were about twenty thousand of these in Latin America at the time, and as luck turned out, the second one to be formed, in 1966, was San Pablo Apostol, close by in one of the eastern *barrios* of Managua. It was also named *14 Septiembre*, after the date in 1855 when the Nicaraguans expelled William Walker, the first North American imperialist invader of Central America.[8]

Of course, Peter Marchetti was well-connected and could help. He interceded for me with his friend Pedro Joaquín Romero, *jefé* of San Pablo Apostol, assured him that I was no William Walker, and arranged for me to stay there for the duration, indeed in Pedro's own house.

These events were recounted in my somber little book, *In Nicaragua*, published in 1988 in the UK by my ex-Yalemate Bob Young, now of the UK.[9] *In Nicaragua* was written to build solidarity for the beloved revolution, but it also reflected my sadness and rage that the *enemigo* was having its way with it during the time of composition.

As for my own Pilgrim's Progress along the path of Jesus, the experiences of 1986 can be seen from a number of perspectives. No doubt, 1986 had been a major turning point in a life full of swerves,

PEDRO JOAQUÍN ROMERO AND SON BEYARDO ARCE

notably in years that ended in the number six, my point of entry. I had suddenly turned away from physical and mathematical science to medicine at age twenty in 1956; 1966 witnessed my choice for the vocation of writer and the stance of a political radical; 1976 was the year I met DeeDee and began a major change in my personal life; now in 1986, approaching age fifty, I began to confront Christ Jesus.

How these things tend to happen at ten-year intervals is an enduring puzzle—or perhaps a mere coincidence. Perhaps we are like cicadas. Something burrows deep underground; something else resists it until one becomes spring-loaded; the tension builds up, and then, triggered by asynchronous forces, pop! goes the transformation. Ernst Bloch writes of this asynchronicity, as my brilliant departed friend Bill Livant pointed out to me. Our self is, as it were, a woven cord, each thread extending both inside and outside as in a Moebius strip; the distinct temporalities overlap and tug at each other, until a slippage occurs and now the string extends, becomes taut for a while, and the process renews. Long live asynchronicity!

Still I was not yet ready, could only take it so far. My experiences in 1986, especially those at San Pablo Apostol and the *Casa Jesuitica*, were deeply moving. However, there was simply too much that needed to be moved. No longer a tourist of revolution and the workings of the Holy Spirit, I remained unready to become a full participant.

External factors played a role. Once the Sandinista songs and the raptures of Sta. Maria de Los Angeles died down, I returned to a cot in the hallway next to the bathroom in Pedro Joaquín's crowded and hectic household; along with lack of privacy and space for meditation, there was the cursed heat, the chronic hunger (yes, we were on a starvation diet thanks to the *enemigo's* sabotage; I lost about fifteen pounds during my stay), the dreariness of working at the Managua psychiatric hospital along with other bureaucratic nightmares, and the stupendous difficulty of getting around broken down and confusing Managua *sans* street signs, all of this (compounded by poor Spanish) had me struggling just to get by day-to-day, with little strength left over for so profound a decision.

THESE ANNOYANCES WERE of the moment. More deeply, I had to contend with something within myself that conditioned the snail's pace along my path to discipleship, and made it a process of decades punctuated by flashes of illumination through the lattices of my mind. When Richard Sewall opened the gates for me in 1953 with his evocation of 1 Corinthians 13, it was his artistry that did it, molding a breach in the mind of a youngster trembling in the process of a major turning point. Aside from that, there was nothing to receive, shape, and interpret Sewall's message. I had never heard of an apostle, had no idea what the word meant, had never stepped inside a church.

Nor did exposure to actually existing Christians accommodate the process. The Christians I knew in my Brooklyn years were unreal to me, mainly shadowy Catholics from surrounding ethnic enclaves. Unhampered by any actual acquaintance, we regarded them as *goyim* with contempt admixed with distant *pogrom*-shaped fear that these Irish or Italians would invade our neighborhood. When it became my family's turn to move to Nassau County—among the first Jews to settle a mixed Christian suburb on the verge of initiation into postwar America—I felt considerable estrangement for a while, and even some bullying with threats of violence for being a "brain," *i.e.*, getting good grades in school. This came close to actual fights, in which I stood no chance; and got so bad that I would have to hide my report card the day it was handed out, or take a circuitous route home. It all was highly unpleasant, even frightening, and was doubtless a kind of anti-Semitism.

While I didn't spend a great deal of time thinking of it as such, the whole process did nothing to make me regard actual Christianity with anything but distaste and a total lack of interest. Had anybody told me that, 35 years later, I would be pondering a vocation as a Christian, I would have scoffed at the prediction. Nor did my readings in literature and exposure to music evoke anything of practical service. Whatever Dostoevsky was brooding about had no connection at all to the existing Christianity of Baldwin, Long Island—though of course he was no stranger to crimes committed in the name of Christianity, and any Christian who is insensible to this possibility is no Christian at all, so far I am concerned.

In any case, there was no pattern laid down in me in my early years which I could relate to my experiences of liberation theology in Nicaragua. I do think that for a religious notion to take hold it needs to be mediated by much more than the ghettoization of early life. The child needs influential figures to represent a faith to him; the grown-up, to have experience within a community where religion becomes part of a sustaining scaffolding of life. It needs to be part of an ongoing conversation so that those who delay their personal religious revival have something available inside them to recall for the purpose.

Viewed from a different angle, one has to be equipped with the building blocks of prayerful seeking. Otherwise one becomes a Joel Kovel, whose intense religious drive breaks forth in odd ways, such as the impulse expressed at the beginning of this chapter. This was really quite dotty. In blurting to DeeDee that we must found a new religion (I'm quite sure of the accuracy of the wording, which struck me as most odd at the time and stuck in my mind) I was combining the unmistakable intensity of a wish with the utter inability to carry it out. Yes, let's *found* a new religion, since I have no idea really what religion means on the ground and can't *find* one in the world I know, being a Lost Traveller.

FOR SURE, THERE WERE MOMENTS of Grace during my Nicaragua voyages of 1986. There were encounters within the humble confines of San Pablo Apostol, evanescent, ineffable and deeply moving. And there was that evening at the *Casa Jesuitica* toward the end of my time when the Jesuits, Gorostiaga leading, announced that Communion would begin. For them, this was routine. For me, however, it was unsettling in the extreme. How could they do this to me? Didn't they know I was a Jew? I felt trapped, even obscurely angry for being placed in such an embarrassing pickle. Meanwhile, the little voice in my head was chiming: after all, this is what they do, you don't expect them to not do it just because Joel the Jew is there, do you? And anyhow you don't have to do anything, in fact, you can "just say no," as First Lady Nancy Reagan would put it, or even leave with some excuse, or do it but fake it, as… well, let's not go there, and since it will be very embarrassing to leave, why not take the lesser evil and just go through with it; in for a penny, in for a pound as they say, and you really do like these people very much, and life is about living, so… oh no, here it comes…!

The little creatures outside were making their sweet noises as the Eucharist began. Actually Gorostiaga didn't lead, since you can't lead a circle and that's who we were as the body and blood of our Lord circulated and as will happen, came to me. And of course I partook, "for the remembrance of me," as it was said and is said, not knowing if anybody had observed me, and for a very rare moment in my life not really caring what anyone thought of me. I just did it, just was… What? Was Jesus there beside me? Had He finally revealed himself to his foolish lost traveller?

We were winding up. I said my goodbyes, went off into the nameless Managua street. And I will swear to my dying day, not that anyone could disprove me or care one way of the other, but as I traveled along I had a very distinct sense of weightlessness, as though my feet were not touching the ground at all, as though I was gently flying—there is no other word for what I was feeling.[10] When

I got to Pedro Joaquín's the house was dark and I lay for a very long time in my cot neither staring nor not staring, just being there. At length my thoughts resumed.

This was certainly the zenith of my spiritual life up to that point and the moment when I could no longer doubt the reality, to me, of Christ Jesus. Inevitably, it led to the question of where I would go next. The prospect of a formal conversion loomed before me like a gown. I tried it on, thought matters over, and concluded painfully that it would not fit. I was not ready, this I already knew; more to the point, I was not even willing.

Conversion had to be into a definite church. The only church I could think of in this respect was that of Roman Catholicism. And I simply could not see myself belonging to that institution, no matter how wonderful some of its priests. Whether looked at from the perspective of Pope John Paul II and Joseph Ratzinger, his Vatican *consiglieire*, or of its basic organizing principle that celibate male priests rule, the prospective of redirecting my life this way made my skin crawl.

The prospect of conversion also forced me to confront what remained unresolved about my Judaic identity. Jews and Christians were basically Others to each other; I could see that unless I worked this out, the horrid history of Christian–Jewish interrelations would weigh like a millstone around my neck. Yes, I despised Jewish tribalism and the religion wrapped around it. But there was no indifference in my soul about the massive crimes committed by Christian Europe against the Jewish people, not to mention against the indigenous people of the Americas. No Holocaust denier I; long before the catastrophe became a fashionable lament among American Jews after the 1967 war, I had brooded about it, seen the films, read the novels, the tracts, the histories, and felt its immensity. And now I was pondering transforming myself into a Christian because Christ Jesus had called?

At the very least, I realized I still had a lot of work to do, including work of the intellectual kind. There was relief here, since I am never more happy than when allowing myself to become a browser and a bookworm. Thus was launched many an intellectual expedition over the next five years, and beyond: the study for Paul Sweezy of *Monthly Review* of the Vatican's campaign against liberation theology, the twenty-five-thousand-word monograph about Wojtyła I called "The Theocracy of John Paul II" and published in *Socialist Register*,[11] and the book I will describe in the next chapter that was to be published in 1991 called *History and Spirit*, written in response to my inundation by so many spiritual questions in so short a time.

Alas, sorrow and rage continued to prevail. My return in the summer of 1986 was the most painful parting I had ever known, indeed, had I not a beloved family to return to I might very well have stayed on, in effect and maybe in reality, defecting from the United States and beginning life anew in the South.

Christ would have us forgive... but how is one to forgive an empire willing to lay waste to whole countries in cold vengeance for stepping out of line? When I arrived in Managua in November 1983, a case could be made that the FSLN might just pull off their revolution. By the time I left in July 1986, the Regime Change Gang had pretty much had its way with Sandinista Nicaragua—mining its harbors, "making the economy scream," to use the phrase applied to Allende's Chile, creating the Contras who gave to barbarism new levels of meaning, using unparalleled control over the media and propaganda systems for the purposes of demonization, as still continues,[12] intimidating solidarity movements (including the setting up of concentration camps by the newly hatched Federal Emergency Management Administration, just in case things got out of hand[13]) and so forth.

I could see the demoralization happening before my eyes by 1986, as internal splits emerged in the Sandinista directorate along with the corruption that would follow, and it broke my heart.

Hate became searing disgust and loathing upon landing in Miami, perhaps my least favorite place on earth. Henry Miller's phrase, "the air-conditioned nightmare," comes to mind—the neon joy, white sun glinting off acres of sunglasses, flabby suntanned legs sticking out of Bermuda shorts, predatory smiles. I could not bring myself to phone Rose Kovel, ninety miles to the north in Century Village, and tell her I had landed in the good old USA. Anything remotely honest could have given her a heart attack.

The rage continued. When the electoral defeat of 1990 happened and senile Ronald Reagan was brought forth to bless the result, I literally had to be restrained from attacking the TV set on which his image appeared and smashing it. A sore loser, I, and a world-class hater.

Notes

1 Erdman, "The Marriage of Heaven and Hell," 39.

2 Today we speak of "indigeneity" or "First Peoples," eschewing the negative connotations of Primitive, whose chief definition Stanley gave as "primary." Sometimes the designation of "state-free peoples" is used. The difficulty is intrinsic to the human condition.

3 Reports confirm a wave of triumphalism in Washington after the toppling of the Maurice Bishop government of Grenada and the murder of Bishop himself. For a while in November, an actual invasion of Nicaragua was actively being discussed, a matter of habit as the U.S. had landed troops there 14 times in the past 150 years.

4 A great earthquake had largely leveled Managua in 1972; and Somoza's frank absconding with the relief funds both left the city a wreck and sealed his own fate by turning the liberal bourgeoisie away from him and to a degree toward the FSLN. This in turn played a role in hamstringing the revolution—the U.S. Embassy remained opened and the CIA worked freely on behalf of the counterrevolution. In those years, Nicaragua was a close second to Haiti as the poorest country in the Western Hemisphere.

5 Four of our six children spent time in Nicaragua. Besides Ezra, Jonathan went down to help build a school; Peter wandered extensively through the country and nearby Costa Rica; and six year old Molly accompanied DeeDee and me in 1985, at which time the photograph of her on my shoulders at a rally in support of Miguel D'Escoto's hunger strike was taken.

6 Many years later, in 2010, D'Escoto would continue to irk the *enimigo of humanidad* as President of the UN's General Assembly.

7 Ernesto Cardenal, *The Gospel in Solentiname* (Maryknoll: Orbis Books, 2007).

8 This date does not correspond to the moment of Walker's expulsion recognized by U.S. historians, which was sometime in December 1857. But the Nicaraguans are entitled to their own recounting. In any case, Walker's story is compelling and paradigmatic in the extreme, *viz.*, the two remarkable films, Gillo Pontecorvo's *Burn*, of 1969, and Alex Cox's *Walker*, of 1987.

9 Joel Kovel, *In Nicaragua* (London: Free Association Books, 1988).

10 A confession: I wrote of this incident in *In Nicaragua* and rendered it as less transporting in two senses, making the feelings less intense and their site of action more localized, taking place within the Casa and not on the journey back to Pedro's house. The reason was to keep focus on solidarity with Nicaragua and not on my own inner change.

11 Joel Kovel, "The Vatican Strikes Back," *Monthly Review* 36 (1985): 14–27, and Kovel, "The Theocracy of John Paul II," *Socialist Register* (1987): 428–479.

12 In September 2013, Bill de Blasio, running for Mayor of New York, was softly skewered by *The New York Times* for his youthful indiscretion of working in Nicaragua and loving the Sandinista Revolution. In March 2016, Hillary Clinton, the Deplorable candidate, denounced Bernie Sanders for similar sentiments.

13 My deceased friend, economist Herbert Schiller, recalled to me an incident in the 1980s when he overheard two tycoons conversing about the Central American solidarity agitation of the time during a high-level meeting at which he was presenting. "Yes," said one to the other, "if this gets any worse, we'll have to install fascism."

Chapter 9
No Direction Known

"If it weren't for the honor I'd just as soon not have been blacklisted."—Lee Hayes, of "The Weavers," from the film, *Wasn't That a Time?*

The reader may have been wondering during the recounting of my voyages to Nicaragua, how did this Professor of Psychiatry, once the director of a training program at a prestigious medical school, find the time in the midst of his busy career and clinical practice for such an extensive journey? Well, that's no problem at all if one does not have a psychiatric career and clinical practice to be in the midst of. And in fact, by the time of my extended journey to Nicaragua I had been forced from my academic post and closed my clinical practice. I was out of a job and without an income. As Dylan's "Like a Rolling Stone" put it, I was, if not a complete unknown, at least a man with no direction known.

Trouble surfaced late in 1978, when my promotion from Associate to Full Professor at the Albert Einstein Medical School was denied by the committee in charge of such things on the grounds that I was not teaching my trainees proper psychiatry but rather corrupting their minds with the writings of a certain Herbert Marcuse. That was upsetting but also somewhat amusing, and even a bit flattering. After all, who wouldn't be pleased to be placed in the same company as Socrates?!

The personal crisis passed before I had to bother with mustering a defense. As soon as the Old Left Guard[1] got wind of the redbaiting, they stormed the promotions committee and sternly warned them they could not tolerate the recurrence of the McCarthyism that would have destroyed their careers twenty-five years ago had not America's most progressive medical school arisen to give them a haven. They were not about to see Einstein lose its identity. In no time, I had become a Full Professor of Psychiatry.

There was no ground for complacency, however. The Old Guard, was just that: old, and fading as time had its way with them. And Einstein was in fact losing its identity under the pressure of the neo-liberalism set loose by the great accumulation crises of the 1970s. The class polarization that has reached atrocious proportions today, engorging the upper echelons and battering those below, was gathering then. It pretty well annihilated the aura of populist progressivism that had eased my early days in the profession, leaving me feeling increasingly exposed and isolated, and forcing me to contend with ideological currents that had been muted during my early days as a psychiatrist.

One response was to write my first Marxist publication, "The American Mental Health Industry" (see Chapter 7), which regarded the rampant reduction of mind to brain that characterized the loudly cheered "biological revolution" in psychiatry as a replacing of living with dead labor, while bringing the whole system under authoritarian control—in other words, trouble ahead for this radical doctor. As the decade of the '70s drew to a close with neoliberalism's foot firmly on the accelerator, I could expect the arrival of a personification of the shift as a kind of nemesis.

His name was Herman van Praag, and he showed up in 1981, fresh from Holland's Utrecht medical school as our new Chairman of Psychiatry, a vigorous, thickly accented man who liked to peel and consume grapefruits at committee meetings. Nobody knew who chose Herman, or how, save that it was the work of a hidden power with a solid interest in biological psychiatry. Said power was remarkably insensitive to certain details of van Praag's history, such as the fact, discovered from Dutch contacts, that he had been driven out of Utrecht by a coalition of students, junior psychiatrists, and patients because of certain shenanigans in his research methods. His swift transfer to the United States made one think of our country's receptivity to other deposed right-wing dictators like the Shah of Iran and Imelda Marcos.

We now had a chairman who firmly believed that the mind was a secretion of the brain and who meant to shape Einstein psychiatry accordingly. Van Praag held other views pertinent to a medical school affiliated with Yeshiva University. He boastfully opened his inaugural address before the massed department (being nicely sensitive to the protocols of European universities): "My name is Herman van Praag. I am a Zionist, and I am a psychiatrist...": first things first for Herman. This was a long way from the position of our founder Milton Rosenbaum. However it was a way along a definite path, and set me thinking about Zionism in a quite different light, seeing it as a component of empire. It was, recall, the time when the Likud Party had taken more-or-less permanent command of the Israeli state. This soon enough degenerated into the massacres at Sabra and Shatila, and appeared in domestic phenomena such as the Jewish Defense League under Meir Kahane. Nor could I overlook the announcements in our public relations handouts that our dean had spent the weekend in Palm Beach—no longer, it goes without saying, the exclusive watering hole for *goyim* aristocracy—and returned with big bags of money for the nourishment of medical science at Einstein.

The writing on the wall now had acquired an additional meaning. Though quite a while remained before I became an active antagonist of the State of Israel, the presence of van Praag deepened my alienation from Zionism in context of a sharp decline in authority and prestige. Once active in all academic decisions, I now stood by and watched my influence vanish along with the "red residency" program.

It drew me closer to Stanley Diamond's program at the New School, which helped lead me toward Sandinista Nicaragua in 1983; indeed, any destination that could take me away from those cold white buildings in the East Bronx was welcome.

I did not realize how far downhill things had gone until the day, I believe it was in 1984, I looked at my desk calendar at the medical school and realized that there had been no entries for three years— years of fruitful activity essentially external to my Einstein professorship. As the connections frayed, the question became not whether a forced separation would happen, but when and how.

I was taken aback by the crudity of the blow. Would Dr. Kovel please come to the director of the service on which he worked at the Bronx Municipal Hospital Center, and make arrangements to begin filling out time sheets for the hours of each week's work there? For he is an employee of the New York City Health and Hospitals Corporation, and since all employees have to fill out time sheets showing they put in their forty hours a week, so must he begin doing the same. A simple syllogism, this, which rested on imposing a reductive identity between myself and other workers. This was rather clever; it essentially said to me, well, Professor Kovel, you have been defending the salaried workers all these years; now we will rub your face in the fact that you are one of them. Nobody bothered to point out that my intention was not to join the workers in filling out timesheets, but as a socialist, to raise the workers to the level where nobody would have to fill in timesheets, an odious reminder of capitalist exploitation.

As matters unfolded, Jerry Oppenheim, the shrewd Jewish-Buddhist lawyer I had hired, told me that what they were trying to do was a breach of my contract with Yeshiva University. Chairman van Praag and Medical School Dean Purpura knew very well that this would not stand up in court. They just wanted to give me a hard time and drive me out. To respond on the best possible terms for myself, I would have to give them a hard time also. And so, on advice of attorney, I took to wearing a "wire," a nifty little Sony tape recorder in my inside jacket pocket. Having mastered the technique of turning it on and off surreptitiously, I carried my wire into the goodly number of heated and nasty meetings that lay ahead between myself and the administration, during which I refused to comply with their demands and endured their bullying. At length a one-on-one meeting was arranged with Dominick Purpura, a rather nice man when he was not being a Dean. After the pleasantries, I got directly to the point: that thanks to my wire I had in my possession a great deal of evidence that a judge would enjoy reading as examples of violations of my basic rights by Einstein psychiatry and medical school. "Hmmm..." said Purpura, and excused himself. He returned a few minutes later to say that inasmuch as almost twenty years of exemplary service to the medical school seemed to be running down, how would I like to have a sabbatical leave that, unlike the ordinary kind, would not be accompanied by a pledge on my part to return at the end? In other words, he was offering me a "terminal sabbatical": half a year's salary and gone. I thought it over for about ten seconds, agreed, and put an end to twenty-eight years of medical career.

I did not take my parting from Einstein with philosophical detachment. Twenty-eight years may be instantaneous in relation to the universe, but not at all to the time line of a human life. There was much to miss from my Psy days, much to regret, and frankly, quite a bit of fear, too, not yet offset by faith in God's grace.

Happily, I was not alone. DeeDee was a great source of strength, love for my children Jonathan, Erin, and Molly, sustained me, friends rallied to my side, fond farewells took place among Einstein folk, and Gerry Oppenheim, with wry humor, steady countenance, and sagacious repertoire of vignettes from his beloved Japan, provided expert guidance and calmed my nerves.

But this is a way of saying that there was a lot of nervousness that needed to be calmed. I had been slammed against the fact that for all my quirkiness and Sturm und Drang, life had until then been rather easy and sheltered. The years had succeeded each other each with a plan, a provision for my care, and with little worry as to how I was going to make my way in the world. There was this, too: that however I may have rebelled against Rose Kovel's program for worldly success, I was by no means indifferent to success itself. I was accustomed to being lionized, to be quicker-witted than others, the brightest boy in the class, the rising academic star. And now…? Well, Humpty Dumpty had had a great fall, had he not? I had felt the hot breath of rage from those in power; they had wanted to get rid of me, and they succeeded. Now I was on my own, no direction known… How does it feel?

Well, complicated. Deeper emotional currents would emerge, as major decisions surfaced and forced my hand, chiefly in planning my major trip to Nicaragua in 1986 and deciding what to do about my small private practice. Until then a sidelight, being a psychotherapist now loomed as the most reasonable way of making a living. It

JOEL AND DEEDEE

AT WORK ON *THE AGE OF DESIRE*

would have been quite possible to do so. I had a good reputation and a professional niche as the shrink for leftists and free spirits concerned lest they be steered into conformist pathways. I also had a nice office in one of New York's fabulous locations, the Apthorp at Broadway and 79th Street, where during our clandestine courtship DeeDee and I had done certain pleasant things to test the versatility of a psychoanalytic couch.

SO IT WENT across the board: a relaxation of the fetters of professionalism, a becoming of the irregular person

I happened to actually be. She was a wide-ranging artist, filmmaker and educator of radical propensity with a tremendous range of connections. I became friends with a number of these, for example, Richard Serra, Nancy Holt, Yvonne Rainer, and Joan Jonas. In 1977 I worked alongside Serra in filming DeeDee's great documentary, *Bronx Baptism*, and testified on his behalf in 1985 when the government took down his sculpture "Tilted Arc" in front of the Federal Office building in Lower Manhattan.[2]

I owe the expansion of my life to DeeDee, including a freeing up of my writing, or at least the process thereof: witness a photo of me from the summer of 1979, taken by DeeDee great with Molly in her womb, as I sat wild-haired on a yellow plastic milk carton working on *The Age of Desire* in longhand on an oil drum at fiddler Joe Kennedy's place in Inverness, Nova Scotia, while Jon, Erin, and Tovey scampered around. Yes, it was quite wonderful, for all the rough edges.

Now, eight years out, my career had tanked, despite, or rather, because of how much had been freed up in me. Meanwhile DeeDee, ceaselessly active, was finding new pathways of recognition. It came about that one of her radical ventures, "Paper Tiger Television," an Anarcho-Brechtian dissection of the capitalist media, had as its inaugural guest Professor Herbert Schiller, critic extraordinaire of the consciousness industry, on leave from his post at the University of California San Diego's Communications Department. Schiller was so taken with DeeDee as to secure for her a Visiting Professorship for an academic quarter at UCSD in 1984. This resulted in an invitation for a full-time post in the department with "security of employment," *i.e.*, tantamount to tenure: not half bad for an Antioch College dropout with a high school diploma.

AND SO WE WENT WEST, albeit back and forth, to become a "bicoastal" family until 2001, enjoying—if the word may be used—about a dozen transcontinental drives—though I would also say that these road trips, on which I eventually completed my inventory of all 48 lower states, were in their concentrated *ennui*, seediness and natural splendor, deeply unforgettable, and essential for grasping what a strange country is our United States.

The move entailed liquidating my Psy career once and for all, as the prospect of moving a psychoanalytic office to San Diego proved to be prohibitive. The *coup de grace* came wrapped in sticker shock: $4000 up front for bare bones malpractice insurance. It was money I did not have, for a practice I would have to build from scratch, in an office I would have to find, in a city I did not know, and for the sake of a profession that made me queasy. What could go wrong? So goodbye Apthorp with the magnificent courtyard, goodbye to the good things and the bad. I had been forced finally to do what I should have done years before.

Bill Schaap, dear comrade, and with Ellen Ray—both departed in the past year—a leading voice of the anti-imperialist left, pronounced the city to be "a fur-lined coffin." Not to be outdone, Bob Adelman, Professor of History at UCSD, explaining his decision to commute 150 freeway miles from Los Angeles, saying of the university that it was a place where "the bland teach the blond."

San Diego itself, speaking through its PR apparatus, calls itself "America's favorite city"; or is it our "finest" city? Take your pick. But keep in mind that what is fine about San Diego is pretty much the setting: the sky above, the ocean to the west down spectacular cliffs, the mountains and desert to the east, and Tijuana and Baja California to the south.... Oh yes, it also featured one of the first iterations of Trader Joe's, apotheosis of intelligent consumerism.

The city inside these wrappings was as desolate as dishwater beneath its sheen, riddled with militarism when we arrived, and with a mixture of hi-tech blather and ultra-consumerism by the time we left in 2001.

UCSD had been constructed amidst eucalyptus trees on a defunct marine base in the spectacular suburb of La Jolla, overlooking the Pacific. In its early years the school had been the home of Herbert Marcuse and the site of much agitation. As this withered, so, it seems, did Herbert, who passed away shortly before my arrival. Meanwhile, the university—to whose spontaneous protests Marcuse added a rare degree of philosophical depth—had settled down to become the economic engine of San Diego, sowing the land with high-tech blessings as the bland taught the blond. (Did you know it had a whole building to develop the magnetic stripe on your credit card?)

It was not a total loss, but a dead-end nevertheless. I easily found some visiting-professor jobs teaching at UCSD and San Diego State, enjoyed them to a degree, and even toyed with the idea of staying on. But the shoulder encountered for this was cold, and my ambivalent reaching out for a permanent post found no takers.

I rolled with the blow and began casting about for some grant support to do a writing project. The Guggenheim Foundation came to mind as a source potentially open to odd fellows like myself. On one of my visits to New York I sought out friend and benefactor Ping Ferry. We conversed about this and that until eventually the name of Joseph Needham came forward, who happened to be a close friend of the marvelous Ferry. I had admired Needham from afar as the polymath who forsook a brilliant embryological career to chronicle the history of science in China, a stupendous intellectual achievement, and one of the greatest single enterprises by a scholar (a Christian socialist, no less) ever achieved. This was very much after my own heart, though it would be more precise to say that it was after my own frustrated hopes for myself.

Ferry and I hammered out a grant proposal, contacted Needham, and won his support. The plan was for me to go over to Cambridge and spend time with Needham at his research institute, returning to do a kind of portrait of the man and his work. I put it into the application form required by the Guggenheim people, sent it off, and awaited the reply. It was not my first such application, and as I knew it to be a kind of a stretch, awaited the usual perfunctory and polite rejection.

It was rejected all right, politely though not perfunctorily. There came back a substantial statement that my proposal was indeed unsupportable by the Foundation, chiefly because it seemed as though I was trying to reinvent myself, which the Guggenheim did not support. But there was more, and it shook me: why not, wrote the man whose letter is buried deep in disorganized files in my attic… why not be true to yourself and seek to extend what you have already done, building on your encounter between great intellectual traditions and adding to them other dimensions? The implication was clear: the foundation actually wanted to support me. All I needed to do was to be true to myself and a Guggenheim Fellowship was mine.

It was not lack of achievement that had held me back but lack of faith in myself, faith to go onward despite external rejection, faith to offset the baying of the "yaller dog," the savage specter that has accompanied me through the years, nipping at my heels.

How nice that a mainstream, "bourgeois" foundation (which the proper Marxist is to dismiss as a tool of capitalist reproduction) filled in that blank, doing for me what I was incapable of doing for myself, urging me to act on a favorite proverb of Blake: that if a fool were to persist in his folly, he would become wise.[3] It seemed that my whole life had been a wrestling with angels and devils, pausing to drag some figure into service as a scaffolding for self-construction until, wearying, I would toss him aside and resume the quest. So it had been for Bernard Knox when I was an undergraduate; or the Unknown Physician the reading of whose obituary suddenly led me in the direction of medicine; or Freud himself in the summer before P&S, when I actively mused on the points of similarity between us; or any number of psychoanalytic supervisors, all sacked in short order as having feet of clay; or a pantheon of great Marxists galore, ditto… and now Joseph Needham, discharged with full honors.

Two years had passed since I was bounced from Einstein, and a year and a half since I had hit a wall in Nicaragua. I had looked down on writers who write the same thing over and over. But repetition is one thing, continuity another, and development is its talisman. The decision to persist gave hope of continuity to a writing career that until then had been rather disjointed and *ad hoc*: first racism, next psychotherapy, next Marx, Freud and my Psy career, next Freud and Marx from all angles, next nuclear terror, next Nicaragua; what now?

Pondering this, I arrived at the obvious yet difficult truth that I could be nobody other than myself, and that there was enough in me to warrant following the path I had already staked out. Standing on the ground offered by the Guggenheim letter, I realized that what had to be done was to incorporate the sundry spiritual phenomena that had come forth over the years into a comprehensive study of the human spirit itself in relation to the world we make and inhabit. So many spirit-forms emergent, so many that one would have to conclude that spirit was a natural, existent power of humanity, as basic and integral as the capacity to transform nature... ultimately, the Self that marks us as a distinct species; is it not equivalently a voyager through the cosmos, as the open gaze of a newborn unifies human being and nature?

> Every Night & every Morn
> Some to Misery are Born
> Every Morn & every Night
> Some are Born to sweet delight
> Some are Born to sweet delight
> Some are Born to Endless Night...[4]

Blake would be my Virgil, accompanying me through the forests of the night, not tracking the rationalized logic of Hegel but an eternal dream of a lost traveller, seeking to awaken at land's end.

It was child's play to comply with the Guggenheim request. In short order a fellowship was mine, enabling eighteen months of delighted browsing and synthesizing. *History and Spirit: An Inquiry into the Philosophy of Liberation* had been launched.

I went to the ziggurat-like UCSD library and spent some days poring over the twenty-plus pages in the big *Oxford Dictionary* devoted to occurrences of the word "spirit" and its congeners in our wonderful English language. And then I classified them. There was "spirit" as the manifestation of power, especially through the breath, hence a materialist aspect (as in "inspired," or used by Reich); there was "spirit" in the sense of an occult person (as in demons, ghosts and poltergeists); there was "spirit" in the sense of an inner truth (the spirit of an agreement); there was "spirit" in the sense of negation to the flesh, especially in the erotic sphere; and there was "spirit" in the sense of the deity, or Supreme Being. Five chapters now, and with some introductory and concluding material, I was ready to go.

Well, somewhat ready... because *History and Spirit* was like a train I had been waiting to ride for a long time, and when I climbed aboard, it was with a lot of baggage in tow, with other baggage to be picked up and dropped off here and there. Its writing resembled that of *White Racism,* each worked on during a hiatus of meditative leisure along the Pacific Rim: the earlier, Seattle-bound venture, a reflection on a variegated experience of race and being under the thumb of the war machine; the later, San Diego *opus,* a pondering on cliffs over the vast blue-green sea of the adventures I had undergone since the awakening to Christ in 1977, and the retribution by the System for my getting out of line. Its context remained the wars waged by Empire to control lands inhabited by the wretched of the earth. I had foolishly thought my ideas *ipso facto* had transformative power, not taking into account that they were not rooted in any concrete praxis on my part aside from writing....

Who would have thought that my eminent, and eminently civilized, Boston publisher with a glowing progressive resume, Beacon Press, which had carried Herbert Marcuse to fame on these shores, would treat me so coldly once they received the manuscript? Could it have been that my growing hostility towards the treatment of Palestinians by Israel was taken with resentment by the publisher? Or that this response would foreshadow the kind of treatment I would receive in similar so-called progressive enclaves twenty years later after the publication of *Overcoming Zionism*?

Well, I don't actually know. I just know that Beacon became remarkably uninterested in *History and Spirit,* which passed sedately away, leaving scarcely a trace behind. It was doubly bitter, in that to publish in the U.S. I had to take *History and Spirit* away from Robert Young, my Yale friend from Texas turned British publisher (and radical historian of science, ex-Cambridge Don, and Kleinian psychoanalyst), who really wanted to work with me on the book. And so I ruined what had been a strong friendship, as well as a fruitful alternative to my Psy career.

All in all, it was a lowpoint in my life—though, as is often the case, life went on. Even *History and Spirit* went on, finding favor in Turkey, of all places, where left-oriented folk wanted to find a way to overcome Kemal Ataturk's ruthlessly anti-spiritual modernization. And a bit later, two very dear and great-spirited Vermont friends, Grace Paley and Bob Nichols, started an alternative publishing house, Glad Day Books, named after a Blake watercolor, and gave my "Inquiry into the Philosophy of Liberation" some renewed shelf life.[5]

Vermont increasingly came into focus during this period, and I often contemplated moving there, as the Green Mountain State became known as the People's Republic of Vermont. There had arisen two centers of

WITH GRACE PALEY AND BOB NICHOLS
IN THETFORD, VERMONT

radical activity that caught my attention: the Institute of Social Ecology, of Burlington and Plainfield, directed by Murray Bookchin, whom I had known since *Telos* days in the mid-seventies; and the Bread and Puppet Theater, of Glover in the Northeast Kingdom, Peter Schumann, director.

Bookchin's group attracted me first, as it was evidently congruent with my intellectual interests and the search for a radical political alternative. One large factor got in the way, however: Bookchin himself, a most peculiar person, who left a trail of broken relationships behind him that clouds his authentic legacy, which was to draw attention to the rootedness of the emerging ecological crisis in a pathological society.

I wrote a long critique of Bookchin in the mid-nineties, and will leave the discussion there, except to say that a good friendship survived the unpleasantness: that of John Clark, the anarchist philosopher who was for a while a disciple of Murray, and with whom much has been shared over time.[6]

Bread and Puppet was a different story entirely. It goes back fifty years, to the time that DeeDee and her three young boys encountered Elka Schumann and her five children on New York City's Lower East Side. Many years later, the firstborns of each—Tamar and Ezra (now my stepson)—having started as playmates in a sandbox in Tompkins Square Park, now joined in a life partnership. So the Schumanns and I are family. Long before, DeeDee had begun associating with Peter's workshops and political street theater, and after the entourage had moved to Vermont, with his expanded pageantry and communitarian projects.

After 1982, I came aboard, and we began more extensive contacts in their rural setting. It has been a rare year since then that some time has not been spent with Bread and Puppet and its extended network; and the major friendships that grew out of this nexus, such as dear departed Grace Paley (beloved writer) and Bob Nichols (my companion in Blake, and sometime publisher), have been integral to our lives.

Peter Schumann remains *sui generis,* a man hard to imagine in this etiolated age of panderers and compartmentalizers. A simple chronicle of Bread and Puppet will take years to compile; indeed, I doubt it can be done. There is one pedantic literal account by a chronicler, Stefan Brecht (yes, the son of Bertolt), comprising two very thick volumes and breaking off in 1986. Meanwhile Schumann waits for no one—though the shadow of age has begun to appear on his brow. This is not to say that he works under any pressure or is in any kind of rush, only that he never ceases and barely pauses. Nor seems ever to doubt—this in the sense given by Blake, that "If the Sun & Moon should Doubt / Theyd immediately Go out"[7] —that is, the creative force is a function of direct access to universal energy, subjectively registered as spirit-power.

Blake had severe down-spells; we all have down spells, so I suppose Peter Schumann does, too. I would not make super-human claims for him; he is certainly not flawless. He just keeps rolling along, amazingly oblivious to what the world thinks of him, never rushing, yet flowing prodigiously. In 2014, Schumann, nearing eighty, did a colossal mural at the Queens Museum. It must have covered two-thousand-square-feet, and he finished a draft without benefit of cartoon in two-and-a-half-hours, working on a spindly ladder, supported by assistants feeding him gallon cans of black paint.

Schumann's prodigious output—in dance, painting, puppet-making and other sculpting, theatre both large-scale and small, even literature (he turns out hundreds of illustrated booklets, along with other texts written in a fine hand) and musical performance (he plays two horns simultaneously to announce his pageants, and gives screeching "fiddle lectures," on the foibles of the world)—is predicated on a number of core themes: the torments of history rendered in monstrous form, the resistance of common people *en masse* to this, and hovering over all, a distinct though never explicit Christian eschatology with pagan, chiefly Celtic, overtones.

Thus his circus is called "Bread and Puppet's 19th Annual Domestic Resurrection Circus." The monster Peter painted on the wall of the Queens Museum was called "The Shatterer"; it was a central theme of his 2013 work, and an adaptation of what J. Robert Oppenheimer, walking away from the "successful" Los Alamos nuclear test, channeled from the *Bhagavad Gita*: "Now I am become Death [i.e., Shiva], the destroyer of worlds".... It represents all that is meant by the plague of nuclear power/weaponry down the decades and since the first machine was employed for desolation.

The paramount theme for Peter is enacted each day at dawn when he walks from his house toward his brick kiln to begin the day's baking. As he likes to say, you can't eat art, but it feeds you. He and I talked about this once, and why the theater was named Bread and Puppet and not Puppet and Bread: it is because feeding of the audience with bread baked that day from whole grains freshly ground and mixed with water is the foundation of his aesthetic, and of the remarkable theater through which thousands of young and old artists and artisans have moved over the past half-century. What other artist has ever fed those who work with him and those who witness the work—and so consistently! No doubt, Peter Schumann, born in Silesia in 1934, victimized by the Second World War and forced to migrate by the war machine and hence a charter member of those refugee populations whom he has unceasingly created over the years, is the materialist artist supreme.

If so, then what is built on that foundation is not simply art- work, but also what produces it: the Bread and Puppet community, especially as it has developed at the Glover site in northern Ver- mont into a veritable city of art populated by intertwining circles ranging from the Schumanns to various kinds of cadre that pro- duce the theater and reproduce the means of its sustenance. Much has passed through the Bread and Puppet farm, and much has ra- diated out from it.

THE READER MAY RECALL that I was stage-struck as a junior at Yale when I played Sir Toby Belch in *Twelfth Night* and later acted in a few radical films; so there is something drawing me in from that direction. But at Bread and Puppet, during our ten or so extended stays, I saw my place to be mainly a member of the mass, a hauler of props, or in the performance itself, a spear-carrier or donner of an outrageously ill-fitting and very large mask forcing me to stagger around an open field, often unable to see anything through the eye- slits and getting lost right in the middle of a crowd.

There were some peak performative moments as a member of the supporting crew, as when I got to be one of the three carriers of the right hand of the gigantic Mother Earth puppet as she came over the crest of the hill to save the population from the Evil One; or when we sang Bach chorales or shape-note classics. And there were also times when I could put to some use the concentrated knowledge I had managed to acquire over the years about the ways of the world, advising this group here or there, and of most significance, introducing Peter to the thought of Karl Marx—for he had had no formal education in these sorts of things, even as he produced them spontaneously out of his own being and intuition. But the core of my experience in Bread and Puppet derived from the fact that a sophisticated left intellectual was now contributing common physical labor enabling a vantage from below on the whole of Bread and Puppet as a model society.

I now saw, in living color as it were, the lineaments of what George Dennison, a dear friend of Peter's, had put as the title of the last book he wrote before he died, namely, *An Existing Better World*. Not a perfect world, that is, not a utopia, but something both possible and really better than what exists, something that can be made with the tools and the human beings on hand, something, moreover, that can be seen in sequence with what exists, an intermediate form between the fallen world and the revolutionary transformation it needs. It was a future to our present, a not-yet to the future we demanded. I saw before me the living concept that was to be distilled later on in my ecosocialist work as prefiguration.

Dennison had children who participated in Bread and Puppet from toddlerhood to adulthood. The younger, Michael, began as a prodigy on stilts, perfecting the movements of a very-long-armed gorilla as he whirled about the ring. As he developed into a strapping youth, Michael reached out, or rather, down, to join various work crews who would take care of those spaces where human / natural needs, *viz.*, shitting and pissing, are carried out. That is, he joined the outhouse detail, a considerable effort when audiences in the thousands and performers in the hundreds are expected for the Bread and Puppet experience. After all, what is to happen with the bread and aioli? Eventually, Michael Dennison became, so to speak, the foreman of the outhouse crew, seeing to it that these structures were built, maintained, rehabilitated, and cleaned as needed. He would announce whatever had to be done at the morning meeting where tasks for the day were allocated, and then met with the volunteers later on.

Now, if we were to take a kind of straw poll here, I warrant that the average person would foresee difficulties in recruiting sufficient numbers of workers for Dennison's tasks, given the widely recognized fact that latrine duty is pretty much the nadir so far as the social hierarchy of labor goes. That's what the Untouchables are for, inasmuch as cleaning up excrement pretty much defines the bottom of society's pyramid of value. Important philosophical glosses indirectly surround this principle, for example, the notable Marxist/ Hegelian dictum that "the realm of freedom begins where the realm of necessity ends," there being little that more combines necessity, displeasure and unfreedom in everyday life than dealing with piss and shit. And who has not heard—or even said so him or herself— that the reason socialism or communism would not work is that we are always going to need lesser kinds of people to do lesser kinds of work like cleaning latrines so that the higher people could do higher things?

How strange, then, that Bread and Puppet would draw to itself such bizarre folk as would actually want to do Michael's outhouse duty, and think of it as a kind of privilege. For they—which to be sure, included myself—would volunteer in droves to clean out the wastepits. We didn't go alone to clean up, however, but to do so in the presence of others, a presence livened by jokes, laughter and often enough, singing. It was another example of the truth that production is first of all a matter of social relations. That we puppeteers went gladly to do jobs considered onerous by a repressive society had to do with the fact that this was freely-associated labor: outside the money circuits that comprise capital's brain, non-hierarchical except for Michael's benign delegated organizing, and collectively carried out.

Under such circumstances a transvaluation occurs, lightening the weight of civilization and its repression of nature and the body, excrements included (the release of which nature provides as highly pleasurable, for all the disgust it provokes in so many). It all came down to the quality of the labor as expressed through the relations among those who exercised it. The power of this was shown one summer when compelling obligations forced Michael to be unable to take part in the actual theatrical events. But he would not be kept away, rather hopping into his car for a two-hundred-mile drive to Glover from Maine, arriving just in time to assume the leadership of the outhouse brigade, helping to get things ready for the performance, and leaving when he achieved this goal.

It all cut very deep, these lowly matters, deep and far back in our lives, or, as George Dennison titled another of his books, *The Lives of Children*—a phenomenon to which the Gospels are by no means indifferent. Indeed, another remarkable feature of Bread and Puppet, is its fundamental openness to the lives of children, from the extraordinary rendering of consciousness afforded by puppetry, to the sharing, insofar as possible, of production with the children themselves.

This included music-making, as shown by a little incident involving five-year-old Zamir, the adopted son of Grace Paley's daughter, Nora. A whiz and enthusiast on the drums, Zamir could be seen rapping away whenever the Bread and Puppet pick-up band assembled. One morning, in the middle of July, Nora was awakened at the ungodly hour of 5 AM by the importuning of her five-year-old boy:

> "Mama! Mama! Get up! It's time for rehearsal."
> (Rubbing her eyes): "But Zamir, rehearsal isn't for
> another six hours."
> "But Mama, they *need* me!"

THE OLDEST OF THE EXTRAORDINARY PEOPLE I met during the decade of the '80s was Alger Hiss, who was close to ninety at the time. Our friendship came wrapped in thick layers of irony. Hiss had first burst into my awareness at the absolute zenith of the Red-Hunting era of the '40s and '50s, through the sensational espionage trial at which he was accused of passing state secrets to the USSR while working at the State Department in the 1930s. The Satanic trinity of Richard Nixon, Whittaker Chambers, and J. Edgar Hoover succeeded in ruining his career through a perjury conviction which sent Hiss to Federal prison for 44 months. My early acquaintance with Alger, therefore, was drawn from large-type headlines in the daily press as refracted by the fervid imagination of Lou Kovel, who assigned him to the domain of the Evil One. Alger Hiss—Take-One, then—was the fiendish betrayer of everything that was good and American.

Take-two: By the time I met Hiss in the flesh, I would have a very hard time designating *anything* both good and American. Lou Kovel had been gone more than ten years and Alger had spent thrice that amount of time in obscurity, though not inactivity. He had a wide network of friends, some of whom were readers who compensated for his fading eyesight, many of whom he helped with his formidable skills, and who were engaged in proving Hiss' innocence against the massed forces of the anti-communist New York intellectuals—a more or less hopeless task, though it maintained a life-sustaining sense of integrity. Needless to say, Lou Kovel's contrarian older son had studied the case and, having long taken Alger's side, was doubly happy to get to know him in person.[8]

We met at a restaurant for lunch, with indispensible Stanley Diamond the go-between. He thought Alger and I would hit it off, and he was right, at least from my perspective. I found a trim elderly man of courtliness and dignity, exceptional intelligence, and fiercely radical-left views. When the conversation passed into a hot topic of the day, the pounding that Nicaraguan President Daniel Ortega was taking in the bourgeois press for a visit to the USSR, Hiss lashed out with startling vehemence: How dare they! Don't they realize that Nicaragua is a sovereign state, and so forth. The feistiness of spirit endeared him to me, even as it jolted me with the insight, that here was why the American Inquisition wanted his scalp.

In fact, Alger had been a definite threat to the United States ruling classes from the 1930s. Because of capitalism's virtual collapse they had to put up with the New Deal, in which a Hiss could come to prominence. But the last thing they wanted to see was the emergence of a left wing of the New Deal comprised of traditional elites.

The rise of Communism was a major threat, which, however, could be dealt with by anti-Semitism or other nativist devices. However, once blue bloods like Hiss (whose family could be traced back to Maryland in the early seventeenth century) began promoting radical-left change, the possibility for structural alteration in the system was materially enhanced.

Alger fit this bill, precisely because he was not a foreign-derived radical leftist[9] but an American aristocrat of universalist ideals. What a range the man had! Knowing Hiss, one could instantly move to the head of the line for playing the "Degrees of Separation" game. FDR had chosen him to be a top aide at Yalta in February 1945. In other words, he who shook Alger's hand was only one degree removed from shaking the hand of FDR, and that of Churchill and Stalin as well, with all the radiations. Then, immediately after the war, Hiss moved into a top planning position, and became essentially the leading figure in putting together the United Nations, with hands galore from all parts of the world to be shook. He did get around.

To my mind, had this nation moved in a worthy direction after its victory over fascism instead of becoming a National Security State, Alger Hiss would have been a leading figure in the process, perhaps, even, our Secretary of State. That calamity befell him was anything but trivial to the imperial ambitions of the United States and its accompanying rise to Superpower status, bathed in oceans of blood and the ruin of whole societies. There would certainly never have been a Vietnam war in which I could "serve," and experience such desolation as would force me to the radical left. By wrecking Hiss, the powers-that-be had removed his powerful voice. More basically, the Hiss case, like the trial of the Rosenbergs—indeed, the whole anti-communist crusade—were show trials in a reign of terror; they gave the left a battering from which it has yet to recover, all the while leaving some twenty million (and counting) corpses behind.

Hiss never cracked under the pressures of his ordeal, nor in the years following his release. Disbarred and forced completely out of public life, he found outlets for his talent and generosity. One of these was to come to the aid of the youngest college president in

American history, Leon Botstein, whose family of physicians had known Alger in a medical capacity and who had undertaken to be president of two threadbare colleges: Franconia in New Hampshire, and soon after, an equivalently nearly dead-broke institution, Bard, in New York's Hudson Valley.

Lacking experience in the ways of the world, Botstein turned to Hiss for advice, and soon enough, Alger had found yet another outlet for his talent, which helped Leon steer his charge toward solvency. Grateful, imaginative and daring, Botstein did something courageous as well: he bucked the tide of vindictiveness, including significant opposition from his own Board of Trustees, and raised a chunk of money from a wealthy Arizona woman who had been Alger's secretary[7] and wanted to honor him. Thus was born the Alger Hiss Professorship of Social Studies at Bard College, otherwise known as the Hiss Chair.

A big problem with an endowed professorship named after a man so disgraced in the public eye as a traitor and perjurer is finding people willing to bear the obloquy of taking it. The Hiss Chair had been set up on a yearly basis, which dried out a not-very-deep pool of candidates, even as it reduced the exposure of its members to the hazards. Stanley Diamond was one of the first chair-holders, but he was one of the least typical academics one could imagine, and manifestly failing in health to boot. Collectively scratching their heads, the powers that be at Bard College pondered and pondered. What kind of odd fellow with a modicum of academic credibility could be found, what Quixote, to saddle up his Rocinante?

I was in California getting ready to return east when the call came, sonorous and educated. I had been recommended by Stanley Diamond... an endowed chair named after Alger Hiss... what did I think? A presidential appointment, not a tenured academic path, though I would come aboard as a full professor... an interesting college... perhaps we could meet at the Harvard Club and talk it over...?

What!!? After all this time on Highway 61? All the wandering, all the doubt? An endowed professorship, on the left! named after Alger Hiss!

Ah, Fortuna!

Notes

1 Led by pediatrician Lewis Fraad, whose daughters Harriet Fraad and the late Rosalyn Baxandall both became my friends.

2 Joel Kovel, "Statement on Richard Serra's Tilted Arc," in *Richard Serra's Tilted Arc*, eds. Clara Weyergraf-Serra and Martha Buskirk (Netherlands: Van Abbemuseum, 1988): 93–94.

3 Erdman, "Marriage of Heaven and Hell," 36.

4 *Ibid.*, "Auguries of Innocence," 490–493. See especially line 119 to end.

5 Two editions of *History and Spirit*, then. That of Beacon Press in 1991, in hardcover; and that of Glad Day Press in 1997, in paperback. Pretty much the same except for some prefatory material.

6 Joel Kovel, "Negating Bookchin," *Capitalism Nature Socialism* 8 (1997): 3–36, and John Clark, *The Impossible Community* (New York: Bloomsbury, 2013).

7 Erdman, "Auguries of Innocence," 492.

8 And still do. I have no intention of dragging Hiss through these pages except to say that all efforts to establish his guilt can be shown to collapse from tendentiousness, including the preposterous circular "proof" dredged from the Soviet files (which also positively affirm his innocence) in which so-and-so says a man named "Ales" was really Hiss, and then who-and-who discovers this "fact," and repeats it, the dance going round and round through the anti-communist machinery and bulking up, until the "overwhelming proof" was squeezed out of its anus. I pass briefly in this memoir over my 1994 work, *Red Hunting in the Promised Land*, which has a lot to say about the climate of persecution in which such as Hiss have been caught... and me as well, needless to add, as *Red Hunting* became shredded in the *New York Times Sunday Book Review* and disappeared from view.

9 Like economist Harry Magdoff, a major figure at *Monthly Review*, for example, who had been tossed out of the government after WWII, whence he went into business and made enough money to join Paul Sweezy.

CAMPAIGN POSTER DESIGNED BY JIM MELLOR, IMAGE BY BRUCE ACKERMAN

Chapter 10
From Apocalypse to Revelation to Praxis

In June, 1988, it seemed that the Willow Valley would burn up. Day after day the Sun rose in a cloudless sky and radiated intolerable heat upon the earth. Wells ran dry and corn planted in hope withered in thirst. We had owned for seven years by then the 1850 house, its timbers taken from its own trees, and while accustomed to patches of brutal winter, had always looked forward to a heavenly summer. Now Hell had supervened. What had happened?

As it turned out, only a random variation, for heavenly weather arrived by mid-July, nor has a heat wave of such severity returned since. But this one had already set me fiercely brooding. Musing in my garden, I recalled something just read—I believe it was by James Hansen—to the effect that carbon emissions from industrial activity can build up in the atmosphere, trap heat, and lead to climate change, including global warming.

The writer who had conveyed this news had omitted the fact that we lived within a social order dominated by the compulsion to endlessly expand the economic product and its industrial base, from which it follows that industrial expansion is another face of imperialism, and both are subsumed into the accumulation of capital, or as the world calls it, economic "growth." Looking further, one could see that the problem wasn't limited to climate change, as immense as that was, but the whole range of destabilizations of nature wrought by the reigning capitalist mode of production. And if capital was hell bent on expansion, well, we were really up against it, weren't we? The locomotive of history, as Walter Benjamin had put it, was heading straight for a cliff; an abyss lay beyond.

I stopped and looked around at the beautiful valley, and saw it now not statically, as a set of natural and man-made forms, that is, ecologies in themselves, but dynamically, as ecology-at-large disintegrating under the influence of nature's human pest. It made sense to speak of an ecological crisis, emerging from history and reconfiguring history, the resolution of which defines the contemporary epoch and presents it with a radically novel challenge. Had I not been a worry-wart of cosmic proportions, I would not have stumbled through apocalypse and upon this revelation. In any case, the big question loomed: just what are we to do about it?

For everything had objectively changed. I realized, too, that there was a kind of destiny here in which everything I had done up to that time was preparation for the adventure that lay ahead. And therefore everything had subjectively changed as well. All had become grist. The days of dilettantish moping were past.

We are told to look askance on those who profess the intention of saving the world. But what if the world objectively needs saving—or, to put it closer to home, what if those grandchildren one loves so much have been placed on a train to desolation—or on the larger scale, what if we, and innumerable other species, face extinction? Is one to sit back and say, well, it's too big for me to comprehend or to try to change their lot?… or to fall back and put oneself in the hands of the state whose ultimate job as a capitalist state is to ensure accumulation?

How can the infinities Blake tells us can be held in the palm of one's hand overcome the infinite greed of capital's expansive drive? Well, that was my task, which I would have to work out by finding others to share it with. I was both objectively and subjectively in the position of Quixote, no longer young but refusing to go downhill to pasture. Recently reading *Fidel y la Religion,* I learned that Castro had read *Don Quixote,* his favorite novel, six times by the mid 1980s. Well, if it was good enough for Fidel, so be it for me. The time had arrived to go forth, and make of revelation, praxis.

But where?

We now lived full-time in the old farmhouse in Willow, a hamlet of Woodstock, "Colony of the Arts," purchased for a song in 1981

with funds given by Pantheon as an advance for *The Age of Desire.*
At the time Woodstock still retained a considerable aura from its
two streams of glory: politically, as home to three surviving veterans
of the Abraham Lincoln Brigade, I should think, a *per capita* record;
and counterculturally, as having been not only the eponym of the
legendary concert (which took place fifty miles away), but home to,
among other luminaries, Bob Dylan, until he couldn't stand the in-
strusions on his privacy.

Alas, the neoliberal era moved in with us, to bring on the "bou-
tique-ification" of the Colony of the Arts, and a steady erosion of its
radical political edge. We did our best to contest this, but our best
could not overcome the structural ascendance of the local bourgeoisie.

The case of Rotron is instructive: a small fan manufacturer
founded by—who else could it be in Woodstock?—a local Zen Buddhist just after the Second World War, it was the firm base of the
local economy and the best of citizens. Nobody looked closely at
this demure little factory until a local antimilitary collective decided
to do so years later, during the second Bush Administration's Heart
of Darkness in Iraq. We found to our shock that the little fan-maker
was part of a transnational weapons conglomerate, inasmuch as
every weapon system more elaborate than a rifle builds up heat and
requires a fan.

Of course our Peace Collective sprang into action with a full bore
Anti-fan-as-weapon-component campaign. It was perfectly suited
to rouse what we thought to be the slumbering pacifist conscience
of our cutesy little art colony… and found it to be like organizing a
bowl of Jello, for there was no political conscience left in dear old
comfortable Woodstock, once the fount of the counterculture, and
now site of my worst political setback.

A KINGDOM OF THE LIBERAL ARTS

BUT WOODSTOCK WAS NOT ALL that gave me hope after 1988.
I now had an academic home base, a nine-hundred-acre campus
overlooking the Hudson River. There were magnificent trees, a few
traditional buildings and a few modern ones, a pathetic library, and

a lot of peace and quiet. As a boy in love with learning I used to fantasize about a place like this (though not the library), where I would walk about—in academic garb, no less—and talk of high things with high-minded people. There would be no father yelling imprecations, no strife-torn world invading the Arcadian sanctuary of learning. I had nearly forgotten this dream since I stepped into the turbulence of medicine and for many years thereafter. Now it seemed I had arrived in Arcadia, and at a senior level, no less. It was a glory to drive there from my Willow home across the gorgeous Hudson River. I could teach what I wanted and how I wanted, with no more than seven classroom hours a week for two courses, and students of a generally progressive disposition. There were no departmental limits, as I belonged to no department yet circulated through all; there was nobody looking over my shoulder, no need to jockey for academic turf, no need to get caught up in the endless minutiae of committee work, no bureaucracy in my way, plenty of tennis courts, and parking so abundant that I never had to worry about getting a place in my whole twenty-one years at Bard College, in the ghost town of Annandale-on-Hudson, New York. What could go wrong?

The man presiding over this riverine Shangri-La was tall, of a frowning, owlish aspect and formal ways. Reason tells us that Leon Botstein once must have been a tiny baby who needed his diaper changed. But sometimes one thought Leon might be a space alien planted in storied Annandale complete with bow-tie and Adorno-esque affectation, sent by the Gods to rule over the little fiefdom of Bard. This he did by the time-honored means of artful control over the funding process, by which the mainstream of the college's fiscal blood supply originated from a hand-picked Board of Financiers held in place by his charisma, to be dispensed by Leon according to an ethos of Liberal Reason and Academic Freedom.

Bard therefore had a leader who preached a pure progressivism while governing a pure despotism. It was an excellent web to ensnare the liberal will, and it made Botstein larger than life in the eyes of the Bard community. Many a time in my early years did I wonder how the college would ever get by if he were hit by a bus, or was lured to another institution (indeed, it was rumored that he was being considered for Secretary of Education in the Gore administration). Would not the financial spigots be immediately turned off?[1] Would not our tycoons go elsewhere? How helpless the school was against Botstein's power; how fortunate that he was so enlightened. And how ridiculous that power was so centralized in one executive's hands; how much would a decent new-fashioned bureaucracy have been appreciated instead of this arbitrary exertion of authority.

Soon after my arrival Leon and I had a few lengthy and interesting conversations in which we staked out, so to speak, the ground between us. I found him to be always on stage, always wary, and very bright—though not so bright as he thought. It also seemed that Botstein was trying to recruit me as a kind of agent to report to him about the Social Studies Division to which I belonged. He professed a considerable contempt for the hacks working there as he tried to set me up as a trusted insider working with him in a strategic way. So I inferred, and so I desisted—and after a while our intimate conversations wound down and I settled into a long and, for the first twelve years at Bard, pleasant routine.

I soon noticed that the first-rate circumstances of the college had done little to improve the *esprit* of the faculty. A cheerless bunch, they were united only by discreet hatred of their President, which they mainly shared endlessly with each other. By and large, I liked them and they seemed to like me, though there was quite a bit of circumspection in our interchanges, and none of the passion that bubbled so often through cracks in my rambunctious soul. Politically they were mostly on the left-liberal side of things, and seemed grateful for my presence and vicariously sympathetic to it, calling me "the conscience of Bard" and such for my various enthusiasms and outrages.

Hatred of Leon welled forth from his exploitation of the tenure process. I assume it is any college president's prerogative to intervene in tenure. But no one I know of routinely turned this into a show trial, in which, after all the evidence had been painstakingly gathered, the college community would bate its collective breath and wait the definitive decision of the Lord High Executioner concerning the wretch whose career had been placed in presidential hands. It was impossible to avoid the conclusion that every so often Leon would perversely overturn a tenure decision that had seemed overwhelmingly positive according to all the recognized criteria of academic virtue, simply to show everybody who was boss and in whom all the power lay as to the future of Bard. Never did any importuning or petitioning move the Liberal King to reverse an opinion of strategic importance. The inevitable results of these manipulations were, first, to stimulate a coterie of toadies and informers who would sidle up to mid-level administrative posts in the Permanent Botstein Administration; and, second, to secrete the elixir of fear and loathing that flowed through the collective veins of the faculty.

I SAW ALL THESE THINGS THROUGH FILTERS of detachment provided by my professorship. Notwithstanding, I had also to some degree fallen into Leon's web: first, for being a "presidential appointment" structurally outside the circuits of ordinary faculty

ALGER HISS

processes like tenure; and in truth, because I was genuinely grateful to him for salvaging what had been a career in trouble, and with the Hiss Chair, no less. So long as there was no ostensible conflict between us, it would have been bad faith to complain openly about Leon's autocratic ways. So long as I was moving along with my writing and teaching (I was at the time working, first on *History and Spirit*; and later, on *Red Hunting in the Promised Land*), there seemed little reason to stir the waters. I felt the detachment to be a self-betrayal, but could see no other course of action for the near future.

There are times when change comes on little cat's feet. About a year after arriving at Bard, I was asked to welcome the next holder of an honorary Chair in Social Studies, one James Chace, who arrived as the Henry Luce Professor in Freedom of Inquiry and Expression. Here was a title guaranteed to curdle the blood of anyone who had acquired some competence in reading the entrails of the bourgeois ideological apparatus. More troubling still was the chief item on Chace's *resumé,* that he had recently stepped down as Editor of *Foreign Affairs,* flagship publication of the Council on Foreign Relations, steering mechanism of the United States ruling class.

Not to worry: Chace was at pains to dispel my doubts and eager to establish himself as my friend. He was a slender, buttoned-down type who wasted no time establishing that we shared elite Big Three Ivy League status, Harvard to Yale. By way of mollification in advance, Chace also made perfectly clear that, yes, he was very critical of American foreign policy in places such as Nicaragua, and overall, of America's Manifest Destiny grandiosity, about which he had written copiously. Most of all, Jim wanted me to know that his liberalism was *bona fide,* witness the fact that he was at work on his *chef d'oeuvre,* a biography of Dean Acheson, who, as we all knew, had brought down rage upon his head for saying that he "would not turn his back on Alger Hiss." I imagine Chace was very proud to learn that George W. Bush claimed to be reading the Acheson biography during the 2000 presidential race, whether to prove his openness to enlightened imperialism or literacy cannot be determined here.

Many a lunch lay ahead with Chace and his coterie, full of chatter and name-dropping, perquisites of the pleasant life at Bard, with its comforts and Mr. Chips moments. What it was not, and manifestly could not be, was a setting in which the radical implications stirred up by my revelation about climate change could be carried forward. I had found a nice perch, and that was all. A different line of approach would be needed.

THE GREEN ALTERNATIVE

I SPENT A GREAT DEAL OF TIME with the Green Party during the decade of the 90s, building to a full-bore candidacy for the United States Senate in 1998, which I lost by a few million votes—why quibble over the exact amount?—to Chuck Schumer; and as if that wasn't silly enough, an actual race for the Green Presidential nomination in the year 2000. Had only a few things gone my way, these memoirs might be written instead of those of George W. Bush as an ex-President, for he and I, along with a few others, were legitimate candidates for the office up to March, 2000, when a crushing defeat at the hands of Ralph Nader terminated my political career and deprived humanity of all the gifts recounted in these pages.

But I get ahead of my story... and truth to tell, it is not much of a story, for though I could spell out lots of sensible reasons why I, as a man dedicated to overcoming the ecological crisis, should do so as a Green, I never felt comfortable in the actual doing, being too much of an unruly romantic to sit so many hours in stale-smelling church basements, all the while obeying Roberts Rules of Order (or is it Ordure?) and seeking consensus, that refined method of domination.

For the Greens were hopelessly fragmented; worse, they were proud of being fragmented, indeed, celebrated it as a kind of healthy diversity. The more helpless the party, the more removed from power, the more did this *faux* pluralism prevail, generally speaking, as a pack of single issues which could be shuffled about like a deck of cards. Here was a voting-reform Green; there was a vegetarian Green; and over there, an anti-pesticide Green, an animal-rights Green, or a LGBT Green, or a prisoner-rights Green, a zero-population-growth Green, a legalize-marijuana Green, and even a nativist- and anti-immigration Green—or these days, a Green with the temerity evinced by their present leader, Dr. Jill Stein, for a "Green New Deal."

Most vexing was the refusal to foreground the transformation of capitalism among the Ten Key Green Values. The proper Green Alternative to the capitalist beast was to opt, with pride, for the vapid goal of "community-based economics"—a fetish of "small is beautiful" that seals off revolutionary aspiration, not to mention, the dynamics of why and how capital foregrounds the economy as the supreme institution of bourgeois society as it ensnares the masses in debt, tosses millions on the scrapheap, and sacrifices their children to Moloch.

One could sum it up as a structural disability of imagination and intellect, or, from another perspective, a loss of aspiration toward the universal—the notion of totality, or wholeness, that gathers the building stones for Blake's visionary city of Golgonooza. Aspiring toward the universal is, in no sense, escapism. It does not offer a formulaic guidebook like the astrological column of the newspapers. It looks through, not beyond, to the horizon, where the whole and the part maintain their identity and differentiation, where we see the world in a grain of sand as we see the sand in itself. And in so looking, the horizon itself opens. In one of his flights of imagination, Blake called this a "minute particular," saying that "General Forms have their vitality in Particulars, & every Particular is a Man, a Divine Member of the Divine Jesus."[2]

The creative imagination is a sealed book to Green politics, locked into petty electoral mechanisms. Radical politics, in text or on the streets, is like that dance upon which Emma Goldman insisted if she were going to join the revolution. Radical politics, in short, is serious fun, though it can break one's heart as well. I was fortunate to share in some of this during the last decade or so of the second millennium.

AUGUST 1989: MARCHING ON VÖRSTER SQUARE

LIKE MANY OTHERS, I HAD JOINED the upswing in anti-Apartheid politics of the 1980s, and watched with horror and rage as the South African state, assisted by the United States and Israel, sank into an abyss of violent intransigence. As the years wore down toward 1990, some cracks appeared, and a sense that something was afoot.

I was surprised but not astounded then to receive a communication toward the middle of 1989 from the United Democratic Front, the collective of some hundreds of civil-society groups coordinating domestic resistance to the apartheid system. It had decided that the time had arrived to take down the blockade for certain Western intellectuals, who on returning home would spread the news of growing struggle. Knowing of my work, they wondered whether I would like to join one of the first contingents for this purpose, specifically, by contributing to a radical psychology conference to be held in Johannesburg, and following it with lectures at universities in Cape Town and Durban.[3]

I was heading South again, this time to witness the incipient breakdown of a racist/fascist state: not in revolution yet, but poised on its edge. It was also an introduction to a place that would concern me greatly in the years ahead, since my son Jonathan and family have taken up residence in Johannesburg as I continued to be involved across various phases of South African politics. This first visit differed from the dozen or so to follow in being carried out amidst violence. It was a ten-day-long peak experience peaking at its very beginning, when my greeter met me as soon as I went through customs with the urgent message that, "we must hurry, else we will miss the march." This, he explained in the car, was to go to the center of town and proceed to John Vorster Square where police headquarters was located, for purposes of protesting unspeakable violence by the authorities to the resistance, as called forth by a considerable number of broken bodies found at the base of the building, having, as the officials delicately put it, either committed suicide or accidentally fallen from the tenth-story holding area.[4]

I did not realize until we got to the assembly point that I was to be in the first row of marchers. I had of course been on many marches before, many protesting state crimes that were certainly comparable in magnitude to what we were protesting: witness those from the Vietnam era. But their magnitude had been "overall"; and the actions, therefore, were to a degree diffused and abstracted from the locale of what had provoked them. Never had I been at an event of such intensity and immediacy, so adjacent to a major scene of its perpetration, and so confrontational toward its immediate perpetrators. Never had I so felt the actual density of evil; and never had I been so close to its immediate victims, many of them my fellow marchers. I submitted to being used on their behalf in the reasonable expedient of being placed at the head of the column as a white presence from the great American republic in manifest solidarity, even as my feelings of the moment were quite a jumble.

The sensation of incongruence became accentuated when I looked to one side and beheld my immediate companion, Winnie Mandela herself, wife of the incarcerated leader of the ANC, and a fiercely militant figure in her own right. She greeted me cordially.

Later, Winnie was to court considerable trouble in those entanglements that come with the territory of revolutionary aspiration. At this incandescent moment, she was simply radiant, the rays dissolving away the grime of my twenty-hour flight.

The strongest impression came from the mass of marchers in whose midst I now found myself. A mass, yes, but not in the metaphoric sense of the "masses" who are said to be the repository of the hopes of revolutions in a state of latency. That is indeed the status for the great mass of black South Africans, but it was not the case at this moment. In the streets of Johannesburg that day it was no longer a potential but now an immediate, activated force, like the "critical mass" nuclear physicists talk about, that moment in the unfolding of matter when the radiation from each atom extends to others and exponentially can become mutually generative, causing the whole to ignite and be transformed. Here the alpha, beta and gamma rays appeared as the "toy-toying," or yipping war-chants, as in Zulu times and at other, immemorial occasions.

Nobody, certainly not I, is so cut off as to be unable to resonate to such animating calls—nor able to respond with equanimity, for who could not tremble at the implication produced by bodies kicked about so long by Boer overlords. Such is the comparative morphology of the peak experience, by definition a moment of disorder and at the edge of chaos.

It was no kind of smooth elation as I became tossed by currents of solidarity, fear, affirmative joy and hope at being part of this churning mass, which then, however, as if on cue, broke apart and disappeared into alleyways as the gendarmerie appeared with their formidable Kaspars, cartoonish "personnel-carriers," hybrids between tank and paddy-wagon to enforce the Law.

The intensity was sustained over ensuing days, albeit with a more spread-out rhythm and admixed with sightseeing—in Durban, Gandhi's ashram and school where Satyagraha was born; in Cape Town, and its splendor of mountains within a city. Giving lectures was a peak experience, too, for who could remain unmoved speaking amidst barbed wire, tanks, Kaspars, and machine guns? Or by students like the ones who were being slain daily, their solemn images displayed in cenotaphic newspapers? Martyred, then, it seemed self-evident that these supreme sacrifices could never be in vain, as we felt the apartheid system falling apart slowly before our eyes like a mountainside-cleaving avalanche, crashing into the future on the way down.

There was great joy about this among comrades, mixed with good sober thinking that much work lay ahead, that formulae cannot be imposed on history, that contingency will always remain as residue. But there was also something dark and snarky hovering, an idea one wouldn't admit openly to others and scarcely even to oneself: suppose that this was somehow rigged, that the battle between visible adversaries took place against an unseen backdrop behind which it had been settled beforehand.

Nowadays the truth is known though kept out of general view. But there was something of the sort known in 1989 as well. I learned of it shortly before my return home during a somber meeting of insiders from numerous points of the political and racial map, namely, that a deal had been cut between finance capital, especially the big bourgeoisie of Britain and the United States, and key representatives of the ANC. The contours were simple enough: bye-bye to the Afrikaner apartheid order, vanquished and delegitimized, though still capable of much havoc; hello to the new stewards of the South African nation, Blacks in power, provided they would take care of global capital and keep it secure from the Marxist threat. Though Mandela had talked of nationalization and similar breaks with the ruling economic system, it became increasingly evident that he had signed on to the grand compromise, selling his birthright for a mess of cash as he turned the nation over to the International Monetary Fund.

I was to bear some witness to this, indeed, watched Mandela giving away the economy on TV during a later visit in 1997. Eventually I came to play a peripheral role in the struggle over the years ahead, visiting South Africa about a dozen times. These visits were shared with Jon, Pat, Rowan and Liam, who settled in Johannesburg, where Jon became a leading cinematographer and Pat a producer of documentaries, and included a range of radical activities, in Johannesburg and chiefly Durban, at the Centre for Civil Society, where I found connection with Patrick Bond, Dennis Brutus, Ashwin Desai, Trevor Ngwame, Shannon Walsh, and Desmond D'Sa, among others, and finished writing *Overcoming Zionism* in 2006. It was a tough place to be, and the only place where I have been street-mugged (twice). Nonetheless South Africa leaves one with an abiding sense that if you've not shared in its agony, you've not lived. Of course, if you've not lived in pain and sorrow, you've not lived either, and South Africa is structured to deliver world-class misery of social origin. What else can one expect if forty percent of a nation's humanity is thrown on the trash heap for the sake of the accumulation of capital, while year after year the ANC deteriorates into endless, and I should think, inevitable corruption.

FEBRUARY 1994: A FIRE ON THE MOUNTAIN

LUCIUS WALKER WITH FIDEL CASTRO

HOW MANY REMEMBER that Fidel Castro was the Guest of Honor at the inauguration of Nelson Mandela in 1994, while Al Gore watched from the sidelines, gnashing his teeth on behalf of the United States? Or that about five thousand Black Americans ecstatically cheered Fidel at Harlem's Abyssinian Baptist Church a year later, for his contribution to the anti-apartheid struggle? There were about five Whites in the audience that day, one of them myself, as the guest of Reverend Lucius Walker, director of Pastors for Peace, a blockade-breaking organization designed to hamper U.S. imperialism in the Western Hemisphere. The five thousand cheers were for the contribution made by Cuba in the blood of its soldiers, a sacrifice made not in South Africa but in neighboring Angola, where Cuban troops stymied the marauding South African army in 1977, and again, decisively, in 1987. Fidel had intervened in defiance of his supposed master, the USSR, who forbade such "adventurism." But one man's adventurism is another's solidarity, here for the sake of revolutionary brotherhood and because the bulk of Cuba's African slaves originated in what is now Angola, which happens to be on the same latitude.

The standard explanation for apartheid's demise in South Africa is the powerful global boycott movement. This was no doubt an important factor, but a case can be made that Cuban military intervention was decisive, as revealed in the reception given Fidel. I was in Cuba with DeeDee in 1989, and we chanced to see a documentary made by a friend, Brooklyn-born Estella Brava, which shows the reactions of families who lost sons on both sides in the decisive battle of Cuito Carnevale. All mourned and grieved in sorrow. But there was more to it; and the difference was compelling. To draw from the terminology of Ignatius of Loyola: the families of the Cuban soldiers felt consolation from solidarity with the universal, while the South Africans perceived their loss as a desolation in which bodily death became magnified by the collapse of self justifying ethnocentric delusions.[5] As revolutionary solidarity is the universalizing negation of racism, so was defeat at the hands of "kaffirs" no simple military reversal for Boer loyalists, but annihilation of one's imperial being. Hence it was that with their defeat at the hands of Cuba, the masters of South Africa began the liquidation of apartheid.

The lessons loomed large for me, and made me question the strict nonviolence I had reflexively shared with many fellow leftists, to the point of becoming so deeply involved in the War Resister's League in the early 1980s as to be elected to their national Executive Committee. But had not Gandhi said that a man whose house has been invaded is entitled to use violent means to expel the intruders—a principle capable of being extended to those victimized by colonialism and all forms of slavery, where possession by another person extends across all of one's selfhood?

Setting aside the many rough edges of Gandhi himself, I came to believe that one of the great challenges posed by critical discernment is to define a zone of legitimate violence against the depredations of empire and its colonization of the subjugated—not, however, "by any means necessary," or the spirit of vengeance that would send suicide bombers into crowded marketplaces or schools. In sum, ruthless criticism applies to means as well as ends, so that these comprise an organic unity.

John Brown was one of the greatest figures the United States ever produced. His espousal of armed struggle was done under the profound recognition that the depth of evil sedimented into slavery surpassed nonviolent forms of restitution. As he put it just before his execution: "I, John Brown, am now quite certain that the crimes of this guilty land will never be purged away but with blood."

Brown failed in his 1859 raid on Harper's Ferry, though not completely. But the fact is that he need not have failed at all had fortune gone his way. What then, if the raid had succeeded? Could the hoped-for outcome of a widening slave rebellion have occurred? Could escaped slaves and their Maroon counterparts have gone into the Appalachian Mountain fastness and built enclaves of armed resistance impossible for Federal troops to smash? To extend this into a metaphor and also an actual possibility, could there have arisen a kind of "Fire on the Mountain" scenario such as an evocative recent book has called it?[6] A Black Republic, like Haiti, but in contrast to that island nation, unable to be subdued because built on a mountain merging with the great eastern forest, all the while attracting growing numbers of African-descent slaves, along with Amer-Indians, Haitians, and Mexicans, and Bolivarians from around the South into its redoubt, so many were the people who held a deep grudge against the Yankee power whose Monroe Doctrine Simon Bolívar had declared was plaguing the hemisphere in the name of Democracy? Could a victory by John Brown have become so destabilizing a force as to inhibit the development of the United States itself into the predatory capitalist super power that burst upon the scene in the twentieth century, and keeps on rampaging to this day, its racist core playing out in the indisputable revelation of recent years that, indeed, Black Lives *do not* Matter? Might an unafflicted United States have been able to actually develop in the direction of socialism? Only failure of imagination—prevalent in these times—could rule out the possibilities that might have arisen out of the "Old Man's" uprising, had it but a modicum of luck.

It seems to me that over the past half-century Cuba has been the John Brown of nations, and twice fits this bill: first, the survivors of the Granma, luckier than Brown, went into the Sierra Maestra mountains to build a fiery redoubt until they could come down in January 1959 and reclaim the island on which the Yankee overlord had built his plantation and whorehouse. And, once in power, the second phase: the island of Cuba itself became the fiery mountain that Uncle Sam could not subdue for more than a half-century, despite the most ferocious assault ever visited on another country short of actual invasion. Like the house of the Practical Pig in the children's tale, the Big Bad Wolf huffed and puffed, huffed and puffed, and could not blow it down—though needless to say, there were some extremely dicey moments—never forget October 1962!—in which this came close to happening, indeed, when blowing up, instead of blowing down, would be the figure of choice as to Cuba's fate.

When the revolution triumphed in 1959 I was a medical student at P&S, preoccupied with my Reichian experience. Had I the nerve and the political vision, I might have found some way to haul myself to the site of the revolution, as did my late friend Saul Landau, who had become a confidant of Fidel long before Saul and I knew each other. In any case, Cuba would have to wait until I grew into it.

Then 1994 proved the year, and Lucius Walker provided the opportunity. The religious impulse of my Nicaragua period having been displaced into the *History and Spirit* project, its political concomitants raged on, their fires continually stoked by one degree or another of United States imperial violence and perfidy. In 1988, I joined with comrades in ideology critique—DeeDee, Bill Schaap and Ellen Ray, Abbie Rockefeller and Lee Halprin, along with Ed Herman (informally known as the "brains behind Noam Chomsky"), Bill Preston, and others—and undertook a series of initiatives to bring down the beast of anticommunism. We put together a major conference at Harvard in November 1988; and this in turn led to a contract from Basic Books for me do an in-depth study of the overall phenomenon of political persecution in the United States: *Red Hunting in the Promised Land*—the "Red" signifier shifting about between "Red Skins," i.e., the indigenous folk set up for extermination so that the Great American republic could thrive; and Red Radicals, i.e., the "Commies" who stood in the way and also had to be eliminated, "by all means necessary."

The range of this signifier was revealed after the Soviet Union collapsed in 1989. Far from abating the anticommunist savagery, this only freed it up for direction against a prime target, the Republic of Cuba, whose "special period" had dawned. Uncle Sam was definitely not kidding: all stops save direct invasion (which might have succeeded, but at excessive cost) were pulled. It was hard to imagine how this could not succeed; but also impossible to foresee the *élan* with which the defense of Cuba could be mounted.

And so we pitched in, and Lu Walker conceived of a brilliant instrument to actualize this: caravans that would break the thirty-year-old blockade whenever and wherever it could be done. By the end of 1993, Walker had already organized two of these—he called them "friendshipments"—with considerable success, and he was putting together the third as these reflections were taking place.

Lady Luck came once more to my aid, for the Third Caravan would coincide with my first sabbatical from Bard, in the winter of 1994, and would be quite workable from San Diego, though far removed from its sybaritic way of life. San Diego would, however, be one of its points of origin, along with others on a semicircular wheel of sorts touching upon much of the circumference of the country, twelve spokes standing for routes along which material aid for Cuba would be gathered and transported to the launch.

Our path was the most southwesterly, taking us for the first night to Tucson, the second to El Paso, and the third to the hub in San Antonio, Texas. In each spot there were to be rallies and celebrations, the gathering of items and the sleeping on church floors; and at the proximate destination, several days of consolidation and then on to the next main stop, Laredo, where the seventy vehicles carrying some 250 people and a quite impressive cargo—ranging from bandages and ECG machines to some of the trucks themselves—would be readied for the assembly at the entry to Mexico, the crossing of the border, and the long trip to Tampico, at which place the objects would be put on a ship and the *caravanistas* on planes to Havana.

Fun it was, for those suitably disposed. Not fun in the trivial, shallow sense we idly ascribe to children and wrongly oppose to the seriousness of the "grown-up"; rather, fun that follows Blake in invoking the couplet from the *Auguries of Innocence,* where the "Childs Toys & the Old Mans Reasons are the Fruits of the Two seasons."[7] And a fully humanized life claims the whole sequence and moves back and forth through them according to circumstance, sweeping away formalities with a childlike intensity, in a succession of moments that will not let you go even as you are thrilled to let yourself go, on this whirlwind escapade of flouting Uncle Sam, of being part of an actual engagement with the revolutionary world. At last, some payback, after all the *scheiss.*

Here is a culling of memories and reflections from those fleeting days:

• I have endured about a dozen cross-country drives, mostly in moving back and forth from San Diego to New York. These journeys were for long stretches awful, but beyond the boredom, the discomfort, and the bad food, there has at times occurred in the later phases of the trip a kind of mystical unity with the land that compensated for much of the dross. In the case of the 1994 caravan, however, there was no prologue, no deferred mystical unity. I felt exhilarated from the outset, and all the many discomforts and fears blended into and spiced the travail, turning it into, if the phrase be permitted, "a firmament of ecstasy." This stemmed from the consciousness of just how large and how far beyond us was the goal. It entered into and intensified relations with many of the 250 or so who shared the experience, so that we grasped the whole of this landscape as a function of our collectivity. It set off the chronicle of the land and the conquests and genocides and ecocides having taken place on it, now seeking to once more reclaim the prized semi-colony of Cuba[8] over the bones of the dead. Hatred and love commingled, spilled onto the land, and made it more beauteous.

• As for my fellow travellers themselves, some became long-term friends, like Kurt Berggren, a lawyer from Ann Arbor and my roommate and chess companion; others were boon companions of the moment, or, like Jim Mellor, would later join me to direct my campaign for the U.S. Senate. Still others were known according to political type, the merits or lack thereof becoming revealed in the white heat of the political moment, when cohesion and discipline were essential. It was gratifying to see how representatives of distinct political tendencies could pull together under the pressure of circumstance, except for beng nonviolent. Thus would old anarchists and old Communist Party Stalinists set aside their differences and their stubborn individual tendencies under the leadership of Lucius Walker.

There was but one exception to this harmonious tendency; and that lay in the behavior of a good-sized and compact contingent of Trotskyists under the banner of the Socialist Workers Party. These chaps insisted upon absenting themselves either in the middle of or directly after every political meeting, and not sharing any of their councils with the rest of the caravan. This eventually led Walker to lose his temper—and, when admonitions proved ineffective, actually go to the extent of throwing them out of the caravan, to general relief. If only the pestilence of sectarianism could be as effectively contained in all cases, the better world would be much closer.

• Gathering at San Antonio and then Laredo, the caravan ceased being a rollicking excursion through nodes of solidarity. Now we were exposed to the very real enmity of ultra-right terroristic Cuban bands known as *gusanos* (the word refers to a kind of worm) as well as the US border authorities under the jurisdiction of the Treasury Department. One never could be sure of the degree these were acting in concert or simply as bearers of a common interest. In any case, we now had to create a guarded perimeter around our vehicles while these were being loaded for the later stages of the journey, lest some creep would sabotage the caravan by planting drugs, or worse,[9] aboard our conveyances. I had to do several two-hour night-time vigils to guard against this.

• I had no idea after all this fuss whether and how we were going to actually get into Mexico with seventy cars and trucks loaded with necessities for Cuba. Not to worry, said Lucius Walker, Jim Mellor, and Cathy Scott. It still seems preposterous; there we were, a long line one moment; then, as the first truck pulled up to the window, there was a pause… and next, just like a Bruce Willis action movie or a Roadrunner cartoon, down went the pedal and away she roared, the others in hot pursuit, all through before the authorities could muster a response. I was part way down the line, in the passenger seat, which I can remember gripping as I bemusedly watched the brown and sluggish Rio Grande laze below. The next thing I knew, I was in the Neuva Laredo parking lot hopping up and down, ululating, high-fiving, and hugging my co-conspirators. Talk about a peak experience!

• The trip to Tampico was 756 km long, slow, hot, dusty, bumpy and mostly lonely, through some of the poorest and least scenic parts of Mexico. Yet it was anything but anti-climactic in itself, and after arrival at the port city, our voyage suddenly ramped up to full celebratory mode.

• In Cuba… To list the events of this eight-day tour as "Heroes of the Revolution" would spoil its essence. Yes, I was thrilled, and also uncomfortable, given good old-fashioned Freudian conflicts about showing off and all that goes with it, admixed in this case with rueful thoughts of how remote this was from the chronic relegation to the status of loser and crank the radical leftist faces back home.

Nothing, however, spoiled the moment. Despite the reality that we encountered, everyone—Cubans included—was still willing to do a little dancing in the streets to celebrate our arrival. How not feel the sorrows and pain of this noble people? For example, the young lady of a house I visited who said that malnutrition made her too weak for the customary bicycle trip to her work at a biology lab where vaccines were developed for the ill? Everyone looked so thin (some priests excepted!) that one thought there must be something wrong with our eyes. And yet they soldiered on, in spite of the imposed austerity.

WE ARE MADE TO FOCUS OUR GAZE on what is wrong with Cuba: the state press, the bureaucratic weight of things, the restiveness of a minority of the population, and not on its greater contribution to emancipation. The result has been acquisition of tunnel vision so that the citizen of an advanced "democracy" will see the world as global capital demands: to damn the upstart for those unfortunate repressions that are bound to arise when the boundaries of survival are defined by the superpower, to blot out the greater good by foregrounding the lesser evil. Meanwhile the reverse applies for the superpower itself: the good American celebrates its consumerist "diversity of choice," its freedom of speech subject to the principle that one can say anything just so long as it is understood that it will make no difference. Che put it best: how wonderful is capitalism; where one can choose the brand of razor blade with which to slit one's throat.

Traveling on the Friendshipment was to learn what makes a difference, and what prices have to be paid in this hard world. Our much-awaited session with Fidel brought this home. He kept us waiting a full hour, and was so distressed by the fact as to open his talk with an explanation of its reason. It entailed recounting a day in the life of a Communist Dictator, entirely given over to scrounging and juggling funds to get the cash so that a shipload of medicines could dock and be paid for its cargo. Hardly anyone realizes, he said, the day-by-day character imposed by the blockade. The worst of it was being squeezed out of global finance. Cuba's imposed pariah status was such as would, for an individual, correspond to not having access to credit cards, or even checks. Every transaction could require, in effect, shaking out the cookie jars, looking under the couch cushions, or pawning grandfather's gold watch.

The high point of the evening came when El Presidente received a gift from one of the *caravanistas* of a pre-publication copy of the latter's most recent work, *Red Hunting in the Promised Land*. As Castro read prodigiously, I could hope that his acceptance of the book might actually have led to something of use—this in contrast to the *el norte* publication about a month later, when its ruin was secured by the one-two punch of a savage review in *The New York Times* (which it took seriously enough to post on the second page of its weekly book review) followed by immediate removal from circulation by publisher Harper Collins, prop., Rupert Murdoch.

HERE ARE MY THREE MOST AFFECTING memories from Cuba, in reverse temporal order:

• A small notice in the back pages of the daily newspaper, that after extensive discussion and despite the ongoing shortages of food and other essentials, it had been decided to continue the program of free violin lessons (instruments included) in the schools to all interested students.

• The announcement, upon arrival in Tampico, that the dockworkers had declared a one-day strike, or however long it took to load the caravan onto the boat to Cuba. No problem from the bosses.

• The appearance, along the way from Nueva Laredo to Tampico, of groups of peasants cheering us on and waving banners extolling the Cuban Revolution and Fidel Castro. This happened perhaps five times. I have no way of knowing how they knew we were coming or connected with each other along this 470-mile stretch of road, but they knew and we felt it.

THE REVOLUTIONARY HANDBOOKS stress the importance of alliances between workers and peasants. They would also add that it is important to have a fire in the mountain, or its equivalent: a beacon of hope and a timeline of struggle. Cuba has been such, and to our eternal gratitude, we had been given the role of a little contributory blaze for a while. The year 1994 was 35 years into Cuba's revolution, and the empire never succeeded in bringing it down. Doubtless, while we were in Havana, Hugo Chavez was planning his Bolívarian revolution in Venezuela, which surfaced in 1999.[10]

Castro did more than tend the fire. Through the development of organic agriculture, he also led Cuba out of its Special Period, one of whose chief blows had been the sudden loss of the oil sent by the USSR. Cuba continued on this track and now regularly earns the praise of the UN and like bodies, as being the world's most ecologically sustainable society. There can never be socialism in one country alone, and these days, Cuba is stepping down from the mountain, according to the law that all things must pass: a new period has dawned and a new phase of struggle.

I COULD'A BEEN A CONTENDER

IN THE YEAR 1998 I SOUGHT election on the Green Party line for the US Senate from New York. Two years later, I compounded the folly by seeking the Green Party's presidential nomination. This meant running against Ralph Nader, the eventual candidate, in the California primary, and getting thrashed.

Mark Dunlea, a hard-boiled and faithful Green operative from Albany, New York, told me that a major political campaign was like running the marathon at the speed of a hundred-yard dash. He forgot to add that when this was on behalf of the Green Party, it was also like running with one's feet shackled together around a circular track in front of a scattering of observers staring off into the distance.

AN UNCHARACTERISTICALLY
DOUR JOEL KOVEL,
BY BRUCE ACKERMAN

Still, the Greens in 1998 were on the verge of a breakout into the Promised Land known as ballot status, in which, by getting a certain portion of the gubernatorial vote, a party also gets to run candidates for the next four years without the torture of petitioning. We already had a cracker-jack team, with the ancient and raffishly radical Grandpa Al Lewis (of "The Munsters" TV fame) to run for Governor, and for Attorney General the excellent Ann Greene, to add appeal to the African-American community. Now the ticket needed to be rounded off by a suitable candidate for the Senate seat held, forever it seemed, by the Nassau County (scene of my high school days) Republican hack Alphonse D'Amato, now challenged by the rising Democrat superstar Charles "Chuck," also the "Chuckster," Schumer, as Jewish in his Brooklyn heritage as I.

A professorial type was called for, to give a certain gravitas to the ticket, considering that Grandpa, his heart in the right place as well as phenomenally well-informed and articulate, was also, shall we say, a bit rude in his speech at times. After mulling for a while, I decided that, being a man of destiny, it was time to put aside my reservations about the Greens, buy a few cheap suits in the discount stores, and have a go.

It was a distinct pleasure to find Leon Botstein more than tolerant when I told him that a campaign for the Senate was bound to compromise at least the first half of the fall 1998 term at Bard. He positively encouraged it, with the proviso—which I was thrilled to accept—that whatever I did, I should bring the students into the process. Ten years into my professorship at Bard, relations with the school had reached their zenith. I was never closer to the students, never had more fun with them, never found them so helpful to me, nor so appreciated the college as a kind of refuge from a harsh world.

There was a little wrinkle, to which I paid scant attention at the moment, as Leon explained—to me and in other contexts to the campus—that this policy was no whim but a manifestation of a structural change. No longer would Bard be the sleepy, countercultural place we all knew and loved. Now it had awakened to become a nexus of worldly activity, a player, small but active and growing, on the world stage. The name of George Soros, famous and associated with liberal intervention, was brought forward. Bard was now a fiefdom in Soros world—and as I learned shortly, Leon Botstein, liberal activist college president extraordinaire, was now a principal lieutenant of Soros, global entrepreneur of liberal democracy. No wonder the Quixotic campaign of its Hiss Professor received Bard's blessing.

The boundaries between politics, theater, and religion cannot be neatly drawn, as they are all played with imaginary characters and made-up lines. In the case of political campaigns for major office, where one must dip a toe in the waters of worldly power, the mental balance sheets for the venture are curious in the extreme. For though one cannot afford being delusional about one's chances of success, lest one get lost in the landscape, it is also the case that one must be more than a little crazy to seek election to a high office. Part of this craziness is the chance to impersonate a candidate who must believe he is really better than the other guys, and moreover, highly qualified for the post. In other words, one has to have a bit, or maybe quite a bit, of grandiosity to put up with the ordeal of such a campaign, from the horrors of fundraising to its protracted daily frenzy and frustration and, as a Green, guaranteed ignominious failure. The tissue between such ambition and delusion is narrow and frayed; or to put it slightly differently, whether one is truly crazy or not depends pretty much on how deeply one scratches the surface. Thanks be to God for granting to humanity, or at least some portion of it, a sense of humor to get through the day.

THE BARKING YALLER DOG forbids my saying whether this applies to me. But I certainly qualified as grandiose, and saw myself destined to take on the injustices of the world. Had I not been seething for 35 years at the abomination that is medicine under the regime of capital, strangling in its cradle the universal access to health care that should be an elementary benchmark of a decent society? I loved whacking away at the medical-industrial complex on the campaign trail; loved, too, reminding appreciative audiences that I was a doctor who left the profession in part because of its systemic injustice, and more, that I was not just talking about "single-payer" insurance, as worthy an issue as such was, but about socialized medicine—"that's right, socialized medicine, God-dammit!"—as practiced in outposts of a better world such as the island of Cuba.

There was a yet greater and more urgent issue that stemmed from my Climate Revelation of 1988. It compelled me to pick up my lance and saddle my nag Rocinante, inasmuch as a potential turning point in civilization's coming to grips with the ecological crisis had been achieved at UN's climate conference toward the close of 1997 at Kyoto, Japan. This set before the nations certain "protocols" designed to bring under control the emission of carbon into the atmosphere. It was at the least a flawed concept, and even a crooked way to bypass real change and to create a new mechanism for the accumulation of capital—which happens to be the core of the problem in the first place. But it was a start, a crack in the edifice, and with the potential for being expanded. What really got me going was the response to the news by one of our Senators, Frank Murkowski of Alaska, who proclaimed of this measure requiring Senate approval as a treaty, that it was "dead on arrival" on Capitol Hill.

Genug!—Enough!—quoth I, now I've got to run for the Senate and give these bastards what for! Tipped me right over the top, it did. And landed me in the soup of a marathon to be run as a hundred-yard dash with one's legs in chains and exposed to the indifference, stupidity, and hostility of the world, including especially the world of what are called "liberals."

Alger Hiss had told me shortly before he decided to pack his bags for eternity[11] that regarding the multiple defects he suffered on account of age—virtually blind, virtually deaf, virtually mute—what brought him down was "not so much the infirmity as the indignity." Thoughts along these lines occur to me as I ponder how to describe the stew of emotions that accompanied these campaigns, continuous as they were with years of futility in face of the contumely of power, of hurling against barricades, of recognition never received, not to mention being the first to enunciate in a major political campaign the demand for a post-carbon economy, necessarily under socialist auspices.

Humiliation cascades over the heads of also-rans in a rat-race society, in spades when one is a candidate of a "minor party" facing the Big Boys anointed by the System to disburse its favors and lubricate its wheels. The more crooked the System, the more cruel its humiliation of those below. Yet one would be hard put to find a more loathsome, scary politician than Chuck Schumer. Republican D'Amato was a comical good-for-nothing, and at worst a petty crook who cheated on the repair of his South Shore home. Schumer, however, was an imperialist dog, a Zionist toady[12] and an inquisitor with a cruel smile, not to mention a servant of Mammon as Wall Street's Chosen One. I

SCHUMATO

first saw him in action in the 1997 documentary, *Waco: The Rules of Engagement*, hounding witnesses and boosting mayhem by the FBI. As a congressman he became a mainspring of this display of state terror. I was alarmed watching him at work.[13] Kyoto provided the weight behind my decision to run, the visceral reaction at Schumer's role in the Waco massacre gave it a special urgency.

This became a wellspring of frustration, however, for no matter how hard I tried during the campaign, the liberals whom I had to reach to get anywhere refused to budge. Were they secretly sympathetic to Schumer's role in eliminating a weird cult of right-wing Christians? In any case, all they could focus on was that they had endured three terms of the oafish "Senator Pothole" D'Amato, and were not going to take it any more.

Progressives from across the Upper West Side, Greenwich Village, and Park Slope and into the bowels of *The Nation* magazine (which gave me the coldest of shoulders) were burning to avenge D'Amato's unlikely victory in 1980 over divided liberal icons Jacob Javits and Elizabeth Holtzman. Mere truth, for example, sordid betrayals by actually existing Democrats, and their evident bankruptcy as worthwhile political alternatives, *viz.,* Bill Clinton's role in ramming NAFTA down their throats, or the gutting of welfare, in short, his *bona fides* as a neoliberal marauder and hence a betrayer of whatever goodness the Democratic Party had achieved when it stood to a degree for workers—all this was swept aside in their frenzy—and with it went any hope for a decent showing by myself.

An especially unkind cut came from a liberal friend at NYU Law School, who labored hard to give me a fundraising party, only to tell me as we were cleaning up, "Good luck, Joel, but I'm voting for Schumer; can't bear the thought of another six years of D'Amato." In other words the best we can aspire toward in this sad world is to have a grinning, smooth-talking Democratic Senator from New York escort the Ship of State toward the abyss.

I had one small triumph over the Chuckster, as we called him. We had been scheduled to meet at the Goddard Riverside Community Center on Columbus Avenue to discuss health care before an audience of senior citizens. Schumer declined with some excuse and sent his mother instead. She turned out to be a lovely lady and scarcely the type of mom, Jewish or otherwise, who would produce such a *putz.* Anyhow, we did our routines, myself hammering away with the well-worn rant on socialized medicine. When we were done I went to pay respects to Mme. Schumer. She responded, "You are such a nice man, much nicer than my son; why can't you be running in his place?" A shocker and no doubt, a sign of superior discernment. Not since my 1954 summer at the Hotel Del Mar had a Jewish mother said such a thing to me. What would Rose Kovel, five years in her grave, have thought?

GREG FITZSIMMONS

There were other kind moments, from generous spirits like my future son-in-law, Greg Fitzsimmons, who along with another stand-up comedian, Barry Crimmins, gave nobly of themselves to liven up my events. But this only offset the drudgery of the grind from one end of the state to another, chiefly by motorcar, which disclosed a society enclosed by inertia, such as the members of the Kingston Kiwanis Club, whom I tried to alert concerning the dangers of climate change, though I might as well have addressed the ten-pins at their bowling alley. Or for that matter, the editorial staffs of the various newspapers (forget the New York City press; the only place of merit was Albany); none of them could get the need for some fundamental change if catastrophe is to be averted. After all, they still can't get it after fifteen years and endless calamities; so why then?

Lo! The marvelous structure of how liberals serve their masters. Our finest caper of the campaign[19] was pulled off by a team consisting of Jim Mellor, my one-man campaign staff, working with Mark Dunlea, the liaison with the Green Party, and some young-blood field organizers of that pillar of the environmental establishment, the Sierra Club. It consisted of simultaneous demonstrations in front of all four of D'Amato's offices in New York state, along with a statewide promotion campaign about climate change. Not bad for a dazed bunch of grass-consuming ruminants. If roofs around the state did not rattle as a result, we could take pride in having brought the Sierra Club aboard; at least such was the explicit promise made by said young-bloods, wildly enthusiastic at finally finding some kick-ass action coming from a registered political party. "Yes, we're with you Joel; this is the start of something big." Ah, but starts are only a small part of the picture, especially when dealing with a large environmental bureaucracy relying on mass contributions from worried middle-class folks and foundations whose job in this world is to help reproduce the established way.

Bitter was the moment, therefore, when the Sierra Club's recommendation for U.S. Senate came out, *sans* mention of my name and giving the laurel of top environmental candidate to that protector of nature, the Chuckster. A similarly unkind cut came from the League of Women Voters, a civil-society group whose spotless reputation feeds the delusion that the System works. Again, I simply didn't exist on their final tally sheet, despite doing what I could to inform them, including hours spent filling out a detailed information sheet. Yes, the System works... but to what end?

And then, the unkindest cut, from our comrades in the progressive media. Over the years since writing *White Racism* I had made scores of appearances on the Pacifica bellwether radio station, WBAI. There was no more favorable place to get the word out during the campaign. I did what I could on quite a few occasions, including a couple of appearances on the morning show, "Wakeup Call," with co-hosts Amy Goodman and Bernard White, where my campaign was copiously discussed, yay and hooray. Then came the morning of election day. I had to drop DeeDee off at Newark airport, and on the way back became stuck in the mother of all traffic jams in front of the Holland Tunnel. I turned on WBAI and listened to "Wakeup Call," and heard Bernard White lamenting the fact that there were no decent alternatives to the Democrats in this day and age. It was like that moment in *A Clockwork Orange* where the protagonist is forced to watch, eyes forced open, scenes of extreme violence. Sitting there, bathed by fumes and surrounded by (indeed, driving) that commodity which was eating the whole world, I felt myself to be inside a corporeal nightmare, as though I had wandered into the Hell Panel from Hieronymus Bosch's "The Garden of Earthly Delights." But then the traffic started moving again, I paid my toll, and entered the tunnel.

> Suffering produces endurance, and endurance produces character, and character produces hope, and hope does not disappoint us, because God's love has been poured into our hearts through the Holy Spirit that has been given to us. Romans 5:3–5

LITTLE MORE THAN A YEAR LATER I was back on the campaign trail to mark the new millennium with an even more audacious escapade, though substantially smaller in scale than the Senate race: January and February as against April through October; pointing toward a party primary as against a general election; and to be carried out with virtually no staff and no budget except those expenses incurred by the travel, food, and lodging of the Principal, myself, as I traipsed alone by car though the state of California seeking to become the 43rd President of these United States, a goal that required as its first step in the path to challenge Ralph Nader in the March 3rd primary.

Strictly speaking, I was not the only alternative before the Greens to Nader in 2000, as two others—Stephen Gaskin, leader of The Farm Collective in Tennesee, and Jello Biafra, left-wing musician—had also declared. However, they had not actually registered for the primary in California: an arduous task requiring a certain percentage of Party locals in the state to endorse one's candidacy, whereupon the wheels of the electoral machinery would commence spinning and one would be rewarded with a spot in an election brochure sent, if I recall, to nineteen million citizens of California. I do not even want to think about what fraction of nineteen million would equal the sum of all the copies of other publications in which my name appears. I still have my copy where I am listed with Al Gore, George W. Bush, Nader, ex-Knick Bill Bradley, and a number of people even more unknown than myself; and I must say, that for all the contempt I feel for our system and the psychopaths who scramble to the top of its heap, I cannot help feel a little thrill of pride when I view this or even think of it. What better way to garnish one's *resumé* for presentation at the Pearly Gates!

WALT SHEASBY

There was a project of sorts to bring this about, and in this case, a leader. His name was Walt Sheasby, and I had known him since 1997, from the Greens and also a journal I had gotten involved with, *Capitalism Nature Socialism,* which I will write about shortly. This made Walt not just a Green, but in contrast to all other Greens I had known, a *bona fide* Marxist whose proficiency in matters Red and Green along with a commitment to a synthesis of socialism and Green politics led to a strong and deep friendship. Walt disdained worldly reward, and, although he had rejected his Catholic background, matter-of-factly and with no vanity, called himself a monk.

I loved visiting his home in the foothills northeast of Pasadena, built by his father and shared with his nonagenarian mother and a bunch of dogs, where he worked out of what had been a capacious California two-car garage now lined with political and philosophical books and papers, including a serviceable set of the *MEGA—Marx-Engels-Gesamtausgabe*—fifty well-marked volumes. He did keep the faith, even if the word "faith" was scarcely heard in his presence. Walt had a first-rate mind, far outshining the academic Fancy Dans who pushed the Marx-this and Marx-that buttons on the elevator to intellectual prestige, while he uncomplainingly eked out a marginal life in community colleges east of L.A. He was also a considerable figure in Trotskyist circles, and connected me with one of their groups, Solidarity, as part of our grand scheme to bring Reds and Greens together, albeit in the reverse path from my Green Party experience, and equally dysfunctional.

Like myself, Walt had some hope that the U.S. Greens could grow into a genuinely revolutionary party based on the only revolutionary doctrine worth a damn. Inserting me into the presidential mix might at least set going a debate on the subject in a race that was catching fire, since Ralph Nader, an authentic legend and one of the half-dozen or so best recognized names in American society, had declared interest in running as a Green.

Nader's candidacy awoke the Greens and allowed them to fancy arriving on the national political landscape. Of course, there was that little detail: Ralph wasn't leading the Greens, he was leading their ticket, being no more in this regard than a stately flagship sailing ahead of a bunch of rowboats. Yes, they would be lifted by the swells of its wake; but this was a very long way from having a living relationship. Ralph's claims about helping bring in money and new members to the Greens were true. But his persistent refusal to join the Party was a thinly veiled insult that made the Greens vulnerable to empty enthusiasm when what they needed was patient, dedicated organizing grounded in a coherent theory of their own. Lacking such, they became hooked by another's charisma.

Some said that Nader's giant Madison Square Garden rally in September was unforgettable, a peak experience that transported them into an ecstasy of religious proportions. But as a student of the spirit I would say that, lacking praxis—the unity of vision and practice—this was more an instance of those boats bobbing up and down as the magnificent lead vessel sailed on ahead than an authentic spirituality. Capitalism's "society of the spectacle" specializes in mass-produced, celebrity-driven ecstasy. Some grow out of it; others become addicted; others turn it to nefarious ends, for such is the germ of political pathology. I saw neither Nader nor the Greens heading directly that way; but there was quite a bit of posturing in these displays, and some troubling shenanigans, as I'll discuss presently.

As for how I spent that two-month sojourn on the byways of the Golden State, the formula was simple in the extreme: hop in the Saab, drive until I find the next appointment with a Green Party chapter or community television station, meet folks, and try to persuade them of the reasoning sketched in above. At times the drive turned from means to end, a way of rekindling a love affair with the Golden State that had begun in fitful and diminishing degree since a visit in 1964 led me to get a California license to practice medicine.

Well, I was long since done practicing medicine, and California's numinous splendor had long since been largely paved over. But there was still something to trigger the imagination if the conditions were right. And how delicious it was to escape the madding crowd on the kind of drive that mostly exists in car ads these days. A six-hour trip from Arcata to Redding on State 299 as it followed the Trinity River did the trick; nobody to answer to, no time to make or make up, no voice blaring in my ear. I don't make a fetish of meditation, and don't care for the New Age airheads who do; but there is definitely a space for silence—well, let's say the humming of the car on the road—in the midst of the hellish intrusions of capitalist culture.

Once at my destination I didn't attack Nader, a man who had shown so much grit and done so much good, but I did want to criticize Nader from a radical perspective, in line with the ideas Sheasby and I had been developing. My thoughts seem to spontaneously take on a trinitarian aspect—hmmm, I wonder what that can mean!—and so it was with Ralph, whom I found myself pinioning thus: first, with the critique of his not joining the party; second, with confrontation of Nader's tendency to reduce politics to legislative or legalistic actions, which led to a truncated practice divorced from lived life and particularly weak in addressing core themes of gender and race; and third, and most important, his abjuring of socialism in favor of various populist themes of citizens organizing to offset corporate power, as by taking control of pension funds and using them to fund reforms.

Obviously, it would take a debate between us to fully develop these points. I asked him directly and received a polite but firm refusal. I stood a good chance of winning, given the advantage of attacking the anointed Apostle of Progressive causes from a thought-through left perspective. I suppose Ralph may have realized this, though I doubt he gave the matter any thought at all, given the vast difference in our organizational power and name recognition by the electorate. It was no surprise to see him simply acting reflexively according to the front-runner's standard strategy of staying away from a place where he had nothing to gain and everything to lose. Needless to say, this did not endear Nader to me, and I felt no sympathy at all when he made a big fuss about being excluded from the debates between Bush and Gore.

If truth be told, I really did not fight to press my demand, given my extreme isolation, and frankly, because I was by now utterly fed up with the ritual abasement of these campaigns. As my friend Schiffrin told me back at Yale, quoting civil-rights leader James Foreman, himself quoting e. e. cummings, "there is some shit I will not eat."

As the day of the primary approached I encountered some more of said shit. We had all gathered in San Francisco for the final pre-primary rally, billed as a chance to see all the Green Party candidates for elected office, high and low, from City Council member to President. I had applied and been accepted, but when I arrived in town, there were the fliers and posters everywhere with Ralph's name all over them, and below this, the names of City Council candidates… and that was all. I showed up at party headquarters in a fury, to be told that they were terribly sorry, somebody must have misplaced the application, but that's all right, we can give you forty dollars to print up your own posters and fliers and post them. I forget which curse word I chose to embellish my parting.

But at least I could speak the next evening, and before some three thousand good citizens of America's most leftward city. Before we began, the organizer emphasized that what with one thing and another, we had to limit ourselves to 15–20 minutes tops. Fair enough. Ralph was not there yet, but the assumption was that he had been given the same message. Usually I speak off the cuff, but the occasion deserved my best effort. And so it was, every word in place, precisely spoken, lots of stirring metaphors, cadences all down pat, even delivered without my usual fidgeting.

And then, a hush, and then, Heeeere he is!!! Our Savior![14] Raaaalph Nader!! And he shuffled out, looking homespun and Lincolnesque, and pontificated and rambled for a full 100 minutes, as the audience cheered and whooped.

Lots of people came up to me afterward, led by my two Bay Area sisters-in-law, Pinky and Fritzi, and brother-in-law Peter Kushner, to praise what I had done. And I was in fact happy with the effort, and knew that a few souls had been touched. But I still can't help thinking that here in this cradle of Democracy, the dreadful Republocrat Parties whom we gleefully savage somehow manage to see to it that pre-primary events allow for all legitimate candidates, whether great or small, to have equal time to make their case… so that, given the facts that this was a pre-primary event, and that Greens were trying to be a party of the same stripe with a chance to vie for the highest office in the land, and that Ralph Nader and I were the only two candidates of the Greens with equal legitimacy before the law, wasn't giving Ralph a five-to-one advantage in time to make his case (which left aside many of the points I made, especially about climate change) therefore crooked and a violation of the law… and didn't this shine the clearest light possible on just how corrupting the so-called breakthrough of the Greens into the territory of major league politics, thanks to the charisma of Ralph Nader, could be? Yes, they were on the way to the big-time—and so far as I can tell, oblivious to the implications.

HERE IS AN INTERESTING SPECULATION on what was a hot topic of the year 2000, the infamous triumph of George W. Bush over Al Gore, a monster midwived by the Supreme Court, and in fact a good old-fashioned *coup d'etat*. We know that Gore had the election won, roughly by five hundred thousand votes, if mere numbers were the only criterion. But Gore didn't have quite the margin needed to suppress the shenanigans that were set loose in places like Florida. This was observed to be in large measure the result of Ralph Nader managing to garner three million or so votes as a Green. Assuming that these would have otherwise gone to Gore (a contested assumption, by the way, but irrelevant here), Nader's absence from the race would have given Gore so large a margin as to make the crookedness of the Bush forces impossible of being exercised.[15]

Now suppose that Ralph Nader had become incapacitated, say, by a stroke, on March 3rd, the day of the California primary; and suppose, too, that I had as a result ended up with the Green presidential nomination: crazy but not outside that well-known realm of possibility. I can't imagine I would have won more than three-hundred-thousand votes. This would have given Al Gore a shenanigan-proof margin of some 3.2 million votes, and altered the course of events: no 9/11, no invasion of Iraq, no War on Terror, etc, etc… or would it? In any case, I would have backed into history!

After the primary, a number of friends urged me to stay in the race and fight on. But I declined, though agreeing to go to the Nominating Convention in June. I was fed up, my political career over. And besides, there was another book I wanted to finish.

Notes

1 Strictly speaking for me, no, as my funds were locked down in securities of the Hiss Chair. But the system as a whole was as spectral as anything under capitalism could be, with Leon and his Vice President, Dmitri Papadimitriou, the only people with any real power, and the financiers of the Board looming behind the curtains in lieu of a decent endowment or significant public money, as is normal.

2 Erdman, "Jerusalem," Plate 91, 251.

3 I remain unsure of who had initiated this measure or been its intermediary. Perhaps it was Ezra Susser, a trainee from South Africa in my later years at Einstein who is presently a Public Health Psychiatrist of great distinction.

4 Vorster was Prime Minister from 1966 to 1978, then President, and forced out by scandal in 1979. He presided over the opening of this eponymous state of the art charnel house of torture, torment and murder.

5 Dean Brackley, *The Call to Discernment in Troubled Times* (New York: Crossroad, 2004). See more on this in Chapter 14.

6 Terry Bisson, *Fire on the Mountain* (Oakland: PM Press, 1988).

7 Erdman, "Auguries of Innocence," 492.

8 General Leonard Wood had written President McKinley that the island was worth any two Southern States, so long as one was not Texas.

9 These fellows were definitely a lethal menace known to blow up jetliners in flight and get away with it, thanks to the protection of the National Security State. On another occasion, when I was on the road to give solidarity to another caravan at the San Diego-Tijuana border in 2000, a car under the control of one of

the groups, Omega 7, tried repeatedly to run our van off the I-5 Interstate. This time we had video recordings of the event, which certainly was an intention to commit vehicular homicide. IFCO took them to court, with myself as a witness, and won a large decision, which effectively destroyed the terrorist organization.

10 The beast never sleeps. As this is being written, Obama and Co. are in process of the nth U.S.-spurred coup against Bolivarian Venezuela, as Nicolas Maduro holds the fort a year after the great Chavez's death.

11 Like an Eskimo elder going off on an ice floe, at age 94 Hiss simply decided to stop eating and passed away on his own terms.

12 He boasts that his name signifies a guardian of the Shetl in the Old Country, now transferred to the role of a protector of the State of Israel.

13 I am not alone in this: "I remember [Schumer] on the nightly news when [Waco] happened…. He was absolutely giddy with joy that all of those people were murdered. It was fucking sickening then and still is…. Ya know, you'd think a Jew wouldn't be so enthusiastic over the massacre of women and children. But there he is, smiling and condemning…. The guy just seemed giddy to have a bunch of women and kids burned alive." Post on AR15 Discussion Board, January 30, 2013, http://www.ar15.com/forums/t_1_5/1433505_.html.

14 Well, not really, but it felt that way.

15 No point in entering into the storm of controversy that ensued on the leftward side of things about this, with huge numbers of people cursing Ralph for running at all. I would just say that my support here was with Nader, who had every right to run. The sufficient fact is that Gore lost the election, which was his to win, because of a combination of ineptitude, cowardice, and/or complicity.

Chapter 11
The Enemy of Nature

I must Create a System, or be enslav'd
by another Mans. I will not Reason &
Compare: my business is to Create...
Striving with Systems to deliver Individuals from those Systems; [*sic*]¹

From the beginning of the 1990s I fancied that overcoming the ecological crisis was a question of "synthesizing" the "Red" and the "Green," that is, a kind of combining the anti-capitalism of socialist movements with the many efforts to contain the damage wrought by civilization on nature. The more I looked into it and tried to make a difference, however, the more hopeless and in need of theoretical revision did the whole matter appear.

The heart of the matter is—if you will forgive the extreme brevity of this introduction—that all political parties, non-governmental organizations, etc., are bound up with one aspect or another of the system, and do not address the Archimedean point, that place from which the system can be changed. This is the "mode of production," production being the transforming of nature by conscious human labor, organized across a society and controlled by states. Our mode of production is given through capitalism; its signature, so to speak, is generalized commodity production organized according to private ownership of the means of production and ruled over by the money power, or the regime of "exchange value." This form of value comes to overpower the "use values" of traditional ways of production. It is the most powerful, the most expansive, and the most destructive mode of production ever devised by humanity, and it will destroy us, and goodly portions of nature as well, unless we overcome it.

No political party can do this, nor can any legislative or regulatory means. Only a social transformation that is sensitive to the spontaneous emergence of openings toward new life, and can build ecosystems of an integral kind. Our hope resides in three major principles.

Firstly, that events of resistance to and breakdown of capitalism occur spontaneously, simultaneously as threats to life and openings toward the protection of life. I would call this the interstitial principle, and it continually brings forward openings toward transformation.

Secondly, that what is done with this depends upon our God-given visionary power to prefigure a world beyond capital, to envision our horizon and move towards it through cooperative socialist practice, and crucially, to connect with others, both by production of integral, non-monetized ecosystems, and the production through activist and cultural as well as intellectual means, of modes of resistance to the capitalist order.

Thirdly, and focusing closely on the core processes of the new mode of production, we need to develop and incorporate a third form of value—the Intrinsic Value of Nature—to offset the deadly dance between use value and exchange value that marks the evolution of capitalism.

So much more to be said! But perhaps the above will serve as a suggestion as to the direction of my work in this sphere. I write in 2016 and am busy planning the development of ecosocialism through a joint effort with my young colleague, Quincy Saul. However, that is not for a memoir but the near future. As for my memoir, we may pick up the thread as it appeared at the beginning of this journey, soon after I decided to focus my energies on overcoming the ecological crisis.

Finding my way

I HEARD EARLY IN THE 1990s of a man, James O'Connor, five years my senior and a professor of Economics and Sociology at the University of California, Santa Cruz, who had founded in 1988 a

JAMES O'CONNOR

journal nicely called *Capitalism Nature Socialism*. *CNS* was focused on rethinking things, including Marxist things, in light of the ecological crisis, and its spirit was iconoclastic.

Jim had made a Long March through the institutions, studying rural proletarians in revolutionary Cuba, the fiscal crisis of the capitalist state, and such matters, until, like myself, he was jolted awake by the ecological crisis and its radical implications. Jim's prime response was to restructure basic concepts within Marxism. His "Second Contradiction of Capitalism" was an expansion of crisis theory in order to embrace the degradation of nature alongside exploitation of labor in determining the flux of society and modes of struggle.[2] It became the point of reference of *Capitalism Nature Socialism*. Some four years later I picked up the trail, and once I did, knew I had found a home base.

I called, introduced myself, and found that O'Connor knew of me and was eager to have me aboard. I became an Associate Editor and developed a New York editorial group (regional editing being a key feature of *CNS*). Over the years I moved from being a supervisee of O'Connor in matters pertaining to the Second Contradiction to his functional co-editor. These were good times for me. Despite— or maybe because of—the frightful specter of ecological catastrophe, the *CNS* collective was a happier and more collegial bunch than the back-biting *Telos* group of twenty years before.

By the mid-'90s I was ready to develop my own contribution. I first envisioned a trilogy: Volume I, the critique of capitalism; Volume II, the building of the ecosocialist alternative; and Volume III, for unspecified theoretical matters. That this was a bad idea became apparent as soon as I finished a draft of the first volume. It was longer than the eventual work, and more telling, a litany of accusations leading nowhere. No, I would have to go back to the drawing board, and produce a compact and articulated version, in which theory emerged from the critique of capital and led into the making of ecosocialism.

After summarizing the ecological crisis and identifying its "efficient cause" in the production of capital, I ventured into an *exposé* of how actual capitalist production and reproduction was implicated in the process of destroying humanity and nature. The work then entered into "ecosystematics": an advance patrol for an as-yet-barely-begun endeavor, developing a rigorous account of the "ecosystem" as influenced by human being, from its disintegrated form under capitalism to its integral form under ecosocialism. With that, the way now lay open to a transformed mode of production. The essential change would move away from the ever-expanding production of commodities to production, through "freely associated labor," of the integral ecosystems whose life develops within the essential terms of the Second Law of Thermodynamics, and by so doing, leads toward a wholeness impossible under the aegis of capital. All of this allowed me the pleasure of re-awakening the love of science that marked my youth. The development of the Intrinsic Value of Nature briefly emerges here, as do essential concepts like "prefiguration."

O'Connor proved indispensible for the project. It was not that Jim and I were optimally aligned; indeed, he never formally endorsed the concept of ecosocialism, but he was a man of open mind and powerful intellect, an intellectual of a kind I had not known since Stanley Diamond and just as crotchety, a warrior of Blake's mental fight, and a true lover of the editorial process. He must have been a terrific sportsman as a young man, all 6'5" of him on the hockey, soccer—or would it have been rugby?—field, thriving in scrums and the like. There was a tragic aftermath: spinal injuries that never satisfactorily healed and whose sequelae of chronic pain and restless leg syndrome could never be treated, except by palliative and addictive narcotics that brought him down. But before this happened, Jim, to me, was a magnificent colleague and a magnificent editor.

Though never in the same league as Jim, I became a pretty good editor myself and helped bring some bright younger folk along. I preferred the odd stuff that brought derision at editorial conferences, but where I could discern some gemlike flashes amidst the debris. I loved the hard work of nursing a fragile draft into premonitory elegance, bringing the tyro along until her or his contribution shone—though I would not have you believe that these happy moments were frequent occurrences.

In 2003 declining health led Jim to step down and ask me to succeed him as Editor in Chief. It was akin to Don Corleone's "offer he can't refuse," not from external threat but from fear of the Yaller Dog conscience that would hound me into eternity if I forsook this scrawny and impecunious quarterly journal that was also a kind of social movement spanning six continents with the modest goal of transforming history in order to rescue nature from capital.

Unhappily, O'Connor's turning over the reins of *CNS* took place in context of a worsening of his condition. Even as the corporeal body continued, then, the framework of our friendship waned and there was to be no further collaboration. But life, as we know, had to go on, and I had to make the best of it. The project required raising some funds from my friend Abby Rockefeller to supplement monies disbursed by the British publisher, Taylor and Francis. Or as they liked to call themselves, the "Taylor and Francis Group." Jim's long-suffering wife, Barbara Laurence, stayed on a while as managing editor (to be replaced by Karen Charman); and she and I went over to Oxford—home to Chaucer's clerk, who would gladly "lerne and teche"—to see how our beacon of ecosocialist hope was being crafted in the mills of T&F.

I learned to my disbelief, first, that *CNS* was one of more than a thousand scholarly journals slickly produced in a large factory bursting with electronics that could just have well been slickly producing ultra-violent video games. Yes, Oxford had come a long way from its medieval origins. Second, that we were managed by "teams" of rather bright, very nice, and progressively inclined young folk in cheesy suits and ties, who got to know us for a while and then were shipped somewhere else within the group, never to be seen again. Third, that T&F could not give a flying fart for anachronisms like individual subscriptions. The name of the game was to place one's journal in university libraries with tightly restricted access to the commodity form of choice, the downloadable article, available for a mere $19 or so, payable from the purchaser's research grant or whatever. Fourth, and summing up, it preyed on my mind that we producers of the discourse of ecosocialism, though on a very long leash—that is to say, never chided for political content nor snooped upon[3]—were nevertheless in the same boat with all producers of surplus value for capital: that is, we turned out a commodity that sold for more value than was consumed in its production. That's right, we helped our publisher make a profit and were praised when we did, as the dancing monkey is praised for doing a nice job by the hurdy-gurdy man. So, when our assigned manager told us that Taylor and Francis Group was very pleased with *CNS,* in that our labor was yielding money over the allotment received, I may be forgiven for feeling a tad less revolutionary ardor than, say, Marx and Engels did by helping out the Young Communist League with the *Manifesto.*[4]

This is no small point: it discloses an iron tendency toward the corrupting of opposition inherent to capitalism, corruption that can vitiate the most ardent activism and cheapen the name of revolution. The happy thousand (nowadays fifteen hundred) journals published by such as Taylor and Francis had that magical property of being refereed, that is, they were places wherein publication would be counted in favor of the author's elevation to the careerist *summum bonum* known as tenure. My ambition was to move the journal somewhat leftward by changing the motto chosen by Jim that *Capitalism Nature Socialism* was a journal of a "Red-Green Synthesis," to the statement that it was "A Journal of Ecosocialism," thereby establishing it as the first refereed academic journal to openly declare its intention to bring about revolutionary transformation of the capitalist system. How about that! We so declared our identity without a flicker of complaint from the publishing group.

Why should anyone complain when the whole thing was covered by the logic of exchange? We got our concept, not yet graced with a dictionary definition, out into the public sphere, even if only in eight-point type on an inside cover page; our young Turk academics got a slight glimmer of hope they could write something politically worthwhile without being squashed like a bug in early career; and the group got that warm glow which comes from subsuming intellectual labor into the expansion of capital, knowing, moreover, that one or two ecosocialists among a thousand or so exponents of one or another tendency in the world's great Marketplace of Ideas is not a bad deal at all.

Some derivatives of these thoughts took shape during that phone call in 2003 when Jim O'Connor offered me the editorship. Though bound to take up the challenge; I insisted on asking myself nonetheless, what could be done to offset the creeping academization that afflicts radical dissent, and will diminish *CNS* unless I brought in some offsetting structure... or person.

If I recall correctly, the name came to me even as I was speaking to Jim about taking on the editorship: Walt Sheasby, my monkish Marxist friend distinguished by not being able to advance further in academia than a pissant community college in the smoggy wastelands of eastern Los Angeles County, and close companion since the 2000 Nader campaign. Walt responded instantly to my suggestion that he come aboard as co-editor and join with me, not only in guiding the editorial direction of the journal but more importantly, in undertaking together the strategy of enabling *CNS* to break loose from the chains imposed by the Group and become reborn as an independent focal point of revolutionary ecosocialism.

Walt opined as well that he was tired of L.A., and that the time might be coming for a move northward to the San Francisco Bay region, for which purpose he planned to obtain a portable home, stuff it with the fifty volumes of the *MEGA* and other essentials, and park it in a trailer park somewhere in the East Bay. A more auspicious headquarters for the new Ecosocialist International could not be imagined.

There was no problem so far as O'Connor was concerned. An ancillary reason to his letting go of the journal was the breakdown of the previous publishing arrangement; and the deal with Taylor and Francis as well as the entire setup of academic journal-making held as little attraction for him as myself. More, his opinion of Sheasby was as high as my own. I think he would have been delighted with the prospect of a new life for *Capitalism Nature Socialism*, even if incapable of contributing to it.

In fact, Walt and I were at that time agreeing to disagree, specifically, about supporting Ralph Nader in the 2004 presidential race. Affected by my 2000 experience, I considered this a fool's game and of no conceivable benefit for the Greens; Walt agreed that Nader had his problems, but that we had to stick by our guns, so to speak, and hunker down for the long run. To that end he was busy organizing Southern California and couldn't foresee breaking loose until the latter part of 2004. Meanwhile he would work with me and dedicate himself to his book project of definitively dealing with Marx's relation to nature. Two chapters were to appear in the 2004 *CNS*, the first volume under my editorial tutelage.

And then, the blow: Sometime early in the summer of 2004, Sheasby began complaining of headaches. This grew, swiftly, horribly, and forced a call to the ambulance. Two days later, the word came from our mutual friend, Sam Fassbinder: Walt Contreras Sheasby, 55 years of age, had perished. The diagnosis was bitter: West Nile Virus, a mosquito-borne offspring spawned by the ecological crisis.

My zeal for remaking *Capitalism Nature Socialism* died with Sheasby and never returned. There remained much good and useful work to do, plenty of companionship—and after turning it over to my young colleague Salvatore Engel-Di Mauro, some good signs as well, including a growing presence on the masthead of folks with the descriptor, "Independent Scholar" after their name. But for me, eight years of deadlines and bickering was enough. I never wanted to be the editor of a journal any more than I wanted to be a psychoanalyst; and it was easy to let go of the helm of *CNS* and assume the identity of *eminence grise*.

OTHER PATHS HAD MEANWHILE opened. In the closing years of the millennium I became an acquaintance and then a friend of the eminent Franco-Brazilian intellectual, Michael Löwy, a man generous of spirit and proponent of a wide, deep and humanistic Marxism. Again, a convergence induced by shared agony over the ecological crisis, this connected me with Fourth International Trotskyism at a high level, along with Löwy's networks in Latin America and Europe. During the late 1990s we gathered several times in Vincennes, outside of Paris, for one of those conferences labeled something like New Developments in Marxism where everybody gets to rant and prate. In 2001 Löwy and I shared in a panel on ecology; and it was there in the back of the room in the midst of another presentation that notes were passed, one of which reflected something that had just flashed into mind and went something like this: "Why don't we write an Ecosocialist Manifesto?" "Yes! Yes!" immediately came the response.

WITH MICHAEL LÖWY AND A FRIEND IN PARIS

It would be a humble project with immense ambitions. I sent a draft to Löwy soon after returning to New York; he sent it back, revised, and so on and so forth, until we had something we agreed upon. And so the first *Ecosocialist Manifesto* was launched to an unexpectant world. Though it seemed a bit grandiose to place ourselves in the path begun in 1848, yet we were definitely heirs to it, even if, having no good idea what channels to use, we just sent our *Manifesto* off to whatever email list happened to be on our computers.[5] It was equivalent to putting a slip of paper with the text into a bottle, sealing the top, tossing it into the ocean and sitting back to see what would happen.

Very little happened for quite a while, although occasionally some word about the *Manifesto* would drift by. Life went on and our thoughts and contacts widened, until in the very busy year of 2007,[6] Löwy and I, in association with our Canadian comrade, the historian Ian Angus, decided that the time had come to declare ecosocialism what it had to be, an international movement with a global voice in the struggle for a livable post-capitalist world.

So we notified and gathered likely people—chiefly, for starters, Northern Europeans, Greeks and Latin Americans, mostly from Brazil. And on a fine October day seventy or so souls from thirteen countries gathered at Montreuil, on the outskirts of Paris, virtually next door to the studio of that Great Illusionist, Georges Méliès.

Wonder of wonders, more than a few, especially the Greeks, had come across the *Ecosocialist Manifesto* at some time in the past six years and were there on its account (moral: never give up if on the side of justice, no matter how foolish one may appear.). By evening, we had introduced the Ecosocialist International Network (EIN) to the world.

There is no doubt in my mind that the EIN was a good idea, indeed, essential if the world is to move in the direction of ecosocialism. For me it reawakened old dreams, as I began looking South once more, after the travels in Suriname, Nicaragua, and Cuba, tracking the strategic advancement of ecosocialism across Latin America and especially Brazil, the leading country represented at the EIN launching and, so far as is known, the place where the word "ecosocialism" was first used in the 1980s.

We also sought places like Turkey, where two of my books had been published, DeeDee and I had friends, and we had been actively involved in the World Tribunal on Iraq. After all, how could one be indifferent to a town like Assos where (thanks to ex-Bard friend Ahmet Tonak) one could stand where Aristotle stood and look off to the island of Lesbos? I had already visited Argentina in 2002 and Brazil's Porto Alegre in 2005 to promote *The Enemy of Nature*. But the EIN put everything into a wider, though not necessarily better, perspective.

I had not realized that among the Brazilians at Montreuil in 2007 were staff members of the amazing Marina Silva, daughter of rubber tappers, illiterate until age fourteen, and soon after, a disciple of the legendary Chico Mendes, the great martyr of ecosocialism assassinated by rubber barons in 1988.[7] By 2007 Marina was President Lula's Environment Minister; and the next year I found myself the keynote speaker at the National Environmental Meeting in Brasilia before two-to-three-thousand ardent supporters of her as the next President of Brazil.

This was a joyride no doubt, but not a strong horse for a long race, as Marina proceeded from here to nowhere, making an ill-conceived alliance with evangelical Christianity and a hopeless and short-lived one with the Greens. She was briefly in play for the presidency, and could possibly rise again; but there is no reason to take this seriously or even as a good thing given her wobbly judgment.

The chief lessons, which apply across the whole planet, are first, that nothing ecosocialist can come into play from the modern state except piecemeal reforms, and second, that patient, creative organizing from below in a myriad of circumstances is the true way forward.

The EIN, however, had some post-Marina Silva Brazilian life. Its high point came with the World Social Forum held in January 2009, in Belém, at the mouth of the Amazon. Dear old Belém, the navel of the world, longitude, latitude and altitude a triple zero, and the days mainly distinguished by whether it rains twice or thrice therein. The town was eminently forgettable, though from its edges one could see so colossal a flow of water as to imagine the days of Noah.

The Social Forums I have attended aside from Belém—Mumbai in 2004 and Nairobi in 2007, both extremely trying, and Detroit in 2010—were pageants of fecklessness; but I would submit Belém for the Grand Prize. No, it could not surpass Mumbai for teeming humanity, ghastly traffic and horrid air, nor Nairobi for menace, which included armed robbery on the premises. But Belém had a kind of loony quality to it that won the laurel, for at what other international conference were things set up so that the majority of attendees could never find out where things were to be held, or how to get there if they did? The Belém Forum was Kafka on the Amazon. And yet in one event I was able to attend, thankfully downtown and away from the two widely separated universities where the bulk of non-events took place, there was indeed a meeting of North and South under the auspices of the EIN, which finally and for the first time merited the "I" in its acronym. People from the deep forest had been arriving all along, some by canoe over the Amazon waterways and some with head dress and tribal regalia. Now some were in the room with Northerners and by their very presence made of the EIN a living network.

The central figure in the meeting was Hugo Blanco, of Peru and the World. Blanco is one of those unique people whose rarity stems from the breadth of his association, the linkage to global struggles certified by a lifetime of activism South and North, accompanied by serious imprisonment and definite threats to his life, not just from the firing squads of the capitalist state but also at the murderous hands of neo-Maoist groups like the Sendero Luminosa of Peru.[8]

Blanco and I shared a platform in Vancouver, British Columbia in 2007 and crossed paths from time to time in London, where Derek Wall and others on the Green Left have sponsored him. His genius is to include the *campesino* liberation movements, and from this Southern base, to connect with and expand the scope of International Trotskyism, and then gradually to move away from that as the locus of struggle shifted, not so much to the South as such but the planet itself, in which core indigenous peoples are foregrounded at the foundation of the New Earth. For Blanco—and I have often wished to include myself in this assessment, but lack the first-hand acquaintance necessary to develop it adequately—the Zapatista enclaves in Chiapas are paradigmatic for the direction of planetary struggle as a whole, in that they do not try to seize existing power but to build power, i.e., produce it from ecosocialist praxis, for such is the common property of ecosocialist ensembles everywhere they arise, interstitially and prefiguratively building integral ecosystems, unionizing, uniting, universalizing, and undermining the rotting capitalist order.

We were doing what we could at *CNS*, chiefly by building a strong ecofeminist presence with the journal. This was spendidly augmented by the leading German ecofeminist, Maria Mies, author of *Patriarchy and Accumulation on a World Scale*. We had met at the

Mumbai 2004 World Social Forum; and in 2005 Maria had keynoted a *CNS* conference in Toronto in a stirring speech which began with ancient foundations: about the Mesopotamian mother goddess Tiamat and her murder by her son Marduk, which brought about the world patriarchal order.

JOEL WITH MARIA MIES, MUMBAI, 2004

And so when Hugo Blanco, declaring himself an ecosocialist, signed his name to the *Second Ecosocialist Manifesto* in a nondescript, packed room in Belém, Brazil, he contributed to what history—should there be such a thing down the road—will recognize as a true turning point in humanity's quest for an integral existence.

Ironically, this also marked both the high water mark of the Ecosocialist International Network and also the beginning of its decline and stagnation. When we met again in Paris in October 2010 it was plain that the EIN had effectively used up all the oxygen allocated for its assigned moment. Webs can be too tenuous to hold together the nodes to which they are attached. In this case, the ecological ensembles were simply too diffuse and too scattered—in any case, insufficiently developed—to sustain an organization assigned to look over them and keep decent records of the state of global ecological struggle while being guided by a tiny, dispersed, and unfunded directorate of six intellectuals who scarcely knew each other.

In a word, impossible. Löwy remains the most active and hopeful, while I have been focusing on Ecosocialist Horizons, founded in New York in 2011, which suits my temperament better. But the EIN was definitely a start, and as the scale of struggle will inevitably expand given the unending crisis, something along these lines, I should think, will emerge in the not-too-distant future, most likely in Venezuela, to pick up its thread.

A COSMOVISION

GRAMSCI WROTE THAT every person was her or his own philosopher by virtue of that organ of human nature which compels us to make sense of our existence regarded as a whole. To the degree such philosophizing addresses the fate of the earth, conceived now in relation to Nature, which is to say, all that is real and exists, whether perceptible or conceivable according to the development of our faculties, it becomes relevant to these tormented times. Now the mind holds a mirror to nature under threat, and to society as a battleground; the metaphor expands and is shaped by the larger narrative: the "whole" becomes now the whole of existence: we have entered, or to be more exact, returned to a condition of being that generates the Cosmovision.

Stanley Diamond taught me that Cosmovisions are axiomatic[9] in every aboriginal society, and therefore "natural" for humans to construct. They define the boundaries between humanity as part of nature and nature as such, where there is neither state, academia, nor fetish of the commodity to mask reality, and where the mystification produced by industrialized media misshapes consciousness. This is why it is impossible for the "good citizen" of an "advanced" society such as ours, who plays by the rules and tends to his/her lawn—metaphorically, a rationalized portion of nature serving as a barrier to perception—to come to grips with the ecological crisis.

SHAWHEEN AND SON DESMOND

DESMOND PROTESTS

How can a Cosmovision take hold when the notion of environmentalism prevails, an anti-cosmogony that hopelessly frays the relationship between humanity and nature and inserts both into capitalist relations, thereby defining nature in the terms of its enemy, with its "icy waters of egotistical calculation." Environmentalism absent the ecological dimension is very much part of the problem—and the failure to recognize it as such, a kind of annihilation.

It seems to me, then, that every coherent approach to the determining crisis of our times—all of the modalities of recognizing injuries to the ecosphere, and all of the strategies for their remediation, needs to declare itself through the lens of a Cosmovision centered about the flourishing of life through a rigorously developed politics of ecosystem integrity, in other words, ecosocialism. Here is the nucleus to one such, which I discovered serendipitously in a letter by its author:

> A human being is a part of the whole, called by us
> "Universe," a part limited in time and space. He ex-
> periences himself, his thoughts and feelings as some-
> thing separate from the rest—a kind of optical
> delusion of his consciousness. The striving to free one-
> self from this delusion is the one issue of true religion.
> Not to nourish it but to try to overcome it is the way
> to reach the attainable measure of peace of mind.[10]

The author: Albert Einstein. Yes, our Einstein, one of the greatest natural scientists ever, claiming the imprimatur of science for radical spiritual speculation, establishing, here, that the discourse of spirit belongs in nature and that there is no a priori contradiction between true religion and science. Einstein, who gave his name to a medical school that gave me my best years as a professional; who agitated for Julius and Ethel Rosenberg as they awaited execution by the National Security State; who led a movement to keep the terrorist-Zionist and future Israeli Prime Minister Menachem Begin from visiting the U.S. in 1948; who was as stalwart an anti-racist as we have ever seen and a friend to Paul Robeson; and who wrote a wonderful essay, "Why Socialism," to help launch the Marxist journal *Monthly*

Review. This inspired me during my happy years of working with Paul Sweezy, America's foremost Marxist, before he entered senescence, human failings intervened and brought my relationship with this journal to a bitter end that will not be discussed here.

What matters is the destination of universality through the overcoming of the egoic self. Thus ecosocialist production, by unmasking the commodity through the Intrinsic Value of Nature, opens upon the heavens. It can never be a merely technical intervention.

Notes

1 Erdman, "Jerusalem," Plate 10–11, 153–154.

2 James O'Connor, *Natural Causes* (New York: Guilford, 1997).

3 Except in one instance, when off-color language tickled the publisher's legal antennae.

4 They were seriously late, however, and kept putting the task off to go to demonstrations and such until begged by the Young Communists, at which point they holed themselves up for a week and did the job. I would tell my Bard students this to rouse the slackers among them.

5 The first version was limited also by being drafted in the shadow of 9/11 before I had arrived at an understanding of that nightmarish event. It contained a number of more or less un-reflected references to "terrorism," all of which demanded that revisions be issued. The most representative version of the *Ecosocialist Manifesto* is that passed in Belem, Brazil in 2009, and is available on the website of Ecosocialist Horizons. As for the questions raised by 9/11, an allusion will appear in the following chapter as to how I came to regard it. It should be no surprise considering my rule of thumb that one rarely goes astray by assuming the worst case for U.S. imperialism. This, however, cannot fit in these memoirs.

6 For me, publication of *Overcoming Zionism*, and the second edition of *The Enemy of Nature*.

7 Mendes named his youngest son "Sandino," which definitely completes a circle for me.

8 See http://www.ww4report.com/node/7756, an interview with Bill Weinberg from later in 2009. See also Derek Wall, *The Rise of the Green Left*.

9 Thanks to Quincy Saul for re-acquainting me with the term.

10 Alice Calaprice, *The New Quotable Einstein* (Princeton: Princeton University Press, 2005), 206. (Letter dated February 12, 1950.)

Chapter 12
My Jewish Question

> Vengeance is Mine, and retribution, In
> due time their foot will slip; For the day
> of their calamity is near, And the impend-
> ing things are hastening upon them.
> — Deuteronomy 32:35

THE NEW JEW COMETH

As the Pauline epiphany that would eventuate in Baptism some 59 years later was taking place at my Yale matricula- tion in September 1953, my beloved aunt Betty, youngest sister of Louis Kovel, lay dying in Brooklyn of ovarian cancer. About a month later, I found myself in the dreary circumstances of her fu- neral; and it was at the reception afterward that I overheard as in a dream or emanation from *Macbeth* the harpy whispering of a trio of aunts, spewing hatred of Betty for abandoning Judaism and depriv- ing them of the satisfactions of mourning a Jewish death. This pro- voked another epiphany, now of rage against Jewish tribalism. I fled the home that had been Betty's, made my way to Grand Central, and was soon back in New Haven to resume my academic career.

Until that time I had no special animus against my ancestral re- ligion, though I found services a boring waste of time spent mum- bling stuff in a language I had no interest in learning, while standing up and sitting down and making a fuss over the Torah, said to be our sacred record, and inscrutable. Most of the kids I knew felt the same, and none of us foresaw any future crisis in life about being

Jewish. I would have scoffed at anybody who saw a religious future in my boyhood self.

We never paid much attention to the Bible in those years—the Old Testament, that is—but some of it was explained in Hebrew School. I was told that Jews were very special people, first of all, because we had discovered very long ago that there was one God ruling over the universe, and that, moreover, we were the chosen people of said God, therefore morally superior, with the insinuation that envy of this status on the part of Goyim had contributed to their anti-Semitism and the hardships that lay across our path through history.

I would have been hard put at the time to say just what Judaism was except a name assigned to various practices around which the family gathered every now and then for holidays and ceremonies that meant nothing to me — and, as far as I could see, nothing much to them, either. For as Jewish families went we were pretty representative of the sociological type of those hell-bent on bourgeois assimilation, in the Kovel instance as in countless others, by trekking to the suburbs where a kind of generalized deracination of traditional identity and its replacement by capitalist consumerism took place. Indeed, my aunts' hatred both repelled and surprised me, as I had never seen any evidence in them of caring for what they had accused Betty of betraying. In truth, Betty was the sole member of the family, so far as I could see, who cared enough about Judaism to feel it as a fetter on her life.

Amidst it all, The Kovel-Farber clan, present company excepted, played the game of assimilation smoothly. The surviving cohort from the immediate families of both parents exceeds in wealth and status that of all of our parents. It includes four lawyers (Alex, Neil, and two Roberts), three doctors (Richard, Jeffrey and yrs. truly), a prominent ad executive and purveyor of real estate in the Hamptons (Gary), an owner of a chain of art supply stores (Steve), and a famous coach of hockey technique to the National Hockey League (Laura), whose photo gallery shows her teaching rough and tough men twice her size how to properly skate. I'm sure the authorities would be pleased with having reaped 90% of the generation, so what if one became an irregular fellow as long as the rest were decent, caring solid citizens, vaunt-couriers of the New Jew; aside from Neil none so far as I know religious though they tend to be observant of Seder, and none with whom, my brother and Steve excepted, I could have a serious conversation about the state of the world. Since I was the oldest and passed through a gateway of academic and professional success while the others were growing up, I was able to watch their eyes shine as "Joel the Doctuh!" appeared before them, and then watched them surpass me in economic reward.

JOEL AND COUSIN DANNY

One who did not survive was Daniel,[1] Betty's only child, and the saddest person I have ever known well. At times I felt that Betty neglected him and saw me as the son she actually wanted. This was not a comforting idea. Dan was a bachelor and had a string of lady friends with whom he traveled on the funds accrued from being a mid-level executive with Grumman, an aerospace company whose fighter-bombers needed the materials and parts he would gather for them. Daniel Horne (the name had been Hirschhorn but his father thought this insufficiently American) was a cog in the Military-Industrial Complex and helped its bombing campaigns and other defenses of Freedom. He despised the System that rewarded him yet reconciled himself to it with quiet desperation as it enabled him to buy his retirement chateau in a gated community on an artificial pond in the wonderfully named Boca Raton, that is, Rat's Mouth, Florida, where no birds sang nor insects chirped, thanks to copious quantities of pesticide assiduously applied as the inhabitants played endless rounds of golf on fine private links. Danny regretted buying his sepulchral dwelling and wished he had gotten retirement digs on a street overlooking the ocean. But he regretted everything, including the politics of Rat's Mouth, known for being one of the top ten Zionist enclaves in America.

I had serious conversations with Danny, who of all my cohort showed the deepest curiosity about what I had gleaned from life. We would meet for a meal on his occasional trips back to New York City and talk about the fallen world and what he could do about his life. Danny was a heavy man, of a scale that had to be treated surgically, whose "weight problem" began with the death of his mother and contributed to the well-being of various high powered clinics in places like Durham, North Carolina. It seemed to have an alchemical effect on the air around him, shrouding joys and desires in a soft, impenetrable gloom.

Often we would talk about—or more exactly, Danny would ask me what to do about—his father and Betty's widower, grim Herman Horne, who was chugging into his last harbor as he passed ninety. Herman had been a science teacher in the New York City system, and in his retirement, an avid botanist and bird-watcher who frequented Jamaica Bay. A body builder in his youth, we found some "I never would have imagined" photos of Herman flexing like Charles Atlas on the Coney Island boardwalk. Herman had been my sole source of information about the Kovel apartment in Williamsburg, where he had gone courting Betty, and told of how strange it was to sense the shadow of the unnamed older sister, likely schizophrenic, who lived in a back room neither seen nor talked about.

After Lou Kovel's death, Herman made certain overtures toward Rose Kovel of an unmistakable kind, which she swiftly rebuffed. It would have been hard to live with Herman Horne. He was a wet blanket of a man who introduced me to a kind of pseudo-Marxist cultural criticism with stern exhortations as to how "they"

were attempting to delude bright youths through false representations of the world like baseball. I was too timid to ask, "But Herman,
is not Duke Snider a real part of the world?"

As Danny worried to me about his father in the latter's dotage, so
did Herman worry incessantly to me about Danny as a motherless
child and an unhappy, obese grownup. Ill fortune brought them together in a dreadful way, when Herman suffered a stroke and a fall
with fractures, and entered Beth Israel Hospital for what looked to be
his final illness. Danny and I would visit him as his only functional
family. One day shortly after Herman's admission, Danny related to
me the terrible news that he himself had been stricken: diagnosed—
no! no!—with lung cancer; and had to go directly to surgery at Mount
Sinai. Surely it was caused by the years of smoking away his nervous
tension—and also, I suspect, the pesticide-full air and water of Rat's
Mouth Condo, not to mention a life of despair and his father's passage
toward death. In any case, a couple of years of unimaginable suffering
lay ahead for Danny, with a hideous death by asphyxiation at its end,
and for me, a number of excruciating trips to Florida.

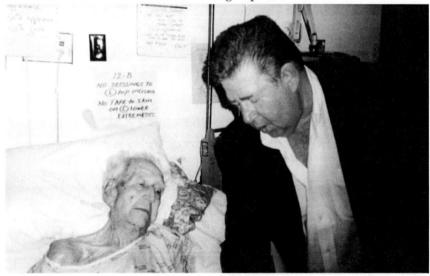

DANNY AND HERMAN

In the awful moment of revelation, Danny focused on hiding the
fact of his illness from Herman by concocting a story. He recruited
myself and a group of his friends to convey to Herman the news

that his boy had been suddenly called away for a month on urgent business and would see him again upon return. A little white subterfuge, it was, for great suffering and pain did not stop Danny Horne from getting a job done.

Herman seemed at first to accept the story. But I could not help noticing that his mind was slipping, so that by the time Danny was released from Mount Sinai his father scarcely noticed. By then Herman had stipulated the conditions of his own death with characteristic severity: neither try to prevent it, nor slow it down; and once it happened, no funeral, no memorial service, no announcement in the papers for the various clubs through which his life had been given attachment and meaning. Nor was there to be burial or cremation: only take the corpse and dump it into the equivalent of Potter's Field. Herman died angry that the world was such a shitty place, which I suppose meant that he had once hoped for a better one, difficult to imagine but a logical possibility. A bitter hard man was Herman Horne, no saint yet a kind of anti-hero, forthright in his radical unbelief and willing to discard all that had meant so much to him. For the Hornes, father and son, were representative of the modern type who live without faith, hope, or expectation of God's grace.

As for Danny, we were able to illegally sneak some of his ashes into Jamaica Bay. Right under the eyes of the Park Police, by God.

> Every Night & every Morn
> Some to Misery are Born…
> — Blake, "Auguries of Innocence"

SHADOWS OF THE SIX-DAY WAR

I HAD FOLLOWED THE FOUNDING of the Jewish State with some interest and considerable confusion stemming from parental discord. The difference from my parents' other quarrels lay in the fact that this time, Rose Kovel spoke out forcefully for the Jewish State and challenged her husband's dominance in matters political. I was twelve in 1948, and Israel's conquest of Palestine had been a blur. By 1953 and for a considerable time thereafter, I had no particular attitude toward these events except to vaguely share in the buzz of excitement that suffused the virtually exclusively Jewish—and heavily pro-Soviet—Midwood-Flatbush neighborhood of my boyhood and its extensions into the suburbs of Nassau County.

Rose Kovel became even more active as soon as we moved to Baldwin in 1949, doing Zionist support work through the women's auxiliary, Hadassah. Meanwhile, Father raged against treasonous divided loyalties, even going so far as to join the American Council for Judaism. This had been founded in 1943 to advocate a bi-national state, a concept of considerable importance that held no meaning for me at the time but was anathema to my mother. I wish I knew more than this of Father's thoughts about Israel. No doubt, his antipathy was accentuated by the originally socialist character of the Jewish State. This of course was exactly what pleased the Midwood Jews, though it turned into a quaint memory as Israel became a colonial power and an epicenter of world reaction—which very likely would please the Midwood Jews of today, for the old neighborhood is filled with ultra-Orthodox, and 1139 East 10th Street, once the place of utmost familiarity, is now a zone of radical culture shock, though no less Jewish.

In any case, since my parents quarreled about everything, I couldn't take the matter regarding Israel *per se* very seriously, though its capacity to stir deep unrest was evident from the beginning of my awareness. Just how deep would become clear almost two decades later.

LATE IN MAY, 1967, I WAS SITTING in the kitchen of our pre-fab home in Seattle's University District where Virginia and I had passed close to two years enduring military duty with the U.S. Public Health Service, Mount Rainier shimmering eighty miles in the distance. I picked up the *Post Intelligentsia*, and there, blaring on the front page, was an eight-column headline to the effect that Israel faced imminent annihilation from the massed armies of Egypt, Syria and Jordan.

What had been calm instantly became panic. It was the worst fright I had ever experienced over a political matter, not so extended as that of the Cuban Missile Crisis, but more visceral, even though, in sharp contrast to the events of October 1962, neither my nor my family's lives, not to mention those of humanity as a whole, were at stake. The fear stemmed from threats to an obscure portion of my identity concerning a country I had never visited, nor wanted to visit despite mother's endless importuning to see the miraculous Jewish State, the tab to be on her account. Although the idea occasionally flickered through my thoughts how exciting it must be to build a new society from the ground up (disregarding, of course, the fate of the indigenous), by and large I had little regard for Israel, and even held it in some disdain because of an obnoxious Israeli co-resident psychiatrist.

Now, reason was swept aside as deep circuits opened, linking the Israeli present and the Jewish past with memory of the Holocaust and what the Holocaust signified in the inner chambers of Jewish being, even of a Jew who had ostensibly put Jewishness behind him fourteen years before. Here it was, about to happen again; and I became Every-Jew, feared what Jews are made to fear, and identified a nation-state with Jewry itself, as Zionism demanded. I was a Jew and, in a moment of supreme danger the Jewish people—*my* Jewish people—were about to be thrown into the sea and exterminated! What was to be done?!

Actually, nothing externally, because what was happening was not integral to the actuality of the person, Joel Kovel, but the splitting-off of a "spirit being," a concept I was to develop in *History and Spirit*. In this instance of the phenomenon, a demon drawn from the collective Jewish soul had taken up residence in my own, a lodger of sorts, the door of whose chamber had been pried open by events. Or maybe a kind of Golem awakened by an alarm in historical time to torment me with what has passed. Its source was not direct experience, rather, the imagined outcome of reading and brooding about the Holocaust once I got wind of it in the 1940s. I saw again heartrending photos of cachectic prisoners and terrifying images of smirking Nazi troops with long coats rounding up Jewish victims on city streets.

A ruthless critic am I, but no denier of Shoah. Being a brooder, I would brood over the Holocaust as it became disclosed and wonder how such evil could happen. And as I brooded the circuits of reason resumed. I brought the tracings of Shoah into myself by photo and text, packed my brain with them, combining them with stories of pogroms such as my parents' families would have experienced before their birth in 1901 and 1908; or during the Nazi invasion, the supreme pogrom that befell to those still living in Ukraine, especially near the infamous Babi Yar, a ravine in the vicinity of where the Rose Farber branch of the family lived and where the corpses of many thousand Jews, Romani and Poles were dumped by *Einsatzgruppen* and fascist Ukrainian militias in the autumn of 1941. Were the corpses of Farbers hurled down as well? It was another, supremely bitter motif of the sense of disconnection with my past, to be gound in my inner mills, and sequestered until the tremors of the Six-Day War began to subside. Thus I made for myself a Shoah-demon, and suffered, shuddering, its release with the threats to Israel.

The notion of a "demon" and its identification as Golem is meant to introduce a feature of Ashkenazi Judaic being. Leon Botstein described it, in the days when we were on speaking terms, as a perennial condition of anxiety awaiting the knock on one's door by authorities coming to get you in the middle of the night. This fear had been inscribed in the collective Jewish psyche over centuries and especially in the extended nightmare that hung over the last one.

IT WORKED OUT DIFFERENTLY, however, for me. Set loose, my demon didn't stick around but wandered off, never to haunt me again. Perhaps it could sense that, in contrast to the majority of Jewish psyches, it had been staying in inhospitable quarters, where it endured by virtue of being unconscious. It wouldn't have taken a very smart demon to arrive at this conclusion, inasmuch as I had by June 1967, declared myself a lifelong enemy of the National Security State and was gathering materials for *White Racism* while eagerly awaiting return to New York where I had every intention of joining the anti-war movement. Having lost so much connection to Jewry over the years and adding to this over the past year the development of an anti-imperial mentality, there was no reason for my rising consciousness to head in the Zionist direction that was to be the destiny of the great majority of American Jews, along with the remarkable surge in Holocaust awareness that followed upon the Six-Day War,[2] and the burgeoning of ties between Israeli and United States foreign policy elites, or neoconservatives.

We all are responsible for our being. As the Talmudic rabbinate made clear, the Golem demon—and *pari passu*, all demons—are human-made, and if of a Jew, shaped by Jewish actuality, which is to say, as a function of the life one lives and the choices and values one lives by. For the great majority of American Jews, the process of bourgeoisification had settled in by 1967 and provided the matrix for an augmented loyalty to Israel. Alongside these a small fraction became what we would call "neo-cons," for whom the expansion of U.S. imperialism and the defense of Israel were essentially identical. Meanwhile the larger body of American Jewry sat back, prospered, and by losing the prophetic edge that had redeemed Judaism over the centuries, facilitated the unification of the two states under augmented Israeli control.

AS FOR MYSELF, I AM ASHAMED to say that I enjoyed a rush of exultation with the rapidity and fury of Israel's triumph. But it subsided under the pressure of my growing left-wing identity. And as things calmed further I began to wonder about certain facts of the matter, to wit, that Israel had instantly routed forces who seemed only a day or two beforehand to be preparing to push Jews into the sea. What had happened to the Arab juggernaut? Was there such a behemoth in the first place? Could there have been a mistake… or, heaven forbid, a deception? If so, my world had been turned upside down. In spite of my alienation, I still held it as axiomatic that ethically superior, long suffering, and eternally victimized Jews, my ancestral people bearing Yahweh's Covenant, would, by definition, never do such a thing.

Chico Marx had asked: "who are you going to believe, me or your own eyes?" Now I was in such a dilemma internalized. The "me" was my socially constructed self and its attachment to the ideology machine churning myths of Jewish moral singularity; meanwhile, "my own eyes," were those of an awakening ruthless criticism.

Having been conditioned to think that Jews were by definition incapable of such behavior, I now had to rethink definitions, including those of "my ancestral people" and Yahweh's Covenant with them. As I realized over the months ahead that Israel's goals in 1967 went far beyond self-defense to include occupation and colonization of the seized Palestinian territories, and that this was no random event, but integral to Zionism, a transformed world began to take shape before my eyes.

From a Zionist perspective, "self-defense" requires occupation and colonization of seized Palestinian territories. But what is the "self" here? Not the physical body of society but its identity, that which holds it together and gives it purpose. That the Zionist Self takes its identity from imperialism as an occupier and colonizer is a simple matter of historical record, certified with the 1917 Balfour Declaration and implicit since the days of Herzl. As Zionism requires forcible removal of the indigenous Palestinians from Palestine—a great crime on its face—it cannot go forward without an enabling legend to obscure the criminality of ethnic cleansing,[3] for which purpose the Shoah provides context, justification, and legitimation. Seizing upon the facts of Holocaust, Zionism arrived at a self-reproducing tautology in which a colonialism of Palestinians and endless aggression toward Arabs became a closed circle locked into place by establishing extreme Jewish victimhood on the one side, and on the other, absolute impunity.[4] For this purpose, imperial patronage became a necessity.

I LEARNED ALL OF THIS, AND MUCH MORE, during the years since realizing I had been suckered in 1967. The fact that millions of other Jews had gone through 1967 to become incorporated into a Zionist identity accelerated my alienation from American Jews as well as from the American empire. Increasingly, this made me not a "self-hating Jew"—an asinine phrase demanded by inquisitors as self-mortification for having betrayed the Tribe—but very definitely a "Zionism-hating" and therefore a free-thinking Jew, which is to say in the framework offered by Einstein, a "human being [who] recognizes the Self as a part of the whole, called by us, 'Universe'." As this made one less of a Jew it also contains the possibility of not being a Jew at all.

THE RISE OF THE POWER JEW

> If there is an intellectual movement in America to whose invention Jews can lay sole claim, neoconservatism is it. It's a thought one imagines most American Jews, overwhelmingly liberal, will find horrifying. And yet it is a fact that as a political philosophy, neoconservatism was born among the children of Jewish immigrants and is now largely the intellectual domain of those immigrants' grandchildren.[5]

I HAD BEEN CLOSE TO A TAP ROOT of a humane Judaism through my close friendship at Yale with Tom Cohen, whose father, Elliot (Yale, '21), was the founder and presiding voice of *Commentary*, the *raison d'etre* of which was to bring Jewish intellectuals into the liberal mainstream of American intellectual life. The brilliance of *Commentary*'s Elliot Cohen Period lay in its openness to many voices, thereby suffusing the identity of Judaism with universal values. Thus Cohen welcomed friends-to-be of ours, for example Conrad Lynn, a brilliant Black lawyer with strong communist sympathies.

In the late '50s, an extremely aggressive young editor, Norman Podhoretz, entered the picture, took over the journal after Elliot's much-lamented death by suicide in 1959, and after a brief hiatus, proceeded to turn *Commentary* into a flagship of neoconservatism.[6] Remarkably, this seemed as if coordinated with Israeli victory in 1967. It is worth noting that seedlings of neoconservatism appeared across the whole post-WWII era bursting forth *before* the advent of neoliberalism in the mid to late 'seventies. In fact, they broke through the ground precisely in the aftermath of the Six-Day War of 1967 that so rattled everybody's spirits, including mine. This can be pinpointed to a shocking event from the war's fifth day, the destruction of the *SS Liberty*, a U.S. surveillance ship, by Israeli bombers and PT boats, and even more shocking, President Johnson's exoneration of Israel and imposition of a blackout about the catastrophe—even though transcripts between Israeli pilots and their base prove it was a deliberate attack.[7]

All this passed me by as I settled into the good life of the psychiatric professoriat, the high point of whose year was the August family trip to places like Truro and Wellfleet on Cape Cod. It was a Jewish scene, along with being a Harvard scene, with plenty of tennis and all kinds of edifying talk about how awful the Vietnam War was as we watched the wind-blown beach grass and the deep blue sea beyond. Virginia and I soon acquired new friends in this happy place, the Thernstroms: Stephan, a historian at Harvard, his wife Abby, and their children Melanie (a future author of note) and Sam.

ONE EVENING AT A PICNIC ON THE BEACH I met their dynamic friend, Martin Peretz, a rising poor boy from the Bronx who was making an impact in the Harvard Department of Government. Some time later I heard that Marty was no longer poor, having wed the heiress to the Singer Sewing Machine Company. Next, he purchased the venerable liberal news magazine, *The New Republic*, declaring it had drifted too far to the left and too far from the interests of the State of Israel, which he, an ardent believer in the rising power of Jews, was going to rectify.

Some years afterward I learned that Marty had joined the Board of Trustees of a progressive liberal arts college on the Hudson River, Bard, under the direction of a polymath named Leon Botstein. When Botstein was offering me the Alger Hiss Chair of Social Studies at Bard in 1987, he mentioned in passing that he had to convince people like Peretz to close the deal. Roughly eighteen years after that, I severely criticized Peretz in my *Overcoming Zionism* for his vicious attack in the *Los Angeles Times* on the anti-Zionist martyr Rachel Corrie, who had been crushed under an Israeli bulldozer while defending the home of a Palestinian friend. My attack on Peretz undoubtedly did not help my cause at Bard, but I could not allow his calumny against this heroic woman to stand uncontested.[8]

UPON THE BREAKUP OF MY MARRIAGE in 1977, Abby and Steve went 100% over to Virginia's side. We never saw each other again, to nobody's regret, as the political divide between us widened. They became Republicans and with support from conservative foundations, wrote an influential book, *America in Black and White*, arguing against the dire influence of affirmative action and generally denying that racism was still a major problem in America, something possible to do from a position of empiricism such as Steve espoused. Sharp-tongued Abby served as Vice Chair of the U.S. Commission on Civil Rights and became useful in various respectable gatherings fostered by our self-proclaimed First Black President, Bill Clinton. I wonder what Steve and Abby think now of the aggravated racist mayhem wrought against Black and Brown people that has generated the phenomenon of Black Lives Matter.

I also remember them as friends who were close to us during my marriage to Virginia, who took care of Jon and Erin while we traveled in Mexico, and who were the first line of help when five year old Erin suffered a compound fracture of her left humerus falling off a bunk bed in Wellfleet, a calamity that set her back several years. But with the breakup of my marriage and spurred by political differences we drifted apart. I imagine they consider me a menace to Western Civilization.

BY THE TIME OF THE MUNICH HOSTAGE CRISIS and the 1973 Yom Kippur War I had substantially distanced myself from Israel and could not share the anguish that surged through the faculty and staff of the Einstein Psychiatry Department. It was not until I read Seymour Hersh's *The Samson Option* while preparing *Overcoming Zionism*, however, that I realized how bad things had gotten—how the Israeli Prime Minister, Golda Meir, facing a major defeat from Arab forces, had called Henry Kissinger and threatened to use just that option unless the United States bailed out Israel. Yes, the Prime Minister of America's client state was going to use the nuclear weapons that we had illegally enabled the Jewish State to build, bringing down the whole region as Samson (impersonated by Victor Mature) brought down the Temple on all. Kissinger complied, Israel was re-armed, and the war passed by until the next atrocity.[9] Doubts about Israel solidified slowly into hostility, inhibited, I am ashamed to say, by tensions with Mother that lasted right up until her death in 1993, though we became kinder to each other in the final stages. My views as to Israeli barbarism were largely formed by the time of the Sabra and Shatila massacres in 1982. Shortly after, a hot-headed—though wholly accurate, in my view—assertion by DeeDee that these events revealed deep Israeli affinities with Nazism provoked a fearsome reaction from a visiting Rose Kovel, who walked out of our recently acquired country house and down Sickler Road, passing through the deep woods where roughly one car an hour went by, and demanded to be taken home after I caught up with her. That her home at the time was in West Palm Beach condoland while our rickety manse lay deep in New York's Catskill Mountains underscored the rift between us, which lingered for years.

Even after Rose's death, my guilt proved hard to dissolve. Little by little, however, her grip on my psyche weakened, as the violence intrinsic to the Jewish State grew. Matters came to a head when Psychopath-in-Chief Ariel Sharon, en route to becoming Prime Minister despite having been declared a war criminal by Israel's High Court for Sabra and Shatila, led one thousand armed thugs to the Al Aqsa Mosque in September 2000, setting off the Second Intifada and causing the proverbial last straw to flutter downward and topple my Jewish identity—and about time, too!

I REMEMBER SITTING IN A Green Party meeting, chafing as usual at the torpid discussion while the Zionist question kept roaring in my head, until something snapped inside and I said to myself that I was sick and tired of beating my head against the wall of Green electoral politics and sick and tired, too, of my dithering at coming to grips with this surpassingly existential issue seven years after the death of Rose Kovel, God-dammit! And so I resolved to concentrate my energies on bringing down the Zionist Beast, the Devil take the hindmost. And he did, as we will see in the next chapter. But first, this concluding digression.

IN WHICH WE REFLECT ON SOME
OF THE DIVERSE WAYS OF BEING A NON-JEWISH JEW

NO LONGER A JEW, I WALK BY A SYNAGOGUE and hear the voices chanting in Hebrew, and walk on. They do not speak to me or for me. I go to Riverside Chapel on Amsterdam and 67th for the funeral of Cousin Neil's wife Linda and I feel the loss of a human being but do not respond to the prayers; they are in a foreign language, not for me or of me. I receive mailings from Jewish Voices for Peace, or Jews Against the Occupation, or Jews for Racial and Economic Justice, and I hit the delete button. I do not like the way they cling to the notion of a special, "chosen" voice and do not venture into the critique of Zionism…. Here it goes again, I think to myself: always holding the mirror of the special people. And I walk on.

But human nature does not function by switches. Identity may be a kind of hegemony of mutually reinforcing elements, but it is no totalization except in pathological extremes. And in this ex-Jew's mind, there are plenty of leftover tendrils of old affection: some simply memories, some cultural tidbits, some actual relationships, all testimony to the glorious unruliness of human being. I am not going to aver that some of my best friends are Jews, but it is certainly the case. And I remain inordinately fond of Yiddish culture, witness an enduring affection for lowbrow Mel Brooks, despite his maudlin Jewish chauvinism—even because of it as in his evocations of Borscht Belt grandeur, which remind me of my vehement Uncle Hy, who grew up in the Esther Manor near Monticello and fought in the Battle of the Bulge. I still crack up with friends and my older children as we circulate lines from Brooks' films, like the sublimely corny *Spaceballs* ("let the Schwartz be with you!") or the masterpiece, *Young Frankenstein* (Dr. F. to his servant Eigor: "wasn't that hump on the right side?" Eigor: "What hump?"—when a patient shared this with me during a therapy session, we both laughed helplessly—I still laugh while reading the line again and again as I rationalize the need to do so as copy-editing). More, Brooks (with Carl Reiner) created the only Jewish

Jesus joke that ever set me rolling with laughter when his 2000 Year Old Man complained that Christ "always came into the store but never bought anything." Perhaps Brooks' charm has something to do with the fact that, as my daughter Erin and son-in-law Greg Fitzsimmons reported after a chance meeting on the street in Venice, California, he is a genuinely sweet and lovable person—in contrast to my boyhood chum Allan Koningsberg, *a.k.a.* Woody Allen, the most famous graduate of P.S. 99's class of 1949, whose comedic gift has become barren with the passage of time.

BILL KUNSTLER

THEN THERE WAS BILL KUNSTLER, not lovable but magnificent, with whom I worked on maybe a dozen cases as—excuse the expression—an expert psychiatric witness, most notably pairing up to free Salvador Agron in 1977 through convincing the jury that his escape from the Fishkill Correctional Facility, where he was about to be paroled for the "Capeman Murders," was due to incipient psychosis. Once I asked Bill, like me a New York Jewish Yalie, how he could be so insouciantly outrageous in the Courtroom, in so doing, infuriating legions, and he replied:

> Joel, before I enter the court each day I pause to remind myself that the Judge, the Jury, the opposing lawyers, and all the others in the courtroom, as well as those outside, all the way up to the most powerful figures in society, even the Pope and Queen Elizabeth, everybody has six inches of shit in their rectum, just like everybody else… and as I realize that, I take a deep breath, fear nothing, and go to work.[10]

In other words, a great humanist, not to mention fighter for justice.

HEREWITH, SOME FURTHER OBSERVATIONS on this theme:

WHEN the voices of children are heard on the green,
And laughing is heard on the hill,
My heart is at rest within my breast,
And everything else is still.

'Then come home, my children, the sun is gone down,
And the dews of night arise;
Come, come, leave off play, and let us away
Till the morning appears in the skies.'

'No, no, let us play, for it is yet day,
And we cannot go to sleep;
Besides, in the sky the little birds fly,
And the hills are all cover'd with sheep.'

'Well, well, go and play till the light fades away,
And then go home to bed.'
The little ones leapèd and shoutèd and laugh'd
And all the hills echoèd.

Allen Ginsberg loved Blake as much as I. He especially loved putting to music the *Songs of Innocence and Experience*—of which the exquisite poem above is the "Nurse's Song" from the former—and singing them in his reedy, rich baritone. His rendition was unique, taking off once the final line had been reached into dithyrambic improvising in which Ginsberg, along with the players accompanying him and the audience, would freely repeat the final line, echoing it for an immoderate length of time. During the summer evening in the mid-1980s in which I took part, echoing lasted more than a half-hour and fairly lifted us all into heaven. The experience wove together a number themes of interest to this memoir: the option, drawn from the Synoptic Gospels (as in Mark 10:12–16) for the "little ones" whom we must take in our arms and bless if we are to enter the Kingdom of God, which belongs to them; the flowing, ever-re-peating songs of nature like the gurgling of brooks, the booming of the sea and the soughing of the wind; the Nurse's peaceful unity with the little ones and nature; and the phenomenon of echoing, which both differentiates and unites.

On this summer evening we were singing in Woodstock's Byrd-cliffe Barn. Allen was the guest of the Fugs, a survivor anarchist band of the late '60s, founded by Ed Sanders and Naphtali, or "Tuli" Kupferberg.

Ed is still active in Woodstock, while Tuli and Allen have passed, the former in 2010, at age 86, and the latter, in 1997, at age 71.

TULI KUPFERBERG

They all were remarkable, but Tuli was special. He had been part of the Beat move-ment, and appears in Gins-berg's *Howl* as the man who jumped off the Brooklyn Bridge (except it was really the Man-hattan Bridge). To me, there was something about him that compels a place at the head of a list of exemplary Jews, unless one counts the late song, "Backward Jewish Soldiers," a ditty consonant with his lifelong loathing of the war-making machine. And yet who could be more Jewish, a Jewish troubadour, profanely holy, who else could give us gems like "Shake, Shake, Whore of Babylon," "CIA Man," "Nothing" (an ex-istential rendering of the Yiddish song about potatoes), "I'm Just a Septuagenarian in Love," "After the Balls are Ova," and scores of other ballads?

I loved Tuli for being radically outside the pincer-grip defined by late-capitalist professionalism and Zionism that afflicts Jews of my ken and cohort. Tuli was Jewish by assuming its immemorial un-rootedness—the voice in the wilderness and not the pharisaic accomplice. It had to be a Yiddish-installed voice, the language spo-ken in his New York City childhood, all praise to Tuli Kupferberg and this city I love.

AND TO ANOTHER YIDDISH-SPEAKING CITY of my dreams, Odessa. Though I never got closer to it than Istanbul, Odessa fired my imagination through its native son and Yiddishkeit genius, journalist and short story writer, Isaac Babel, who roamed through Ukraine and Poland during the wars with the White Russians, and afterwards became a leading Soviet writer, only to be murdered in 1940 by Stalin's purge. One of the fabricated creatures who inhabit my imagination, Babel's is scarcely a life I would actually want to live. It serves, rather, as a harvesting of my dreams and a *recherche* of ancestral roots, all gone, leaving me adrift on a sea of self invention.... And how about this! Babel, perhaps Russia's greatest twentieth-century writer, actually wrote of Kovel, the place!;[11] and was the kind of communist I would want to have been, a participant in a youthful revolution that seemed to have a chance. And, also a general condition: a Jewishness completely outside the clutches of Zionism; and of course, a brilliant literary gift totally beyond me. But what a gruesome ending! The worst and most ignominious! Still, poor Babel sleeps with the immortals.

There is no Judaism these days completely outside Zionism's grip; and so to me it has become like a beach with a lot of empty shells scattered about, some pretty, some interesting, none with a worthwhile future in a world dominated by Israel and capitalist hegemony. But what do I know?—once a Jew who felt no pulse from his heritage but the deadly brutality of its Zionist derivative, and decided, by bits and pieces, to let it go?

I AM IN THIS REGARD A MEMBER of a diffuse class, the "Non-Jewish Jews," who live, thanks to the conquests of Zionism, in one degree of separation or another from their ancestral identity. The great Isaac Deutscher, Polish-Jewish Communist and biographer of Trotsky (himself an example), coined the term some time ago, and respected friends, notably Bertell Ollman, who opened the gates to the Young Marx for me, and French/Israeli-historian Shlomo Sand, have honorably claimed the distinction as well.[12] Albert Einstein is a charter member of this club, needless to say, whose deeply etched connection with Judaism gave way in face of the rise of Zionist Israel, and was left behind by his philosophical universalism. Freud, of course, is ritually added to the list despite his ambivalent spiritual posture, generously described as stoic. I cannot help seeing in any case that he never left the side of "civilization" and what he called Reason, and which an honest yet severe view must call patriarchy dedicated to the capitalist project.

And the most important figure of all, Karl Marx, I would not call a Non-Jewish Jew at all, despite what many Marxists say, because he was not Jewish at all, unless being the scion of rabbis who is baptized Lutheran at age seven, and takes a Christian identity seriously thereafter, is still Jewish. It is remarkable how deeply imprinted is the chauvinism of "Once a Jew, always a Jew." But a fact is a fact.

One more major figure of this sort, Simone Weil, steps forth as the most religiously profound of all the non-Jewish Jews, and perhaps the most radical as well. Simone came to loathe the Old Testament for its violence and cruelty and saw this in Judaism itself—an outrageous view according to the prevailing Judaeophilia, but not without substantiation by a discerning mind. She also developed a sensibility for the victim worthy of Christ's self-identification with the "least of these" in Matthew 25:31–46. Combining this with Marxism and passionate engagement with the French Resistance, Weil sacrificed herself with an early death of tuberculosis and self-starvation in 1943.

ROSA LUXEMBURG

To my mind, however, the greatest of Non-Jewish Jews is Rosa Luxemburg: of Jewish origin yet who never, so far as I know, showed more concern about being Jewish than in the color of her eyes. The key was Red Rosa's disdain for another pillar of chauvinism, that Jewish suffering is special, as well. Luxemburg's universalism appears in this light as compassion for all human or non-human creatures who suffered, *per se*. It defines the whole direction of her socialist revolutionary doctrine, the most promising of all traditional Marxist writings from an ecosocialist standpoint.

DEEDEE WAS WILLING TO NAME our precious daughter born 5 December 1979, after our favorite Marxist, as an expression of our deepest values for the little one. I could not bring myself to do this, however, as it would mean somehow informing my mother, Rose Kovel, that she was there as a second-string candidate. Chalk up another scar of ambivalence, love and accusation in the same breath: the Human Condition in quotidian garb. Get thee behind me!

We rummaged… and came up—I believe it was on a beach— with Mariana! Who? Well, not a girl at all, but a sixteenth-century Jesuit, Juan de Mariana, who wrote an epochal treatise, *De rege et regis institutione* (Toledo, 1598), the argument of which, that it was lawful to remove a tyrant from power, could not be refuted.

And so Mariana Louise Drosten (for Lou Kovel, and MaryLou and Louise Drosten) Kovel entered humanity… and grandmother Rose was well pleased, as was everybody, especially when the top notch nickname "Molly" was added for everyday use. Its origin was equally strong: the famous Molly Jemison, a woman from western New York State of the sevententh century, taken captive by Indians, who refused to go back to "civilization": a distinguished inheritance indeed.

Notes

[1] Another, David, brother to Steve and Laura, was killed by friendly fire while serving in Korea, while Anne, sister of Neil and Gary, died of medical causes.
[2] Peter Novick, *The Holocaust in American Life* (New York: Houghton Mifflin, 1999). Novick gives a comprehensive account of the phenomenon.
[3] This is not the place to take up the question of the degree to which Zionists were complicit with the Third Reich in order to get Jews into Palestine, alas, significant. See Lenni Brenner, *Zionism in the Age of Dictators*.

4 Ilan Pappé, *The Ethnic Cleansing of Palestine* (Oxford: Oneworld, 2006).

5 Gal Beckerman, "The Neoconservative Persuasion," *Jewish Daily Forward*, January 6, 2006, http://www.forward.com/main/printer-friendly.php?id=7102. In 2003, Note the source, a still-functioning Jewish journal with roots in a now-gone Left, especially the ILGWU. Halle Lasn, publisher of *AdBusters* magazine, inquiring into the Jewish contribution to the Iraq war, listed fifty indisputable leaders powerfully involved in the invasion. Twenty-five were Jewish. Since Jews comprise some 2% of the population, this is also twenty-five times the incidence that would obtain in a random distribution.

6 Compounding this, Podhoretz's son-in-law is Elliott Abrams, who directed State Department policy toward Latin America in the 1980s and the National Security Council's policy toward the Middle East under Bush II—in the interim convicted of perjury during the Iran-Contra crisis, and pardoned by Bush I.

7 A great deal of material can be found about the *SS Liberty* incident at http://ifamericansknew.org/us_ints/ussliberty-res.html.

8 Joel Kovel, *Overcoming Zionism* (London: Pluto Press, 2007) 127–129.

9 Seymour Hersh, *The Samson Option* (New York: Random House, 1991). This study of how Israel got the Atom Bomb has essentially been banned despite Hersh's tremendous reputation.

10 Bill also told me my favorite lawyer joke: "What's the difference between a Lawyer and a spermatozoon?" I give up. "The spermatozoon has a one in six million chance of becoming a human being."

11 A city and railroad hub of about seventy thousand originating in 1300 and located in the northwest corner of Ukraine close to Poland.

12 Shlomo Sand, *The Invention of the Jewish People* (New York: Verso, 2009).

ANDISHEH HAZRATI

DESMOND HAZRATI

ERIN AND OWEN

JOEL AND JOSEPHINE

LIAM KOVEL

ROWAN KOVEL

Chapter 13
Free at Last

As an active member of the Jewish community, I recognize that the American Jewish community is disproportionately generous to American higher education. For the president of an institution to express his or her solidarity with Israel is welcomed by a very important part of their support base.

— Leon Botstein, *Chronicle of Higher Education*, Jan 5, 2014

Bard College, where I spent the last 21 years of my academic career, was touted by the gaming pages that announce such things as the school that had "put the 'liberal' in liberal arts." In this spirit the college's van was turned over to students to drive the 250 miles to Washington, DC for a hearing ensuing upon arrest for protesting on the steps of the Supreme Court. As for myself, during my years as its Alger Hiss Professor, the college generously supported my race for the Senate in 1998, essentially giving me a leave of absence so long as I made it an open tutorial for students who wanted some rough and tumble exposure to the harsh world of electoral politics.

The name of Bard College and that of Leon Botstein, its "President for Life," may be regarded as freely interchangeable. It was Botstein *cum* Bard who saved my floundering career when I was down and out. This gave me the space to teach what I pleased no matter how contrary to established wisdom, to publish four substantial books, and do interesting things like march against the Apartheid regime of South Africa, cross the U.S. blockade of Cuba, or take over the reins of a quirky journal with the modest goal of bringing down the capitalist system to save the world from ecological degeneration and collapse.

And it was Bard *cum* Botstein that crushed the selfsame career. In remarkably short order, hard times befell me: first, estrangement around the turn of the Millennium, then increasing exclusion, and finally, in 2009 upon return from the Belém Social Forum where we had launched the *Second Ecosocialist Manifesto*, outright expulsion.

THE BATTLE TOOK PLACE ACROSS two fronts. The first evolved from a funding mechanism to keep Bard afloat by turning the Board of Trustees into a reliable year by year source. Wealthy folk were needed, generous and eager to be swayed by a charismatic president; not old money then, but new and fluid money, such as comes from finance. In this way, small, dreamy Bard became an instrument of finance capital, the most dynamic sector of the Number One society of the United States of America.

Capitalism, based in the endless accumulation of money, calls itself the "liberal" society. The same word is advanced by "progressives" who stand for modernity, for example politicians like Barack Obama and Hillary Clinton, philosophers like Karl Popper, and tycoons like billionaire George Soros — notwithstanding that capitalism widens the gap between rich and poor, leaves nature in ruins, and for the last forty years, has inflicted upon our world the devastation we call "neoliberalism." Thus liberalism breeds upon itself, and turns into nightmare.

Soros was introduced to Bard, along with my Senate campaign of 1998, when Botstein announced association with the acclaimed financier as a structural change for the once lethargic college, not directly (though his wife was to join the Board of Trustees), but as a sort of a Godfather, with Leon Botstein as *consigliere* to carry out the global agenda of Soros' Open Society Foundation and its numerous projects of "democracy enhancement."

It was not long before the Open Society college combined with the far more powerful forces of the Council on Foreign Relations, the beachhead for which was created when James Chace joined the faculty in 1989, a year after I assumed the Hiss Chair. Now poor Alger had to endure the further indignity of being posted on ground taken over by the National Security State that had made him an outlaw. Soon, CFR was joined by the U.S. Military Academy at West Point, just across the Hudson River, the combination transforming the school that put the liberal in liberal arts into a bastion of neo-conservatism.

It got worse. Early in the new Millennium I returned from a leave of absence to learn that one Walter Russell Mead had occupied my office while I was gone. Mead was, believe it or not, the Henry A. Kissinger Senior Fellow of the Council on Foreign Relations, a post he held until 2010. *Quel Honneur!* He became full-time at Bard after 2004 as the James Clarke Chace Professor of Foreign Affairs and Humanities, a redoubt from which he could cheer on the invasion of Iraq.[1]

THE SECOND STRUCTURAL CHANGE leading to downfall at Bard was to declare myself an anti-Zionist at an institution whose president would later write in the *Chronicle of Higher Education* on the significant value of appealing to a "very important part" of Bard's "support base" by "expressing" his "solidarity with Israel."

By 2000 the Oslo Accords were coming apart and the Second Intifada loomed in reaction to the clearing of great swathes of Palestinian houses through the brutal expedient of crushing them with giant bulldozers donated by America. Water was stolen as well, for the use of "settlements" that resembled the suburbs of San Diego and whose toilets flushed directly onto the Palestinian villages below.

Being unable to stand by, I stepped forth.

A SURGE OF HOPE CAME EARLY IN 2001 with the arrival of Peter Linebaugh, co-author, with Marcus Rediker, of the brilliant study of resistance around the Atlantic to oppression and slavery, *The Many-Headed Hydra*. It was the first radical left senior appointment made by Bard since my arrival in 1988. We became friends and sharers of discourse on the Commons and William Blake, who had been as beloved by Peter's mentor, the great Edward Thompson, as by me. But we could not follow through at Bard, which for reasons I have never understood, was bent on undoing Peter's hire and sending him packing.

In the process, Linebaugh became shunned by the History Department and the Social Studies Division.[2] I found myself not just his only friend, but the only member of the faculty who would talk to him; and hence the only person to argue on his behalf to persuade the Division to allow this distinguished scholar—who soared far above Bard's historians—to be admitted to meetings. I won the battle. But it was nasty going, the first ugly moment with faculty I had experienced in my years at the college. I could not help feeling it as a harbinger of worse.

The boom was lowered in October 2002, when I was asked to come to the wood-lined office of Leon Botstein, where I was informed that the Alger Hiss Chair of Social Studies was no longer mine. It was, Leon averred, the decision of the Hiss family, who wanted the Chair turned over to cultural purposes and restored to its yearly rotation (neither of which was to happen; indeed, the Hiss Chair sank into oblivion).[3]

Then Botstein abruptly changed the subject: of course, that article about Zionism I had just published played no role in the decision. Notwithstanding, he had to tell me how wrong-headed I was. For Zionism was just and here to stay, and he was proud to sign high profile ads in *The New York Times* to that effect. Leon concluded with the well-worn trope that as the French people are entitled to France so are the Jewish people entitled to Israel, their ancestral homeland — an atrocious argument I was too stunned to answer.[4] As for Bard, I saw no alternative to hunkering down and working for as long as possible. This turned out to be about seven years, mostly under the auspices of a half-time contract that gave me one semester on and one off, defusing for a while some of the pressure while increasing my alienation.

The article Botstein chided me about was a study of how the contradiction between Jewish moral exceptionalism and the conquest and colonization of Palestine generated a vicious cycle of racism and violence. Called "Zionism's Bad Conscience," it was the first major product of my decision to focus on the Jewish State of Israel and the penetration of American society by Zionism. For publication I sought the cooperation of Michael Lerner, founder and editor of *Tikkun*, a journal of Jewish affairs constructed to fill the vacuum created by the move of *Commentary* to the right. Lerner agreed to publish, and so we resumed an uneasy relationship that began in the sixties when we worked together on various political and psychological projects. The uneasiness grew over time given our opposed relationships toward Judaism: estrangement on my part as I have already sketched, and for Lerner, the centering of his life about a Judaic vocation.

Michael had studied while at Columbia with the legendary refugee from Nazi-occupied Poland, the late Abraham Joshua Heschel.[5] He was active in the New Left, got a PhD in philosophy from UC Berkeley, and was ordained in mid-life, becoming an influential rabbi with a following in the San Francisco Bay Area and a widespread readership through *Tikkun*. The name derives from a notion of Heschel's signifying the healing of the world, all well and good. Though Lerner has espoused a reasonably wide range of left liberal policies toward the world-in-general for his "Network of Spiritual Progressives," it is that portion of the world occupied by the Jewish State of Israel where the call for "transformation," and the trouble between us, arose.

HOW CAN ONE ADDRESS A JEWISH STATE unless the "Jewish Question," the very same that has long vexed me and hexed me, is addressed with it? And how can the Jewish Question for such as me do aught but swirl together as in a Witch's Brew its threefold fronds, first, dissolution of tribal-familial bondage, second, emergence of ruthless criticism as a Marxist, and third, the cumulative illumination by moments of God's Grace, gathering for more than fifty years as a vantage for viewing Israel through the prism of universal Justice.

I was bound, then, to read Lerner's *Tikkun* with considerable skepticism, seeing in his fine talk about transformation, the "politics of meaning" and the "Network of Spiritual Progressives" a claim of universalism staked while clinging to the 3000-year-old covenant of God's uniquely chosen people: in the phrase of Matthew, the mark of a "Hypocrite Pharisee." I looked, therefore, with a cold eye upon the title of Lerner's book: *Healing Israel/Palestine*, as though the settler-colonials have a bellyache from digesting the victims of Zionism;[6] and I was shocked to learn that Lerner asks of the spiritual progressive that s/he love both Israel and Palestine. Really?

Lerner's endless hectoring over the internet (on several occasions I tried to remove myself from his list with no success) brings to mind nothing so much as huckstering. My mother used to tell me about the Orchard Street merchants who would run out and drag you in by the button hole in to see the merchandise. Was this not an atavism? After all, here is a man who would shamelessly write:

> Here's what is spiritual: Ethics, aesthetics, love, compassion, creativity, music, altruism, generosity, forgiveness, spontaneity, emergent phenomena, consciousness itself, and any other aspect of reality not subject to empirical verification or.... Those aspects of reality that cannot be reduced to publicly observable and verifiable behavior we call spiritual. What Is A Spiritual Progressive? (Hint: You don't have to believe in God or Be Part of a Religion...)
> *YOU are a spiritual progressive if* you endorse the New Bottom Line....

Ah... the New Bottom Line replacing the old gods. No wonder contemporary Judaism has become so fragmented.

EVEN THAT SPIRITUAL FIRST LADY, Hillary Clinton once seemed ready, in the early 1990s, to adopt the Politics of Meaning and Michael Lerner with it. I discussed this at the time with him and felt I should supply some wet towels lest his head explode with excitement and pride. But Hillary lost interest and Lerner went back to the grind of building his global network of spiritual progressives by hectoring people through the internet.

From my side of things, I pressed on, pretty much alone in confronting Zionism. My reconnection with Lerner had briefly kindled a hope that I had found a community within which to continue the quest. Acquaintance with *Tikkun* quashed that and made me realize that liberal anti-Zionism suited me as little as the Democratic Party. I simply had to get closer to the root of things, and for the nonce, on my own.

The result was an essay called "Anti-Semitism on the Left and the Special Status of Israel." It began with a critique of Lerner, who had charged some Marxist-Leninists (of my acquaintance though not comrades) with this hackneyed canard for having said some hostile things about Israel, thereby going over the line as Zionists customarily define it. I differed and wrote that the line had to be re-drawn with a look at the essential character of Israel itself. Here one encounters a profound contradiction at the heart of Zionism, which demands a democratic façade for the legitimation of the state, while at the same time insisting that the character of the state remains Jewish until the end of time even as it is built in the midst of a conquered and colonized people. Hence the tediously repeated slogan of being "the only democracy in the Middle East" is not only empirically false (inasmuch as Lebanon happens to be a democracy) but also destructive of its own ideal since the Jews always need to come out on top, if necessary by violent suppression of the indigenous Arab population; indeed, its ultimate logic— a final solution, if you will— is extermination of the Palestinian natives. Therefore a Democratic-Jewish State is a living oxymoron, because Zionism breeds a monster that destroys universalist principles and curses its own land with racism, eternal war and human rights violation.

I had gone over to the unthinkable: a One State Solution for Palestine derived from the conclusion that the Zionist State, structurally racist, does not have the right to exist—because no state does, being a contract, and therefore has to earn by a certain respect for human rights which Israel has long forfeited. I knew as well that I had also made a whole lot of trouble and ostracism for myself among my "people," beginning with Michael Lerner, who plainly hated what I had done, but could not simply reject it lest I embarrass him by moving it elsewhere. Instead he ran it with a panel of attacks by three liberal anti-Zionists (one of them Heschel's daughter Susannah). Of course, I had to reply, and found doing so a pleasure.

In any case I had crossed my Rubicon, and awaited what would happen next. It took a little while, then came in the shape of an enthusiastic letter from Edward Said, praising my essay and expressing a hope that he could work with me on developing its message. It was a nonpareil bittersweet moment — because there was nobody whose praise meant more, and no voice I would miss as much, knowing that he was in the terminal phase of leukemia. Our correspondence was as fleeting as its influence on me was profound. I never sat down with Said face to face, but his name is on the acknowledgments page of *Overcoming Zionism* as the man whose encouragement enabled the book to be written. How could I not write it now? Who else could have enabled me to set aside my doubts and fears?

AND SO MY TENTH BOOK WAS UNDERWAY. It followed the pattern of teaching myself about a subject and then teaching it to others. It differed in two respects: it was especially difficult to find a publisher within a society so controlled by forces deeply hostile to the ideas I was advancing; and also in demanding that I visit the subject in person. Were it not insurance against allowing people to dismiss the book on grounds that I had never visited the country, I would not have gone at all. But this would have been wrong, as it would have cost me the chance to meet up with courageous Israelis who fight a lonely battle for a just society under such fiendish conditions—though not at all encouraging to realize now, eleven years since my visit, that Israel has so regressed under the corruption induced by Zionism that its number of human rights activists are ever scarcer, perhaps now in the three-digit range.

In any case, I met some admirable people who became friends and from whom I learned much — among them Ilan Pappe, the leading historian of ethnic cleansing (soon to be driven out to England); Michel Warschavski, a profound and radical observer of Zion; Eitan Bornstein, whose Zochrot was a perpetual thorn in the side of colonialist amnesia; and Ingrid Jaradat Gassner, of the NGO, Badil, who opened many Palestinian doors for me. And of course, how could I not be deeply moved by seeing Old Jerusalem, especially at that moment when, stumbling with my bags on the Via Dolorosa, I raised my head in sweat and confusion, and saw that I was on a well-defined Station of the Cross.

By and large, however, my trip did little but confirm and accentuate the ideas that had been gathering over decades. Old Jerusalem may be a treasury of Spirit. Jerusalem under Zionist rule, however, is a zone of spiritual death. It generates a sense of desolation in anyone who refuses the logic of Jewish chauvinism and racism, a despair I felt every minute on Zionist soil, including five hours in the good-quality art museum of Tel Aviv, where one sees not a single Arab face, neither in the exhibits (which include lots of photographs) nor amongst the other visitors. Despair and mean-spiritedness inhabit the stones of Israel's built environment[7] and the bearing of the people one meets. There is a word for a willed malevolence that creeps out of every stone and twists so many faces: "evil." Is there a more apt term when the crimes of violent expropriation and ethnic cleansing are committed through unending impunity guaranteed by a captive Superpower? What surer way toward moral degeneration?

No surprise, then, that I found the negative of this to be true among the subjugated Palestinians. It is inflected concretely as the oft-heard "Sumud," a word that conveys in Arabic a kind of synthesis of patience, forbearance, hospitality, and even good will, none of which should fool us into thinking that a clear-headed fury is not also present and deeply set into place. The Palestinian inhabitants of their occupied country have been dreadfully served by a Quisling-style leadership that relishes the parasitic comforts of accommodation far more than principled struggle. I have been greatly heartened, however, by many brilliant and fiery Palestinians I have met who are active in the diaspora. I only wish I live long enough to see their triumph.

THE FOLLOWING YEAR, 2006, DeeDee and I spent a good portion of the time away from Bard in South Africa, where I had an appointment at Patrick Bond's Centre for Civil Society at UKZN in Durban. This allowed for family visits — Jon, Pat, Rowan and Liam in Johannesburg—and considerable tooling around in an indestructible ancient yellow Mercedes Jonathan purchased and then resold for us after our departure. I deeply love South Africa, and just as deeply despair about it, as the forebodings put forward in my 1989 visit as to Mandela's Faustian compact with global capital have become more evident with each passing year. They stand as a grim object lesson for those with their sights set upon the transformation of Israel, too, into a non-racist state: above all, do not sell out to global capital.

Notwithstanding, South Africa is a good place from which to launch a rigorous critique of Zionism, and in my case, to bring *Overcoming Zionism* to a conclusion in a subtropical setting suffused with the anti-racist and anti-imperial principles supplied by Bond and associates like the great Dennis Brutus, at the time approaching the end of a beautiful life, and the combative and brilliant Ashwin Desai. It was good, too, to be able to lecture before an audience of Brown and Black people who knew the truth about Zionism and the long-standing bonds defined between Israel and the Apartheid State. It was a blight Americans shared, and which I would have to confront when I returned to the United States.

THERE WAS AN OMINOUS FORESHADOWING. I learned while away that Leon Botstein had added to his leadership of the American Symphony Orchestra the directorship of the Jerusalem Philharmonic. By 2006 Leon was an official cultural consultant to the Israeli government, making some ten trips a year to advance the Zionist cause. Now he organized an American tour: first stop, Annandale on Hudson, where the Frank Gehry-designed Fisher Performing Arts Center (cost: $75 million)[8] at Bard awaited the JPO. Leon has suffered considerable criticism of his musicianship over the years, but no one doubts his imaginative talent as an impresario. In any case, as I sat sunning myself in Durban, RSA, 8,200 miles away, some two thousand well-dressed citizens of the Hudson Valley came to a glittering auditorium for a February concert which began as follows:

1. Botstein leads the JPO in "Hatikvah," the Israeli national anthem. Audience, all but two, rises.

2. Botstein leads the JPO in "The Star-Spangled Banner,"
another national anthem. Audience, all but two, rises.

It was most dismal to learn that aside from these two—my good friends from Woodstock, Cambiz Khosravi and Liz Simonson, who were scolded for disrespect and wrote me with the news—there was only miniscule protest, perhaps half a dozen forlorn students and community people posted outside with signs. In other words, nobody else on the Bard faculty within 8,200 miles of Annandale saw anything wrong with a concert hailing a serial human-rights abusing foreign state and celebrating its special relationship with America.

I brooded about what this revealed about the alienation and passivity of people in the United States in the face of Zionist influence. I revolt inwardly at the thought of standing for any national anthem. To do so for a foreign country as criminal as Israel, I find obscene. To allow this to go unchallenged is enough to send me through the roof. Couple this with my helplessness to intervene at such distance, and we have a fine, pressure-cooked stew on our hands, made worse by realizing how much worse my position at Bard would be after I spoke out, alone, months later. But I feared my conscience more.

The lecture was delivered on a frosty late-autumn evening, the sparse audience included one faculty member, Richard Gordon, who left without speaking as soon as it was over, along with some students and community members from an organization that had been launched that summer, myself a cofounder, during the Israeli war with Hezbollah. This made the experience tolerable and offset some of the estrangement that had increasingly become my lot at Bard.

We called it Mid-East Crisis Response, or MECR, and it eased my isolation on campus by enabling me to focus on surrounding communities and to work with a growing network of anti-Israel activists from the mid-Hudson Valley. When we began operations, the local scene was dominated by the Jewish Federation of Ulster County, who picketed our meetings, heckled us mercilessly and blasted us in the local paper. Maurice Hinchey, the Hudson Valley's left-of-center congressman, told us at a private meeting to expect this, and added that, even though he agreed with our position, we would first have to undercut the Federation's power before he could help. Maurice was a *bona fide* leftist, who had given me his card when I went off to Cuba in 1994, in case I got into trouble. He often identified himself as a socialist on the stump—though he found me irritating on the occasions I would discomfit him for cozying up to U.S. foreign policy.

Zionist power, like any other, evolves and devolves. Victory depends on understanding its ways, and seizing the emergent moment to actively intervene in order to hasten downfall. By 2006, the times were getting set for change. MECR's presence was a sign of this, as I set out to converse with grassroots activists everywhere I could while chipping away at the Beast and stirring the spirit of revolt. I knew we would lose battle after battle, and despite it all, had faith and hope that the war would be won.

ONE OF MY FONDEST WISHES has been to live long enough to see the collapse of Israel. I don't see this happening in my lifetime, but the freedom to dream is itself life-giving. Meanwhile, the wave of sympathy for Israel generated by the horrors of Shoah and the propaganda triumph of wars in 1967 and 1973 was beginning to recede as Zionism's genocidal potential came forth, along with its latent fascism, causing divisions to appear in what had been a seamless Jewish community. Along with the reaction to the Second Intifada and the massacres in Gaza to come, the Lebanese war in 2006 exposed Zionism's Moloch in its wanton violence against children and women. And sure enough, through countless vigils, public addresses, letters to the editor and broadcasts over community radio, the power and verve of the Jewish Federation of Ulster County began to crumble.

By mid-year I had at hand the just-completed *Overcoming Zionism*. Indeed, I was able to give some seminars on the subject to the group at MECR. I will spare the reader tales of frustration with the liberal and academic presses that were predictably involved, along with, perhaps, Rabbi Lerner, if some back-channel disclosures were accurate. At length I was able to find comradely publishers, Pluto, of London, and Between the Lines, of Toronto, along with Pluto's contractual surrogate for distribution, the University of Michigan Press, in Ann Arbor.

IF I MAY PAUSE FOR A NEWS ITEM... In the midst of preparing *Overcoming Zionism* in the autumn of 2006 I received a call from James White, a lawyer, psychologist, and Associate Rector of a small, mostly Black, Episcopal Church in Harlem, St. Mary's. They were planning a weekend conference on racism and would be pleased if I would give the keynote lecture... and while I was at it, perhaps I could preach, you know, give a sermon. A sermon? Yes, a sermon, anything I wanted to preach about; it was understood that this was something I had never done before.

Oh, well, in that case... how about something on "Prophecy" with a focus on William Blake: I had studied him a lot. Sure, fine, whatever you say. And so I gave my sermon, which people seemed to like; and I met, and liked, Jim, and Earl Kooperkamp, the Rector, both of whom brought to mind the radical Jesuits and Franciscans I had known in Nicaragua, being at the same time radical left and cheerful, so unlike the doleful inmates of my academic dungeon on the banks of the Hudson.

OVERCOMING ZIONISM HAD A HOPEFUL COVER showing two Palestinian chums walking hand in hand down a blasted Gaza street. In the position I was in, one is schooled to expect nothing like a review from a world such as ours, and nothing I got. But there was a stirring from the underside: small meetings, radio interviews, sustained by the murmur of person to person. It was all I could hope for, and all I got—and it was enough, as David Castle of Pluto happily informed me in mid-2007 that, yes, despite the blackout, *Overcoming Zionism* was steadily if modestly growing in sales.

Survival in the face of malign neglect meant we could soon expect the enemy's offensive. This arrived shortly in the form of hostile letters and the rising, as if from under a flat rock, of broadsides from Zionist websites. One in particular, *Stand With Us*, had a chapter in Ann Arbor and informed the citizenry with hysterical broadsides that there was an evil book out there: Israel-hating, unscholarly, and thoroughly crooked (no evidence given) as well as anti-Semitic. It had to be stopped. This caused quite a clamor, and provoked Phil Pochoda, the Director of the University of Michigan Press, who by an odd turn of fortune had been my Pantheon editor 25 years before for *The Age of Desire*, to write me a reassuring note that, not to worry, he would stand by me to protect my rights of free speech. Thanks, Phil, said I.

Alas, not for long: a few days later, a friend wrote to say that *Overcoming Zionism* had mysteriously disappeared from the UMP website. I informed Pochoda by email, who replied that his first letter had been written before the reading of my book, which made him realize that this wasn't a matter of "free speech," but *hate speech*. Had he known so, he would have banned it right away. Phil was evidently unaware that the essence of free speech is to respect the right to express even those views one finds noxious and hateful. To his mind, therefore, *Overcoming Zionism* had to be removed from the market in order to protect the citizens of the United States from exposure to immoderate hatred of Israel.

And so *Overcoming Zionism* had been *de facto* banned, and I became a cause, forty years after the shock of the Six-Day War had set me on an anti-Zionist path. It was a real honor, and the occasion for some serious organizing. A group of friends, mostly lawyers, swiftly gathered, and the next thing we knew, another organization had been born, the Committee for the Open Discussion of Zionism, CODZ, pronounced "Cod-Z" for short.

It was rough, but fun, and of course, good for the book. From a legal standpoint, it was also, to borrow the argot of basketball, a slam dunk; for by pulling the book precipitously from his list, Pochoda flagrantly violated a contract, which is something any nitwit in America knows not to do. We were of course prepared to go to court. Too bad the University caved in within a week, restoring *Overcoming Zionism* to its catalogue and depriving me of a solid chance of considerable wealth.

Have no fear; the conflict was not over. In swift order, the faculty board of UMP convened and, admitting they had to bring the book back on line, nevertheless made clear that as established academics at one of the world's great universities, they really, truly and sincerely loathed my calumny on the State of Israel, and would take measures to protect humanity from such arguments in the future. The way of doing so would be to terminate the contract with Pluto when it came up in a year. This they did, which harmed Pluto a little[9] and the University of Michigan Press a lot, through losing sizable income from the leftist British publisher. Collusion with the Zionist Thought Police caused UMP to languish in the later Pochoda years. An announcement of May 2, 2011 that Pochoda was "technically retiring" extolled his great contributions in bringing about the exciting digital age of academic publishing, and concluded with the somber statement that COMMENTS ON THIS ENTRY ARE CLOSED. Way to go, Phil!

At the height of the brouhaha, some 650 letters had reached the university administration, almost all supportive of me, as I was informed by Kurt Berggren, my lawyer friend since days of breaking the blockade of Cuba, on the basis of inside contacts. I don't think any came from Bard faculty, and I know none came from the President, for when I asked Leon Botstein whether what I had heard was true, that he, the great defender of unfettered freedom of speech, had not supported one of his faculty whose speech rights were grossly violated, the reply was airily, "we thought you could take care of yourself."

The banning happened in August 2007; and by November the atmosphere at the University of Michigan (which happens to be located just north of the largest concentration of Arabs in the United States, in Dearborn and northern Ohio), had so changed that I was invited back to give my side of things in a public address in one of the main lecture halls. It was delightful to see all the muscular campus cops there to keep order, and charming to see the phalanx of chunky, dour lads and lassies in the upper balconies with their black t-shirts upon which were written the proud words, "MICHIGAN ZIONIST," and looking… well, I don't know how to describe it except that it was very Zionistic.

FEROCIOUS STRUGGLES OVER ISRAEL continue to roil academia, but the balance has changed, making it very hard to imagine such a scene today, as the popularity of Zionism withers amongst the young. To be sure, the wealth and power commanded by the Zionist power structure remains immense, and extends across the entire range of state and civil society. But times are definitely, and structurally, changing. It was sheer joy to see my good friend Phil Weiss's web-zine, *MondoWeiss,* reporting in 2014[10] the results of a Brookings Poll that 34% of a sample of more than one thousand Americans in 2013 now affirm a One State Solution for Israel/Palestine, a rise from 24% over the past year, while 39% affirm the Two State Solution, unchanged from last year. No less remarkable, fully 71% of respondents affirm a One State Solution in the event that a Two State Solution is not possible—which *Overcoming Zionism* among other works, argues is precisely the case.

I should think that any sentient being should be able to see that the Two State (or Bantustan, for that is all it promises) option is nothing but a con game perpetuated by the fraudsters to give Zionists time to do their damage. No less an authority than Ehud Olmert, Israeli PM (now imprisoned for fraud), announced in 2007 that were the Two State Solution proven impossible, then the Zionist State would have to face a "South African solution," in which case, "Israel is finished." One might add that Omar Barghouti, progenitor of the (presently menaced) Boycott Divestment Sanctions movement and a leading spokesperson for the Palestinians, has stated that an absolute majority, whether in Israel, Diaspora, territories or camps, want a One State Solution as well, regardless of what their Quisling bureaucrats are telling them to want. Nevertheless, the battle rages on, with tremendous amounts of money backing the Zionist cause; indeed, it is hard to imagine my living long enough to see the downfall of the Jewish State.

NONETHELESS I FEEL REWARDED for all of the hard work and trouble. For when *Overcoming Zionism* was published in 2007, I would guess that no more than 1% of Americans would have affirmed the argument for One State put forth by that book. All kinds of people, friends as well as foes, were advising me that the doggedness mentioned just above amounted in this case to a barking at the moon of an endlessly remote desire. Nobody, that is, "really" wanted anything other than two separate states. But what is real about "really"? I regarded this then, and still do, as a manifestation of what Sartre called the "practico-inert," that sedimentation of thought in order not to confront either the nightmare or the hope of history, thought unable to see beyond the dead-end of a Jewish State (which by the way, Sartre, reeling from the Holocaust, endorsed). But there is a dustbin for really bad ideas, and more and more people are ready to add one of the worst, Zionism, to it.

I am definitely not the only one-stater, nor would I claim that the polemical *Overcoming Zionism* did more than contribute at the edges to this change. The idea was active before I came aboard and it will persist after I leave. Indeed I, along with DeeDee, attended a congress on the theme in Geneva in 2006, which came to naught when it was discovered that the man who convened it, a Palestinian physician, had had run-ins with the law beforehand, putting a serious crimp in the process of organizing. Still, there were others who have written notably on the logic of One State, including Ilan Pappe, Virginia Tilley, Ali Abunimah, Cathy Christison, Ghada Karmi, Jeffrey Blankfort, Oren Ben Dor, and others. We all have our own perspective and generally shore each other up. The important thing is to sustain the idea, as a filament, perhaps no more, to connect with other people and through them, with other ideas, keeping hope alive as contradictions unfold and recombine, until the future is born.

It requires going into the communities even if this means taking a lot of crap from Zionists. For me the worst of these seemed to be located in towns with a reputation of progressivism, for example, Boston, so civilized, so culturally advanced, yet a repository of ferocious Zionist repression, for example, CAMERA and The David Project, all of which were vociferously heard at the Brookline movie theater my supporters reserved for a stormy lecture on the evils of Zionism during the winter of 2008.

Then there was Burlington, Vermont, home base of Bernie Sanders, where a session organized by anti-Zionist and Bread and Puppet comrade Marc Estrin drew a large contingent from a local synagogue, the members of which barely let me begin before becoming vituperative. Matters degenerated rapidly into a simulacrum of

Gunfight in the OK Corral, rather like the quarrel with the three Lerneroids over my essay in *Tikkun*, but much more nasty. A similar event took place at the western end of the continent, in Victoria, British Columbia, a town renowned for balmy weather, extreme progressivism, veganism, and political correctness. Here the folk from the local Synagogue left their seats and began charging the platform, stopping only when the house moderator threatened to pull the plug and end the evening if they didn't desist and sit down.[11]

These events evoke the argument that was used against publication of *Overcoming Zionism* by liberals, namely, that putting forth radical views such as mine would undercut efforts by such as Rabbi Lerner to build coalitions of well-meaning "spiritual progressives." To this I would say, that such undercutting was exactly my intention insofar as such coalitions included a dominant strand of "soft anti-Zionism," which means, logically, soft Zionism as well, the kind of wishy-washy "I feel your pain" pabulum that blunts the ruthless criticism necessary to do the job and benefits the Jewish State. With declining support for Israel across the world, the validity of an unrelenting critique of Zionism can no longer be doubted. The history of Israel's conquest of Palestine is a harsh, blood stained history, and the more people realize this, the more ready we will be to bring a just end to all forms of racism.

I ALSO DID A CONSIDERABLE AMOUNT of speaking in the UK and Ireland, where the reception bore little resemblance to what I had encountered in the United States and Canada (Montreal and Quebec contain rabid Zionist enclaves). London is dear to me, yet I found that the concentration of Jews introduced a degree of ambivalence that led to stagnant discussions. Not so for the outlying areas, sparkling Liverpool for instance, where bashing of Zionism encouraged two attractive Arab ladies to vie with each other in asking for my hand in marriage on the spot (let the record show I firmly rebuffed their advances).

Galway, on the west coast of Ireland, provided another exemplary human in the figure of Tommy Donnelon, a retired rail worker assigned by the Solidarity Committee as my minder, who personally stapled some 200 fliers to lamp-posts to rouse folks for the lecture, and personally took them all down the next morning before joining me for breakfast. The Irish, by the way, need no lessons in the ways of expropriating colonials who tear apart indigenous communal spaces, witness a postcard they distribute under the heading of "House Removal—Then and Now." The present case is illustrated with a pane showing a Caterpillar Bulldozer crushing a house in the Occupied Territories; while the former case was graphically depicted by the image of a team of louts using a large tree trunk as a battering ram to achieve the same effect on the home of an Irish peasant.

There is a special place in my heart for the SPSC—the Scottish Palestine Solidarity Campaign, headquarters, Edinburgh—Mick Napier and Sofia Macleod in charge. By dint of unceasing militancy, they have done a fine job making Scotland a nearly Zionist-Free zone where even the Israeli ambassador trembles to go. Ah, Scotland, land of fierce intellectuals… had I only been born there, perhaps all these troubles would not have befallen me… Dreamer!

MEANWHILE, IN ANNANDALE ON HUDSON, the *dénouement* of my Bard career was bring prepared as the calendar crept up on 2009 and the days of my contract dwindled down to a not-so-precious few. Having endured the first course in Zionism I had taught at Bard, I was off to Belém over Christmas for the World Social Forum and the Second Draft of the *Ecosocialist Manifesto*. I looked to my six months off campus coming up, but my five-year contract was expiring, and Bard had prepared a reckoning: too dreary to detail but necessary to ponder and in any case, to document. And so I will compress my version of what occurred to supply a selection of bulleted points before turning to the next stage of my travels.

• My situation differed from most others of this kind in that the last thing I wanted was to have my job back, a fate akin to a prison sentence. My best hope was modest, a gracious departure, without rancor; and I tried to make this wish known. Whether because of sensitivity that any separation agreement might be seen as prejudicial on their part, or from sheer vindictiveness—or more likely, from both of these motives—Bard elected to claim that of course there was no question at all of any political motive by the college, and chose to get rid of me by alleging incompetence and irrelevance at a time of budgetary hardship (the "Great Recession" was then raging). It appeared as a hastily prepared letter from Dean Michele Dominy with all the charm of a Pink Slip telling me to leave my identity card at the door.

• I refused to accept what amounted to an allegation of senility, and protested. This triggered a Blitzkrieg on the college's part in which vindictiveness was rampant and all stops were pulled. Botstein turned a routine full-faculty meeting which I missed, into a character assassination, alleging my lying, psychopathy and paranoia; similar charges were launched over the faculty email list serve; Dean Dominy and Professor Amy Ansell from the Social Studies Division called a meeting of students in which my defects were laid forth. This provoked a revolt among sectors of the student body, my only ally in the furor, which included allegations from students assigned to the committee handling my case, that there seemed to be actual tampering with the evaluations used as evidence.

THIS WOULD HAVE BEEN VERY INTERESTING evidence for a lawsuit I could have brought alleging defamation of character. There were other major irregularities, for example, the fact that the faculty committee evaluating me was chaired by Prof. Bruce Chilton, an arch Zionist who among other things had spoken on national radio during the destruction of Gaza taking place at this time, opining that the havoc could be legitimated by Just War theory. Yes, that's what the man said; after all, he was a theologian, the Episcopal chaplain at Bard (a fact of some interest in view of my forthcoming religious turn) and director of Bard's extensive programs in this area. In better times at Bard, Chilton had been supportive of my work, including *History and Spirit*. He even said that he had supported my rehiring and had been deeply offended by my hostile reaction to his role, poor fellow.

• All of this (and there is more) requires no further comment. My position was that I was being subjected to what amounted to an inquisition and that I had the option to seek recourse in a law suit that if won, could be devastating to the college. I also had a lot of people on my side, including the group founded during the 2007 fracas with *Overcoming Zionism,* Committee for Open Discussion of Zionism, which contained a number of fine and prestigious lawyers, for example, Michael Smith, Michael Ratner (deceased, a great loss to humanity, in 2016), Abdeen Jabara, Barbara Harvey, and Dennis James, the latter of whom who served admirably as my first-line legal adviser, and added top-notch anti-Zionist intellectuals like Terri Ginsberg and Jonathan House, a psychoanalyst who had organized The NY Hospital System when we both were House Officers.

PERSONALLY, I THOUGHT THE SUIT could be won, and that it would have positive political impact aside from the settlement itself. I was emotionally disposed to do so, having been driven into a fine rage by the treatment I had received over the years. Weighing against the decision to sue was a definite prospect: that suing would almost certainly ruin the later years of my life. I knew this myself and all my legal advisers felt the same—and that was that. So I had to forego the fond dream of seeing Leon Botstein, Bruce Chilton, *et al.* squirming in the Dock under oath. I wanted to be Free from Bard, Free at Last!, and a lawsuit of this kind is at base, nothing but a set of leg-irons.

• I even wanted to be free from writing and talking about that desolate place, but not so free as would have been the case had I accepted the final terms demanded by Bard's legal team, namely, that in exchange for a package of unspecified paltry "benefits" that is, "an "amicable settlement," all I needed to do was to pledge: a) to never write or speak publically about anything that transpired between the college and myself regarding this affair; and b) that in the spirit of this, I would see to it that all references to it as had found their way onto the internet, would be deleted. Rather akin to peeing while bathing in the ocean and removing all traces from the briny waves. Oh, and also: that I could never write this memoir. Next case!

• An endnote of some interest: In mid-March, the supportive students, bless them, went out of their way to bring to Bard the great Noam Chomsky, champion of freedom, academic and otherwise, in support of me. The largest hall at the college, Olin, was reserved for the event. I arrived somewhat early and greeted Noam in the ante-room. His wife having recently died, he looked sad, but was otherwise the same fit and prepossessing person who had graced a thousand lecterns over the past half-century. I had known Noam since the early 1970s, when I had him come to the Albert Einstein College of Medicine to give his standard talk, powerful and tirelessly delivered, on the perfidy of empire; and he had endorsed *Red Hunting and the Promised Land*. Most important to me, as I have related, Chomsky had been the heroic figure of the '60s whose speaking truth to power had inspired my own vocation as an intellectual pledged to do the same.

We chatted in a friendly and desultory way for a few minutes, and then I got up to join my party in the packed auditorium and give Noam some time to rest up. As I left the room I met with an official from the college who with some urgency, asked after Chomsky and said that President Botstein wanted to say hello to him.

Soon after, the lecture began, before some 500 people from the college and the community. I settled in, wondering how Chomsky was going to develop the theme he had been invited to present. I waited, and waited, and waited — and heard instead the standard Chomsky speech familiar to anyone with an ear and a progressive mind: there was this power, the United States, that strove to rule the world, and did so through brutality, chicanery, lies, moral blindness, and the complicity of elites. As ever, the speech was dotted with many concrete points, masterfully arrayed and scathingly delivered, in support of his thesis. There were also references to the state of Israel, familiar to the follower of Chomsky's reasoning: to wit, that though Israel did many bad things, in contrast to the allegation of Zionist control over America, the United States remains fully in charge, and anytime it wanted to, could force its client state to give up its territories and submit to a two-state solution — which, needless to add, was Chomsky's preferred outcome.

What was missing from the lecture was any reference to the local situation at Bard, and in particular, to that individual whose cause he was supposed to be there to defend: me. When this was pointed out somewhat plaintively by a student early in the question period, Chomsky replied curtly, that it was something for the students to do on their own.

WHAT HAD HAPPENED? I WAS STRUCK NUMB, as I unfortunately tend to be on occasions of this sort, although a number of my supporters were furious. I feared that it was too shocking for me to take a critical view at the moment, although the outlines of the problem are not hard to surmise: Noam Chomsky, when all is said and done, has been Zionist at least since some adolescent years spent in the *Yishuv*. He has admitted this as such on occasion, and the preference for a two-state solution means essentially support for a Jewish State and therefore a lifetime pass for Zionism. In itself, the admission is remarkable, as any observer of Chomsky over the years will have noted an inflexibility of character and inability to ever question his basic views, in other words, his genius does not extend to the self scrutiny required by Marx's view of the ruthless critic. As Noam has achieved godlike status among progressives in an epoch of reaction and defeat, it has proven most difficult to criticize him from the left; hence his influence been outsize in matters like academic boycotts of Israel, or in other areas, questioning of the official versions of the Kennedy assassination or what happened on 9-11-01, since his rigid rationalism abhors the notion of "conspiracy." Notwithstanding, a number of active critics have intervened to hold Chomsky accountable before a higher tribunal.[12]

As to the role of Botstein in this, I have no way of knowing whether he took Noam aside, so to speak, to warn him of supporting so reprehensible a figure as myself to any right-thinking Zionist. Either interpretation casts a bad light; though I should think it is worse for Chomsky to have accepted such an invitation already planning to sabotage my cause, than to have yielded to Botstein's pressure on him to do so. Not that it mattered to his fortress-like and avuncular reputation, which endures in hard times.

And it really did not matter to me, for whom the only immediate goal was to free myself of Bard. Yet there remains a qualification. I titled this chapter "Free at Last," because of the strong sigh of relief at finally severing ties after years of alienation. But it would be very wrong to convey the idea that there was an all-good period at Bard succeeded by one that was all bad. In the second, downward part, there still occurred much good, indeed, one of the more memorable achievements of my academic career: being granted permission by the Literature faculty to teach an advanced seminar on William Blake, an honor in four of my last five years.

And there were regrets that separation from the college could not heal. Of these the most enduring pain remains the virtually unanimous lack of support by the faculty during the period of my ouster. Twenty-one years of thinking of people as friends, twenty-one years of being told that I was "the conscience of Bard," all washed down the drain: this will never be undone. There are explanations deriving from the school's tyrannical structure behind its liberal façade; or from my partial withdrawal over the period of harassment; or deriving from the general rightward shift of these times; and other reasons as well. But these did not make the pain go away.

IT CAME TO A HEAD ON A WEEK DAY in Spring Break, 2009, when DeeDee and I visited the empty campus and my office, #208 Aspinwall, to clean it out, books, student projects and evaluations, files, junk, all of it, that is to say, to "free" myself of things pertinent to Bard gathered over 21 years. But it turned into an exercise in disillusioning me of the fancy that I was too grown up to fall apart at giving away hundreds of books, many of them beloved. And the quarrels between the two of us as these twenty years were triaged, packed, and hauled away to various chambers: such was pain meted out.[13]

THE CROSS

WHILE WRITING THE FINAL PASSAGES of this penultimate chapter of my *Lost Traveller's Dream* another object was in my study, though I didn't realize the fact until a day ago. It is a cross, of the Celtic kind, made of some nondescript metal and suspended on a soft, violet cord. I purchased it at the St. Mary's 2014 Christmas fair for $10, and proceeded to lose it that evening. I must have pulled it over my head as I took off my shirt. Fallen to the floor, its colors and pattern overlapped those of the complex Persian rug (gift of my Iranian in-laws) underfoot, and as I am not just a Lost Traveller but also one who routinely loses

things, nor has the sharpest eyesight, I didn't notice its absence until the next day, and never thought of looking at my feet but went about in misery until three days ago, when the cross caught my eye, just below the chair where I have been sitting writing this book. It had been waiting for me all this time like a faithful little dog, perhaps the white Maltese sitting patiently behind St. Augustine in Carpaccio's great painting of 1502 — though I must admit that Augustine's desk and his mind were much more orderly than mine.

What a blessing is my Cross! Serene, plain, and enduring, it casts my time at desolate Bard into a large dustbin. Hear Luke (6:22) on the theme:

> Blessed are you when people hate you and when
> they exclude you and revile you and spurn your
> name as evil, on account of the Son of Man.

Yes, that's it! At no point in the long and lonely fracas with Bard did
I reflect that I was doing this on account of Christ Jesus — a.k.a. the
Son of Man. I was, rather, preoccupied with the fact that Bard had
become part of what Jim Petras has called the "Zionist Power Configuration" in America, which does immense harm to the world, beginning with the Palestinian victims of Zionism, proceeding to our
frail democracy and including moral damage to Jews themselves. I
knew I was going to lose the battle, being weak and exposed, but
would not give in.

My defeat had its moments of great bitterness and pain, as I have
told, but also the deeper happiness for having fought the good fight.
And as this settled into my being, so did the spiritual realization, as
the great hymn has it, that "we shall overcome." For Christ Jesus
awakens in us, becomes us as we open and connect to a righteous
cause. This is how I read Luke 6-22. It is Jesus-building, if you will,
insofar as the Being of Jesus is Full of Grace, Grace that does not belong to any religion *per se,* but to humanity when and wherever we
cast aside the ego and reach toward universality.

IN THAT SENSE, I WAS INDEED FREE, after all the comings and
goings, to do in depth what I had been circling around since Richard
Sewall's speech at Yale in 1953. It may be said that the Pauline message finally found me in the hour of my expulsion. For that, I thank
you, Bard, and all the characters within. Everything and everybody,
even Bruce Chilton, even Leon Botstein, has a purpose. And may
Leon find his Soul once he realizes it cannot be from the Jewish sup-
port-base of a Zionist controlled liberal-arts college.

> Oh, Lordy, how happy I am
> My feet are washed in the blood of the Lamb
> Glory, Halla-loo.
> The Reverend Gary Davis[14]

The seeking of justice in this world pretty much guarantees persecution by those in power, aided by the cowardice and indifference of followers and functionaries. All of which materializes into the Celtic Cross. It gave me great joy on a trip to El Salvador in March, 2015, of seeing one identical to it, except for being twice as big, in the personal collection of Msgr. Oscar Romero in the plain and tiny flat he lived in just a few feet from where he was gunned down in the course of giving Mass in the hospital chapel. Romero is a great martyr in the Christian tradition, that is, one who draws in a larger body by his sacrifice. His assassination, carried out with complicity by the US Security apparatus on March 25, 1980, was one of the seminal events of the middle phase of my spiritual journey. It set me on the path of going to Nicaragua in 1983 to learn from and defend the Sandinista revolution, which in turn brought me within an ace of conversion to the Roman Catholic faith. The martyrdoms within El Salvador left a mark deep within. When the eight slayings at Casa Jesuitica in 1989 were announced I was so moved as to write the UCA and offer my services as a teacher in their time of trouble. Well, that got nowhere, needless to add; but when I finally got to Salvador, thanks to School of the Americas Watch and Roy Bourgeois, to visit the places of martyrdom, not just of Romero (and his friend Rutilio Grande) and the Jesuits, but also the four American nuns who were raped and murdered deep inside the country in December, 1980, also with the connivance of our Security Forces, it was plain that currents of God's Grace were flowing within.

Then the Cross ceases being static and becomes a "Crossroads," not of place but of spirit, a meeting place and finding of new direction. I am drawn to the Celtic Cross because it connotes resistance to the Roman Empire, which never conquered Ireland or England north of Hadrian's Wall; and also because of the resistance shown by my Scottish, Liverpudlian, and Irish friends to the empire of United States and Israel. Celtic Christianity moves away from the splitting between humanity and nature found in imperialist lines of Christianity to celebrate instead the sacred differentiation of Christ. Thus the intertwining tendrils seen in the arms and post of the Cross tell us something about the intertwining of the sexes and races, and all the intertwining of humanity and nature signified in the notion of nature's intrinsic value, or as Blake gathered it at the close of *Jerusalem*: "All Human Forms identified even Tree Metal Earth & Stone... "[15]

As for those radiating circles extending outward from the center of the Cross: is this not something that Wilhelm Reich would have smiled upon as suggestive of a cosmic energy?... But then, the man one of whose final works was called *The Murder of Christ* had perhaps lost the capacity to smile after the persecutions he suffered.

I associated with Jesuits in Nicaragua during the 1980s, and the idea has often occurred that had I been born a Catholic, I might very well have ended up a Jesuit myself. Well, I have to admit I am too old for that, but a great range of Christian paths remain and will be here as long as I am. More than twenty years later, Jewishness wrung out of me by Zionist Academia, I was ready to resume my travels, the crossroads of which were given at St. Mary's Episcopal Church, 521 W 126th Street, in West Harlem.

Notes

[1] In 2004 I was on a local panel about the Iraq War along with four other faculty. Curious about their attitude, I polled the panel and was astounded to learn that all of them supported the U.S. invasion. If I'm not mistaken, that was the last campus event to which I was invited.

[2] Triggered, it seemed, because the *New York Review* had given the recently-published *The Many-Headed Hydra* (co-authored with Marcus Rediker) a hostile review conducive to their center-Right inclination.

[3] Eventually awarded in 2007 to the Director of the Yale University Press, Jonathan Brent, who, incredibly, did not believe in Hiss' innocence. What began as an honor for Hiss became an insult to his memory. I never found out what Leon Botstein felt about this.

[4] The comparison between the immemorial story of the inhabitation of the land, in the present case, of France, with the tendentious and largely mythological construction of whatever the Zionist wants Jewishness to be, provides framing for critique. See

Shlomo Sand, *The Invention of the Jewish People*. Sand said at a lecture that Israeli universities have dual history departments: one for Jewish History and another for the history of everybody else.

5 Heschel's prestige was augmented through friendship with Martin Luther King, Jr., with whom he had crossed the Edmund Pettus Bridge in Selma, Alabama in 1965.

6 Michael Lerner, *Healing Israel/Palestine: A Path to Peace and Reconciliation* (San Francisco: Tikkun Books, 2004).

7 For example Rafi Segal and Eyal Weizman, *A Civilian Occupation* (London: Verso, 2002).

8 The Fisher Center took Bard out of the humble and funky pre-Botsteinian era and into the big-time academic performing arts circuit. I was told it cost something like twenty thousand dollars just to change the main auditorium from one of its modes to another.

9 Pluto eventually contracted with Palgrave Macmillan, a business-oriented firm, after being turned down by the university presses of Columbia and NYU. Now they work with the University of Chicago Press.

10 "In major shift, one third of Americans want U.S. to push for one-state outcome in Israel/Palestine," *MondoWeiss*, published December 5, 2014, http://mondoweiss.net/2014/12/americans-outcome-israelpalestine.

11 I would not give the impression that all liberal and progressive enclaves were of this sort—in fact, the best evening I had as an anti-Zionist on these shores was in Berkeley, California in February 2008 at the Unitarian seminary.

12 Harry Clark, "Noam Chomsky and BDS: the 'Responsibility of Intellectuals?'," *The Question of Palestine*, April 23, 2015, https://questionofpalestine.files.wordpress.com/2015/12/ncbds_2-10.pdf.

13 A comment of mine at the time of expulsion—Feb 18, 2009—adds some facts: http://jewssansfrontieres.blogspot.com/2009/02/joel-kovel-fired-for-crime-of-anti.html.

14 A wonderful study of Davis may be found in the late Dave van Ronk's memoir. See Dave van Ronk, *The Mayor of MacDougal Street* (Philadelphia: Da Capo Press, 2013).

15 Erdman, 258.

Mural Near St. Mary's

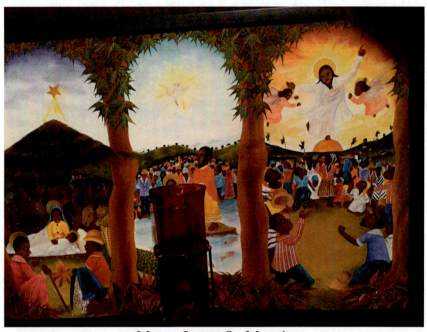

Mural Inside St. Mary's

Chapter 14
St. Mary's

"You did not choose me but I chose you."
(John 15:16)

As Jesus passed along the Sea of Galilee, he saw Simon and his brother Andrew casting a net into the sea—for they were fishermen. And Jesus said to them, "Follow me and I will make you fish for people." And immediately they left their nets and followed him. As he went a little farther, he saw James son of Zebedee and his brother John, who were in their boat mending the nets. Immediately he called them; and they left their father Zebedee in the boat with the hired men, and followed him.

Mark 1:16–20

Such grace is costly because it calls us to follow, and it is grace because it calls us to follow Jesus Christ. It is costly because it costs a man his life and it is grace because it gives a man the only true life.

Dietrich Bonhoeffer,
The Cost of Discipleship[1]

Bard gone, we relocated, choosing to supplement the Willow home with a modest co-op on Claremont Avenue. Molly and Shawheen found a place nearby and brought two splendid

FRED HO

youngsters into the world, Desmond (7/16/10) and Andisheh (5/1/13), to gladden our later years. DeeDee and I kept on doing what we do, in my case the causes of ecosocialism and anti-Zionism, in hers, the advancement of democratic communications. I made new connections with the great saxophonist and revolutionary Fred Ho, tragically ill and not long for the world. This led to Scientific Soul Sessions, a multi-hued collective focusing on the boundary between radical politics and cultural work, in particular, on behalf of the Prison Justice movement, where the collective was able to win the release of Russell "Maroon" Shoats from solitary confinement after 25 years. The outstanding group who did this included Quincy Saul, Kanya D'Almeida, and Ben Barson, all recently graduated from Hampshire College. I happily found in them a superior opportunity to do what I had been struggling to do at Bard. With others, we were able to gather in 2011 to put together Ecosocialist Horizons, which continues to develop as a collective for the propagation of Ecosocialism. At my end, this included substantial trips to China in 2010 and 2013, and the translation into Mandarin of *The Enemy of Nature.*

And then there was the little church on 126th Street, a mere eight minutes by foot from our new apartment, and the promise I was going to keep.

THE TRAVELLER FINDS A HOME

WHEN I INTRODUCED MYSELF to the Rev. Earl Kooperkamp, Rector of St. Mary's Episcopal Church, he not only recognized me but made me feel welcome and that my return had been expected during the four years since my first visit. I learned soon after that St. Mary's generosity of spirit had been singled out by Stephanie Sellers in her *Radical Welcome,* which affirmed it as the true vocation of a Protestant church.[2] One could add that it belonged to what Marx held as what religion could be at its best: the "heart of a heartless world" and the overcoming of estrangement. Radical welcome went to the roots of a person's identity in a basic affirmation of common humanity; it undid chauvinism and isolation as it built a new community.

A church should impose neither marble monuments nor "Priests in black gowns... walking their rounds, And binding with briars, my joys & desires,"[3] but nourish freely developing fellowship and welcome new people, including prideful intellectuals of a certain age who had been driven out of academia, this was what St. Mary's was all about, its *point d'honneur*. And Earl Kooperkamp, of Kentuckian extraction and lively demeanor, who wore black gowns on occasion, was not there to suppress "joys and desires," but to personify such a spirit.

We chatted in his rumpled and cluttered office. I told him something of my bumpy path to this point and he shared with me his own journey, accompanied by his wife, Elizabeth, a child psychologist, and three grown children. They lived in the down and out mid-nineteenth century Rectory whose dilapidation considerably exceeded its quaint charm.[4] As for the job, well, it was fairly easy, said Earl, just prepare for a few formal services each week and take care of the needs of the parishioners, living, dying, in hospice or prison or one kind of joy and desolation or another. To do so, Kooperkamp roamed the streets of Harlem, seemingly known to all as a friend, always available, always helping, always cheerful.

Earl became my counselor and spiritual guide, and enabled me to become an Episcopal Christian at age seventy-five. The external obstacles had now melted away, principally the all-male hierarchy that had blocked conversion to Catholicism in the 1980s. To the contrary, the Episcopal Church, America's successor to the Church of England, has been, of all established religions, the most progressive from the standpoint of gender, and has had no more forward-looking a parish in this regard than St. Mary's.[5] Wealth is another story, lack of it a problem for St. Mary's, but which for the upper reaches of the Church is comparable to that of the Vatican with all of the ominous accouterments, though without the world-power wielded by the Papacy.[6] The Baroque immensity of the Cathedral of St. John the Divine, seat of the Diocese of New York, was for a long time second only to St. Peter's in Rome as the world's largest church. I had often enjoyed wandering through its cavernous nave, where echoing never ceases and sound takes four seconds to go from one end to the other, a reminder that a church (for example, St. Chapelle on the Ile de la Cité) can also be a musical instrument.

As for St. John (Jesse Lemisch, that blasphemer!, called it "the positively divine"), it also has on its capacious grounds a serene close, juxtaposed to the Bedlam of Amsterdam Avenue, that could evoke in a suitably disposed person a whiff of strolling about Salisbury Cathedral. It contained what I knew in the '70s as a crackerjack school, 30% students of color, where Jon and Erin got a fine education for a very modest fee. Alas!, the Great Cathedral, whose original designers proudly held that it would never be finished, as a testament to the subordination of man's works to eternity, is now itself subordinated to Mammon's money-curse to raise yet more of the root of all evil, for which purpose condos now arise on its land surrounding and choking off towers and stained glass apertures.

SO IT GOES WITH THE HEART of a heartless world. Yet I will always remember what Peter Lamborn Wilson told me, that when it was time for William Blake to leave our world, his friends gathered around and asked what he, surely one of the fiercest critics of organized religion to have ever lived, wanted to do in the way of religious solace. This caused Blake to smile, and, say, "why, the Church of England, of course." And so it was. Blake was as happy with this prospect at the end as at the beginning of the choosing, for it is well attested that when the moment of passage arrived, he began to sing, and did so right up to the doors of eternity. So if British Anglicanism was good enough for William Blake, American Anglicanism is good enough for his disciple, me. And that, I hope, settles the matter.

There remained the everlasting "inner reasons" to complicate a transition that appears a good deal smoother from the outside than within. If you question this, try converting to a religion when you are 75 years of age. Even if the faith is welcoming in the best sense of the word, even if it stands before you like the true love bride you always really wanted, and even though you were well fed up with the old path you are leaving, you also have a barnacle-encrusted crotchety old vessel for a soul, that scrapes and bumps against everything under the sun and gets buffeted by the waves, a soul that has learned to survive and live under difficult circumstances and has the scars to show for it, and is still a long way from living into the splendid motto which is pasted all around St. Mary's, to "Be Not Afraid."

One wants, in circumstances of this sort, a guide to get him home, bountiful of spirit yet steadier than Simeon Tropp, my first, Orgonomic, therapist, and much more fun to be with than my saturnine analysts, Dr. C., who perished of a day, and Dr. S., the seven years with whom passed as in a cold fog. And of course you want this person to be firmly grounded in the doctrine whose principles you know you are never too old to learn, and also can still use a booster about, now and then, as when you shyly ask how and under what circumstances does one move one's hand down and up and then across and back on one's chest as believing Christians do in order to create a sign of holiness, and you want to learn this right away so that you can make the Cross with your moving hand thousands of comforting times in what remains of your existence while on earth. In sum, one wants Earl Kooperkamp.

Earl was learned and serious, but self-effacingly so. He liked corny jokes which he told with a twinkle and a shrug, even ones so low down as praising a gift of cheeses to the Church by connecting it to... well, you know who... for he loved reminding us that the Lord Christ was "our Savior and friend," and had therefore in his human aspect as fine a sense of humor as would be expected from any good friend. Earl had a firm grip on Scripture, needless to say, and like every user of the Bible, his favorite passages. I would grant the laurel for Kooperkamp to First Thessalonians 5:16–18, which reads: "Rejoice always, pray without ceasing, give thanks in all circumstances; for this is the will of god in Christ Jesus for you." A gracious passage, whose combination of fidelity, bounciness, and cheer suits Earl to the proverbial "T" even as its tense juxtapositions complement a moody spirit such as mine, and gently wrap themselves about my soul.

WE WOULD MEET AT ODD INTERVALS, often in a nice coffee-shop across from Union Thefanological Seminary. Generally we discussed whatever came up. There were, however, two projects Earl had for me, which were steadfastly put forward, and had considerable implication.

The first was to join a prayer group that met weekday mornings at Lampman Chapel, a small gathering place at Union, facing onto the courtyard and windowed with stained glass images of Luther, St. Teresa of Avila, and St. Francis of Assisi. Earl would lead and readings were taken from the Episcopal Lectionary of the day, typically an Old Testament passage followed by one from the New Testament and then one from the Gospels. These were introduced by the Lord's Prayer; while the background to the session as a whole was from a little book, "Celtic Prayers from Iona."[7]

Celtic Christianity being the version relatively free from Roman influence, there had now appeared at the start of my St. Mary's journey a version of the old option for those unspoiled by civilization. It began in fascination during days of Reich and Stanley Diamond's vision of the primitive, had been sustained by travels and works of literature that tugged at my fancy over the years,[8] were explored during the writing of *History & Spirit,* and became consolidated in my thinking about ecosocialism.

Once I had settled into the church, these values eventually led to the acquisition of the Celtic Cross described at the close of the last chapter. But the settling hit a hidden snag near the very beginning of the process, the instant Earl proposed that I join the Lampman Prayer Circle, to be exact, at mention of the word, "prayer." This set off a soft yet ominous alarm.

THE FACT WAS, THAT FOR ALL my spiritual mobilization, I had trouble accepting the notion of prayer. I knew it to be integral to religion, but prayer wasn't included in those things that had drawn me to Christianity, such as Grace, beauty, high drama, the search for justice and fellowship congruent with communism. It seemed, instead, a leftover from bygone ages of fear-driven superstition. I fan-

cied myself more advanced than that, indeed, a scion of the dis-en-
chanting scientific tradition, well trained in basics and guided by
scientific-medical reason. More than that, here I was, once a fully
fledged Freudian having acquired an at best charitable contempt for
the "magical thinking" we thought childishly evinced in prayer.
And here I was, a student of Marx having learned sympathy for
prayer as an instance of religion's "opiate" function, which may
have been more generous than Freud but nonetheless had not
granted to faith the status of praxis. That is, one would definitely
not expect Marx to endorse prayer as something to emulate in real
life. I knew well the passage in the *Communist Manifesto,* that we had
arrived at that place where Man, "with sober senses," takes stock of
the real world and sets about to transform it, presumably with sober
senses as well, and had little inclination of going beyond it.

Though I had been deeply concerned with the differences between Marx and Freud, I was also aware of common ground between them, and had once been an enthusiastic endorser of Paul
Ricoeur's famous judgment that they were jointly "Masters of Suspicion." The book where this insight was worked out in detailed regard to Freud, *Freud and Philosophy,* had been as intently underlined
as any in my collection and had been given a substantial role in
"Things and Words," my effort to legitimate myself as a contributor
to psychoanalytic discourse (See Chapter 7).[9] What, then, was I
doing submitting to a method in which prayer was a central organizing principle? How suspicious was that?! I imagine that many who
have known me over the years as at least a decent practitioner of
"suspicion" would variously grieve or gloat at the news of my conversion into a practicing Christian. Soft in the head has gone poor
Kovel, some might even have added.

It was a serious dilemma, which threatened the whole project of
conversion. Earl let me be, while I mulled and fretted, and fretted
and mulled: a small, quiet crisis but momentous in its way. At stake
was whether to forsake the Church and fall back to an individualized pathway, like a Jew for Jesus. Whatever else a Church might
be, it is grounded in collective speech, people coming together
around God-talk, the words of which are organized into prayers. As

God is beyond us, prayer is essentially another word for language addressing the Deity, whether as She, He or It. To turn away from prayer is to spurn the very idea of a Church. I could not go further, then, unless I overcame these doubts. And so I mulled and fretted.

ON THE SUNDAY NIGHT well into the Monday morning set as the target date for clearing this matter up, I awoke as is my habit before the dawn and quietly lay in bed, DeeDee's soft breathing audible to my right and the eternal ambulance and/or the 1 train sounding in the distance. Much of this memoir has flowed through such moments, the actual writing largely a matter of stenography and endless subsequent fussing. I was particularly still at this moment, a good sign, as I thought and thought, and counseled calm, until something between speech and an idea passed across the screen of my mind.

Don't be stupid, it thought quietly: the Celtic prayers are not childish or desperate demands, and certainly not magical thinking, but ways of setting up lines of communication toward what is beyond the self, and connecting with others doing the same. You have been travelling a long time and this is the place you have reached. Give it a chance and see what happens....

All right, then. I got up, boiled my morning eggs and made the tea and toast, DeeDee now awake and plugged into *Democracy Now!*; and I left the people on the flat screen, and headed out, stomach churning, turned southward on Claremont Avenue, turned left past the Manhattan School of Music and right on Broadway until I reached the entrance to Union Theological Seminary, where I showed my Columbia University card to the frowning guard, who let me in....

And I couldn't find God-Damned Lampman Chapel!! Lost again!!! Flooded by Panic for the n-thousandth time, an endless, shameful, chain: No!! No!! But calming, I took a few deep breaths and asked a passerby who kindly showed me the way; and I arrived there, breath quieting, no more than a moment late, earlier than Earl if I recall correctly, to meet Liz and Allen Mellen, faithful and more venerable than any anyone at St. Mary's save blessed Bonnie Phelps, along with blessed Janet Dorman, Kansas born, who labors with the choir and keeps the Food Kitchen going, and the remarkable

Lysander Puccio, a small woman with a strong contralto voice, who, upon conversion to Christ searched for a church, choosing St. Mary's when the process was done. Lysander is the St. Mary's parishioner I feel the most comfortable with on matters Zionistic, having endured years in Occupied Palestine working with the International Solidarity Organization.

Earl was very happy when we talked about it, especially with my small, still voice, which he deemed an authentic manifestation of the Holy Spirit. I loved working with the group, as it came and went with the rhythms of life. It is, as the Spirit said to me that Monday Morning, a fabric of lines of communication, plaiting them together. Thus we have inserted "Our Mother and Father" in the opening line of the Lord's Prayer, a small step, but part of the process which is the lifeblood of a functioning faith.

I STILL QUESTION THE LIMITS to the efficacy of prayer and just what it can achieve, whether move mountains, divide the loaves and fishes, or set into motion lesser miracles. Nothing is going to still my questioning but death itself. But I made a kind of peace with the matter following an incident from November 2010, during my first visit to China, when, the conference having ended, I spent a harrowing day in Shanghai, alone and wandering through its vastness under a two-hundred-foot-high image of LeBron James and becoming more and more discombobulated until, desperate and on the verge of melting down even after finally arriving back at the hotel, I laid down on the bed and recited the Lord's Prayer to myself several times… and then peace came stealing over me, a sense of integrity and that everything was going to be alright… and so it was. For sure, I will settle for that, no questions asked! As it is said, there are no atheists in the foxholes. And I am no atheist in or out of the foxhole, an opinion I have drawn from living in a world full of wonder and manifestations of a kind of Love that either comes from God or some similar entity with a different name.

Earl's second project lay ahead, to the world a greater wonder still, passage across that Rubicon called Baptism, with a new identity on the other side. How everlastingly strange it has been, to change who I am so late in life; how truly impossible to encompass in words what this has meant. The words merely surround and trace the outlines of things, like droplets in a cloud chamber bearing witness to the passage of subatomic particles. They are all, as it occurred to me when trying to make sense of the onrushing flow of spiritual presentiment that came over me around 1980, about predicates, that is, the attributes of being and not being itself, which is the ground here. I still can't put my head around it… which if one thinks a bit, is just fine, for if one could figure this sort of thing out, there wouldn't be much sense in trying, would there?

PEOPLE WHO KNOW ME WELL, my physician for thirty years, Marguerite Collins, for example, a righteous woman of great virtue who built a scientifically grounded rural practice in the Catskills that enables her to actually talk in depth with her patients, says that she sees a beneficial difference in me over the time I entered into the Christian faith. I am pleased to accept her judgment. But the words used to describe this, like "centered," or "at peace with oneself," fall short; I, who dwell in language, blush to have to resort to such descriptors of the states of being traveled since I committed to the "Be Not Afraid" church on West 126th Street. Moreover, DeeDee, the person who knows me the best, and therefore sees me at my worst, would be hard pressed to give me a clean bill of spiritual health in light of the wild mood swings that have by no means passed out of my life; after all, though I told Marguerite Collins about them, she has never witnessed me in their throes. And while I always bounce back from the meltdowns, and do see them as slackening, I can never convince myself that these furies have been put to rest.

In this light, the decision for Baptism was no turning point but a confirmation of the changes induced by the ensemble comprised of prayer, new personal associations, continuing study, spiritual music-making and participation in rituals of Grace. The most important—because sustained—of these has been Eucharist, but there are others of searing intensity, like Holy Week's Tenebrae and Maundy Thursday. Taken all in all, they rendered not being Baptized simply unthinkable. It might not have happened at all, however, had not St. Mary's quietly defied the Episcopal hierarchy's dictum that Holy Communion was open only to those who had been baptized, period, a principle whose enforcement would have deprived me of the spiritual nourishment to develop in the faith.

I grew up a smarty-pants hostile to ritual in general. In part this was making a virtue of necessity by a youngster who virtually flunked out of the Boy Scouts because of inability to make his bed or tie more than his shoelaces. Deeply rebellious, I came to think of life as an endless war against what I was told by authorities to do, from shop-teachers who coined the name, "Mr. What?" for me, to all the this-ings and that-ings, and standings and sittings, that characterized my visits to Shul or the rituals of Seder, where, like Pavlov's dog, one was rewarded with some tasty borscht for mouthing the Four Questions.

This improved, indeed, fairly turned itself around once I recognized my mystical moments as instances of Grace and realized that the rituals were dramatic enactments that enabled Grace though collective narratives compressed into and transmitted by symbolic forms connecting the individual worshipper to the community of believers, and through them, to the universe and its deity, or cosmic principle.

EUCHARIST, WHICH I EXPERIENCED ONCE in Nicaragua in 1986 and then resumed at St. Mary's in 2010, is the foundation enabling the soul's opening to that Love, which as in the conclusion to Dante's *Paradiso,* "moves the sun and the other stars." The Freudian still in me supposes this is in part due to its returning the believer to archaic memories of nursing. The growing Christian gathers the narrative and moves it to the present where Love can build a garden and palace within, turning secular time into eternity. If God is Love, and God's Grace the unbidden presencing of Love, then the ritual of Eucharist (Greek for gratitude) provides for a direct re-enactment of the drama redirected through Christ. It simply cannot be done through intellectual means, however essential sound thinking may be.

Words are vital, nonetheless, however, as *les mots justes,* which in poetry enter and cross the boundary, or membrane, between themselves and the original things of the world. Eucharist works by providing words that cross the word-thing membrane, critically, the words of Jesus himself to his disciples and person embarking on Holy Communion: "do this for the remembrance of me." Remembrance… membrane, activity across the boundary. The remembrance of me: memory necessary for human existence, its limiting and its infinite proportion. Had not Freud in the *Traumdeutung* written that every dream contains a kind of umbilicus, a mycelium branching off into an infinitude of association and therefore beyond interpretation?[10]

The passage struck me greatly in 1957 when I first read the *Dream Book*, though it was never developed further, either by Freud or so far as I know (which is not far enough, to be sure), by the Psy tradition. In any event, consider: here is Jesus—for there was such a one, and there are real memories, leading from the disciples all the way forward to our present, nesting, as memory will, in a infinitude of association, the membrane for which is the boundary between verbal and nonverbal existence, the former signifying our membership in the human community and the latter going back through sensuousness, to infancy, into the womb and outward again, dust to dust, to join the matrices of the universe.

In the Eucharist we find, as in the Celtic Cross, an interweaving of modalities. Here word-consciousness is interwoven with thing-consciousness in the unity of sensuousness, as seen in the original speech of infants where a word is from one side itself, and from the other, a thing. This is as primary as the taking in, or knowing through the mouth, at the center of the infant's existence. It is concrete and immediate, like the mycelium of dream thoughts, it enters into the zone of where Marx in 1845 put his First Thesis on Feuerbach, that the real base of [historical] materialism as a living doctrine was not dull scurrying matter,[11] which is the legacy of bad Newtonian metaphysics, loathed by Blake, but "human sensuous activity, practice, not subjectively."[12]

That is, objects are not completely outside the self nor is subjectivity detached inwardness, but inside and outside interpenetrate in the specifically human form of being, consciousness. Engaged with the material, physical world, the human being comes to grips with reality through a concretely organized signal-set connecting the sense organs of an active person—eye, ear, skin, nose, tongue—as well as the other senses we can only surmise and intuit, and that, in the case of Eucharist, conjoins our being into the being of the living, indwelling Christ. This is what the nexus of remembrance and memory means to me in context of Eucharist. Concretely, it is the dry, gnarly wafer on my tongue, the faint yet unmistakable wine buzz in my brain (felt right over the palate), as synesthesia in an ensemble of ideation and sensation and narrative and memory and location… and also, sound put together and realized as music. It cannot be transcribed into syntactical words, nor can it be dissociated, split off, from words as these appear in the shapes of prayer, including foremost, the Lord's Prayer, without which no Eucharist could be fulfilled. It is, thank the Lord, a mystery. All of this induces Grace among fellow worshipers coming together as Church.

Music, most incarnate of the arts, most deeply set in the material core, as mater/mother's heartbeat is known to the fetus, and now we know by recent neuroscience, "hard-wired" into our cerebral cortex. If "God" is a word for the form-giving force animating the universe, then music stands for an immediacy of contact with the deity: it is indeed the divine form itself. Will I live to write another book about this phenomenon, joining the host of voices who have inspired me, extolling my Mozart, my Bach, my Nina Simone, my Otis Redding, my shape-note friends who will travel hundreds of miles to sing "Fa-Sol-La" in squares, and hundreds of others unifying the human spirit in collective music making? Music is no ornament to religious experience; it is the thing itself; and my greatest regret in this life is that I never gained a foundation in music making: blocked as a child by foolish family quarrels, working hard on the piano from 1997 to 2007, and ultimately unable to follow through after my last two books caused an explosion of demands on my time.[13]

NOBODY ATTENDING ST. MARY'S will mistake the rough singing emanating from its pews and choir loft for a fully realized professional musical experience, much less, the Godliness of a Bach. But do not mistake the garment for the person wearing it. The aura of music extending from womb to Cosmos can pick up a charge of energy as it circles, as if by solenoid, around the persons absorbing the "remembrance" of Christ and unites them into a Spiritual body. The Holy Spirit is the executor of such events, imbuing music with spirit, even as hard work is necessary for technique.

I decide as I head back to my pew after Eucharist whether to join in song with the choir or remain silent in prayer. Both options are frequently accompanied by tears, depending somewhat on the hymn. If this is "Taste and See" you will likely find me joining in—because it is beautiful and sensuous at once, and connects the Old—the words from Psalm 34—and New Testaments. Mostly I do this because it is a Black hymn and St. Mary's is a Black Church even though roughly half the congregation is White. I find *Lift Every Voice and Sing,* the African-American hymnal which contains "Taste and See," in its pew along with the standard Episcopal/Anglican 1982 hymnal, and cherish them both.

A CURIOUS MATTER, THIS AFFECTION FOR BLACKS. It runs like a living thread through my life. I initially wrote of it at the end of the first chapter in relation to my summer job at the Hotel Del Mar in 1954 where my sympathies came down on the side of the Black workers; later, I wept reading Blake's "The Little Black Boy" from *Songs of Innocence*; and I chose the freedom struggle of Blacks as the negation of "White" racism in my inaugural voyage as a writer; as I made white supremacy a touchstone of loathing and definitive of a large grab-bag of despicable luminaries over the centuries, for example, Kant and Jefferson.

And then there was Dietrich Bonhoeffer, whom I boundlessly admire, and who, during two brief sojourns at Union Theological Seminary in 1930 and 1939, found himself repelled by liberal Christianity as practiced there and in the neighboring Riverside Church. In both periods he found a desolation at the heart of what these important institutions stood for—and sought a spirituality to his liking in the Black Churches of Harlem, where the depth of oppression entered into the liturgy and the spirituals and Gospel music, all of which he intended to bring back to Germany.[14] I doubt Bonhoeffer ever visited St. Mary's, which began as a rural church in 1823 and did not become a Black congregation until the 1950s. Nor, of course, have Union or Riverside remained as they were during his sojourns. Indeed, both institutions have become bellwethers of African-American influence on Protestant churches, to what effect is not for discussion here. In any case, conscience drove Bonhoeffer back to the Third Reich to join the struggle to get rid of Hitler, for which he gave his life in 1945, hung by Nazis days before war's end.

Martyrdom tells us that in the domain of faith, joy and grace are admixed with sorrow, grief, and moments of abomination and terror as the world's evil impinges on human existence. These are inextricably woven in Christianity—as they are in human existence down through the ages, so that to avoid the darkness means to avoid the light and settle for a conformist and pallid midline existence.

The sufferings of Christ during Holy Week bring it to a crescendo. The potential for sin is never more profoundly realized than here, and expressed in Christian art and music, the limits of which were, I should think, sounded in the *St. Matthew Passion*.[15] From the perspective of Eucharist, the "remembrance" of Jesus is a figure who, viewed from one angle, reveals his Love for us, and from another, the implacable evil that was done to him by the human agency of sin and death. Insofar as we are of the world, the evil potential is ours, as enacted in the drama of the *Passion*.

The *Passion* is not merely what others, out there, do to Jesus. It is what we, as aspiring disciples of Christ, do to Christ. For it is made quite clear in the Gospels that the leading disciple, Peter, leads also in sinfulness among the faithful with his threefold turning away, thereby consigning Christ to the Cross. The passive sins of omission are far more numerous than those of commission, and the operations of power sneakier, needless to say, than hammering in the nails. Just so, do the machinations of the CIA as expressive of the entirety of the capitalist system require more attention than, say, the assassin who pulled the trigger on Archbishop Romero. This, to me, defines the prime challenge to Christian conscience: not to withdraw from the world and sit upon a mountaintop; but to withdraw one's compliance from the world in order to throw sand in the engines of evil and work toward the good, in sum: to conscientiously change this world insofar as is possible.

We are all in this pickle together, the highest as well as the lowest. My much admired Jesuits, who gave so much to the people of Nicaragua and sacrificed so much for the people of El Salvador, have themselves been quite capable of moral heinousness, never more than in 1838 when they sold 272 African slaves to pay off the debt on Georgetown University. "Strait is the gate" and endless the struggle.

Nevertheless, the Society of Jesus, through the genius of its founder, Ignatius of Loyola, defined that struggle in a way that anticipated by some four hundred years the emergence of Freud's psychoanalytic movement and Lenin's codification of Marxism into the praxis of the "Vanguard Party." He did so by setting forth a set of disciplinary directives centered on the praxis of "discernment of spirits," which is in spirit closest to Marx in his early years, a kind of anticipation of the principles of ruthless criticism and the "Theses on Feuerbach," albeit grounded in the gospels of Christ. I find in retrospect that I was groping in the same direction in *History and Spirit*; and that indeed, I have been brought by the work of this memoir to resume the same struggle, and hope to develop it in in the direction of building the movement toward ecosocialism.[16]

A most exemplary Jesuit, Dean Brackley, worked with people who were down and out in the South Bronx in the 1980s—in the course of which he might have had some acquaintance with St. Mary's. He left an academic post at Fordham to go to San Salvador after the massacre of 1989. Brackley eventually became the Rector of the University of Central America and expanded the concept of discernment in a magnificent study, *The Call to Discernment in Troubled Times*,[17] before dying in 2011. I acquired a copy thanks to the abounding generosity of spirit of St. Mary's Jim White, and it has been an invaluable companion as I seek to be a decent Christian through fortifying the quest for justice.

Brackley sees discernment as thinking by embodied and socially determined women and men living in the real world of class, race and gender. But he also regards it in perspective of the light cast by John 8:32: "When Jesus said that the truth will set you free, what he meant by truth was the bad news of sin and the good news of divine love." Discernment is a skill of recognition and differentiation, of not reducing us to what Blake called "single vision." It is not a simple matter, being neither external nor internal, and requiring self reflection as well as engagement with the world. The goal is consolation, a form taken by Grace, where once stood desolation.

IN THE STRUGGLES THAT CONVULSED Central America in the last century, Jesuits took Christ Jesus to the *barrios* and base communities. But at the time of their origin in the sixteenth century, they went to the settlements of First Peoples scattered in the nations of the world, including the forests of North America, working to convert them but also learning from them and respecting their unique arrangements of human being. At least they did more of this than the average missionary, and also with more curiosity, bringing a scientific attitude to bear that includes spirit in the data of humankind. Thus the Jesuit observations on indigenous Amerindians of the seventeenth century informed Lewis Henry Morgan's *Ancient Society* of the nineteenth century, and through that conduit, Engels' *Origins of the Family, Private Property, and the State.*

For me, this opened another window on the relations between Marx and Christ. Reading Brackley on discernment one sees a first-rate mind at work dialectically bringing together radical faith and a deep revolutionary consciousness. And reading the adolescent Marx of 1835 before he became the young Marx of the 1844 *Manuscripts,* we see a genius doing the same, anticipating what the liberation theologians taught me in Nicaragua of the 1980s: *"entre communismo y cristianismo no hay contradiccion!"*

Marx's baptism as Lutheran at age seven opened a path for Christ to return to the source of his mission, as the voice for the "least of these" and against the instruments of empire. In his world the Church had wandered far from this goal. But Gospel supplied the link, as we can see in the first, and shamefully overlooked, of his writings: "The Union of Believers With Christ According to John 15:1–14, Showing its Basis and Essence, Its Absolute Necessity, and Its Effects."[18]

This, the first item in the *Collected Works,* is proof of a deeply Christian calling, at age seventeen, in the form of a magnificent essay on John 15, where Christ names himself as the "true vine," God his Father as the Vinegrower, and humanity as branches of greater or lesser fruitfulness. This unification with Christ, Marx says in the title, is an "Absolute Necessity" for the bringing forth of true life. To be sure, Marx does not stay at this place, which provided little traction for his genius. By his twenties, he is becoming Karl Marx the Revolutionary, providing the logic and insight that will grow into revolutionary socialism as a component of the theology of liberation. Yet I would hold that the basic idea never left him and appears at the foundations of his revolutionary theory: the text summons imagery of grafting smaller branches to larger ones of a vine or tree, an organic connection between beings of common "nature," having to hold them together, a process deeper than mere acquaintance, but recognizing difference and overcoming separateness by caring, protective, praxis.

THE PRACTICE OF GRAFTING dates back at least to the first millennium BCE. It travelled from Central Asia to Europe and can be assumed to have been known in Jesus' day. The holding together of branches is a kind of "abiding," a staying with, dwelling commonly, finding a home for something rootless, say, a loose branch, the alienated working classes, or a homeless person, or a traveller seeking to belong to a larger body in the Church. The word 'abide' appears eleven times in John 15, as in verse 4: "Abide in me as I abide in you... ." It is the verbal firmament for the unification process that brought the young Marx to his rapture. It suggests that discernment, or as it can also be expressed, "ruthless criticism," can be carried out to break fetters and permit the creation of new and liberating connections. Thus the new is built by completing a process embedded in the old, in contrast to capitalism, which, fetishizing the new, "drowns religious ecstasies in the icy waters of egotistical calculation." Abiding with Jesus means making Jesus the presence within our life, unifying the self with him and with other creatures through him. Thus what had been loose branches mutually support each other as living being.

It is ritualized in Tenebrae, Wednesday evening of Holy Week, a ceremony that moved me as has no other. Zenith is brought forth by nadir, as light gradually fades from the nave and the worshiper sits in the growing dark, no longer seeing his companions nor able to read the devotional text. He is alone from a coarse sensory perspective, but really not at all alone, rather with every one, unified in Christ. I have never felt this way before, gasping, once the proud loner, now surrounded with unseen others, reaching out for Jesus. Followed the next evening by Maundy Thursday's foot washings (talk about sensuousness!) one is readied for the vigil in the garden and Good Friday, watching out for Him, protecting the protector, singing "Jesus, remember me, when you come into your kingdom," again and again, no longer worrying about how strange this would seem to those, including myself, who puzzled over me through the years.

As time went by and St. Mary's became integrated into my life, the decision for Baptism was no longer one of whether, but a simple question of when and how. Well, not entirely, witness the moment when I blurted to Earl whether Baptism could be done privately, just between the two of us and maybe a few witnesses. That got a good laugh out of him and an embarrassed chuckle from me, accompanied by the disappearance of the worry. And so it was to be the whole church, sharing in the homecoming of the lost traveller. April 8, 2012, Easter Sunday, was the day, and all arrangements proceeded smoothly. I was happy to not be the only one, rather, accompanied by two children, a slender thirteen year old Latino boy, preternaturally pious, and a robust twenty-month-old Black girl, coiffed by her mother, who was as happy and proud as can be.

It was a splendid day, the Church festive and full, including a considerable number of friends and family, even Alex, who drove down from Boston with his Chinese lady-friend, Haaka, for the occasion and passed along to Peter Halleck his bewilderment that I would so submit my will to another.

Once the service got underway, it became the quintessential initiation rite, taken without a trace of irony. I had donned a plain long-sleeved white shirt from Bread and Puppet Days over my black chino pants and was ready to go. It wasn't full-body immersion baptism but the sprinkling kind, straight from the *Episcopal Book of Common Prayer*, and it made me as joyous as I've ever been. You'll not

EARL BAPTISING

find that kind of smile on me very often, as all the years ran whoosh-
ing from me like a Roman candle taking off toward heaven.

The sad note was the looming departure of Earl Kooperkamp.
He had been rector for twelve years, the upper limit of reasonable
service before burnout settles in, and there were pledges to family,
Vermonters on his wife's side, to be fulfilled. And so on May 20, Earl
bid us goodbye and headed north to Barre, Vermont, where the
Church of the Good Shepherd awaited him.

We continue to meet from time to time, and he has been very
helpful in the preparation of this memoir. As I looked about after
Earl's departure for what to do in order to be useful to St. Mary's,
the logical path turned out to be that of helping to replace him. This
was not as *outré* as it seems. As little as I knew about the ways of
faith, and as wooly, easily flustered, and impractical as I may appear;

there remains a functional and worldly side, compounded out of pretty good instincts for dealing with people, skills at discernment, and a whole lot of life experience. Hearkening back to my time as Training Director at the Einstein Psychiatry department, I recalled a write-up that the residents did about me which went something like this: don't be misled by how out to lunch and distracted this guy may appear: he never misses a trick, never forgets anything, and his mind is both sharp and strategic. After all, I did run for the U.S. Senate and the Presidency with a firm conviction just shy of delusion that all I needed was an efficient chief of staff and a whole lot of money plus values compatible with those of the System—and there would be no stopping me! And I also recalled that, as Director of Training at Einstein, I had taken part in many searches, for trainees and faculty members, hence had fulfilled the requirements for the post at St. Mary's, of chairing the Search Committee for our new rector. When all is said and done, we only go around once down here: and being a living paraphrase of the song from *Oklahoma!* whose title would now be rendered as, "I'm just a boy who can't say no," I decided to remain true to character and give the post a fling.

And so I went for it, the Wardens and Vestry were pleased; and the next thing I knew, I was, I hope, in my last administrative job ever, though one whose emoluments were to be laid up as by an angelic pension plan, in heaven. The job included elaborate rituals of preparation: first, to bring the whole congregation together to discern their desires for leadership; and then the even more elaborate process of working up a "Parish Profile" in collaboration with the officials whose work it was to supervise the transitional processes of some two hundred churches within the jurisdiction of the New York Diocese. Once these labors were accomplished—and it took a painful six months to do—we would open the gates (chiefly via website) and begin the elaborate and drawn out processes of triage, tracking down references, and sorting things out to bring forward the more suitable candidates. We then ran a list of the happy dozen or so by the diocese, they got back to us, removing some they knew bad things about but we didn't and possibly adding more, and turning over to a grumbling committee a list of, so to speak, quarterfinalists, which we would reduce to semifinalists—all six women! I should think, a salutary record—to whom we would make visits in their home parish, and then to a list of three finalists, at which point we would turn them over to the Wardens and rest from our labors, spared the agony of having to choose the winner and negotiate their position with the Church. Whew!

YES, IT WAS DRAWN OUT, A FULL YEAR beyond the preparation stage, and yes, it was intermittently stormy and full of intrigue, with levels of conflict across various institutional fronts and their internalization in the persons of believing individuals: very challenging, all in all. It was also highly instructive; and though I was often wont to tear out the last remaining hairs from this battered skull, as for the brain beneath, I must say that it got in some quite valuable exercise along the way. My style of leadership is deliberately indirect, relying on sensing how things are brewing in the group, waiting to intervene until the time is ripe, allowing people to seize initiative, and taking into account where individual conflicts are liable to go and with what effect. I had been well-trained at the Einstein program's excellent program in group process, and it was good to have this reprise to confirm this and sharpen my wits, and a great learning experience for me, who was by far the least experienced of the group I was leading in the ways of the Church, although the oldest save one: Bonnie Taylor.

2015: NOTES FROM THE WINTER FROM HELL

SUNDAY, FEBRUARY 8, THE WEATHER was bad enough to delay us from going south for a few weeks of respite from the icy blasts. I arrive at St. Mary's just in time, which means a few minutes after 10 AM. Kym Roberts is outside with Shirrell Patterson and a man I don't know, under the faded "Be Not Afraid" banner. Shirrell works closely on a project called Miriam, Mark and Marx, with Jim White, who first brought me to St. Mary's in 2006, and she likes to call me "Noel," with soft, effacing cadence and a shy smile. They won't go into the service though they are tremendous stalwarts of the Church, especially Kym, massive, sleepy looking, and very sharp, who beneath his slouch has taken it upon himself to be all around lookout, mail keeper and guardian of the premises. Exactly a month later, Kym appeared in a white gown on the dias to facilitate the service and hold the wine-chalice at Communion. I am certain that this was thanks to Mary Foulke. He is a good man to know, especially as Rahim Harris, the handsome young Sexton,

KYM ROBERTS

has been quite ill with complications of diabetes. Ah, the terrible health of urban Black folk. Six Black Saint-Mary persons have departed in the past eighteen months, including Robert Jones, the beloved previous Sexton, brought down by an acute asthma attack; gentle, mournful Charles Kelley, who passed of multiple myeloma, a "redeemer"—that is, a homeless man who collects and cashes in on discarded beer and soda receptacles, and sang the Lord's Prayer with aching beauty at Eucharist; Sheldon Garland, a superb singer once long ago with doo-wop quartets, who in 2013 sang a sublime "Taste and See" before a packed Cathedral at the Ordination ceremony, and finally succumbed to a life of imprudent choices and what is called "bad habits"; then there was Delores Jones (no relation to Robert), a very beautiful lady who worked, I believe, in the city tax department as a mid-level administrator. I was happy to recruit Delores for the Search Committee for a new Rector late in 2013, but she soon came down with not one but two kinds of cancer and never took part. Then there were two women in the choir, Rhonda Mendoza and Tamika Scott, both of whom died very suddenly, one of a heart attack, the other of a seizure. Janet Dorman, our music director and organizer of the food pantry, keeps scrambling in her selfless, calm way, and she has managed to bring in decent replacements, one of whom, tall, elegant Dwayne Lavender, adds a flash of style to the choral proceedings, while tending to the Thrift Shop and Fashion Parlor.

Dwayne is inside in his floor-length gown as the choir, including North Carolinian Billy Adams, also of the Search Committee, assembles. I met Billy in November 2011 in front of Occupy "headquarters" on 125th near 12th Avenue, one of the last holdout buildings against Columbia's invasion uptown for the building of its northern campus. He was patrolling the space, and his charisma infused sixteen-month-old Desmond, out for a walk, so that the toddler picked up the call and pranced about pro-

BILLY ADAMS

claiming the clarion word: "Occupy! Occupy! Occupy!"

> He who respects the Infants faith
> Triumphs over Hell & Death[19]

Billy can be ornery at times, but no one manifests better that cardinal Christian virtue of a transforming, self-leaping faith, of the kind that Paul advanced as the centerpiece of his Letter to the Romans:

> For I am not ashamed of the gospel [of Christ]; it is
> the power of God for salvation to everyone who has
> faith, to the Jew first and also to the Greek. For in it
> the righteousness of God is revealed through faith

for faith; as it is written, "The one who is righteous will live by faith" (1:16).

Billy relayed this to candidates for Rector in plain words: we want to hear about your political and theological values; but mostly we want to learn what you are going to do about putting them together, not just in the pulpit, but in the street as well.

St. Mary's is small, and weak, like the quintessential object of Christian care, yet also the quintessential subject of Christian caring. I do not think it will fade away, indeed, the new Bishop of New York, Andrew Dietsche, while accepting the fact of its weakness, seems not at all desirous to see St. Mary's collapse as a heart of a heartless world. And so the "Be Not Afraid" Church goes about its Missions—soup kitchen, free clinic, weekly films, homeless shelter, clothing dispenser, outdoor services and meals in Marcus Garvey Park, feeding the micro-communities of homeless who live in catacombs across Harlem: there is a micro-community in a giant chamber beneath the viaduct that goes over 12th Avenue which could have been imagined by Piranesi. If only the shoppers who crowd the Fairway supermarket mere feet away, knew, or the filmmaker who arranged for a *Spiderman* movie stunt overhead.

As the service drew closer, Dorothy Ross, shrewd of mind, an ex-warden just retired from teaching at Hunter, hands out the week's program, which, typically, consists of three unattached sheets that this elderly and slightly neurologically challenged parishioner has never been able to negotiate without a degree of confusion; indeed, rare is the moment when I can focus my wobbly eyes onto the opening bars of the hymn in time with the congregation. But that's all right, because everybody is there, smiling and greeting one another. There is Celia Braxton, one of our wardens and an adjunct drama teacher in the CUNY System, and Lisa Slocum, a lawyer and warden-to-be who will join her with the retirement of Warden Radford Arrindel, an ichthyologist with the Museum of Natural History; and here is Thomas Hearn, from Liberia, and Marilyn Macmillan from the General Theological Seminary, and Maggie Jarry from Union, who is trying to decide whether or not to stay with her Roman

Catholic origin (late breaking news: she went over to the Episcopals). And here is Mary Foulke, our new Rector, gently commanding in presence, with a radiant smile that I, as Chair of the Search Committee, connected with from the moment we met.

When the congregation gathered afterward for its annual meeting, I was chosen to be St. Mary's delegate to the Diocesan convention next November. At the end everyone was asked to make a statement to round off the meeting. I hadn't given thought to what to say, but when my turn arrived there was no hesitation and the words came out short and sweet:

MARY FOULKE

"I am grateful to have lived long enough to find this church."

Notes

1 Dietrich Bonhoeffer, *The Cost of Discipleship* (New York: Collier Macmillan, 1963) 47.

2 Stephanie Sellers, *Radical Welcome* (New York: Church Publishing, 2006) 19–20.

3 Erdman, "The Garden of Love," 26.

4 Since Earl's departure for Vermont in May 2012, it has been renovated for Mary Foulke, her partner Renée Hill, and their adopted sons, thanks to a committee headed by Liz Mellen.

5 Gender justice for the Episcopal priesthood did not happen without a great deal of struggle. But when the first eleven women were ordained as Episcopal Priests in 1977, two were sponsored by this very modest church in West Harlem (out of some six thousand parishes nationwide). And when the St. Mary's Search Committee came to the round of semi-finalists in 2014 for Earl's replacement, we proudly beheld all six as women. The spirit of

radical innovation goes back to the church's founding in 1823, with two bold initiatives in the early years: opening a school for girls as well as boys, and scrapping the traditional policy of pew rentals, thus democratizing worship among the whole congregation.

6 Trinity Church, at the corner of Wall St. and Broadway, is the richest of all, thanks to land donations by the British Crown in the eighteenth century, now worth billions, and known for its unfriendliness to demonstrators during the Occupy Movement. Ten U.S. Presidents have been Episcopal: Washington, Madison, Monroe, Harrison, Tyler, Taylor, Arthur, Franklin Roosevelt, Ford, and George H. W. Bush. George W. Bush started as an Episcopal but converted to Methodism. Barack Obama does not belong to the Episcopal Church but is said to worship at one near the White House on occasion.

7 J. Philip Newell, *Celtic Prayers from Iona* (Mahwah: Paulist Press, 1997).

8 A diverse collection, ranging from *Moby Dick*'s Queequeg to *War and Peace*'s Platon Karateyev, and *Huckleberry Finn*'s Jim. Blake, of course, is rich in allusion to Celtic myths and deities, including, because he would never rest with single vision, considerable attention to their diabolic negation, the Druidic priesthood. Of further importance, which I employed greatly in the writing of *History and Spirit,* is Jerome Rothenberg, ed., *Technicians of the Sacred* (Berkeley: University of California Press, 1985).

9 Paul Ricoeur, *Freud and Philosophy* (New Haven: Yale University Press, 1970). The trio of Masters included Nietzsche, considerably less influential in my case than Freud and Marx.

10 "The dream-thoughts to which we are led by interpretation cannot, from the nature of things, have any definite endings...[there is a] navel in even the most thoroughly interpreted dream, the spot where it reaches down into the unknown." Freud concludes that the unconscious "in its innermost nature is as much unknown to us as the reality of the external world, and it is as incompletely presented by the data of consciousness as is the external world by the communications of our sense organs." Sigmund Freud,

The Interpretation of Dreams in vols. IV–V of *The Standard Edition of the Works of Sigmund Freud* (1955) 525, 613.

11 A paraphrase of Whitehead's seminal critique of mechanical materialism, as developed in *Science in the Modern World*.

12 Robert Tucker, ed., *The Marx-Engels Reader* (New York: W.W. Norton, 1978) 143. Also see Donald Ault, *Visionary Physics: Blake's Response to Newton* (Chicago: University of Chicago Press, 1974).

13 Aunt Betty offered a free piano; Mother said yes, Father said—as always—no. So they put the choice to nine-year-old me, who was too terrified to think or choose, and simply submitted to the more powerful and frightening figure at the time.

14 Bonhoeffer was a brilliant musician, who could have gone on to a major career had not God called. Eric Metaxas, *Bonhoeffer* (Nashville: Thomas Nelson, 2010).

15 The genius of Peter Sellars' staging of the *Matthew-Passion* resides in his breaking down the boundaries between audience, chorus, orchestra, and *dramatis personae*. The effect is to establish it as an event in and of the entirety of humanity. Simon Rattle, Dir., *Matthew-Passion*, Berliner Philharmoniker, BPHR 140021, 2010.

16 Hopefully, in the forthcoming *The Light of Nature*, to be co-written with Quincy Saul.

17 Brackley, 21.

18 In vol. I of *Marx-Engels Archive Collected Works* (London: Lawrence & Wishart, 1975) 636.

19 Erdman, "Auguries of Innocence," 494.

Epilogue
Ruthless Criticism meets the Holy Trinity

> People were bringing little children to him in order
> that he might touch them; and the disciples spoke
> sternly to them. But when Jesus saw this, he was in-
> dignant and said to them, "Let the little children
> come to me; do not stop them; for it is to such as
> these that the kingdom of God belongs. Truly I tell
> you, whoever does not receive the kingdom of God
> as a little child will never enter it." And he took them
> up in his arms, laid his hands on them, and blessed
> them. Mark 10:13–16

I can't remember when I first encountered Marx's dictum of 1843, in a letter to a fellow editor, but it has proven a trusty and durable guide to the thickets of this world:

> we do not attempt dogmatically to prefigure the fu-
> ture but want to find the new world only through
> criticism of the old.... If the designing of the future
> and the proclamation of ready-made solutions for all
> time is not our affair, then we realize all the more
> clearly what we have to accomplish in the present—
> I am speaking of a ruthless criticism of everything
> existing, ruthless in two senses: The criticism must
> not be afraid of its own conclusions, nor of conflict
> with the powers that be.

I would tell the students in my courses at Bard that if they conscientiously followed this precept the essentials of Marxism would fall into place, inasmuch as ruthless criticism is true to Marx's methodological core of praxis in which knowing and doing can neither be realized without the other. And it anticipates the 11th Thesis on Feuerbach, that "until now philosophy has only tried to interpret the world; the point, however, it to change it."

Passages like this stirred me greatly and caused Marx to displace Freud as my worldly guide and ideal in the middle years of my career. But much has changed since then, including the world itself, in ways that all people of good will, Marxists included, have observed impotently—and, if they have any wit, with the deepest foreboding.

WE ARE NOW CAUGHT UP in the early stages of a massive ecological crisis that inflicts climate change but cannot be reduced to climate change and whose development bids to destroy civilization and could even bring about our extinction along with innumerable other species. Driven by capitalism's rapacity, enmity toward nature and tendency toward perpetual war we now face a conjuncture unprecedented in history, the foul fruit of six thousand years.

I have written and agitated endlessly about it, have a certain reputation based on this, often feel at my wit's end, but will not give up, for the sake of the little ones—my own as reminders of the others, for we do not give up on life, at least I do not. Nevertheless ruthless criticism now contends with a situation that would have been unthinkable for Marx in 1843: that although we cannot prefigure the future, neither can we rule out the real possibility that there may not be a future to prefigure within the ken of people now living or just born.

The horizon of an actual future plays a vital role in the history of thought, providing an essential anchoring point for speculation, whether utopian, dystopian, or somewhere in between. The possibility of no future is deeply disorienting; it can send thought into a tailspin, like an unbalanced paper airplane thrown into the air that swoops, turns helplessly and crashes. The present crisis generates no end of speculative and imaginative responses and much that is hysterical and tawdry as well: just take a glance at the lineup of summer movies, mostly dreadful, some with flashes of insight, all stained by the industrialization of consciousness that keeps the masses titillated and confused.

Rather, the crisis demands we go further, ruthlessly deepening the notion of criticism itself to focus upon what exists beyond the future: eternity, and the voices that give meaning to eternity.

Jesus is the prime voice of this kind... and also that faithful one who has been with me all these years, my lodestar, William Blake. We are fortunate to be able to study a passage where these voices come together in a kind of Holy ensemble.

PROCEED TO PLATE 96 (of 100) of *Jerusalem*, where Albion, who is England but also humankind is having visions...

The end of the Dream approaches...then Jesus suddenly appears...

As the Sun & Moon lead forward the Visions of Heaven & Earth

England who is Brittannia entered Albions bosom rejoicing
Then Jesus appeared standing by Albion as the Good Shepherd

By the lost Sheep that he hath found & Albion knew that it
Was the Lord the Universal Humanity, & Albion saw his Form
A Man. & they conversed as Man with Man, in Ages of Eternity

And the Divine Appearance was the likeness & similitude of Los

Albion said. O Lord what can I do! my Selfhood cruel
Marches against thee deceitful from Sinai & from Edom
Into the Wilderness of Judah to meet thee in his pride
I behold the Visions of my deadly Sleep of Six Thousand Years
Dazling around thy skirts like a Serpent of precious stones & gold

I know it is my Self. O my Divine Creator & Redeemer
Jesus replied Fear not Albion unless I die thou canst not live
But if I die I shall arise again & thou with me
This is Friendship & Brotherhood without it Man Is Not
So Jesus spoke! the Covering Cherub coming on in darkness
Overshadowd them & Jesus said Thus do Men in Eternity
One for another to put off by forgiveness, every sin
Albion replyd. Cannot Man exist without Mysterious
Offering of Self for Another, is this Friendship & Brotherhood
I see thee in the likeness & similitude of Los my Friend
Jesus said. Wouldest thou love one who never died
For thee or ever die for one who had not died for thee
And if God dieth not for Man & giveth not himself
Eternally for Man Man could not exist. for Man is Love:
As God is Love: every kindness to another is a little Death
In the Divine Image nor can Man exist but by Brotherhood

There are many representations of Christ in Blake's works, but none more fully drawn as this. Remarkably, he introduces the Lord, the Universal Humanity, quietly, with no fanfare, in the form of a... man, no less and no more, who converses with humanity as one of us, except for being "the likeness & similitude of Los." Los is one of the central figures of Blake's Pantheon. He appears hundreds of times in the texts as the creative power of humanity moving through various adventures and crises. Like Los, then, we create Jesus according to our passage through the potentialities of prophetic vision and giving of self.

Two anecdotes from Blake's life give some context of his maneuverings with people who were eager to trap him into displaying just how crazy he was, perhaps to enjoy a laugh or two at his expense. In the first he was asked whether he actually saw God or not, and when he replied affirmatively was asked again just where and how this happened, to which the reply was a gentle smile and a pointing of his index finger to his forehead. On another occasion Blake was asked if he actually thought he was God, to which he agreed, smiled and went on to say, "and so are you" and "so are you" to another interrogator. And so they were if only they could bring themselves to the recognition. Blake's moves were undoubtedly meant to shrug off the morons who were pestering him, but they also lead into the very profound exegesis of Plate 96 of *Jerusalem* in which Albion, conversing with the Lord, confesses that "my Selfhood cruel marches against thee" and that he beholds "the Visions of my deadly Sleep of Six Thousand years," that is, the entirety of human history can be seen in light of the sinfulness of Fallen human nature, so deep, it is embedded in the Self itself, or as we can also call it, the "Ego" form of the Self, the Self divided from the other form, that of Soul. Ego is the locus of splitting, arrayed in the ways we normalize and identify the non-recognition of estranged human beings, whether these be gendered differently, or of different racial stock, or "inferior" nations, savages, or workers across the class divide: or, finally, Nature itself which becomes mere instrumentality for the capitalist ego and rebelling, sets the ecological crisis into motion.

To this predicament Jesus gives the answer: "Fear not Albion unless I die thou canst not live but if I die I shall arise again and thou with me." In a glimpse the panorama of struggle appears before us…. I think of what Msgr. Oscar Romero said before his murder that "if I die I shall rise again in the Salvadoran people," which has been the case, and the same holds for Martin Luther King, Jr. and Malcolm X and John F Kennedy who was murdered because he wanted to end the Cold War, the Vietnam War and the nuclear arms race and make peace with Fidel Castro. How long will they kill our prophets? sang Bob Marley, well you see, very long indeed. How can it be and how can Jesus arise and become the Lord, entering into the endless chain, not of Being but of non-being, the "death" of Plate 96, which is at its lower level simply an opening of self to the universe, entering into and transforming being. It is the molecular structure of miracles. Jesus' reply to Albion is expansive: "This is Friendship & Brotherhood without it Man is Not."

Forgiveness is born into the relationship of one for another: to put off by forgiveness every sin and the condition of love and dying for another. Forgiveness, yes—and justice also: the two are not antithetical. Forgiveness is not forgetting, and it is not slackening of resolve. It means, to me and I should think I am following Blake and Jesus, the overcoming of vengeance, the eye for an eye that leaves the whole world blind. As a minimal condition, justice requires the ending of capital punishment, not for instrumental reasons but because it is contrary to the Spirit of forgiveness taught by visionary prophets, another meaning of which is that killing, and especially vengeance killing, should be a power taken away from the State, that cruel institution of legitimate violence, which is to say, justifiable vengeance.

Here a further differentiation occurs for God's sake: life is not just a chain of slaughters and the breaking of the cycle of revenge, no, there is another cycle emerging alongside in the Divine image. For every kindness to another there is a little Death, a death on one side becoming life on the other and generating that Brotherhood without which humanity cannot exist.

IT REQUIRES IMAGINATION but is not imaginary, hence took a real Jesus to happen. I believe in the reality of the historical Jesus because of logic and because it had to have been the case with so many witnesses, even though the outer events seemed unimportant at the time: A flesh and blood Galilean Jew who came into town, a remarkable man from a remarkable tradition of the One God, who took it where it could only have been envisioned before by such as Isaiah. Jesus lived in unprecedented circumstances that split the Judaean class system because of Roman colonization and betrayal of the people by their Quisling rulers and priestly elites. The Nazarene glimpsed as in a flash that the representation of the One God had been corrupted, turning the God of old into the false and bestial Satanic interlopers: Mammon, or money and Empire, for one; and child-devouring Moloch for another. All this was concealed under a carapace of legalisms. Jesus was by his faith drawn to make the supreme sacrifice, dying so that the faith might live and the principle of God's love, or Grace, would endure and prevail for the sake of the forgiveness of sins—not of course, that this would be an easy matter given the radical weaknesses of human nature and its selfhood, as the tortuous history of the religion in his name, Christianity, confirms. But he opened the possibility of communism through the immensely radical ideas from which it stems, the sacredness of little children and all the "least of these."

My path to Christ was blazed by Grace and set about with struggle. It was only when matters settled down that I recognized a startling fact: that theology mattered also, and that the reigning formalization of Christian faith, that of the Trinitarian notion of Godhead, Donne's "three-personed God," made a lot of sense to me.

Ruthless criticism helped clear the way by de-legitimating an uninflected monotheism as has hounded Zionism, and back into time as the exceptionalism of the Jewish people: a very bad, chauvinistic idea. I realized that there was no necessity in this—and indeed, great geniuses like Spinoza ould do wonders with it—but no circuitry could conceal the fact that the monotheism handed down through Torah remains as a massive and permanent stumbling block always at the ready to afflict the world.

Only a structural alteration could suffice, and one true to a deeper truth about the universe, that entities are differentiated and pass the one into another according to the lawfulness of nature. All the sages recognized some variation of this, some of their insights, like those of Heraclitus (the favorite of Marx) and Laozi, becoming suitable in the emergence of what is called dialectic. I think, though this is scarcely the place to develop the idea, that the sages who put together the life and death of Christ into the Trinitarian conception were faithful dialecticians combining the presence of a wonder-producing God-power, the evolution of a creature capable of abiding with God, and a Holy Spirit of boundary crossing, into the threefold God of Love. The Trinity is, fundamentally, then, a reading of the relationships of being; along with the harm done by Satan, the "Accuser who is the God of this World"; and the Faith, Hope and Love set forth by Grace.

I SHOULD THINK THAT RUTHLESS CRITICISM itself is an heir to this processual dialectic-making—and that the young Marx, fresh from his sojourn with John 15, turned this razor toward the creation of his foundational ideas, just as we have to learn to go beyond these ideas into an eternity beyond any conceivable future as the Darkness gathers and demands the building of a new, ecosocialist world.

So the Holy Trinity and ruthless criticism are different nodes on a loop. Not a closed loop, because both nodes open onto the eternity beyond themselves, as have held the universalists: Blake, Einstein, all the Saints who refuse to tolerate the Evil One in the light of the Love that moves the Sun and all the stars....

A CHILD CRIES OUT; it is Leila. I think she wants to go swimming and I must hurry to her side. The savior calls.

This dream, this time, is over.